WRITING TRANSFORMATIONAL GRAMMARS:

an introduction

WRITING TRANSFORMATIONAL GRAMMARS:

an introduction

ANDREAS KOUTSOUDAS
Indiana University

McGRAW-HILL BOOK COMPANY
New York St. Louis San Francisco Toronto London Sydney

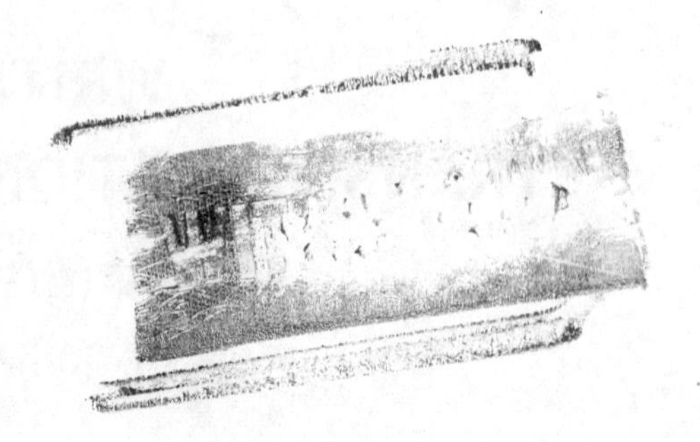

Writing Transformational Grammars: An Introduction

Library of Congress Catalog Card Number 65-22958

35365

1 2 3 4 5 6 7 8 9 0 MP 7 3 2 1 0 6 9 8 7 6

to my wife

Olympia

PREFACE

The purpose of this book is to help the reader learn how to write transformational grammars, i.e. grammars based on a theory of language description originated by Noam Chomsky. To write a transformational grammar, one must have an understanding of transformational theory; consequently this book will also help the reader gain some understanding of that theory. The theory exemplified in this book does not contain a number of changes that have been proposed as a result of ongoing research, in particular those discussed by Chomsky in *Aspects of the Theory of Syntax* (The M.I.T. Press, Cambridge, Mass., 1965); once the reader controls the materials presented here, he should have a proper basis for studying such proposals.

Although this book is written primarily as a text for an introductory course in syntax, it may also be used for a number of other courses, such as an introduction to linguistics or field methods.

The first two chapters of the book provide what I consider to be the minimal theoretical background needed to work with the material in the chapters which follow. The third chapter is devoted to morphophonemics; and each of the last five chapters focuses on a particular syntactic notion, i.e. co-occurrence relations, agreement, permutation, conjoining, and embedding, in that order. While the first two chapters provide the (minimal) theoretical background needed to work through the last six chapters, it is the last six chapters that provide the basis for making the concepts in the first two more meaningful. It is therefore suggested that related sections in the first two chapters be reread while working through the later chapters.

The general format of the last six chapters is: (1) problems, each of which is accompanied by a discussion; (2) solutions (i.e. grammars) for the problems; (3) a discussion of the more important considerations involved in writing the solutions; (4) notes, usually on specific solutions; (5) for some chapters, collateral readings; and (6) a set of exercises for the reader to do on his own.

The problems in each of these chapters are ordered in terms of difficulty. (The exercises are similarly graded.) While each chapter focuses on a particular grammatical feature, some of the features that have been previously illustrated always appear within the problems of the following chapters. The problems are presented in a variety of transcriptions, i.e. broad phonetic, phonemic, or orthographic; and in order to illustrate the grammatical feature in question, the data given not only are restricted but may either be regularized (e.g. tones or stress may be omitted) or the ungrammatical sentences may include sentences that are grammatical, or both.

Because of the controlled nature of the data, the solutions for the problems do not necessarily make valid structural claims about the languages from which the data are taken. The emphasis here is on writing reasonable rules, i.e. rules that are technically sound and that make reasonable claims about the data given, and not on whether a given solution makes reasonable claims regarding the structure of a language.

Doubtless some people will take issue with some of the solutions presented. Those given, however, are reasonable, I feel, in light of the scope and purpose of this book and the readers for whom it is intended.

I am indebted to many people for their assistance during the writing of this book; I would like to take this opportunity to express my sincere thanks to them all.

In particular, I am grateful to Fred W. Householder, Jr., for his encouragement, his comments, and his experimental use of a preliminary edition of this book in his syntax courses. I am also grateful to Benjamin Elson for experimenting with the preliminary edition, as well as for granting permission to use Problems 44, 93, and 95 from the *Laboratory Manual for Morphology and Syntax,* 2d ed., by W. R. Merrifield, C. M. Naish, C. R. Rensch, and G. Story, Summer Institute of Linguistics, Santa Ana, California, 1962.

In addition, I would like to thank Peter H. Matthews, who read early versions of this book, for his criticisms and suggestions. I am also indebted to Charles J. Fillmore and Ronald Langacker for their detailed comments and suggestions on the prefinal draft.

One of the most difficult and time-consuming tasks in writing this book was obtaining data and constructing problems. I am particularly grateful to Robert Blair, Loraine Bridgeman, Ernest Lee, and Gerald Sanders for the help they gave me in this respect. I would also like to thank the following people for contributing data: Kostas Kazazis, Robert Orosz, Mercedes Roldan, and Seok Choong Song.

Not to be underestimated or forgotten are the comments and suggestions of my students, particularly those of Marvin Loflin and Gerald Sanders.

Last, and most of all, I would like to thank my wife, Olympia, for the constant encouragement and the invaluable help she gave me during the writing of this book.

Andreas Koutsoudas
Bloomington, Indiana

[illegible] and Orend [illegible]

[illegible]

[illegible] three of Marvin [illegible]

[illegible] my wife Carmela [illegible] for the writing of this book.

[illegible]

CONTENTS

WRITING TRANSFORMATIONAL GRAMMARS:

an introduction

chapter one

BASIC CONCEPTS

INTRODUCTION

To write a transformational grammar, we must first have some understanding of the following: (1) what we mean by the term "grammar" and (2) what might be reasonable to demand of a grammar.

A grammar is a device that generates (i.e. enumerates) an infinite number of correct sentences of a given language and no incorrect ones. Put differently, a grammar is a device that tells the reader how to construct an infinite number of correct sentences of a language and no incorrect ones.

By equating a **device** with a **finite set of rules, correct sentences** with **grammatical** or **well-formed sentences,** and **incorrect sentences** with **ungrammatical sentences,** we may rephrase the above definition as the following more precise one: a grammar is a finite set of rules which generates an infinite number of grammatical sentences of a given language and no ungrammatical ones.

First, it should be understood that, although not explicitly stated in the definition, by **grammatical** or **well-formed** sentences is meant *maximally* grammatical, i.e. those sentences of which there is the least doubt as to their grammaticality. We make this requirement because we know that in any given language there are both maximally grammatical sentences and sentences whose grammaticality is questionable; i.e. there are degrees of grammaticality. If we were to attempt to generate all sentences at once, we would not be able to account for this distinction in grammaticality. That is, in order for a grammar to generate both these types of sentences and to provide the distinction between them, it must first generate only the maximally grammatical; otherwise there would be no basis for determining in what way the questionable sentences deviate from the maximally grammatical sentences.

Second, notice that by definition we require that a grammar generate an infinite number of grammatical sentences, but that the set of rules that generates them be *finite*. The first requirement is necessary because there is no limit to the number of grammatical sentences in a language, and the second is necessary because otherwise the implication would be not only that a grammar could never be written but, more importantly, that people could never learn a language.

Third, the above definition of a grammar makes it immediately clear that the reader of a grammar can ask the grammar neither to construct a grammatical sentence nor to identify a given sentence as grammatical for him. That is, given a grammar of English, the reader cannot ask, for example, that this grammar construct for him the sentence *the man likes the house,* nor can he ask that the grammar decide for him whether this particular sentence is an English sentence. Both these tasks are his own. The reader must know in advance that this is an English sentence and determine for himself whether he can construct this sentence by applying the rules of the grammar of English given him. If he succeeds, then the grammar is adequate; otherwise the grammar is inadequate.

Let us now see very briefly, using English as an example, some of the features which we know grammatical sentences of languages have and which must therefore be accounted for by a grammar.

One of the most obvious features is that every sentence in English is a sequence of sounds; therefore among the rules of our grammar there will have to be a set which assigns the proper pronunciation to English sentences.

Second, since some sequences of sounds are English words and others are not, we must have a set of rules which provides a list of permissible words (or morphemes); i.e. we must provide the **lexicon** of English. In other words, we must require that there be a set of rules which allows words such as *man, girl, house,* but not **ksan* or **ngan;* otherwise sentences such as **the ksan likes the house* would be specified as English sentences.[1]

Third, the rules must be so formulated that words appear only in positions peculiar to English. These rules will ensure that the words in *the man likes the house* appear in this order, since, if these words appear in any other order, the result will be ungrammatical sentences, e.g. **man the likes house the* and **likes the house the man.*

Fourth, our rules must be so formulated that words comprising sentences are specified not only in terms of their permissible positions (or order) but also in terms of their permissible groupings. This is necessary because the construction of sentences is not simply a matter of the order of words but primarily of the order in which words combine or group with each other; i.e. the structure of sentences is hierarchical. Given the sentence *the man likes the house,* for example, we say that *the man* is the subject, while *likes the house* is the predicate; the predicate is then said to be (or be composed of) *likes* (a verb) and *the house* (an object). For another example, we say that the sentence *they are starving children* is ambiguous, or has two different interpretations, because there are two groupings possible for *starving:* we get the interpretation 'the children are starving' if the grouping is *they – are – starving children,* but we get the interpretation 'somebody is causing children to starve' if the grouping is *they – are starving – children.*

There still remains a large body of ambiguous sentences, however, which cannot be accounted for by either the position or the grouping of the various words in them. For example, the sentence *starving children can be dangerous* can mean either 'to starve children can be dangerous' or 'children that are starving can be dangerous.' The ambiguity of this sentence cannot, like that of *they are starving children,* be explained on the basis of two possible groupings for the words that comprise it. That is, although the ambiguity must be due to some difference in the relationship between *starving* and *children,* there are no alternative groupings for these two words. Our rules must therefore be so formulated as to account for this type of (structural) ambiguity as well as the one exemplified above.

Another feature the grammar should account for is that certain groups of sentences are related to each other while others are not. That is, the grammar should account for the fact that the two sentences *the*

[1] Here and throughout the remainder of this book, an asterisk before a word, phrase, or sentence indicates that what follows is an ungrammatical sequence.

man likes the house and *who likes the house* are related (since the second is the interrogative of the first), while sentences such as *John was shot by the seashore* and *John was shot by the boy* are not related (since the second sentence is the passive of the active sentence *the boy shot John* and the first is simply an intransitive sentence in which *by the seashore* modifies *was shot*).

Finally, the rules should be so formulated as to account for the fact that sentences in a language can be as long as a speaker wishes to make them; in other words, one set of rules must be recursive. For example, a speaker of English can make the sentence *Mary liked the man* as long as he wishes by doing the following: *Mary, John, George, Jim, Bill . . . liked the man* or *Mary liked the man who went to the store, who bought a house that stands in a lot that . . . ;* our grammar must account for this feature of sentences.

If a grammar is to account for all the above-mentioned features that grammatical sentences may have, we must place one more requirement on our concept of a grammar, namely, that the grammar automatically assign a grammatical analysis or structural description to each sentence it generates. We must add this requirement because, having decided that a grammar must account, for example, for the fact that sentences are or are not related to each other, we are thereby demanding that the grammar be a device not only for telling the reader how to construct sentences, but also for explaining how these sentences are understood by speakers of the language. That is to say, to demand that a grammar account for the fact that *the man likes the house* and *who likes the house* are related, is to demand that a grammar not only account for how these two sentences are constructed, but also explain how native speakers of English perceive that these sentences are related. Thus, unless we demand that the grammar assign a structural description to each sentence generated, there is no basis for obtaining the information to explain how a sentence is understood.

Incorporating this last requirement into our definition of a grammar, then, we get the following definition:

> A **grammar** is a finite set of rules which enumerates (or generates) an infinite number of grammatical (or well-formed) sentences of a language and no ungrammatical ones and assigns to each sentence generated its proper structural description.

One type of grammar that meets the above definition is that which is the subject of this book, i.e. that called a transformational generative grammar, or simply a **transformational grammar.** A transformational grammar has two components, the syntactic and the phonological. The syntactic component consists of two parts, each of which is said to be a level for representing the structure of sentences; the first part is called the phrase structure level, and the second, the transformational structure level. The phonological component also consists of a number of parts, or levels, for representing the structure of sentences. It should be noted that it is the transformational level that distinguishes this grammar from any other type of generative grammar; and the term "grammar" henceforth will refer only to a transformational grammar.

The rules of each part of a transformational grammar have certain restrictions imposed on them and have a particular function. In brief, the rules of the phrase structure part of the grammar state the underlying structures of sentences by specifying the syntactic classes, their co-occurrence relations, and the lexicon. The rules of the transformational part of the grammar specify changes in these underlying structures. The rules of the phonological component assign the proper pronunciation to the sentences of a language. The only set of phonological rules we shall be at all concerned with in this book, however, is that set which specifies morphological variations, i.e. those rules that are traditionally referred to as morphophonemic rules. These rules are briefly discussed in 1.6 (see also 3.0).

The rules of the phrase structure part of the grammar are called phrase structure or constituent structure rules, or simply P-rules, and the rules of the transformational part of the grammar are called transformational rules, transformations, or simply T-rules. The restrictions imposed on P-rules and T-rules are discussed in 1.4 and 1.5, respectively, while the function of these rules is discussed in more detail in 1.7.

1.1 STRING AND RULE

To understand the concepts discussed in the remaining sections of this chapter, we must first have some understanding of the concepts string, rule, and initial string.

A **string** is one or more concatenated (i.e. strung together) vocabulary symbols (defined in 1.2.1), e.g. *Name* + *Verb* and *Bill* + *hit* + *John*. Each vocabulary symbol in a string is said to be an element in the string and to represent a bit of structure. In fact, they are the *only* symbols that represent bits of structure.

A **rule** is considered an instruction to rewrite one string (or two strings, as we shall see in Chapter 7) as another string; e.g. $S \rightarrow NP + VP$, where the arrow stands for "rewrite."

Each grammar has an **initial string** which consists of a single symbol, flanked by the proper boundary symbols, and is that string which specifies the boundaries within which the rules of a grammar are to apply; or put differently, it specifies what the grammar generates. This string is given by the theory and is stated before the first rule of the grammar. Thus, if *S* is given as the initial string, it will appear as $\#S\#$ at the very beginning of a grammar and will indicate that the rules of the grammar apply within the sentence boundary, i.e. that the output of the grammar is sentences. (The double cross is a boundary symbol, defined in 1.2.2.)[2]

1.2 SYMBOLS

The rules of a transformational grammar consist of three types of symbols: (1) vocabulary symbols, (2) operators, and (3) abbreviators. Vocabulary symbols are symbols used to represent syntactic classes and other linguistic units; operators, as their name indicates, symbolize certain operations; and abbreviators are devices used to conflate the listing of rules. It should be noted that, unlike vocabulary symbols, none of the operators or the abbreviators are considered elements in a string and therefore none represent any structure.

1.2.1 Vocabulary symbols

(1) **Class and morpheme symbols.** There are two types of vocabulary symbols, namely, class and morpheme symbols. **Class symbols** represent higher order constituents of a sentence, such as *NP* (for noun phrase) and *VP* (for verb phrase), and are **non-terminal** symbols, while **morpheme symbols** represent lower order constituents of a sentence, such as *boy* and *see*, and are **terminal** symbols (see 1.3 for a definition of the terms non-terminal and terminal symbols). The class symbols used in this book are listed and defined in the Appendix.

Morpheme symbols are, in turn, of two types, which in this book will be referred to as **grammatical morphemes** and **lexical morphemes** (discussed in 1.6); e.g. *Pres, Pas* and *door, run,* respectively.

(2) **Cover symbols.** In writing a rule, the necessity for specifying

[2] Strictly speaking, since the grammar generates an infinite number of sentences, the initial string consists of not one but an infinite number of symbols, i.e. one for each sentence generated: $\#S\#\#S\#\#S\# \ldots \#S\#$.

the various strings that may occupy a particular position in a string may be obviated by using what are referred to as **cover symbols.** The capitals of the last four letters of the alphabet, W, X, Y, Z, are most often used in this book as these symbols; unless explicitly defined otherwise they, and all other symbols used as cover symbols, will mean **any string** which the grammar permits to occupy the position indicated by the cover symbol(s). "Any string" includes a null string, i.e. an empty string, or what is often referred to as "no string." For example, if we wanted to write a rule to delete B in the string $A + B$, regardless of what strings preceded or followed this string, we would write the rule $X + A + B + Y \rightarrow X + A + Y$, and, assuming that, according to our grammar, either the string $C + D$, the string E, or *no string* can occur before $A + B + Y$, then X represents $C + D$, E, and *no string* (i.e. we can interpret the rule as defining a string that begins with $A + B$) but not D or C alone. Given, in addition, the information that only $F + G$ and $F + G + H$ can occur after B, then in the above rule

(1) X represents the strings *null,* $C + D$, and E but not D or C.
(2) Y represents the strings $F + G$ and $F + G + H$ but not H, $G + H$, F, or *null.*

It should be understood that (a) each time the same cover symbol appears in a rule, it represents *exactly* the same set of strings in each position in which it occurs; e.g. each X in the rule $X + A \rightarrow X + X$ represents exactly the same set of strings, or, in other words, the use of the same cover symbol in various positions in a rule indicates identity; the converse is not true, however; i.e. the use of different cover symbols in a rule does not necessarily indicate that these symbols represent non-identical strings; and (b) a cover symbol always represents the same strings on both sides of the arrow; i.e. if X represents the strings A, $A + B$, and $C + D + E$ on the left of the arrow, it represents these same strings on the right of the arrow.

It is sometimes necessary to restrict the strings which a cover symbol may represent. That is, it will sometimes be the case that we will want to specify that a rule applies only when *some* (and not all) of the permissible strings occupy a particular position in a given string. Whenever this is the case, it is done in a note below and to the right of the rule in question, using either an equality or an inequality sign to do so. For example, in the following rule, the use of the equality sign specifies precisely what X must represent in order for the rule to apply:

$$X + F + G \rightarrow F + X + G$$
$$X = Det + N$$

That is to say, although the grammar may permit the strings *Name*, *Pron*, and $Det + N$ to occur before $F + G$, the above rule applies only when $Det + N$ precedes $F + G$. If we were to use the inequality sign instead of the equality sign to restrict X in the above rule, that is, $X \neq Det + N$, we would specify exactly the opposite restriction, namely, that the above rule applies only when *Name* or *Pron* precedes $F + G$.

The following examples illustrate how the inequality sign may be used to restrict the strings a cover symbol may represent; i.e. they illustrate some restrictions we may want to put on a cover symbol and a notational convention for doing so:

(a) X is not B: $X \neq B$
(b) X is any string but one beginning with B: $X \neq B + W$
(c) X is any string but one ending with B: $X \neq W + B$
(d) X is any string not containing B: $X \neq W + B + Y$
(e) X and Y represent any string, but both cannot be the same string in any given application of the rule: $X \neq Y$

Any cover symbol (such as W and Y above) which is used to restrict another cover symbol also represents only those strings which the grammar permits in the position specified. If, therefore, a grammar permits W and Y to be *null* in the positions indicated in the above examples, we have not imposed the desired restrictions on X. For example, if the W in example (c) above may be *null*, then $X \neq W + B$ means "X is not B or any string ending with B" instead of "X is any string but one ending with B." To impose the desired restriction, then, we would have to add "and $W \neq$ *null*."

1.2.2 Operators

Operator symbols indicate two operations, namely, concatenation and rewriting.

(1) **Concatenating symbols.** (a) The **plus,** +, is used to symbolize the operation of concatenation and indicates the boundaries of the symbols in a string; i.e. it indicates where the symbols bounded by the plus begin and end and that they form a string. For example, the plus in the rule $A \rightarrow B + C$ indicates that B and C are two distinct symbols and that they form a string.

(b) The **double cross,** #, is also used to symbolize the operation of concatenation and indicates the boundaries of a sentence, e.g. $\#S\#\#S\#$ (see footnote 2). A string of symbols bounded by, but not containing, double crosses is a representation of a sentence; e.g. the double crosses around the string $\#NP + VP\#$ indicate that this string is a representation of a sentence. If a double cross is written before a symbol, e.g. #*NP*, it indicates that *NP* is the first element of a sentence, and if a double cross follows a symbol, e.g. *NP*#, it indicates that this symbol is the last element of a sentence.

(2) **Rewrite symbols.** An **arrow** is used to indicate the operation of rewriting, i.e. that the string on the left of the arrow is to be rewritten as the string on the right. In addition, the arrow indicates the *relation* of the string on the left to the string on the right. An arrow in the phrase structure grammar indicates the relation "is a," while in the transformational part of the grammar, it indicates the relation "is derived from." For example, the arrow in the P-rule $A \rightarrow B$ indicates that A is to be rewritten as B and that "B is an A," while the arrow in the T-rule $A + B \rightarrow B + A$ indicates that $A + B$ is to be rewritten as $B + A$ and that the relation of $B + A$ to $A + B$ is that "$B + A$ is derived from $A + B$." (See 1.7 for a discussion of the relationships postulated in a transformational grammar.)

Several practices are followed in linguistic literature with regard to the type of arrow used to indicate the operation of rewriting: (1) a single solid arrow (→) is used in both P-rules and T-rules; (2) a single broken arrow (-->) is used in P-rules and a single solid arrow in T-rules; (3) a single broken arrow is used in P-rules and a double broken arrow (==>) in T-rules; and (4) a single solid arrow is used in P-rules and a double solid arrow (⇒) in T-rules. The last practice is the one followed in the remainder of this book.

1.2.3 Abbreviators

Since the abbreviating devices defined below are used at boundaries already indicated by pluses, the pluses are then omitted to avoid the redundancy that would result otherwise.

(1) **Parentheses** are used to abbreviate the listing of, or to conflate, (two or more) rules which are identical except for the additional occurrence of one or more symbols. In the conflated rule the latter symbols are parenthesized and are placed in the same position that they occupy in the strings in which they do occur. The absence of parentheses around a symbol in a rule indicates that the occurrence of that symbol is obligatory in every application of that rule; i.e. it must always appear in a particular position in a string. For example, the rule $A \rightarrow B(C)$ is a conflation of the two rules $A \rightarrow B$ and $A \rightarrow B + C$ and specifies that, while the occurrence of B is obligatory, the occurrence of C after B is optional in any given application of the rule. For another example, the rule $B + C(D)E + F \Rightarrow B + C(D)E$ is a conflation of the two

rules $B + C + D + E + F \Rightarrow B + C + D + E$ and $B + C + E + F \Rightarrow B + C + E$ and specifies that the same change applies to two strings which are identical except that in one D does not occur between C and E. The following rules are given to exemplify what the parentheses and lack of them indicate in a conflated rule.

(a) $Y \rightarrow (A)B$ conflates the rules $Y \rightarrow A + B$
$Y \rightarrow B$

and specifies that in any given application of this rule, the occurrence of B is obligatory while that of A before B is optional; this is to say that A cannot occur unless B occurs, but B may occur with or without A.

(b) $Y \rightarrow C(A)(B)$ conflates the rules $Y \rightarrow C$
$Y \rightarrow C + A$
$Y \rightarrow C + A + B$
$Y \rightarrow C + B$

and specifies that in any given application of this rule, the occurrence of C is obligatory while that of either A or B or both is optional, but if A and B do occur, A must follow C (and precede B); this is to say that neither A nor B alone or together can occur without being preceded by C, but C can occur with or without either or both A and B.

(c) $Y \rightarrow C(A + B)$ conflates the rules $Y \rightarrow C$
$Y \rightarrow C + A + B$

and specifies that in any given application of this rule, the occurrence of C is obligatory while that of the string $A + B$ is optional; this is to say that A cannot occur without B and vice versa; they cannot occur without C; but C can occur with or without $A + B$.

(d) $Y \rightarrow ((A)B)C$ conflates the rules $Y \rightarrow A + B + C$
$Y \rightarrow B + C$
$Y \rightarrow C$

and specifies that in any given application of this rule, the occurrence of C is obligatory while that of either B or $A + B$ before C is optional; this is to say that A cannot occur without B; B, in turn, cannot occur without C; but C can occur without either B or $A + B$.

(e) $Y \rightarrow C(A(B))$ conflates the rules

$$Y \rightarrow C + A + B$$
$$Y \rightarrow C + A$$
$$Y \rightarrow C$$

and specifies that in any given application of this rule, the occurrence of C is obligatory while that of either A or $A + B$ after C is optional; this is to say that B cannot occur unless preceded by A; A, in turn, cannot occur unless preceded by C; but C can occur with or without being followed by A or $A + B$.

(f) $Y \rightarrow (B)(C)$ (Choose at least one) conflates the rules

$$Y \rightarrow B$$
$$Y \rightarrow C$$
$$Y \rightarrow B + C$$

and specifies that in any given application of this rule, B, C, or $B + C$ must occur. The instruction (Choose at least one) is added to this rule as a reminder to the reader that at least B or C must be interpreted as part of the rule, since otherwise one of the basic restrictions on P-rules will have been violated, namely, that no P-rule can rewrite a symbol as *null* (see 1.4).

(g) $(A)B + C \Rightarrow (A)B + C + B$ conflates the rules

$$A + B + C \Rightarrow A + B + C + B$$
$$B + C \Rightarrow B + C + B$$

and specifies that in any given application of this rule, the occurrence of B and C is obligatory while that of A is optional, but that when A does occur, it occurs before $B + C$.

(2) **Braces,** { }, are used to conflate (two or more) rules which are identical except for one symbol (or a sequence of symbols) which always occurs in the same position. These symbols are placed vertically and are enclosed within braces. Unlike the symbols in rules conflated with parentheses, however, one of the symbols must always occur in that position in each rule; i.e. any *one* of the symbols (or sequence of symbols) within braces must appear in every application of the conflated rule, and it makes no difference which is chosen. For example, the rule

$$A \rightarrow \begin{Bmatrix} B \\ C \\ D \end{Bmatrix}$$

conflates the three rules

$$A \rightarrow B$$
$$A \rightarrow C$$
$$A \rightarrow D$$

and specifies that either B, C, or D must appear in the position indicated in any given application of the rule. For another example,

$$\left\{\begin{matrix}A\\B\end{matrix}\right\}C \Rightarrow E \qquad \text{conflates the two rules} \qquad \begin{matrix}A + C \Rightarrow E\\B + C \Rightarrow E\end{matrix}$$

and specifies that in any given application of the rule, either A or B precedes C but never both at the same time.

Although all the symbols within braces in the above rules are obligatory symbols, braces can also be used to enclose optional symbols as well. That is, rules such as the following are also permissible:

(a) $A \rightarrow \left(\left\{\begin{matrix}B\\C\end{matrix}\right\}\right)D$ which abbreviates the rules

$$\begin{matrix}A \rightarrow B + D\\A \rightarrow C + D\\A \rightarrow D\end{matrix}$$

(b) $A \rightarrow \left\{\begin{matrix}B + C\\D\\F(G)\end{matrix}\right\}$ which abbreviates the rules

$$\begin{matrix}A \rightarrow B + C\\A \rightarrow D\\A \rightarrow F + G\\A \rightarrow F\end{matrix}$$

(c) $A \rightarrow B\left\{\begin{matrix}\left\{\begin{matrix}C\\D\end{matrix}\right\}F\\E + Y\end{matrix}\right\}$ which abbreviates the rules

$$\begin{matrix}A \rightarrow B + C + F\\A \rightarrow B + D + F\\A \rightarrow B + E + Y\end{matrix}$$

(d) $A\left\{\begin{matrix}C\\D\end{matrix}\right\}B\left\{\begin{matrix}R(L)\\M\end{matrix}\right\} \Rightarrow A + B$ which abbreviates the rules

$$\begin{matrix}A + C + B + R + L \Rightarrow A + B\\A + C + B + R \Rightarrow A + B\\A + C + B + M \Rightarrow A + B\\A + D + B + R + L \Rightarrow A + B\\A + D + B + R \Rightarrow A + B\\A + D + B + M \Rightarrow A + B\end{matrix}$$

When braces are used to abbreviate the listing of P-rules, the symbols need not be placed vertically; instead, they may be arranged linearly and separated by commas, but the braces are then omitted, e.g. $A \rightarrow B, C, D$. One of the most common uses for this manner of abbreviation is to list the lexicon. For example, the linear arrangement and separation by commas of the morphemes in the rule $N \rightarrow$ *man, boy, girl* indicate that any one of the morpheme symbols to the right of the arrow may be chosen in any given application of the rule, but only one may be chosen at a time.

(3) **Square brackets,** [ ], are used to abbreviate the listing of (two or more) rules pertaining to strings which are different and identical in the same places. These rules must differ in at least two places; therefore at least two pairs of brackets must appear in a conflated rule. The symbols which are different are placed vertically and enclosed in brackets, and the rule thus conflated is read across by lines; for example, the rule

$$\begin{bmatrix} A \\ B \end{bmatrix} C + X \Rightarrow \begin{bmatrix} a \\ b \end{bmatrix} C + X$$

conflates the two rules

$$A + C + X \Rightarrow a + C + X$$
$$B + C + X \Rightarrow b + C + X$$

and specifies that a different change applies to A than applies to B when each is followed by $C + X$; in other words, the conflated rule specifies two changes which occur in the same environment. For another example, the rule

$$\begin{bmatrix} A \\ B \end{bmatrix} C \begin{bmatrix} D \\ E \end{bmatrix} \Rightarrow \begin{bmatrix} A \\ B \end{bmatrix} C \begin{bmatrix} F \\ G \end{bmatrix}$$

conflates the two rules

$$A + C + D \Rightarrow A + C + F$$
$$B + C + E \Rightarrow B + C + G$$

and specifies that two different changes occur in the same environment, namely, C. As with braces, optional symbols may also occur within brackets; in fact, all three abbreviating devices may be combined to conflate rules. That is, a rule such as the following is also permissible:

$$\begin{Bmatrix} A(B) \\ C \end{Bmatrix} D \begin{bmatrix} E \\ F \end{bmatrix} \Rightarrow D \begin{bmatrix} E \\ F \end{bmatrix}$$

which conflates the rules

$$A + B + D + E \Rightarrow D + E$$
$$A + D + E \Rightarrow D + E$$
$$A + B + D + F \Rightarrow D + F$$
$$A + D + F \Rightarrow D + F$$
$$C + D + E \Rightarrow D + E$$
$$C + D + F \Rightarrow D + F$$

1.3 DERIVATIONS AND P-MARKERS

If we are given, for example, the following (partial) grammar:

GRAMMAR A

$\#S\#$

1. $S \rightarrow NP + VP + Adv$
2. $VP \rightarrow V + NP$
3. $NP \rightarrow Det + N$
4. $Det \rightarrow$ *the, a*
5. $N \rightarrow$ *girl, flower*
6. $V \rightarrow$ *cut*
7. $Adv \rightarrow$ *yesterday*

and we go through the following procedure:

PROCEDURE A

1. Write down the initial string of the grammar (which, you will notice, is also the symbol on the left of the arrow in the first rule).
2. Apply the rules:
   (a) one at a time;
   (b) in the order indicated (by the Arabic numeral on the left of each rule);
   (c) choosing one expansion for a symbol whenever a choice is given, skipping any rule(s) that expand optional element(s) not chosen previously;
   (d) reapplying a rule as many times as necessary if two (or more) identical symbols result in a string from the application of a previous rule.
3. Each time a rule is applied, place the result under the preceding string; that is, write under the initial string the string resulting from the application of the first rule and under that, the replacing string and the part of the preceding string that remains unchanged by the rule. In other words, replace only *one* symbol in each successive string, until every symbol can no longer be replaced (rewritten or expanded) by a P-rule.

we will get what is called a **derivation** of a sentence.

Thus, by applying the rules of Grammar A as indicated in steps 1 to 3 of Procedure A, we obtain the following derivation for the sentence *a girl cut the flower yesterday:*

Initial string #*S*#

(1) *NP* + *VP* + *Adv*
(2) *NP* + *V* + *NP* + *Adv*
(3) *Det* + *N* + *V* + *NP* + *Adv*
(3) *Det* + *N* + *V* + *Det* + *N* + *Adv*
(4) *a* + *N* + *V* + *Det* + *N* + *Adv*
(4) *a* + *N* + *V* + *the* + *N* + *Adv*
(5) *a* + *girl* + *V* + *the* + *N* + *Adv*
(5) *a* + *girl* + *V* + *the* + *flower* + *Adv*
(6) *a* + *girl* + *cut* + *the* + *flower* + *Adv*
(7) *a* + *girl* + *cut* + *the* + *flower* + *yesterday*

Notice that by comparing the successive lines in the derivation, we can see the order in which the rules were applied to form it; therefore a derivation tells us precisely how a sentence was constructed, or, technically speaking, it tells us the **derivational history** of a sentence.

Note that the last line, or string, in a derivation consists entirely of symbols that can no longer be expanded by any P-rule of the grammar. Any symbol that cannot be expanded further by the application of a P-rule is called a **terminal symbol,** and any string consisting entirely of terminal symbols is called a **terminal string.** Thus there is only one terminal string in a derivation; all other strings are **non-terminal** and consist of at least one **non-terminal symbol,** i.e. a symbol that is expanded further by a P-rule.

We say that every non-terminal string in a derivation is a representation of the terminal string; e.g. *NP* + *VP* + *Adv*, *NP* + *V* + *NP* + *Adv*, *Det* + *N* + *V* + *NP* + *Adv*, *a* + *girl* + *V* + *the* + *flower* + *Adv*, *a* + *girl* + *cut* + *the* + *flower* + *Adv*, etc., are all representations of the terminal string. Notice, in addition, that by comparing successive strings, we thereby know what are the **constituents,** or what is the **constituent structure,** of a sentence. For example, if we compare the second and third lines of the above derivation, we see that the constituents of a noun phrase are a determiner followed by a noun, and if we compare the fourth and fifth lines, we see that *a* is a determiner since it replaces *Det*; by comparing other successive lines, we see that both *flower* and *girl* are nouns since they both replace *N*, etc.

Now, we will get a *formal representation* of the constituent structure of a sentence as shown in a developing derivation if we go through the following procedure, omitting all boundary symbols:

PROCEDURE B[3]

1. Write down the first line in the derivation (which is also the initial string of the grammar).
2. Match it with the next line of the derivation, and under the first line write the symbols that replace it.
3. Match the second and third lines of the derivation, and write under the replaced symbol those symbols that replace it.
4. Continue matching, in pairs, the successive strings of the derivation, placing, as in step 3, the replacing symbols under the replaced symbol, taking care that the correct linear order of the symbols is maintained, until every symbol has been replaced (i.e. until the last line of the derivation appears).
5. Draw lines that connect the respective replaced and replacing symbols.

NOTE: If steps 1 to 5 are performed properly, a unique path will always be traceable (a) from the termination of each line to the initial string (i.e. to the topmost symbol), (b) from any symbol to any symbol (i.e. from any **node** to any node), and (c) none of the lines will cross.

This procedure results in what is called a **labeled (branching) tree diagram** (or simply a **derivational tree**) and is one of several equivalent ways of formally representing the constituent structure of a sentence as shown in a developing derivation. Following Chomsky,[4] we shall call all such representations **P-markers** (phrase markers). We shall use only the labeled tree in this book, however; thus, whenever the term "P-marker" is used, it refers to a labeled tree.

[3] Notice that steps 1 to 4 are essentially the same as Procedure A (the steps for forming a derivation), with the exception that the pluses and the part of a string that remains unchanged with the application of the rule are omitted; in other words, a formal representation of a derivation can be drawn by applying the rules of a grammar and observing the same restrictions as those for forming a derivation.

[4] "On the Notion 'Rule of Grammar,'" in *Structure of Language and Its Mathematical Aspects* (*Proceedings of the Twelfth Symposium in Applied Mathematics,* vol. 12), American Mathematical Society, Providence, R.I., 1961, pp. 6–24; reprinted in J. A. Fodor and J. J. Katz (eds.), *The Structure of Language: Readings in the Philosophy of Language,* Prentice-Hall, Inc., Englewood Cliffs, N.J., 1964, pp. 119–136.

By following steps 1 to 5 of Procedure B, for the above derivation we will get

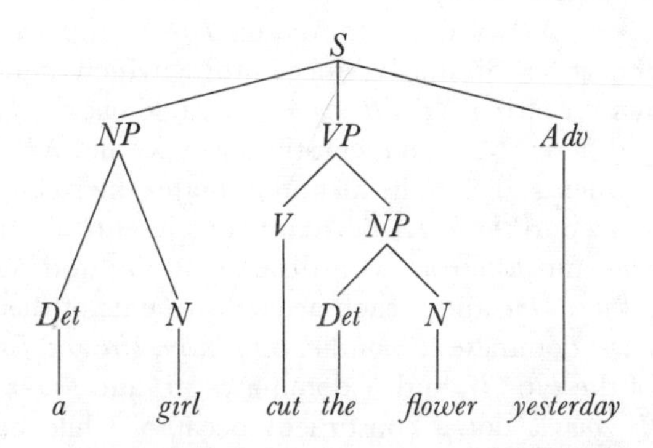

Notice that we cannot tell by looking at the above P-marker in what order the rules of Grammar A were applied to construct it; i.e. we cannot tell by looking at the above tree whether *NP* was expanded before *VP* or whether *Det* was expanded before *N* or *Adv*, etc. We can, however, get this information from a derivation, simply by comparing the successive lines in it. In fact, this is the only difference between a derivation and a tree; i.e. the order of application of rules is preserved in a derivation but lost in a tree. We can therefore draw a tree from a derivation but not vice versa. This does not, however, obviate the fact that a P-marker is equivalent to the *set* of strings in a derivation, and, therefore, that whenever we speak about a P-marker, we are also speaking about the derivation it represents.

Although a P-marker does not show the order in which the rules of the grammar were applied to construct it, a P-marker explicitly shows what strings of symbols are related to other single symbols; i.e. it explicitly shows the constituent structure of a sentence. The fact that certain strings are "uniquely" traceable back to a common label, or node, say *B*, indicates that (a) the string which is uniquely traceable back to *B* is a **constituent of the type** *B*, or is a **constituent-type** *B* (or *B* **constituent-type**) or simply **is a** *B*, and (b) the symbols comprising the string are **constituents of** *B*. The node to which a string is uniquely traceable back is said, in turn, to **dominate** that string. A string is "uniquely traceable back to a common node," say *B*, if nothing immediately preceding or following the string is traceable back to *B*.

In the above P-marker, for example, the string (or sequence) *Det N* is uniquely traceable back to *NP* since nothing which immediately precedes *Det* or immediately follows *N* is also traceable back to *NP*; therefore the string *Det N* is an *NP* (or a constituent of the type *NP* or an *NP* constituent-type); *NP*, in turn, dominates *Det N*, and *Det* and *N* each are constituents of *NP*. Similarly, since nothing which immediately precedes or follows the string *NP VP Adv* is traceable back to *S*, *NP VP Adv* is an *S* or, put differently, is an *S* constituent-type, and *NP*, *VP*, and *Adv* each are constituents of *S*; *S*, in turn, dominates the string *NP VP Adv*. The strings *a girl* and *the flower* both are constituents of the type *NP*; *a* and *girl* and *the* and *flower* are constituents of *NP*; and *NP* dominates *a girl* and *the flower*. *the* and *a* each are constituents of the constituent-type *Det*, and *Det* dominates *the* and *a*. Similarly, *girl* and *flower* each are constituents of the type *N*, and *N* dominates *girl* and *flower*. In contrast, the string *NP Adv* is not a constituent because, while both are ultimately traceable back to a common node, namely, *S*, they are not uniquely traceable to *S*. The same is true in the above P-marker of *girl cut, V Det, V Det N, VP Adv, NP VP*, etc.[5]

Finally, those symbols, or nodes, which occur toward the top of a tree are referred to as **higher order constituents,** while those symbols that occur toward the bottom of a tree are referred to as **lower order constituents.** Thus *NP*, *VP*, and *Adv* in the above P-marker are higher order constituents of a sentence, while *Det*, *N*, *the,* and *girl* are lower order constituents of a sentence, but of different levels.

1.4 PHRASE STRUCTURE RULES

The phrase structure rules are the first set of rules in a grammar, and, as stated earlier, they specify the syntactic classes, their co-occurrence relations, and the lexicon of a language. P-rules are simple string replacement rules; i.e. one string replaces another in the sense that one symbol is expanded into a string. They must be written in such a way as to permit the automatic assignment of P-markers to the strings of morphemes derived from these rules. The P-markers assigned by P-rules are called **underlying P-markers.** So that these P-markers will be automatically assigned, the following restrictions are put on P-rules:

1. Each rule must replace (i.e. expand) only a *single* symbol.

[5] The distinction between "constituent of the type *B*" and "a constituent of *B*" corresponds to the distinction between what in traditional terminology is called "a constitute" and an "immediate constituent." Thus, in traditional terminology, *Det* + *N* is said to be "the constitute *NP*," while *Det* and *N* are said to be "the immediate constituents of *NP*."

2. Each replaced symbol (except the initial) must be part of some replacing string; i.e. every symbol (except the initial) that appears to the left of an arrow must appear to the right of the arrow in some rule.

3. Each symbol must be replaced by a *non-null* (i.e. non-empty) string; for example, *A* cannot be replaced by *B* if *B* is *null* (represents no string). In brief, deletions are not permitted in the phrase structure grammar.

4. The replacing string must be distinct from the original; i.e. *A* cannot be replaced by a string beginning or ending in *A*. In this book, however, this restriction will be such that *A* cannot be replaced by *A* or any string containing *A*.

5. For any two symbols *A* and *B* which concatenate in some strings, giving $A + B$, it must not be the case that there is both a rule (or a sequence of rules) expanding *A* as *B* and a rule (or a sequence of rules) expanding *B* as *A*; i.e. permutations are not permissible in the phrase structure grammar.

It is often necessary to specify that a symbol may be expanded into a string in a certain environment or context. For example, an expansion of *A* may be *B* only when it is preceded by *Y* and followed by *Z*. A P-rule that specifies such an expansion is called a **context-restricted** (or **context-sensitive**) rule, while all other P-rules are called **context-free.**

Context-restricted P-rules have the same restrictions on them as context-free P-rules, with the additional restriction that the context, or environment, of such a rule, if stated with a class symbol, must be the last expansion of that symbol. For example, if *VP* has been expanded into, say, $\left\{\begin{matrix} Vtr + NP \\ Vin \end{matrix}\right\}$, *VP* cannot be used as the environment in which another symbol is expanded.

There are several equivalent notations one may use to specify environments; these are exemplified in the following rules, all of which can be read as the instruction "Rewrite *A* as *B* in the environment *Y*_*Z*" or, alternatively, as the statement "*B* is an *A* in the environment *Y*_*Z*."

(a) $YAZ \rightarrow YBZ$
(a′) $A \rightarrow B$ in env. Y_Z
(a″) $A \rightarrow B \,/\, Y\_Z$

The last notation for specifying environments, (a″), is the one used in this book.[6]

[6] The pluses on either side of the dash are omitted in context-restricted rules, since the dash itself makes it clear what the boundaries of the symbols in the string are.

Context-restricted rules are needed only when there are mutually exclusive expansions for a given symbol; and in this book the following notational convention is used to indicate this:

$$A \rightarrow \begin{Bmatrix} M\ /\ B\_C \\ F \end{Bmatrix}$$

The omission of a specification of the environment for the selection of F means that F may be chosen in *any* context other than B_C; in other words, the above rule specifies that A *must* be expanded as M in the context B_C, and F must be chosen otherwise (or elsewhere). The following rule, however, specifies that M must be chosen in the environment B_C, but that *either* M or F may be chosen elsewhere:

$$A \rightarrow \begin{Bmatrix} M\ /\ B\_C \\ M \\ F \end{Bmatrix}$$

1.4.1 Examples of P-rules and underlying P-markers

The following are some examples of P-rules and the P-markers they assign:

(a) $A \rightarrow B$

(b) 1. $W \rightarrow X + Y$
2. $X \rightarrow A + B$
3. $Y \rightarrow C + D$

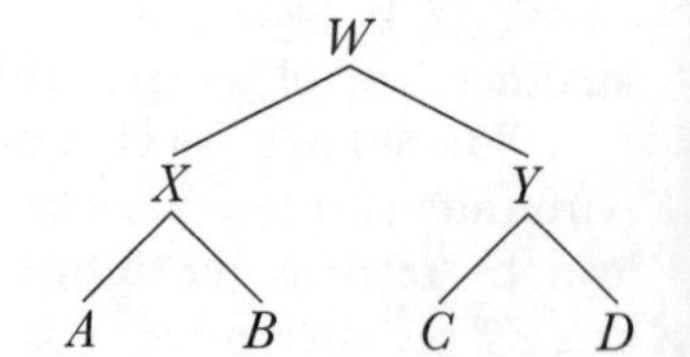

(c) 1. $N \rightarrow Ns + G$
2. $Ns \rightarrow Nsf, Nsm$
3. $G \rightarrow \begin{Bmatrix} M\ /\ Nsm\_ \\ F \end{Bmatrix}$

(1) N and (2) N

Ns G Ns G

Nsm M Nsf F

(d) 1. $S \rightarrow NP + VP$

2. $VP \rightarrow Aux \begin{Bmatrix} Vtr + NP \\ Vin \end{Bmatrix}$

3. $Aux \rightarrow (Neg)T$
4. $T \rightarrow Pres, Pas$
5. $NP \rightarrow D + N$
6. $N \rightarrow Ns + Afn$
7. $Afn \rightarrow G + Nu$
8. $Nu \rightarrow Sg, Pl$

P-MARKERS ASSIGNED BY (d)

(1)

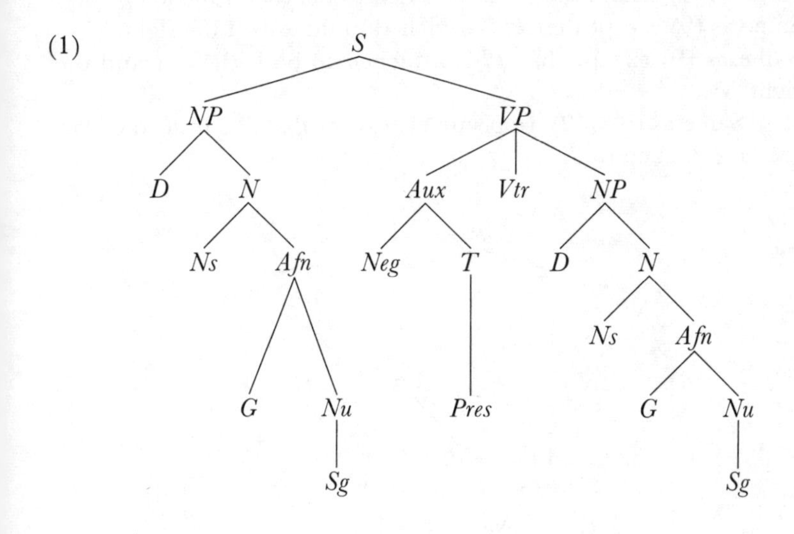

(2) Same as (1) except that *Pl* is attached to the *Nu* on the left.
(3) Same as (1) except that *Pl* is attached to the *Nu* on the right.
(4) Same as (1) except that *Pl* is attached to both the left and the right *Nu*.
(5)–(8) Same as (1)–(4), respectively, except that *Pas* instead of *Pres* is attached to *T*.

(9)

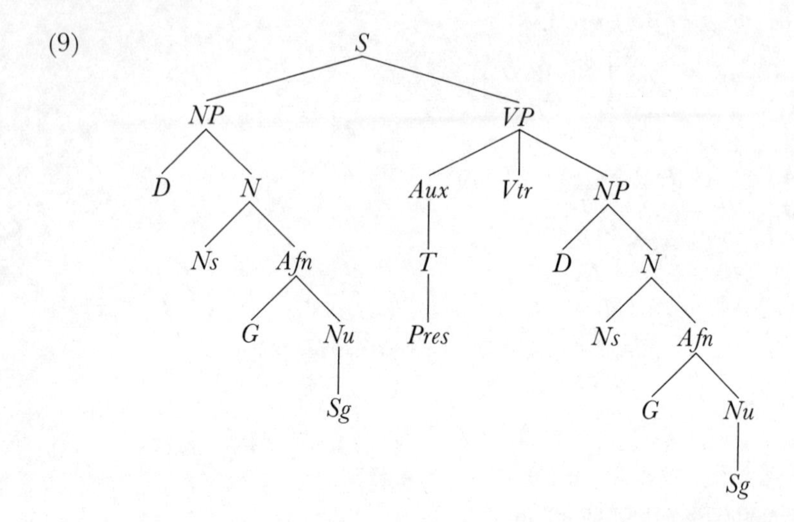

(10) Same as (9) except that *Pl* is attached to the *Nu* on the left.
(11) Same as (9) except that *Pl* is attached to the *Nu* on the right.
(12) Same as (9) except that *Pl* is attached to both the left and the right *Nu*.
(13)–(16) Same as (9)–(12), respectively, except that *Pas* instead of *Pres* is attached to *T*.

(17)

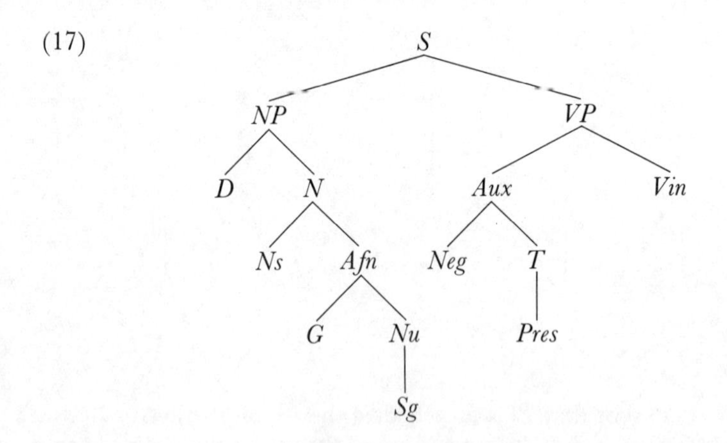

(18) Same as (17) except that *Pl* is attached to *Nu*.
(19)–(20) Same as (17)–(18), respectively, except that *Pas* instead of *Pres* is attached to *T*.

(21)

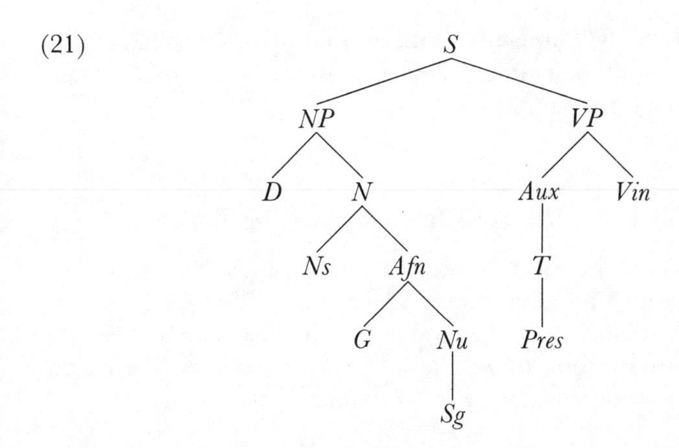

(22) Same as (21) except that *Pl* is attached to *Nu*.

(23)–(24) Same as (21) and (22), respectively, except that *Pas* instead of *Pres* is attached to *T*.

1.5 TRANSFORMATIONAL RULES

The second set of rules in a transformational grammar are the T-rules. Although, as stated earlier, both P-rules and T-rules are rewrite rules, i.e. both are of the form $A \rightarrow B$, T-rules operate on the underlying P-markers provided by the P-rules and produce new P-markers, called **derived P-markers,** which can undergo further change through the application of other T-rules (thus the source P-marker of a derived P-marker may be either an underlying P-marker or a derived P-marker). That is, the A and B of a T-rule $A \Rightarrow B$ are (a set of) P-markers and not individual strings as they are in P-rules.

While P-rules must always be applied wherever they can be applied, this is not the case with T-rules. The application of T-rules wherever they can be applied may be optional or obligatory, or obligatory under certain conditions and optional under others. (See 1.7 for the significance of optional versus obligatory T-rules.) Whether the application of a T-rule is optional or obligatory must therefore be indicated in some way. In this book the optional or obligatory application of a T-rule is indicated by Topt and Tob, respectively, at the beginning of the T-rule. If a T-rule is optional under some conditions and obligatory under others, only T appears at the beginning of the rule and the words "optional" and "obligatory" appear with the conditions in question below the rule; for example,

T

$$X + Y + Z \Rightarrow X + Z + Y$$

obligatory if $Y = Pron$ and optional otherwise

Let us suppose, now, that we wanted Grammar A of 1.3 to generate sentences in which an adverb may precede as well as follow everything else in a sentence, i.e. to generate sentences such as *yesterday the girl cut the flower* in addition to *the girl cut the flower yesterday.* We would then simply add an optional T-rule to Grammar A:

GRAMMAR A′

#S#

1. $S \rightarrow NP + VP + Adv$
2. $VP \rightarrow V + NP$
3. $NP \rightarrow Det + N$
4. $Det \rightarrow$ *a, the*
5. $N \rightarrow$ *girl, flower*
6. $V \rightarrow$ *cut*
7. $Adv \rightarrow$ *yesterday*
8. Topt

$$NP + VP + Adv \Rightarrow Adv + NP + VP$$

The left-hand side of a T-rule is called the **structural description** and specifies the form P-markers must have for the rule to be applicable; i.e. it defines the **domain** of the rule. The right-hand side of a T-rule is called the **structural change** (or transform) and specifies the form of the P-markers after application of the rule.[7] Thus, the application of rule (8) changes the underlying P-marker representing the sentence

[7] It should be noted that there are different notational conventions for writing a T-rule; rule (8) above can also be written, for example, as:

(a) SD: (*NP, VP, Adv*)
SC: $X_1\text{-}X_2\text{-}X_3 \rightarrow X_3\text{-}X_1\text{-}X_2$

(b) $\frac{NP}{1} + \frac{VP}{2} + \frac{Adv}{3} \rightarrow 3 + 1 + 2$

Although both notations (a) and (b) are commonly used in the literature, the notation used in rule (8) above has been adopted for this book.

a girl cut the flower yesterday, formed by applying rules (1) to (7), to the derived P-marker shown on the right below:

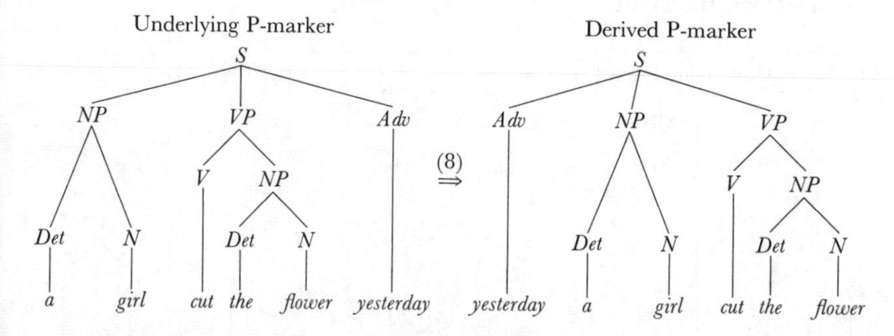

Notice that the higher order symbols *NP*, *VP*, and *Adv* are used in rule (8) rather than any of the lower order non-terminal or terminal symbols that are in the underlying P-marker. This is not accidental. Changes specified by a T-rule pertain to that *set* of P-markers which have the form (or structure) given on the left of the rule and produce a new *set* of derived P-markers. Thus, if *NP* + *VP*, for example, is the structural description of a T-rule, this means that the domain of the rule is *every* P-marker with the general structure *NP* + *VP*, regardless of how different the strings dominated by *NP* and *VP* may be from one P-marker to another. Clearly, then, the more general we want a change to be, the higher the order of symbols we use in a rule, since the more P-markers the rule will then operate on. For example, suppose we modify Grammar A′ as follows:

GRAMMAR A″

1. $S \rightarrow NP + VP + Adv$
2. $VP \rightarrow V + NP$
3. $NP \rightarrow \begin{Bmatrix} Det + N \\ Name \end{Bmatrix}$
4. $Det \rightarrow$ *a, the*
5. $N \rightarrow$ *girl, flower*
6. $Name \rightarrow$ *Mary, John*
7. $V \rightarrow$ *cut*
8. $Adv \rightarrow$ *yesterday*
9. Topt

   $NP + VP + Adv \rightarrow Adv + NP + VP$

Rule (9) above (which is identical to rule [8] of Grammar A′) applies *at least* to the four P-markers on the left below and changes them as shown on the right:

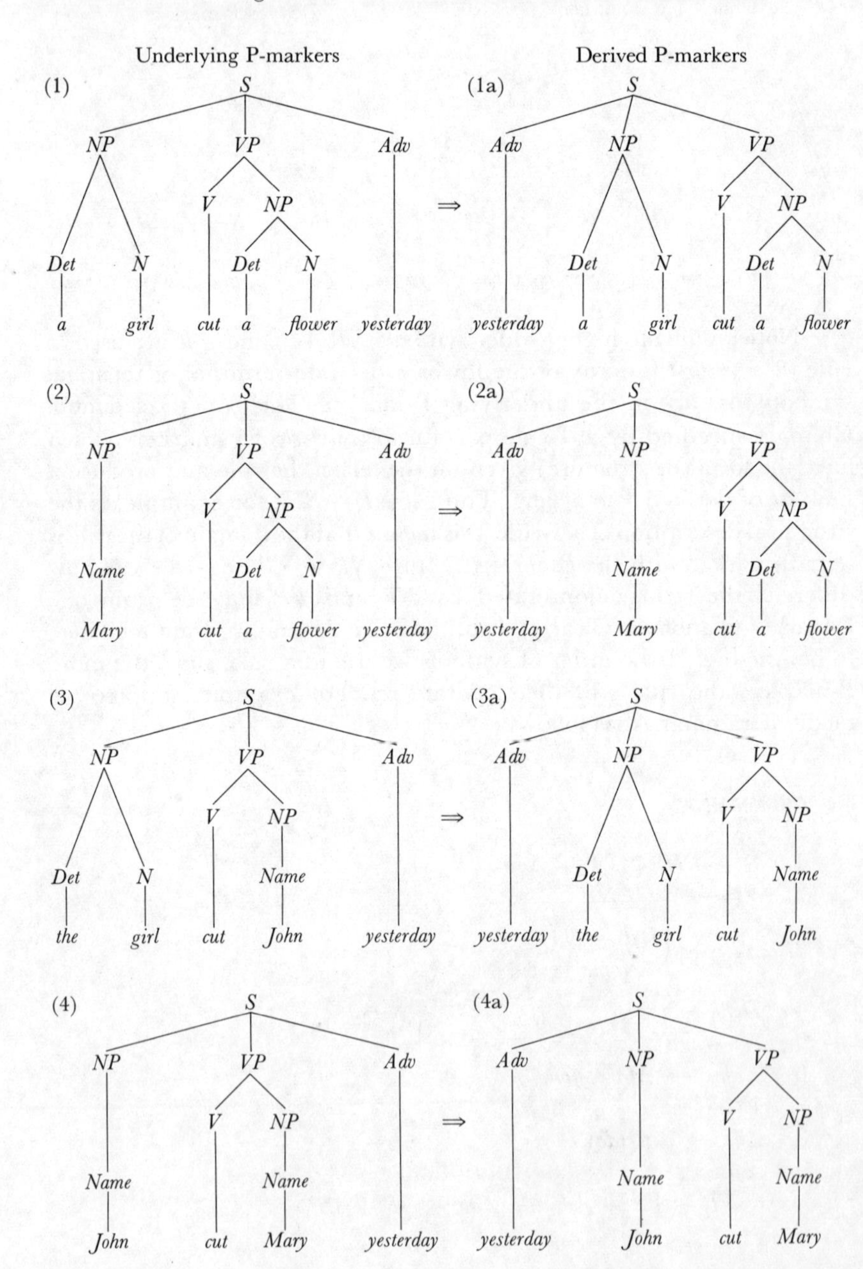

In other words, rule (9) applies to every P-marker with the general structure *NP* + *VP* + *Adv* regardless of what is dominated by *NP*, *VP*, and *Adv*.

Suppose, however, that, instead of generating sentences like *yesterday the girl cut the flower* and *yesterday John cut the flower,* we wanted to generate *only* sentences like *yesterday the girl cut John,* that is, we wanted to specify that an adverb may be shifted from sentence-final to sentence-initial position only if the object is a name. We would then modify rule (9) as follows (i.e. write it with fewer higher order symbols):

Topt
$$NP + V + Name + Adv \Rightarrow Adv + NP + V + Name$$

Of the four underlying P-markers shown, only P-markers (3) and (4) would be changed by the above modified rule into the derived P-markers (3a) and (4a), respectively.

So far, we have discussed only the domain of a T-rule and the structural change in underlying (or derived) P-markers that it assigns. But the domain and structural change are only two of the three parts of what is technically called a **transformation.** The third part of a transformation is the **operation,** or combination of operations, that produces the structural change. T-rules, or transformations, may be made up of one or more elementary transformations. A T-rule which consists of any one of the following four operations: adjunction, deletion, permutation (i.e. juxtaposition), and substitution (or replacement) is called an **elementary transformation.** Rule (8) of Grammar A′ and rule (9) of Grammar A″ are each a transformation which consists of two elementary transformations, namely, deletion and adjunction.

Just as it is required that P-rules automatically assign P-markers to the strings generated by these rules, it is required that transformations automatically assign derived P-markers. Clearly, however, since T-rules do not have the same restrictions imposed on them as P-rules, we cannot construct derived P-markers in the same way that we can construct underlying P-markers. Each elementary transformation therefore has a **convention** (provided by the theory) for properly constructing its respective derived P-markers (See 1.5.1.). P-markers assigned by a transformation that consists of more than one elementary transformation are constructed by applying, one at a time, the conventions for constructing P-markers produced by the respective elementary transformations.

The automatic assignment of derived P-markers by a rule requires that no non-terminal symbol that does not appear in the source P-marker defined in the structural description of the rule replace or be adjoined to another symbol by a transformation. That is, we cannot write the rule $X + B + C \Rightarrow X + D + C$, for example, which would specify that

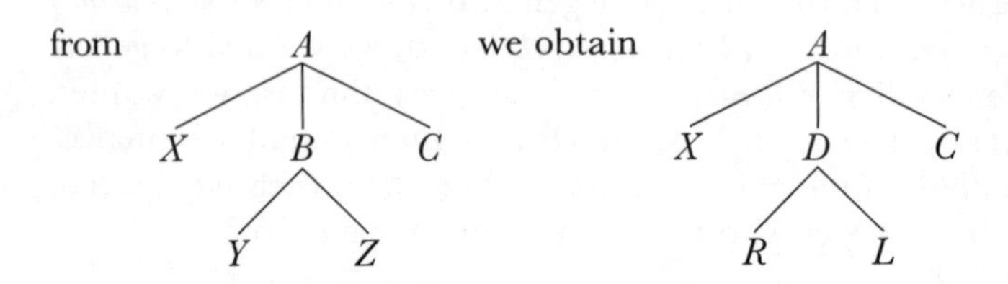

even though there may be a P-rule expanding D into $R + L$, because D does not appear in the source P-marker and we would have to refer back to the P-rules to find the structure of D. In other words, we could not automatically determine the derived structure assigned by the transformation from the rule itself.

Just as which P-rules are applied and the particular expansions chosen in generating a sentence provides us with the derivational history of that sentence (formally represented in its underlying P-marker), those transformations applied in generating a sentence and the particular derived P-markers they assign to that sentence provides us with what is called the **transformational history** of a sentence. It is the derivational and transformational histories of a sentence, then, that constitute (or provide us with) the **structural** (or **grammatical**) **description** of a sentence, which the grammar is required to provide for each sentence generated. Put differently, the structural (or grammatical) description of a sentence is its underlying P-marker(s), the transformations applied in generating it, and the derived P-markers for that sentence assigned by these rules.

1.5.1 Examples of T-rules and derived P-markers

The various elementary transformations and their respective conventions for constructing derived P-markers are defined and exemplified below. Some transformations that consist of more than one elementary transformation are also exemplified.

1. **Adjunction.** One or more strings in a given (set of) P-marker(s) are adjoined to one or more other strings in that (set of) P-marker(s). The string that is adjoined to (the right or left of) a string is attached to the *lowest* node that dominated that string in the source P-marker. For example, given a rule $X + Y \Rightarrow X + Y + Z$, where Z is a morpheme symbol, we may obtain

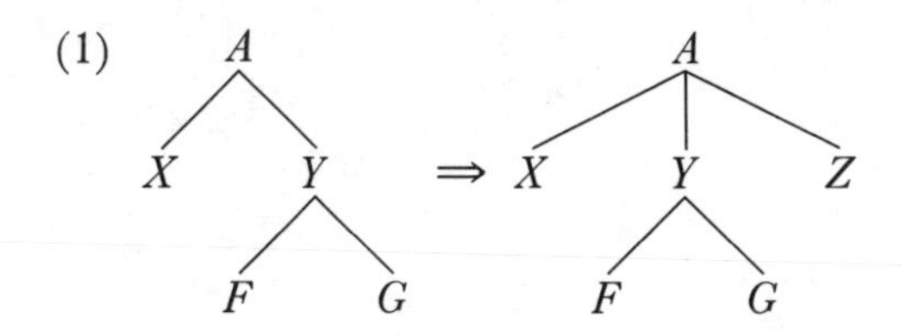

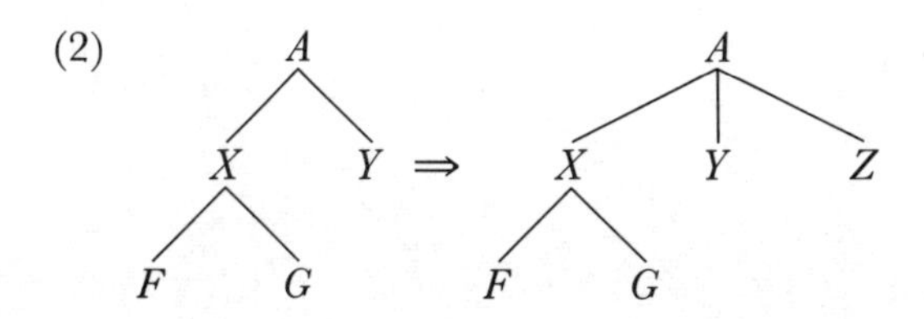

Given another rule $X + Y \Rightarrow X + X + Y$, we may obtain

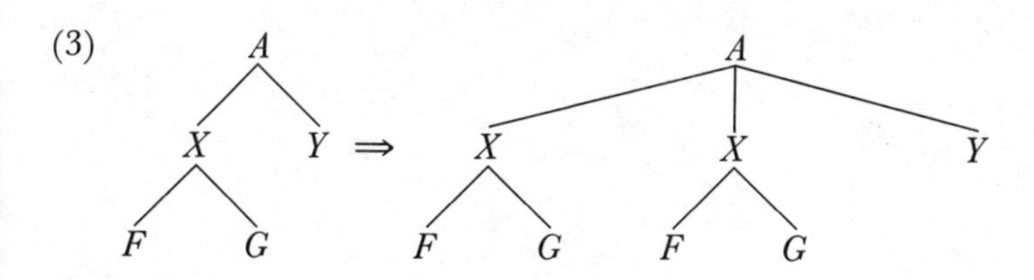

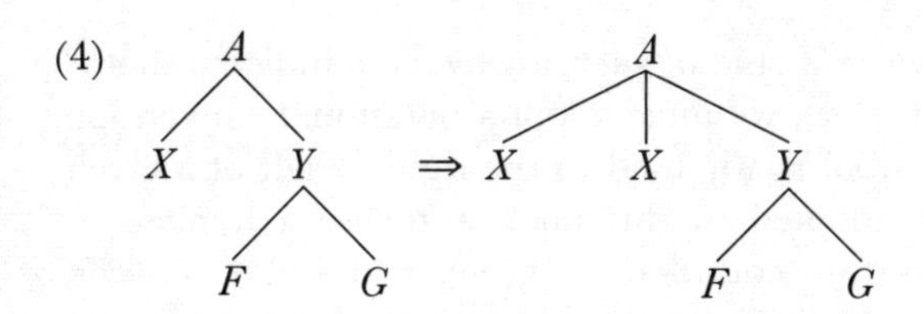

And given a rule $X + Y \Rightarrow X + Z + Y$, where Z is a morpheme symbol, we may obtain

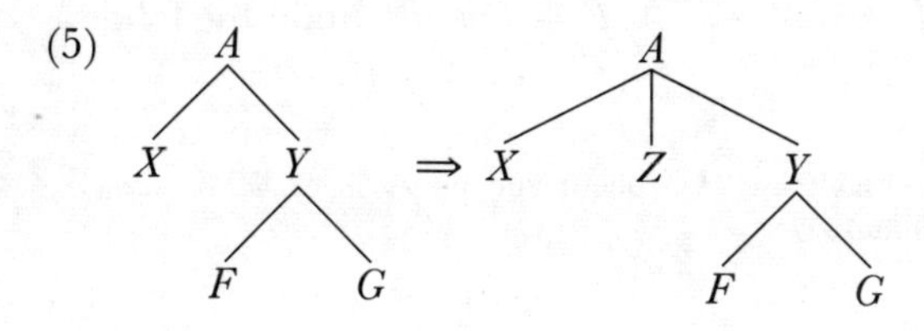

(6)

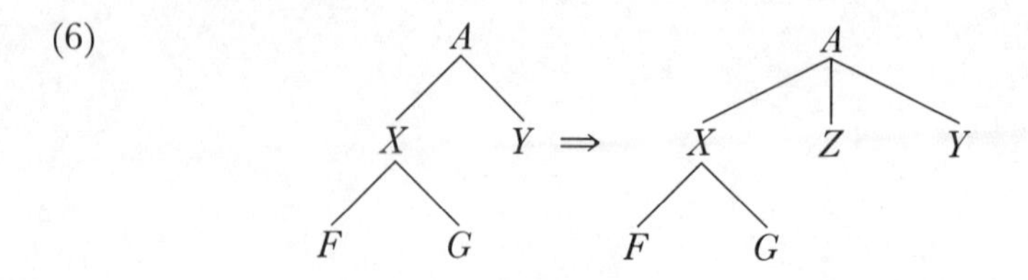

(7)

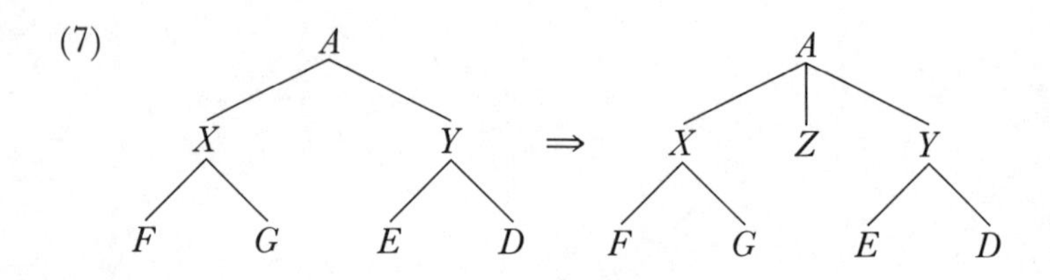

If, however, we wanted to obtain a derived P-marker that looks like, say, the following:

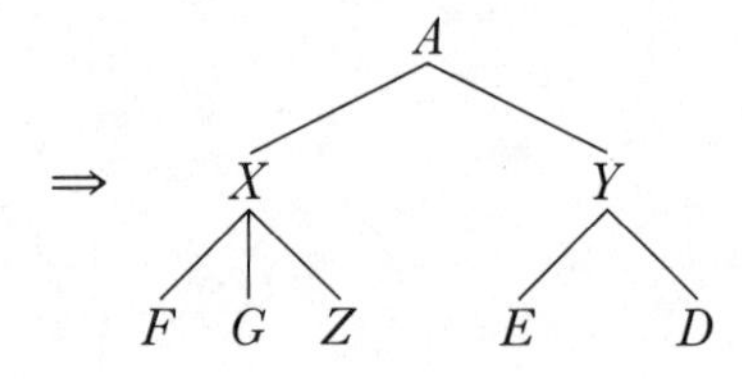

that is, if we wanted to write a rule in such a way as to indicate that Z is attached to X (and not to A), we must adopt a **notational convention** to indicate whether a symbol is adjoined to the right or left of a given symbol. The convention adopted in this book is to use a hyphen to separate symbols that we want considered a group and a plus between the symbols in each group, in both the structural description and structural change of a T-rule.[8] Thus, to indicate that Z is to be adjoined to the right of G, we would write the rule $F + G - Y \Rightarrow F + G + Z - Y$ and would thus automatically get the P-marker we wanted above. If we wanted to indicate that Z is to be adjoined to the left of E, we would write the rule $X - E + D \Rightarrow X - Z + E + D$ and obtain the following derived P-marker:

[8] A modification of N. Chomsky's use of hyphens and pluses in *Syntactic Structures*, Mouton and Company, The Hague, 1957.

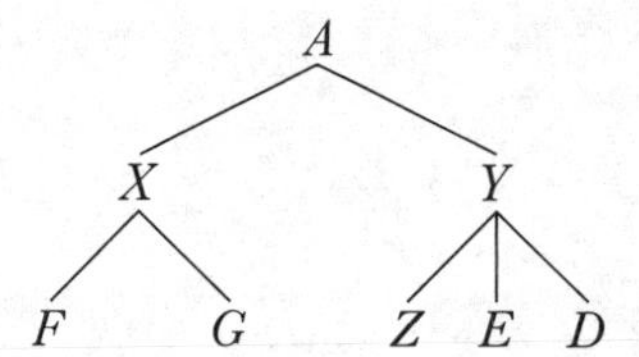

If we wanted to indicate that Z is to be adjoined both to the right of G and to the left of E, we would write the rule $F + G - E + D \Rightarrow F + G + Z - Z + E + D$ and obtain the following derived P-marker:

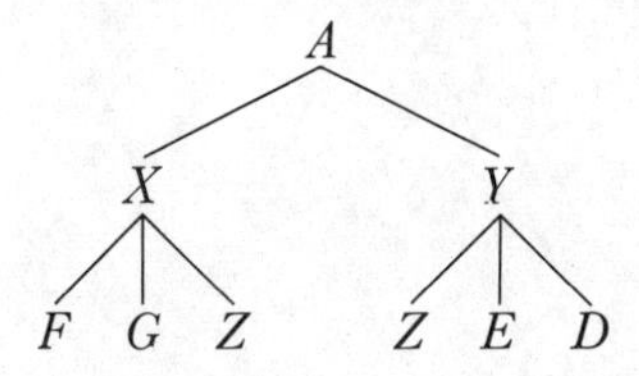

2. **Deletion.** One or more strings are deleted from a given (set of) P-marker(s). The string to be deleted, as well as any nodes that it uniquely dominates and any nodes uniquely dominating it, is deleted from the source P-marker. For example, given a rule $X + Y \Rightarrow Y$, we may obtain

(1) A / X Y ⇒ A / Y

(2)

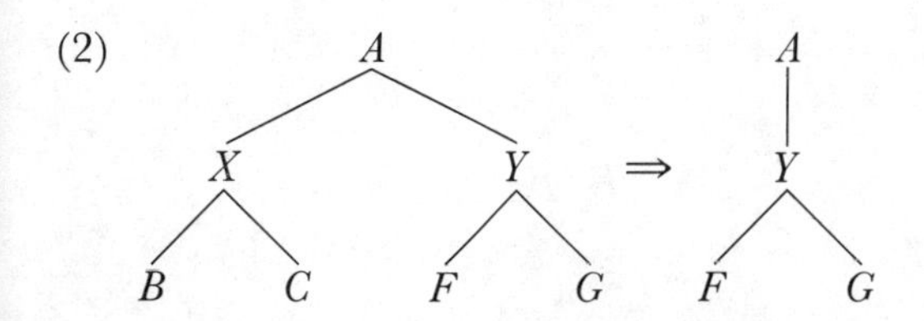

(3)

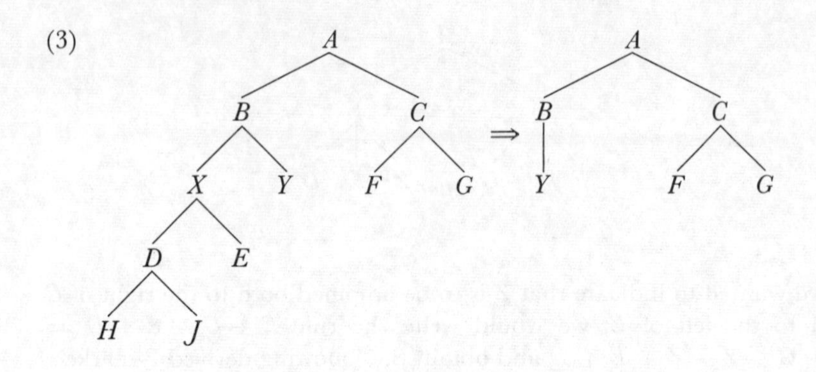

(4)

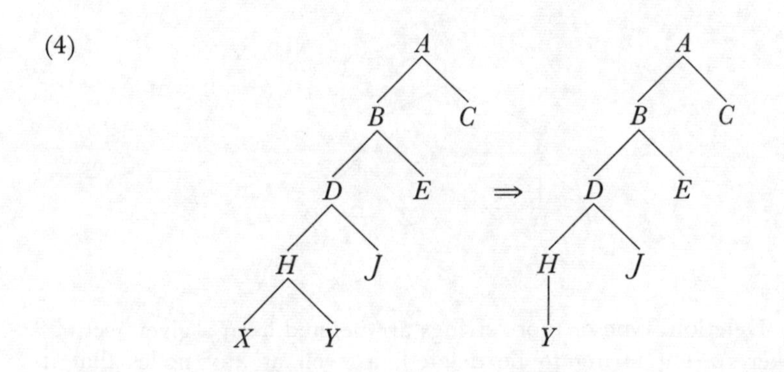

3. **Permutation.** *Two* strings that are *adjacent constituents* in a given (set of) P-marker(s) are permuted (i.e. rearranged or juxtaposed) in relation to each other (see 6.3.4). The strings to be permuted are detached, permuted in the proper order, and reattached to the *lowest* node which dominated both in the source P-marker. Carry along intermediate structure whenever other structure is not destroyed as a result. (See 4.4 for an example of what it means to "carry intermediate structure.") For example, given a rule $X + Y + Z \Rightarrow X + Z + Y$, we may obtain

(1)

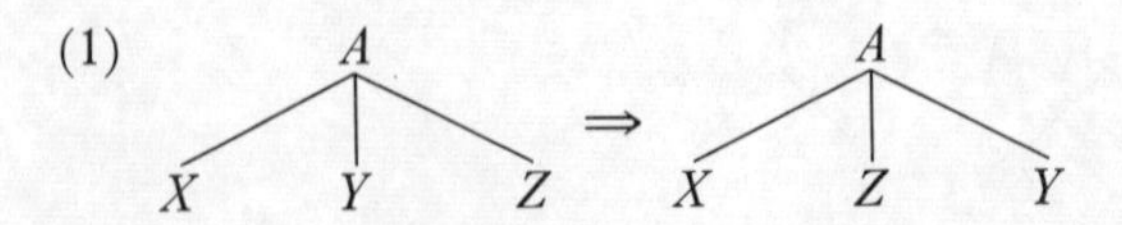

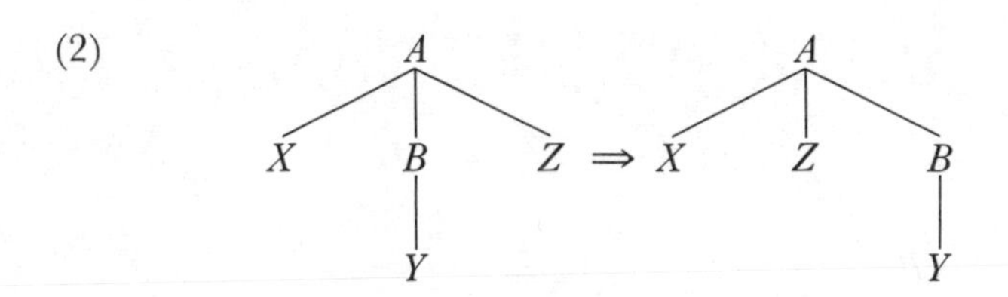

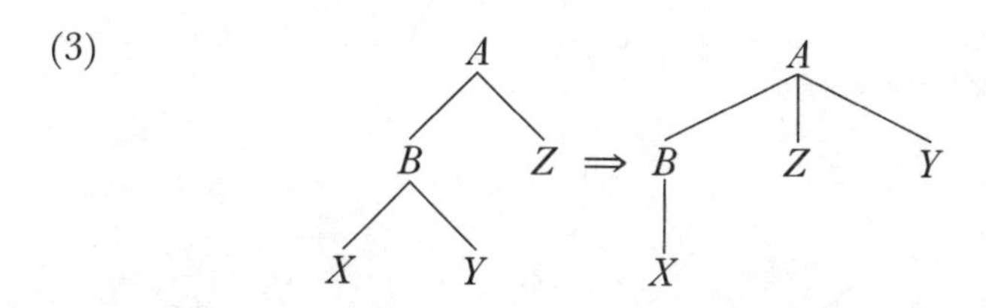

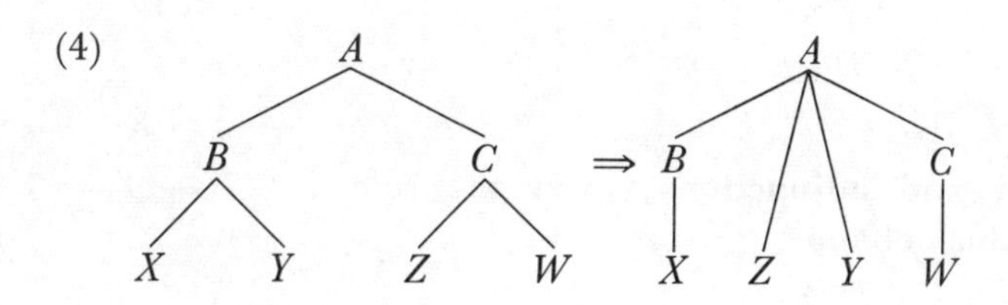

4. **Substitution** (or **replacement**). One or more strings of a given (set of) P-marker(s) are replaced by one or more different strings. The replacing strings are attached exactly to what the replaced strings were attached to in the source P-marker. For example, given a rule $X + B + C \Rightarrow X + D + C$, where D is a morpheme symbol, we may obtain

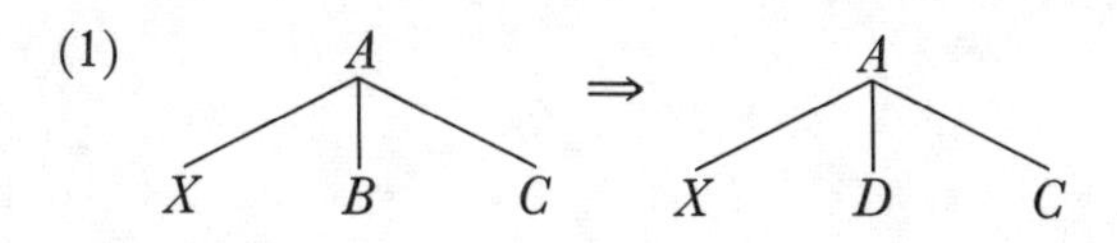

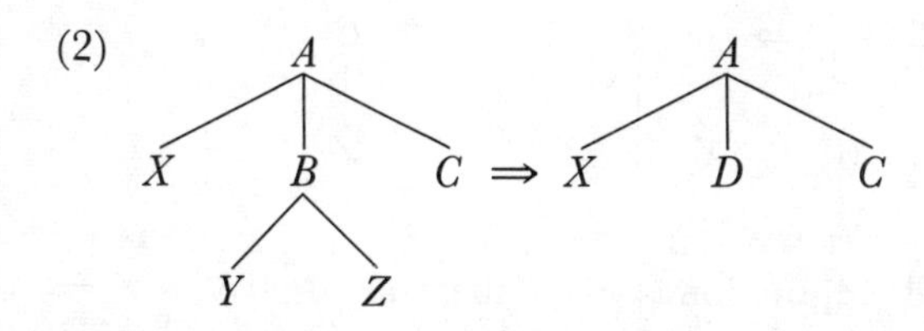

(3)

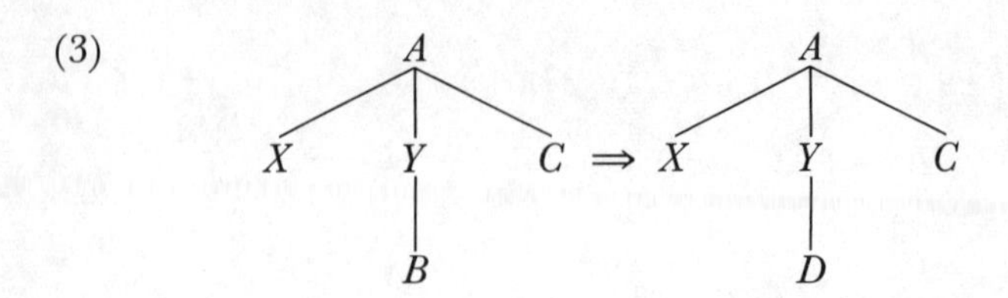

Or, given another rule, $X + C + D + E \Rightarrow X + R$, where R is a morpheme symbol, we get

(4)

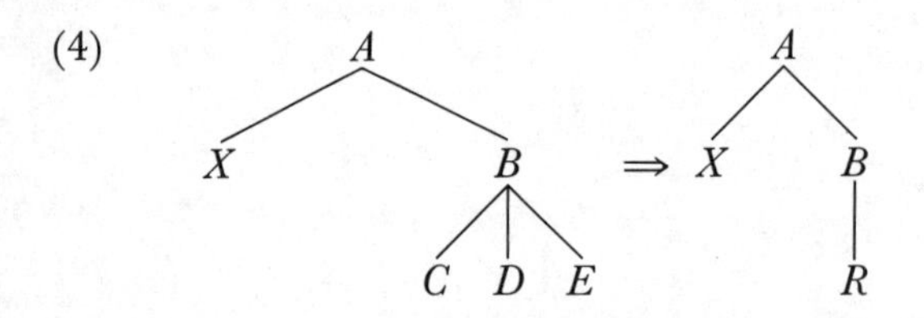

5. **Deletion and adjunction.** Given the rule $B - X - Y \Rightarrow Y - B - X$, we may obtain

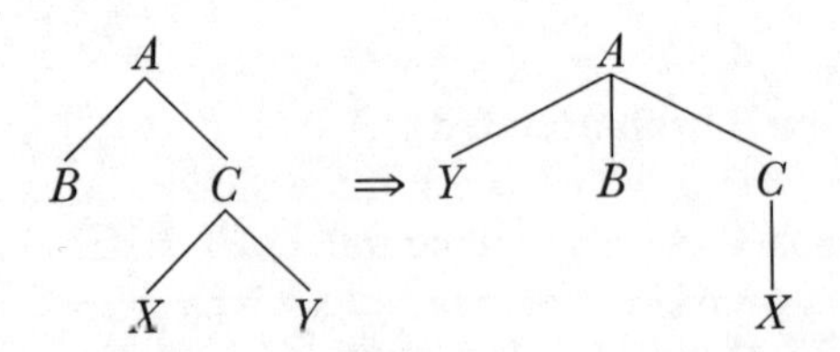

Or, given another rule, $X + Y - Z + W \Rightarrow X + W + Y - Z$, we may obtain

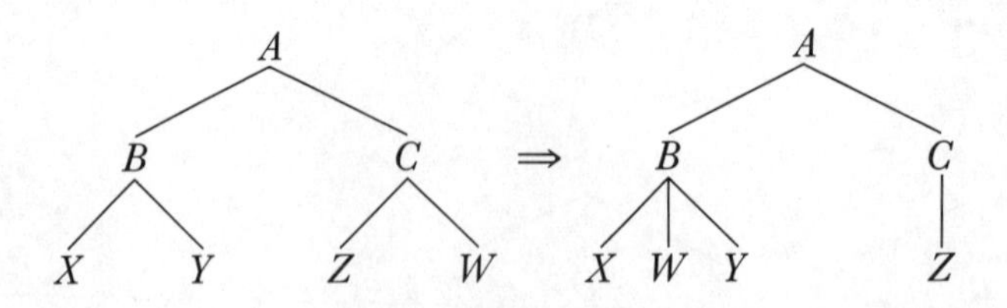

6. **Permutation and adjunction.** Given the rule $B + X + Y \Rightarrow X + B + Y + Z$, we may obtain

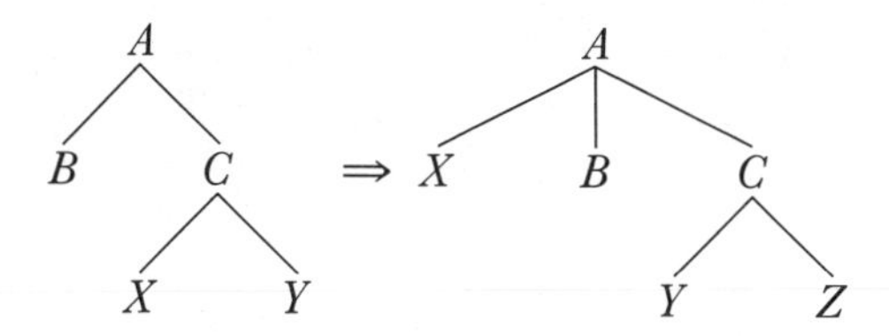

7. **Permutation and deletion.** Given the rule $B + C + D \Rightarrow D + C$, we may obtain

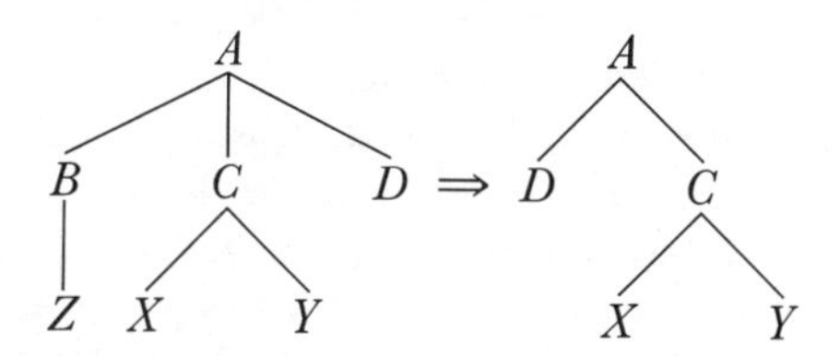

1.6 MORPHOPHONEMIC RULES

The first set of rules of the phonological component would be those rules that assign to morpheme symbols (listed by P-rules and introduced by T-rules) some kind of phonological representation; we call these morphemes **lexical morphemes.** The morphophonemic rules would then apply to strings of morphemes thus represented. In this book we will operate not only as though lexical morphemes have been assigned phonemic and morphophonemic representations, but also as though the orthography used to list these morphemes is also the phonological representation for them. That is, when writing morphophonemic rules, we will operate not only on the assumption that the morphemes *pandofla* and *boy,* for example, have been assigned a phonemic representation but also that this representation is the same as the orthography used to list these morphemes, namely, *p-a-n-d-o-f-l-a* and *b-o-y.*

Morphophonemic rules also operate on strings of morphemes that are not assigned a phonological representation by the first set of phonological rules but by the application of morphophonemic rules themselves; we call such morphemes **grammatical morphemes.**

Since in this book the rules stating morphological variations operate in the same manner as T-rules, they are labeled in the same way and have the same format. For example, the morphophonemic rule Tob $az + C + X \Rightarrow a + C + X$ (where C is a cover symbol for "any consonant" and the operation is deletion) operates on terminal strings (of a particular type of constituent) represented as specified in the structural description and changes them to the representation specified in the structural change.

1.7 FUNCTION OF P-RULES AND T-RULES

The structure of a language is conceived of as a hierarchical system of relationships, some of which can be said to underlie others. Each set of rules in the syntactic component has a particular function with respect to specifying what these relationships are.

In the introduction to this chapter we said that, in specifying the syntactic classes, their co-occurrence relations, and the lexicon, the P-rules of a grammar state the underlying structures of the sentences of a language, while the T-rules of a grammar specify changes in these underlying structures. Later we saw that what this means is that P-rules postulate the underlying constituent structure of sentences, while T-rules, in operating on the underlying P-markers, change the constituent structures postulated by the P-rules. In general, to say that transformations change the underlying structures means that, because of their very nature, transformations gradually break down, erase, or destroy (the latter is especially true of permutation transformations) the constituent structure of sentences postulated by P-rules. In other words, in generating a sentence, constituents and constituent-types postulated by the P-rules as underlying this sentence are eventually either changed or non-existent after the application of the T-rules of a grammar.

Optional transformations change the representations of sentences provided by the P-rules (and other optional T-rules) such that the representations of a different set of sentences are generated. That is, the P-markers derived through the application of optional transformations represent different sets of sentences than the sentences represented by the P-markers from which they are derived. Sentences derived through the application of optional T-rules are called **derived sentences.**

The terminal strings generated by the P-rules and optional T-rules are too abstract a representation of sentences (except perhaps in a pedagogically designed problem) to bear any resemblance to the sentences a native speaker would produce or accept, even if we should be able to specify a pronunciation for these strings. The function of obligatory transformations thus is to adjust the terminal strings provided by the P-rules and optional T-rules such that after we apply the phonological rules to the strings generated by the obligatory T-rules, we get grammatical sentences of a language.[9]

The various types of sentences generated by applying P-rules and obligatory T-rules (as well as the phonological rules) and no optional T-rules are called the **kernel sentences** of a language. Thus there are two general types of sentences in a language, **kernel** and **derived,** the latter of which are derived from the underlying structures of the former by the application of at least one optional T-rule.

Two (or more) sentences are said to be **related** to each other if they have the same underlying structure, meaning that both sentences are derived from the same underlying P-marker.[10] Thus one of the related sentences may have undergone an optional transformation which the other has not (i.e. the other has undergone only obligatory transformations), or one sentence may have undergone one or more additional transformations which the other(s) have not, or each sentence may have undergone a different transformation. In other words, related sentences are sentences whose underlying structure (i.e. their underlying P-markers) is the same but whose derived structure (or transformational history) is not. For example, the English sentences *Mary hit the boy, the boy was hit by Mary, who hit the boy, who did Mary hit, was the boy hit by Mary* are all related to each other since they all have the same underlying P-marker, i.e. that which terminates in *Mary* + *Past* + *hit* + *the* + *boy,* but not to *the boy hit Mary, Mary called the boy,* or *Mary hits the boy,* since all three of the latter sentences have different underlying P-markers.

1.8 ORDERING RULES

We already know that the rules of a transformational grammar are ordered at least in that each *set of rules* in the grammar is presented in a certain order, namely, the P-rules are first, the syntactic transformational rules are second, and, in this book, the morphophonemic

[9] Chomsky has pointed out that there is an analogy between optional and obligatory T-rules and the choice and lack of choice a native speaker has in producing (and understanding) sentences; i.e. the choices are what we specify by optional rules, and the lack of choice, or the machinery which he is not aware of in producing sentences, is what we specify by obligatory rules; see point 3, p. 154, "A Transformational Approach to Syntax," *Third Texas Conference on Problems of Linguistic Analysis in English, May 9–12, 1958,* University of Texas, Austin, Texas, 1962, pp. 124–158; reprinted in Fodor and Katz (eds.), *The Structure of Language: Readings in the Philosophy of Language, op. cit.,* pp. 211–245.

[10] A more comprehensive definition of sentence relatedness is given in 7.3.3.

rules are third. Whether the rules within each set should be ordered, and how, are still unsettled questions. In this book *all* the rules of the grammar are considered strictly ordered (with the one exception being conflated rules).[11] By "strictly ordered" is meant that, while we have a choice as to how to state in what order the rules should be applied, once this order is stated, the rules must be applied in that order only. Specifically, to generate a sentence, not only must we apply the rules only in the stated order, but once a rule has been applied and we move on to another rule, we cannot go back and reapply any rules which have been previously applied, nor can we skip any rule and go back and apply it after applying other rules. Clearly, then, deciding how to order rules will be an important consideration in writing a grammar.

The order in which rules are to be applied is indicated by Arabic numerals at the extreme left of each rule. In this book, the numbering is consecutive throughout the grammar; i.e. we do not start renumbering each time we begin a different part of the grammar.

The following are a few conventions that should be followed in ordering rules and some considerations to be taken into account when deciding how to order the rules within each part of the grammar.

1.8.1 Ordering P-rules

In observing the following guides for deciding the order in which to state P-rules, one should always keep in mind the restriction on environments imposed on context-restricted rules, namely, that only the last expansion of a symbol can be used as an environment in which another symbol is expanded.

1. Rules expanding higher order non-terminal symbols should precede those that list the lexicon; i.e. all the rules that expand a non-terminal symbol as a list of morphemes should be given together as the last rules in the phrase structure part of the grammar (the order in which these are given usually does not matter).

2. Rules expanding higher order symbols should precede rules expanding lower order symbols; more specifically, symbols that will be introduced as part of the expansion of another symbol should themselves be expanded by later rules.

3. In a context-restricted rule the most easily specifiable expansion

[11] It should be noted that we cannot maintain the statements that "rules are strictly ordered" and that "abbreviators conflate two or more rules" without contradiction. If the rules are ordered and, say, two rules are conflated, one of these rules will never be applied, and the grammar cannot, therefore, generate the sentences of the language under analysis. One way out of this dilemma is to consider conflated rules as unordered or as a single complex rule with unordered choices.

of a symbol is given first (i.e. that requiring the least number of symbols) and is followed by the (successively) less easily specifiable.

1.8.2 Ordering T-rules and morphophonemic rules

The T-rules (both obligatory and optional) precede the morphophonemic rules. It should be remembered, therefore, that the following considerations apply independently to each of these sets of rules.

1. Usually the more general (or unrestricted) rules should *follow* those that are restricted or less general; i.e. exceptions should precede the general rules.
2. Any rule, the product of which is to undergo further transformation(s), should precede the rules that operate on its product. In other words, a basic consideration for ordering T-rules and morphophonemic rules (and therefore how to write them) is whether the output of one rule can serve as the input of another rule. It should be noted that this characteristic of T-rules, namely, that the output of one may serve as an input of another, is a powerful device for generating related sentences. It therefore should always be kept in mind when writing a grammar (see 6.3.6).

1.9 COLLATERAL READINGS

Bach, Emmon: *An Introduction to Transformational Grammars,* Holt, Rinehart and Winston, Inc., New York, 1964, pp. 1–85.

Chomsky, Noam: *Syntactic Structures,* Mouton and Company, The Hague, 1957 (2d printing with additional bibliography, 1962), chaps. 1, 2, 4, and 5.

———: "A Transformational Approach to Syntax," *Third Texas Conference on Problems of Linguistic Analysis in English,* University of Texas, Austin, Texas, 1962, pp. 124–158 (discussion, pp. 158–186).

Householder, Fred W., Jr.: "On Linguistic Terms," in Sol Saporta (ed.), *Psycholinguistics: a Book of Readings,* Holt, Rinehart and Winston, Inc., New York, 1961, pp. 15–25.

Lees, Robert B.: "Some Neglected Aspects of Parsing," *Language Learning,* vol. 11, nos. 3 and 4, pp. 171–181, 1961.

Postal, Paul M.: *Constituent Structure: a Study of Contemporary Models of Syntactic Description,* Indiana University Research Center in Anthropology, Folklore, and Linguistics Publication 30, pp. 1–17, 67–80 (*International Journal of American Linguistics,* vol. 30, no. 1, pt. 3, 1964).

Schachter, Paul: "Structural Ambiguity in Tagalog," *Language Learning,* vol. 11, nos. 3 and 4, pp. 135–145, 1961.

chapter two

WRITING A GRAMMAR

INTRODUCTION

In the preceding chapter we discussed briefly the basic concepts in a transformational grammar. With this background, let us now discuss some procedural hints and criteria for writing acceptable grammars.

2.1 PROCEDURAL HINTS

To write a grammar, we must have a corpus consisting of (a) different (maximally) grammatical sentences of the language under consideration and (b) different ungrammatical sentences of the language. If we have at least (a), we can proceed to write a tentative grammar of a language. In this book, however, either a list of ungrammatical sequences or a statement concerning ungrammatical sequences, or both, accompanies each problem.[1] This list, or statement, is headed by *But not* and represents enough patterns or types of ungrammatical sequences to provide some idea of what sequences a solution should *not* generate.

Since some readers may not be familiar with techniques for organizing data to write a grammar, the following procedural hints are given.

1. Guess at the morphemes, list them with a gloss, posit a class membership for each, e.g. adjective, verb stem, verb affix, etc. By "morpheme" in this step is meant simply a minimal meaningful segment.
2. Scan the data and note which classes can be said to constitute the subject, verb, object, prepositional phrase, etc.; i.e. posit a function for the classes posited in step 1. Label the (groups of) classes accordingly. Posit sentence types based on the same order of functionally labeled groups of classes; e.g. all sentences composed of subject, verb, object would be one type while those sentences composed of a prepositional phrase, verb, adverbial, subject would be another type.
3. Beginning with the longest sentence, state, for each type, the classes that occur in each position. Use a column arrangement to do this, leaving blank spaces when necessary so that corresponding elements are under one another.
4. Note which elements always occur and which sometimes occur, i.e. whether the occurrence of any elements is optional or obligatory. Reduce the number of different combinations in each type accordingly. Note any other co-occurrence relations or restrictions.
5. Posit syntactic relations between the members of each type (i.e. posit constitutes), for example, that the combination verb + object + prepositional phrase forms a verb phrase and that the combination determiner + noun or simply a name both form noun phrases.
6. Compare the types and note the similarities and differences between and within them.
7. Write a solution, ordering the rules in accordance with the guides given in 1.8; then draw representative P-markers, i.e. P-markers with the general form specified by the P-rules.[2]
8. Check, in the way indicated in 2.2.1, that the solution works. Make any necessary adjustments. Check again.

[1] The term **problem** is used in this book to refer to data designed for pedagogical purposes. A **solution** for a problem is considered a partial grammar of a (partial) language which generates at least the original data; thus, whenever the term "solution" is used, it is used in the sense of "grammar." Two other expressions that are used synonymously in this book are "solution for Problem A" and "Solution A."

[2] When writing solutions that require a large number of rules, it is a good idea to write

2.1.1 Procedural hints illustrated

Let us now apply procedural hints 1 to 7 to a problem.

PROBLEM A: Artificial Data

1.	gal tasupa bod	*The girl hits the dog.*
2.	ped tagrup buntu bod	*The boy caresses the big dog.*
3.	tagapa umu buntu ped	*The big boy loves the mother.*
4.	bod tagapa umu	*The dog loves the mother.*
5.	tasupa buntu gal ped	*The boy hits the big girl.*
6.	buntu gal tagapa buntu ped	*The big girl loves the big boy.*
7.	ma buntu samak pso	*The man eats the big fish.*
8.	umu ma samak	*The mother eats the fish.*
9.	buntu pso tagapa bod	*The big man loves the dog.*
10.	buntu samak tagrup samak	*The big fish caresses the fish.*

But not:

*umu buntu ped
*gal tagapa
*umu ma
*bod tasupa
*gal tagrup
*Any sentence produced by shifting the subject so that it immediately follows the verb.
*Any sentence containing a verb other than *ma* 'eats' without the prefix *ta*.
*Any sentence with the order object, verb, subject, or subject, object, verb.

From step	We get		
1.	*Morpheme*	*Gloss*	*Class*
	gal	'girl'	noun
	ped	'boy'	noun

---

each rule on a 3 × 5 card, number it, and note (1) the rules it depends on and (2) the rules that depend on it. This provides a quick and dependable way of checking the effects of any particular revision in all parts of the grammar. How the card would look is illustrated below:

Rules which this particular rule depends on →	4, 12, 22 30, 45, 50 Topt $A + B \Rightarrow B + A$ Rule (28)	← Rules which depend on this particular rule

Morpheme	*Gloss*	*Class*
bod	'dog'	noun
umu	'mother'	noun
pso	'man'	noun
buntu	'big'	adjective
samak	'fish'	noun
ta	'present tense marker'	verb affix
supa	'hits'	verb
grup	'caresses'	verb
gapa	'loves'	verb
ma	'eats'	verb

2. Sentences 1, 2, 4, 6, 8, 9, and 10, which we shall group into type *a*, are alike in that in each the subject is first, the verb follows, and an object follows the verb. Sentences 3, 5, and 7, which we shall group into type *b*, are alike in that in each the verb is first, the object follows the verb, and the subject follows the object. Thus the order of the functional groupings in type *a* is subject, verb, object, and in type *b* it is verb, object, subject.

3.

Type a			Type b		
Subject	*Verb*	*Object*	*Verb*	*Object*	*Subject*
A N	Afv Vs	A N	Afv Vs	N	A N
N	Afv Vs	A N	Afv Vs	A N	N
A N	Afv Vs	N	Vs	A N	N
N	Afv Vs	N			
N	Vs	N			

4. Type a: (A)N Afv Vs (A)N. The verb affix occurs before all verbs except *ma*. Both the subject and the object consist of an obligatory noun optionally preceded by an adjective. Type b: Afv Vs (A)N (A)N. The verb affix occurs before all verbs except *ma*. Both the subject and the object consist of an obligatory noun optionally preceded by an adjective.

5. Type a: S = NP + VP; VP = Vb + NP; Vb = Afv + Vs;
NP = (A)N
Type b: S = VP + NP; VP = Vb + NP; Vb = Afv + Vs;
NP = (A)N

6. The only difference between types *a* and *b* is the order of the functional groupings: in type *a* the subject precedes the predicate, while in type *b* the predicate precedes the subject.

7.

Solution	*Read as the instruction:*
#*S*#	The following rules will generate 'sentences.'
1. $S \rightarrow NP + VP$	Rewrite 'Sentence' as 'Noun Phrase + Verb Phrase.'
2. $VP \rightarrow ta + Vs + NP$	Rewrite 'Verb Phrase' as '*ta* + Verb stem + Noun Phrase.'
3. $NP \rightarrow (buntu)N$	Rewrite 'Noun Phrase' as '*buntu* + Noun' or as 'Noun.'
4. $N \rightarrow$ *gal, ped, bod, umu, pso, samak*	Rewrite 'Noun' as any one of the morpheme symbols *gal, ped, bod,* etc.
5. $Vs \rightarrow$ *supa, grup, gapa, ma*	Rewrite 'Verb stem' as any one of the morpheme symbols *supa, grup,* etc.
6. Topt $NP + VP \Rightarrow VP + NP$	Optionally change the order of *NP* + *VP* to *VP* + *NP*.
7. Tob $ta + ma \Rightarrow ma$	Obligatorily delete *ta* before the morpheme *ma*.

P-markers assigned by the rules

Underlying P-markers — Derived P-markers

(1)

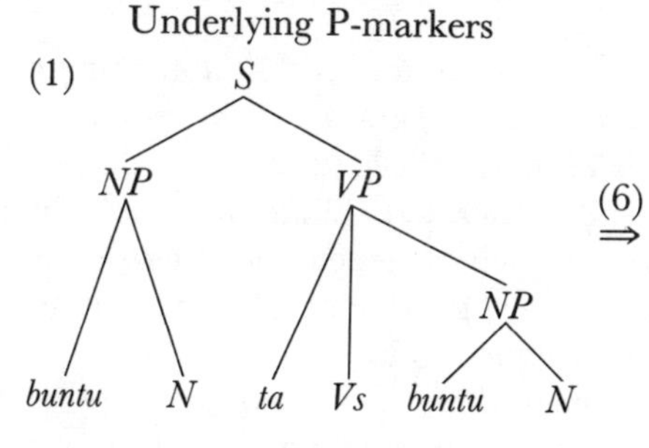

(6) ⇒

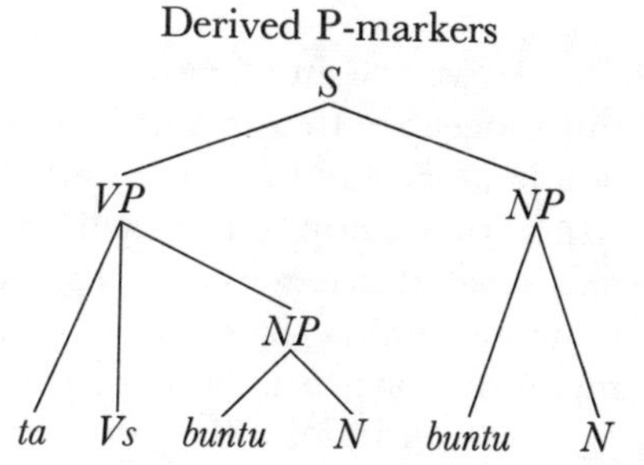

(2)

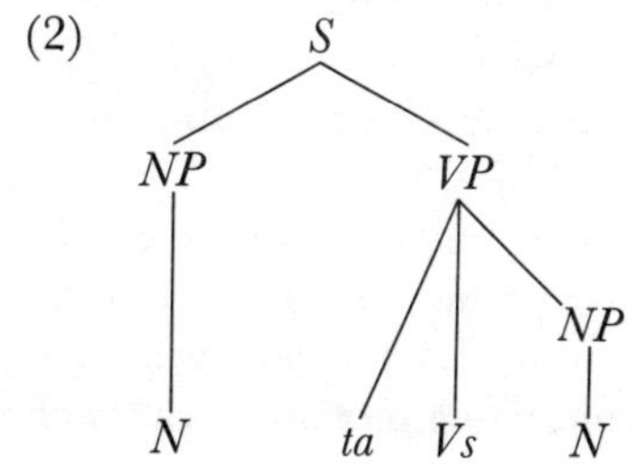

(6) ⇒

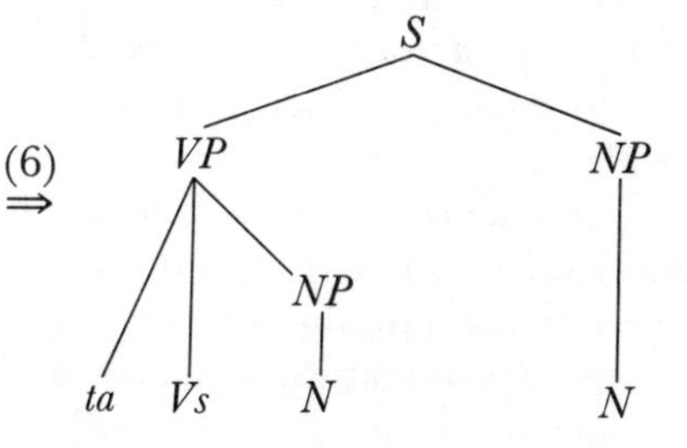

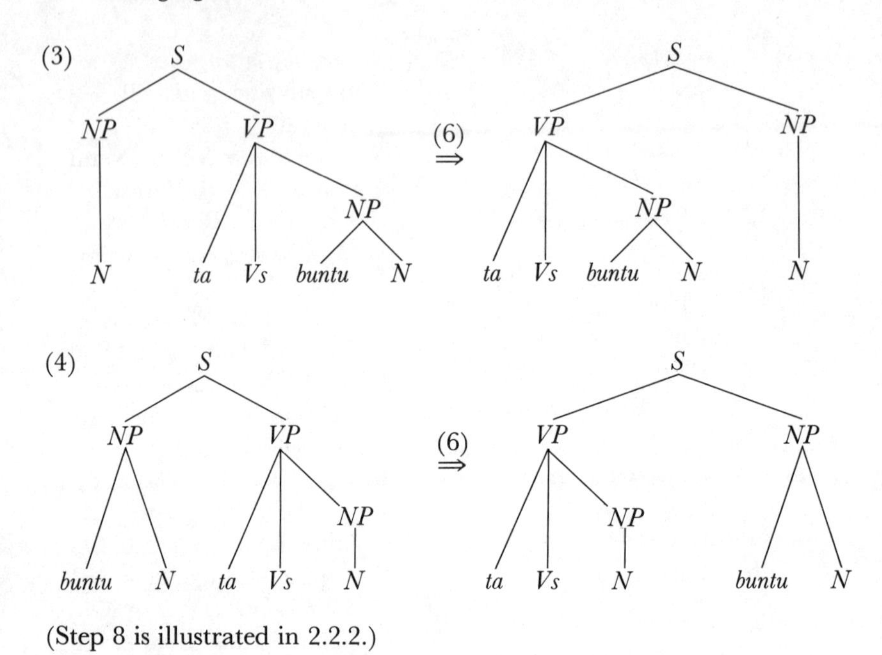

(Step 8 is illustrated in 2.2.2.)

2.2 REQUIREMENTS A GRAMMAR MUST MEET

As we saw in Chapter 1, the basic requirements that a grammar must meet are that it must (1) generate all the grammatical sentences of a language and no ungrammatical sentences *and* (2) assign a proper structural description to each sentence generated. There must be only one structural description assigned to each sentence generated by a grammar, unless the sentence is ambiguous, in which case there will be more than one structural description assigned to it.

Any grammar that does not meet these basic requirements is unacceptable and must be rejected; and any solution that does not (1) generate *at least* the original data *and* (2) assign a structural description to each terminal string generated does not "work" and must be rejected.

Since a grammar will generate sentences beyond those in the corpus (data) on which it is based, the question of whether some of these sentences are grammatical or not is inevitable. Even when we have various ungrammatical sentences of a language, we cannot always answer this question, since it is impossible to have *all* the grammatical and ungrammatical sentences of a language. The only check for ensuring that such sentences are grammatical is a native speaker of the language being analyzed. Whenever a native speaker is not available, however (which very often is the case in a classroom), the analyst should write the most general and plausible grammar possible, given the data he does have, and then modify it, if necessary, as he gains insights or additional information, or both, from a native speaker or, if the language is no longer spoken, from some reliable source.

2.2.1 Checking that a solution works

The following are a number of "checks" that the reader should carefully go through once he has written a solution, to ensure (1) that it works and (2) that it works without violating any of the restrictions on P-rules and T-rules. If any one of these checks is not met, the solution is unacceptable and must either be completely rewritten or modified, depending on the seriousness of the violation.

1. Check that none of the restrictions on P-rules is violated (see 1.4).
2. Check that you have not forgotten to expand all higher and lower order symbols.
3. Check that the guides for ordering rules have been followed (see 1.8).
4. Check that all non-terminal symbols used in T-rules appear in some underlying P-marker.
5. Check that any non-terminal symbols that are adjoined to (the right or left of) another symbol or that replace another symbol by a T-rule appear in the structural description of the transformation.
6. Check that the rules generate *at least all* the data. This is done by forming derivations (Procedure A in 1.3) and checking the results against the data.
7. Check to see that sentences generated by your solution do not contradict any information that you may have concerning ungrammatical sentences.
8. Check (a) that the rules unambiguously assign a set of P-markers (i.e. structural description) to each sentence generated by the grammar and (b) that none of the P-markers violate the restrictions discussed in the note accompanying Procedure B (see 1.3).

2.2.2 Checks illustrated

Let us now apply the checks to the solution written for Problem A in 2.2.1.

For check	We get

1. None of the restrictions on P-rules are violated:
   (1) Each rule replaces a single symbol; e.g. rule (1) replaces *S*, rule (2) replaces *VP*, rule (3) replaces *NP*, etc.
   (2) Each replaced symbol (except the initial) is part of a previous replacing string; e.g. *VP* in rule (2) appeared in rule (1), *NP* in rule (3) appeared in rule (1), *N* in rule (4) appeared in rule (3), etc.
   (3) Each symbol is replaced by a non-null string; e.g. *VP* is replaced by *ta* + *Vs* + *NP*, *NP* is replaced by (*buntu*)*N*, etc.
   (4) All the replacing strings are distinct from the original; e.g. *S* is replaced by *NP* + *VP*, *VP* is replaced by *ta* + *Vs* + *NP*, etc.
   (5) No permutations result from the application of one or more P-rules.
2. Every higher and lower order symbol is properly terminated: rules (4) and (5) expand the constituent-types postulated by rules (1) to (3) into lexical morphemes.
3. The rules are properly ordered:
   (1) The P-rules are all given first, i.e. rules (1) to (5).
   (2) The rules listing the lexicon are the last P-rules (the particular order given within this set of rules is arbitrary).
   (3) Rules expanding higher order symbols precede those expanding lower order symbols. The only time we applied this guide was in deciding whether to expand *NP* or *VP* first: since a noun phrase is part of a verb phrase, the symbol *VP* is expanded before *NP*.
   (4) Rule (6) is a T-rule and as such precedes the morphophonemic rule (rule [7]).
4. Checks out; i.e. both *NP* and *VP*, which are used in rule (6), appear in an underlying P-marker.
5. Does not apply (since the T-rule effects a permutation).
6. Checks out. As a first example, let us take a type *a* sentence, *gal tasupa bod:*
   Given #*S*#
   (1) *NP* + *VP*
   (2) *NP* + *ta* + *Vs* + *NP*
   (3) *N* + *ta* + *Vs* + *NP*
   (3) *N* + *ta* + *Vs* + *N*

(4) *gal + ta + Vs + N*
(4) *gal + ta + Vs + bod*
(5) *gal + ta + supa + bod*

As a second example, let us take a type *b* sentence, *ma buntu samak pso:*

Given #*S*#
(1) *NP + VP*
(2) *NP + ta + Vs + NP*
(3) *N + ta + Vs + NP*
(3) *N + ta + Vs + buntu + N*
(4) *pso + ta + Vs + buntu + N*
(4) *pso + ta + Vs + buntu + samak*
(5) *pso + ta + ma + buntu + samak*
(6) *ta + ma + buntu + samak + pso*
(7) *ma + buntu + samak + pso*

The reader can check that the remaining sentences are generated himself.

7. Picking morphemes at random and following the same procedure as above, we get at least the following ten sentences:
1. gal tasupa gal
2. gal tagrup buntu samak
3. buntu umu ma ped
4. ma buntu pso ped
5. tagapa samak bod
6. tasupa pso umu
7. samak ma buntu samak
8. ma samak bod
9. tagrup umu gal
10. tasupa buntu bod pso.

Since none of these sentences contradict the ungrammatical information given, we shall assume that they are all grammatical.

8. Checks out, but the reader can see for himself by drawing P-markers assigned for the sentences generated.

2.2.3 Problem B

Let us now take a slightly more complicated problem and go through the procedural hints once more.

PROBLEM B: MODERN GREEK

1. i maria pezi	*Mary plays.*
2. afti pezi	*She plays.*
3. pezi	*She (he/it) plays.*
4. i eleni pleni	*Helen washes.*
5. afti pleni	*She washes.*
6. pleni	*She (he/it) washes.*
7. i maria epeze	*Mary used to play.*
8. afti epeze	*She used to play.*
9. epeze	*She (he/it) used to play.*
10. i eleni eplene	*Helen used to wash.*
11. afti eplene	*She used to wash.*
12. eplene	*She (he/it) used to wash.*

But not:

*i afti eplene
*maria epeze
*eplene maria
*pleni afti
*maria i eplene

Procedural hints

From step	We get		
	Morpheme	*Gloss*	*Class*
1.	i	'determiner'	determiner
	maria	'Mary'	noun
	eleni	'Helen'	noun
	afti	'she'	pronoun
	plen	'wash'	verb stem
	pez	'play'	verb stem
	e...e	'past tense marker'	verb affix
	i	'present tense marker'	verb affix

2. Type a: Subject Verb (sentences 1, 2, 4, 5, 7, 8, 10, 11)
Type b: Verb (sentences 3, 6, 9, 12)

3.

Type a		Type b
Subject	*Verb*	*Verb*
D N	Vs Pres	Vs Pres
D N	Vs Pas	Vs Pas
Pron	Vs Pres	
Pron	Vs Pas	

4. Type a: *Subject* *Verb* Type b: *Verb*

$$\left\{\begin{matrix} \text{D N} \\ \text{Pron} \end{matrix}\right\} \quad \text{Vs}\left\{\begin{matrix} \text{Pres} \\ \text{Pas} \end{matrix}\right\} \qquad \text{Vs}\left\{\begin{matrix} \text{Pres} \\ \text{Pas} \end{matrix}\right\}$$

5. Type a: $S = NP + Vb$; $NP = \left\{\begin{matrix} D + N \\ \text{Pron} \end{matrix}\right\}$

$$Vb = Vs + T;\ T = \left\{\begin{matrix} \text{Pres} \\ \text{Pas} \end{matrix}\right\}$$

Type b: $S = Vb$; $Vb = Vs + T$; $T = \left\{\begin{matrix} \text{Pres} \\ \text{Pas} \end{matrix}\right\}$

6. The only difference between type *a* and type *b* is that there is no subject in type *b*.

7. *Solution*[3] — *Read as the instruction:*

#S#	The following rules generate 'sentences.'
1. $S \rightarrow NP + Vb$	Rewrite 'Sentence' as 'Noun Phrase + Verb.'
2. $Vb \rightarrow Vs + T$	Rewrite 'Verb' as 'Verb stem + Tense.'
3. $T \rightarrow Pres, Pas$	Rewrite 'Tense' as either 'Present' or 'Past.'
4. $NP \rightarrow \left\{\begin{matrix} Det + N \\ Pron \end{matrix}\right\}$	Rewrite 'Noun Phrase' as either 'Determiner + Noun' or 'Pronoun.'
5. $Pres \rightarrow i$	Rewrite 'Present' as the morpheme symbol *i*.
6. $Det \rightarrow i$	Rewrite 'Determiner' as the morpheme symbol *i*.
7. $N \rightarrow$ *maria, eleni*	Rewrite 'Noun' as either of the morpheme symbols *maria, eleni*.
8. $Pron \rightarrow$ *afti*	Rewrite 'Pronoun' as the morpheme symbol *afti*.
9. $Vs \rightarrow$ *plen, pez*	Rewrite 'Verb stem' as either of the morpheme symbols *plen, pez*.

[3] See 5.3.5 for the reasoning behind rule (10).

10. Topt — Optionally delete 'Pronoun' before 'Verb.'
    Pron + *Vb* ⇒ *Vb*
11. Tob — Obligatorily change 'Verb stem + Past' to '*e* + Verb stem + *e*.'
    Vs + *Pas* ⇒ *e* + *Vs* + *e*

P-markers assigned by the rules

Underlying P-markers — Derived P-markers

(1)

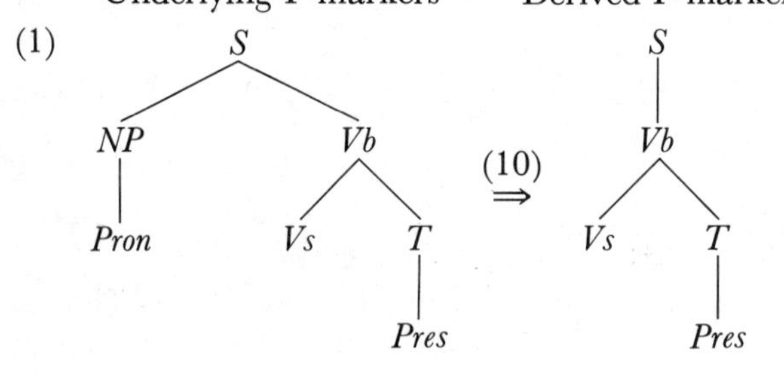

(2)

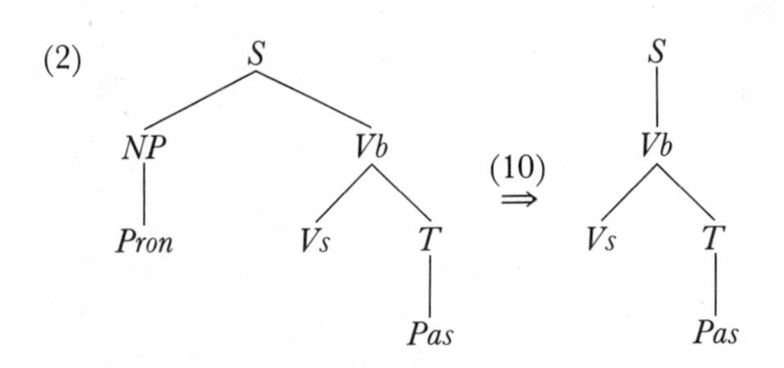

(3)

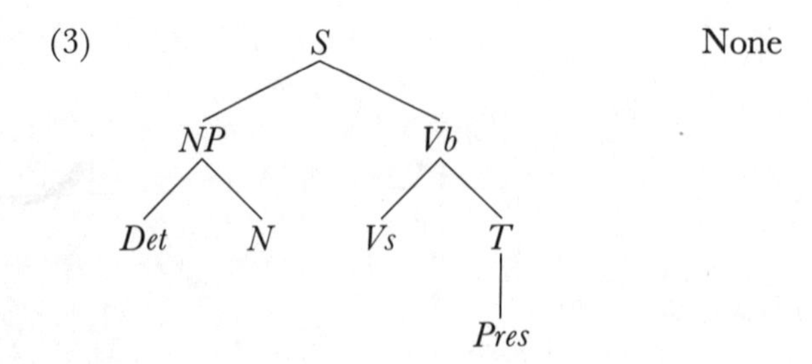

None

(4)

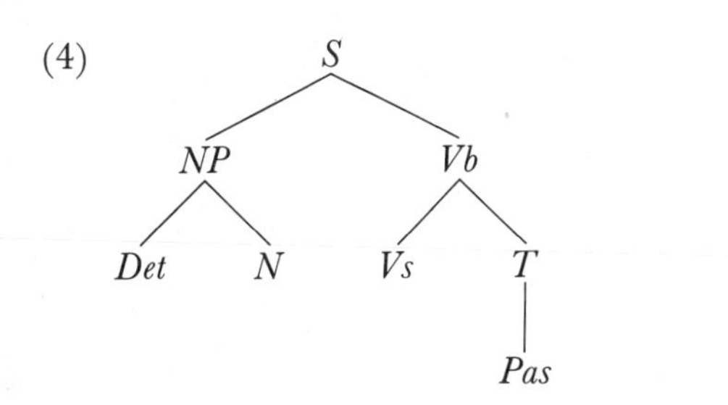

None

8. *Checks:*

For check — We get

1. None of the restrictions on P-rules are violated:
   (1) Each rule replaces a single symbol; e.g. rule (2) replaces only *Vb*, rule (3) replaces only *T*, rule (4) replaces only *NP*, etc.
   (2) Each replaced symbol (except the initial) is part of a previous replacing string; e.g. *Vb* of rule (2) appears in rule (1), *T* of rule (3) is part of the replacing string of rule (2), etc.
   (3) Each symbol is replaced by a non-null string; e.g. *Vb* is replaced by *Vs* + *T*, *T* is replaced by *Pres* or *Pas,* etc.
   (4) All the replacing strings are distinct from the original replaced symbols; e.g. *NP* is replaced by *Det* + *N* or by *Pron.*
   (5) No permutations result from the application of one or more rules.
2. Every higher and lower order symbol is properly terminated: rules (5) to (9) expand the constituent-types postulated by rules (1) to (4), except *Pas,* into lexical morphemes; *Pas* is a grammatical morpheme which is rewritten by rule (11).
3. The rules are properly ordered:
   (1) All the P-rules are given first, i.e. rules (1) to (9).
   (2) The last group of P-rules (rules [5] to [9]) are those listing the lexicon.
   (3) Rules expanding higher order symbols precede those expanding lower order symbols; see rules (1) to (4).
   (4) The one T-rule (rule [10]) precedes the morphophonemic rule (11).
4. Checks out; i.e. both *Pron* and *Vb* of rule (10) appear in some underlying P-marker.

5. Does not apply (since the T-rule specifies a deletion).
6. Checks out, but the reader should check for himself. As an example, we give the following derivation for the sentence *afti eplene:*
   Given $\#S\#$
   (1) *NP* + *Vb*
   (2) *NP* + *Vs* + *T*
   (3) *NP* + *Vs* + *Pas*
   (4) *Pron* + *Vs* + *Pas*
   (8) *afti* + *Vs* + *Pas*
   (9) *afti* + *plen* + *Pas*
   (10) *afti* + *e* + *plen* + *e*
7. Picking morphemes at random, we get at least the following sentences:
   1. i maria pleni
   2. i eleni pezi
   3. afti pleni
   4. i eleni epeze
   5. i maria eplene

   If we check the above sentences against the ungrammatical sentences, we see that they do not exhibit any ungrammatical patterns.
8. The rules unambiguously assign a set of P-markers to each sentence generated, and the P-markers do not violate the restrictions discussed in the note accompanying Procedure B in 1.3. The reader should check for himself, however.

Since none of the checks have been violated, we come to the conclusion that our solution works.

2.3 EVALUATING GRAMMARS

It is always possible to write more than one grammar for a language; therefore we must have a way of evaluating or choosing between alternative grammars. Since, in essence, a transformational grammar of a language is a theory of that language, and since what we want of any scientific theory is a coherent system of general principles, the **generality** of a grammar will be our criterion for choosing between two or more grammars of a language. By generality we mean "that which accounts for the greatest number of cases," and our formal measurement of the generality of a grammar will be in terms of **simplicity.** In other words, that grammar is the most general which has the simplest set of rules.

In this book that grammar will be said to be the simplest whose rules have (a) the least number of vocabulary symbols and (b) the least restrictions; such a set of rules will also be referred to as the most economical set of rules.[4] The number of symbols in a rule is equal to the actual number of vocabulary symbols used in it; two identical symbols count as two symbols, and if a cover symbol is used in a rule, it should be counted as one symbol each time it is used.[5]

In using the criterion of simplicity to judge alternative solutions for a problem, the reader should bear in mind what was said in the Preface, namely, that any grammar written for restricted data will not, in all probability, make valid structural claims about the language from which the data are taken. Thus it may not be the case that whatever is the simplest solution for a problem will be a reflection of the simplest grammar for a language, which is to say that the simplest set of rules for a problem will not necessarily postulate the relationships we would prefer to postulate for the language as a whole.

The notions of simplicity and generality are exemplified by alternative solutions for some of the problems in the following chapters. It may be fruitful, however, to see how the solutions for the preceding two problems might provide some insight into the understanding of these notions.

2.3.1 Examples

Notice that although in applying the procedural hints to Problem A we labeled *ta* as *Afv* and grouped *Afv* and *Vs* under *verb,* neither *Afv* nor a constituent of the type *Vb* is postulated as a constituent in the solution for this problem. The reason for this is that neither can be used to simplify either the P-rules or the T-rules of the grammar. In contrast, however, *ta* + *Vs* + *NP* is postulated to be a constituent of the type *VP* precisely because the postulation of *VP* simplifies the grammar, in particular, the transformational part of the grammar. That is, if *VP* were not postulated, instead of rule (6) we would be forced to write the longer and less general rule $X + ta + Vs(buntu)N \Rightarrow ta + Vs(buntu)N + X$. This rule is less general precisely because it limits the permutation to *X*

[4] There is no consensus among linguists as to what constitutes simplicity. In fact, one of the goals of linguistic investigation is to determine what "the simplest grammar" would be. The approach to simplicity used in this book is thus tentative.

[5] It should be noted that (b) above is required because restrictions are not always stated solely in terms of vocabulary symbols.

and the string *ta* + *Vs*(*buntu*)*N*, while rule (6) does not; i.e. it states that any verb phrase may be permuted with any (subject) noun phrase.

Turning again to the solution for Problem A and comparing what was done in applying the procedural hints with what was postulated in the solution, we see that although *buntu* was labeled as an adjective in applying the hints, a constituent of the type *Adj* was not postulated in the solution. The reason for this is that an *Adj* constituent-type would not simplify either the P-rules or the T-rules of the grammar. While rule (3) is thus justifiable for this particular solution, it will be objectionable, once more data are introduced, because it precludes any possibility of making any generalizations. For example, should a number of words that function the same way as *buntu* (i.e. a number of words that are adjectives) occur elsewhere than before nouns, say as the complement of a verb in copulative sentences, it would be much more economical to postulate an adjective constituent-type which would, in turn, be postulated to be a constituent of both *NP* and *VP*, and then expand *Adj* only once as a list of morphemes than to list these same morphemes once as constituents of *NP* and again as constituents of *VP*. Furthermore, should additional data require any transformations which would involve these morphemes (i.e. the adjectives), we would have to list all these morphemes for *each* such transformation. Clearly, then, the postulation of an adjective constituent-type would result in a more economical and general solution. The same is true of the labeling of *ta* as a verb affix when applying the procedural hints but not postulating an *Afv* constituent-type in Solution A; namely, it precludes the possibility of generalizing should additional data include other verb affixes.

In contrast to the treatment of *ta* and *buntu,* an *N* constituent-type was postulated both in the solution and in the initial analysis. The postulation of *N* in Solution A is justified because it obviates the necessity of listing every noun in every position in which nouns can occur.

Turning now to Problem B and its solution, in the light of what we have been discussing, none of the constituent-types postulated in this solution are justifiable. They were postulated, however, because it is known that they are justifiable given other data (see, for example, Problem 38 in Chapter 5).

In conclusion, it should be clear that (1) there is no one-to-one correspondence between what is posited in an initial analysis of the data and what is posited in the solution for the data and (2) no constituent is postulated in the phrase structure part of the grammar unless it is required by the grammar, i.e. unless it simplifies the grammar as a whole.

2.4 POSTULATING RELATIONSHIPS

As stated in 1.7, there are two general types of sentences in a language, kernel and derived; and the structures underlying kernel sentences also underlie the structures of derived sentences. One of the most crucial decisions that must be made in writing a grammar, then, is what to postulate as underlying and what to postulate as derived. The primary considerations that enter into making these decisions are stated below, the first two of which are briefly exemplified in 2.4.1, and all of which are extensively exemplified in Chapter 6.

(1) Given any two (or more) sentences tentatively of a different type, the first decision to be made is whether or not they are related to each other. The primary criterion for deciding whether these sentences are related is whether the grammatical and lexical constraints they exhibit are such that one can be said to have undergone at least one transformation that the other has not. Put differently, only if the difference between two (or more) otherwise identical sentences can be accounted for simply by postulating that one has undergone one or more transformations which the other has not, can the sentences in question be postulated as being related.

(2) Having decided that two or more sentences, say A, B, and C, are related to each other does not mean that as a result we know which to postulate as kernel and which to postulate as derived. Only if, say, sentence A can be derived from sentence B but not vice versa can we postulate that sentence A is a derived sentence. To determine whether sentence B is kernel or derived, we must compare it with sentence C. If it should be possible to derive sentence C from sentence B but not vice versa, then we know that sentence B is a kernel sentence and that sentences A and C are derived sentences. If, however, it should be possible to derive sentence C from sentence B and vice versa, then that sentence is postulated as kernel which would yield the overall simpler solution. In summary, those sentences that can be derived from another sentence are postulated as derived sentences, while those sentences that cannot be derived from any other sentence are postulated as kernel sentences.

(3) Once we have decided which sentences are to be postulated as kernel, we must decide what constituent structure to assign to them. The main criterion for making this decision is how the kernel sentences behave under transformation, and thus what constituent-types will simplify the statement of the transformational part of the grammar.

2.4.1 Examples

Let us now see how these considerations apply to Problems A and B.

(1) In Problem A, for every sentence in type *a* there is a corresponding sentence in type *b* which differs from the sentence in *a* in the way certain elements are arranged. Since this difference between the otherwise identical sentences can be accounted for by postulating that one has undergone a permutation transformation which the other has not, we decide that the sentences of type *a* and the corresponding sentences of type *b* are related to each other. The decision as to which to postulate as kernel and which to postulate as derived, however, is completely arbitrary, since, regardless of which sentence we pick, we can derive its corresponding sentence from it with no difference in the overall simplicity of the solution.

(2) In Problem B we first had to decide whether those sentences which differ only in that one has a pronoun as the subject while the other has a determiner and a noun as the subject are related. Clearly, they cannot be, since it is not possible to account for this difference as being due to the fact that one sentence has undergone a transformation which the other has not. That is, to derive *afti pleni* 'she washes' from *i maria pleni* 'Mary washes,' for example, we would have to postulate one type of *NP*, namely, *Det* + *N*, in the phrase structure grammar and then replace *NP* with another constituent-type, namely, *Pron,* via a transformation, and this is not permissible (see 1.5).

Next we compared sentences with a subject and those without one (i.e. the type *b* sentences) to decide whether they may be related. Since the only difference between the sentences of these types is that the sentences of type *b* have neither a pronoun nor a determiner and a noun as the subject, and since this difference between corresponding sentences of each type can be accounted for by postulating that one sentence has undergone a deletion transformation which the other has not, we decided that some of the sentences of each type are related to each other. It should be clear that we cannot postulate that the sentences of type *b* are kernel sentences, simply because we cannot derive the corresponding type *a* sentences from them; i.e. to do so would require introducing a non-terminal symbol (an *NP* or *Pron*) via a transformation, and this is not permissible. Thus, having compared the sentences within each type with corresponding sentences of the other type, we came to the decision that type *b* sentences are derived sentences, while all the type *a* sentences are kernels. As said in footnote 3, the reasons why type *b* sentences are postulated to be derived from sentences with a pronoun as the subject are discussed in Chapter 5.

chapter three

MORPHOPHONEMICS

INTRODUCTION

Although this is a book on syntax, it would have been impossible to eliminate morphological variations from all syntactic problems without making them too contrived and, more important, without in some cases making it impossible to illustrate the syntactic notion in question. This chapter has therefore been included in order to provide the reader with a means of handling morphological variations in the syntactic problems of the following chapters. But a discussion of how to write bona fide morphophonemic rules would also involve a discussion of phonological concepts that would not be pertinent to the syntactic material in this book. What is illustrated in this chapter, therefore, is how to write rules that are precise ways of stating the observations for which proper morphophonemic rules should be written in more complete grammars. For the sake of convenience, however, the type of rules illustrated here are still called morphophonemic rules.

The following problems are divided into two sets. The first set illustrates morphophonemic patterns or processes (i.e. morphological variations) which have traditional labels; these are pointed out, labeled, and roughly defined in the discussion of each problem. The second set of problems illustrates morphophonemic patterns that primarily involve stress, tone, or length.

3.1 SET I

3.2 DATA

PROBLEM 1: MAYA, the language of Yucatan

1. cˀon	*gun*	1a. ˀincˀon	*my gun*
2. siˀ	*wood*	2a. ˀinsiˀ	*my wood*
3. kˀab	*hand*	3a. ˀiŋkˀab	*my hand*
4. kab	*juice*	4a. ˀiŋkab	*my juice*
5. bat	*ax*	5a. ˀimbat	*my ax*
6. pal	*son*	6a. ˀimpal	*my son*

Possession is indicated in Maya by a prefix which consists of *ˀi* immediately followed by one of the (nasal) consonants *m*, *n* or *ŋ*. Notice that the last consonant of the prefix and the initial consonant of the following stem both have the same or similar point of articulation; e.g. both the *n* of the prefix and the *s* of the stem in *ˀin-siˀ* 'my wood' are dental; both the *ŋ* of the prefix and the initial consonant of the stem, *k*, in *ˀiŋ-kab* 'my juice' are velar; and both the *m* of the prefix and the initial consonant of the stem, *b*, in *ˀim-bat* 'my ax' are bilabial. This type of pattern is called **assimilation.** That is, if, whenever two morphemes, *A* and *B*, combine, the particular shape of *A* is determined by the shape of *B* such that one or more vowels or consonants of morpheme *A* are similar in point or manner of articulation (or both) to those of *B*, we say that this is the pattern or process of assimilation.

PROBLEM 2: MODERN GREEK

1. pandofla	*slipper*	1a. tin pandofla/bandofla[1]	*the slipper*
2. porta	*door*	2a. tin porta/borta	*the door*

[1] The slant line (/) indicates that the forms on either side of the line are equally acceptable and therefore are in "free variation."

3. tanalja	*pliers*	3a. tin tanalja/danalja	*the pliers*
4. taverna	*tavern*	4a. tin taverna/daverna	*the tavern*
5. kiria	*lady*	5a. tin kiria/giria	*the lady*
6. kori	*daughter*	6a. tin kori/gori	*the daughter*

Notice that the words in the first column all begin with a voiceless consonant and that whenever they are preceded by the article *tin,* this consonant optionally changes to its voiced counterpart. This morphophonemic pattern is assimilation in voice; i.e. a voiceless consonant becomes voiced when it is preceded by a word ending in a voiced consonant.

Now notice how the assimilation in this and in the preceding problem differs: (1) in Problem 1 we have assimilation in point of articulation and in Problem 2 in manner of articulation, (2) the assimilation is optional in Problem 2 but obligatory in Problem 1, (3) assimilation is observed between words in Problem 2 but within words in Problem 1, and (4) the direction of the assimilation is different. In Problem 2 the first consonant of the following word assimilates to the last consonant of the prefix, while in Problem 1 the last consonant of the prefix assimilates to the first consonant of the stem; i.e. in Problem 2 we have **progressive** assimilation while in Problem 1 we have **regressive** assimilation.

PROBLEM 3: INDONESIAN, the official language of Indonesia

1. kursi	*chair*	1a. kursikursi	*chairs*
2. lalat	*fly*	2a. lalatlalat	*flies*
3. ibu	*mother*	3a. ibuibu	*mothers*
4. gadzah	*elephant*	4a. gadzahgadzah	*elephants*
5. rumah	*house*	5a. rumahrumah	*houses*
6. medzah	*table*	6a. medzahmedzah	*tables*

Notice that the plural form of each word above is two identical occurrences of the singular. This type of pattern, i.e. a repetition of identical forms, is called **reduplication.** Since, in this problem, an entire form is repeated, we have an example of what is called **complete reduplication.**

PROBLEM 4: TAGALOG, the official national language of the Philippines

1. bili	*buy*	1a. bibili	*will buy*
2. inom	*drink*	2a. iinom	*will drink*
3. sulat	*write*	3a. susulat	*will write*

4. layas	*leave*	4a. lalayas	*will leave*
5. kain	*eat*	5a. kakain	*will eat*
6. ibig	*love*	6a. iibig	*will love*
7. pasok	*enter*	7a. papasok	*will enter*

Notice that the forms in the first column differ from those in the second only in that the latter have an extra syllable which is identical to the first syllable of the former. This extra syllable is an example of **partial reduplication;** that is, we call a reduplication partial whenever only part of a form is repeated.

PROBLEM 5: TURKISH

1. diš	*tooth*	1a. dišler	*teeth*
2. çocuk	*child*	2a. çocuklar	*children*
3. asker	*soldier*	3a. askerler	*soldiers*
4. kedi	*cat*	4a. kediler	*cats*
5. masa	*table*	5a. masalar	*tables*
6. gece	*night*	6a. geceler	*nights*
7. baba	*father*	7a. babalar	*fathers*
8. kuš	*bird*	8a. kušlar	*birds*

The plural forms in the above data differ from the singular only in that they end in either *ler* or *lar*. Notice that the vowel of this suffix is the front vowel *e* when the last vowel of the stem is either of the front vowels *i* or *e*, and the back vowel *a* when the last vowel of the stem is either of the back vowels *u* or *a*. This similarity between the last vowel of the stem and the vowel of the suffix is an example of a type of assimilation called **vowel harmony.**

PROBLEM 6: MODERN GREEK

1. θa γrafo	*I will be writing*	1a. θa γrapso	*I will write*
2. θa ravo	*I will be sewing*	2a. θa rapso	*I will sew*
3. θa ðjavazo	*I will be reading*	3a. θa ðjavaso	*I will read*
4. θa kapnizo	*I will be smoking*	4a. θa kapniso	*I will smoke*
5. θa lino	*I will be solving*	5a. θa liso	*I will solve*
6. θa aniγo	*I will be opening*	6a. θa anikso	*I will open*
7. θa trexo	*I will be running*	7a. θa trekso	*I will run*
8. θa sfigo	*I will be squeezing*	8a. θa sfikso	*I will squeeze*

Notice that the words in the first column end in *o* while those in the second column end in *so*. Now notice that the fricatives, *f*, *v*, γ, *x*, that occur before *o* become stops having the same or a similar point of articulation before *so*. This pattern is called **dissimilation.** Dissimilation is the opposite of assimilation in that one or more consonants or vowels of one morpheme become *unlike* those of another morpheme whenever these morphemes combine.

In the above data we also have assimilation in voice: all final voiced consonants become voiceless before the suffix *so;* i.e. the fricatives not only become stops before *so* but also become voiceless (because *s* is voiceless), and the *g* in *sfig-o* changes to *k* before *so* (see 8a).

Finally, notice that the *z* and *n* occurring before *o* in the first column do not occur, or are dropped, before *so* in the second column. This pattern is called **reduction;** that is, we label as reduction that pattern wherein one or more consonants or vowels of one morpheme do not occur, or are dropped, whenever that morpheme combines with another.

PROBLEM 7: AMHARIC, a language of Ethiopia

Present

Singular		Plural
1. jigəwidal	*he loves*	1a. jigəwidalu
2. jiwəsidal	*he takes*	2a. jiwəsidalu
3. jiməgibal	*he feeds*	3a. jiməgibalu
4. jikəfilal	*he divides*	4a. jikəfilalu
5. jidəgimal	*he repeats*	5a. jidəgimalu

Past

1b. gəwədə	*he loved*	1c. gəwədu
2b. wəsədə	*he took*	2c. wəsədu
3b. məgəbə	*he fed*	3c. məgəbu
4b. kəfələ	*he divided*	4c. kəfəlu
5b. dəgəmə	*he repeated*	5c. dəgəmu

There are two morphophonemic patterns in this problem: (1) **reduction:** *ə* drops before the plural suffix *u* (compare columns b and c); and (2) **discontinuity:** the present tense is formed by an affix which splits in such a way as to surround the stem. Put differently, the present tense morpheme is discontinuous.[2] The general label, then, for the in-

[2] Alternatively, we could say that the present tense is formed by a prefix and a suffix which always occur together; since one affix cannot occur without the other, however, it can still be said that the stem is included within these affixes and, therefore, that we still have an instance of discontinuity.

clusion of one or part of one morpheme within another morpheme whenever two morphemes combine is discontinuity.

PROBLEM 8: KOREAN

1. johʉn	*good*	1a. jotha	*(it) is good*
2. manhʉn	*many*	2a. mantha	*(they) are many*
3. jakʉn	*small*	3a. jakta	*(it) is small*
4. jopʉn	*narrow*	4a. jopta	*(it) is narrow*
5. talhʉn	*hot*	5a. taltha	*(it) becomes hot*

1b. jokhesso	*(it) will be good*
2b. mankhesso	*(they) will be many*
3b. jakkesso	*(it) will be small*
4b. jopkesso	*(it) will be narrow*
5b. talkhesso	*(it) will become hot*

Notice that the difference between the forms in the above three columns is the suffixes: in the first column all the forms end in *ʉn*, in the second in *ta* or *tha*, and in the third in *kesso* or *khesso*. The new pattern illustrated in this problem is the following: when the suffixes of the second and third columns combine with the stem, if the last consonant of the stem is *h*, the *h* changes position so that it *follows* rather than precedes the initial consonant of the suffix; that is, the change in position of the *h* results in a discontinuity of both morphemes involved in the combination. We thus get *tha* and *khesso* instead of *...h–ta* and *...h–kesso.* This type of pattern is called **metathesis.** That is, metathesis is a change in the order of the elements of one morpheme when it combines with another morpheme such that both morphemes become discontinuous.

PROBLEM 9: SAMOAN, a language of the South Pacific

1. mate	*(he) dies*	1a. mamate	*(they) die*
2. nofo	*(he) stays*	2a. nonofo	*(they) stay*
3. galue	*(he) works*	3a. galulue	*(they) work*
4. tanu	*(he) buries*	4a. tatanu	*(they) bury*
5. leo	*(he) calls*	5a. leleo	*(they) call*
6. atamaˀi	*(he) is intelligent*	6a. atamamaˀi	*(they) are intelligent*
7. alofa	*(he) loves*	7a. alolofa	*(they) love*
8. taoto	*(he) lies*	8a. taooto	*(they) lie*

In this problem there are two patterns which have been discussed previously: partial reduplication (one of the syllables of the singular is repeated in the plural form) and discontinuity (the repeated syllable is inserted into the singular form). Notice, however, that while in Problem 8 discontinuity was a result of metathesis and in Problem 7 the result of an affix including the stem, in this problem discontinuity is a result of the stem including the affix. Whenever an affix is included as illustrated in this problem, the pattern is called **infixation,** and the affix involved is called an **infix.** Infixation, like metathesis, then, is a particular kind of discontinuity.

Although in this problem infixation occurs concomitantly with partial reduplication, i.e. the infix is a partial reduplication of the stem, these patterns may occur independently of each other.

PROBLEM 10: MODERN GREEK

Present (First Singular)		*Imperative* (Second Singular)
1. pleko	*knit*	1a. plekse
2. afino	*let*	2a. ase
3. akuo	*hear*	3a. akuse
4. troo	*eat*	4a. fae
5. spao	*break*	5a. spase
6. piγeno	*go*	6a. ame

Notice that verbs in the present tense end in *o*, while those in the imperative end in either *e* or *se* (the *s* in *se* is a morpheme signaling perfective aspect). Notice further that the stems (the forms up to the final *e* or *se*) of 2a, 4a, and 6a are completely different in form from their counterparts (the forms up to the final *o*) in 2, 4, and 6; that is, some verbs have one stem in the present tense and an entirely different one in the perfective imperative. This type of morphophonemic pattern is called **suppletion;** that is, we label as suppletion the complete difference in form a morpheme has whenever it combines with another morpheme.

PROBLEM 11: HUNGARIAN

1. a cipøø	*the shoe*	1a. a cipøøvel	*with the shoe*
2. a saboo	*the tailor*	2a. a sabooval	*with the tailor*
3. a tyy	*the needle*	3a. a tyyvel	*with the needle*

4. az eke	*the plow*	4a. az ekeevel	*with the plow*
5. a fiuu	*the boy*	5a. a fiuuval	*with the boy*
6. a liba	*the goose*	6a. a libaaval	*with the goose*
7. a haaz	*the house*	7a. a haazzal	*with the house*
8. a tyyz	*the fire*	8a. a tyyzzel	*with the fire*
9. a cukor	*the sugar*	9a. a cukorral	*with the sugar*
10. az ember	*the man*	10a. az emberrel	*with the man*
11. a kanaal	*the spoon*	11a. a kanaallal	*with the spoon*
12. a køteel	*the rope*	12a. a køteellel	*with the rope*
13. a tej	*the milk*	13a. a tejjel	*with the milk*
14. a vaj	*the butter*	14a. a vajjal	*with the butter*
15. az ees	*the mind*	15a. az eessel	*with the mind*
16. a køññ	*the tear*	16a. a køññel	*with the tear*
17. az aall	*the chin*	17a. az aallal	*with the chin*
18. az aaǰ	*the bed*	18a. az aaǰǰal	*with the bed*
19. a kereek	*the wheel*	19a. a kereekkel	*with the wheel*

There are four patterns exhibited in these data. Three have been previously discussed and illustrated: (1) assimilation of the suffix consonant to the last consonant of the noun stem; (2) reduction, i.e. clusters of three consonants are not tolerated at morpheme boundaries; and (3) vowel harmony, i.e. the vowel of the instrumental suffix is *a* when the last vowel of the stem is a back vowel and *e* when the last vowel of the stem is a front vowel.

Now, notice that whenever a word ending in a single vowel is followed by the instrumental suffix, the last vowel of that word is repeated before the suffix; for example, *eke* 'plow' becomes *ekeevel* 'with the plow.' In this case we could say that we have an instance of partial reduplication, but since vowels and consonants may be inserted between morpheme boundaries without being reduplications, it is preferable to say that we have an instance of a new pattern, which we shall label **epenthesis.** Epenthesis is the addition of a segment (phoneme[s] or a syllable) whenever two (or more) morphemes combine; or, more simply, epenthesis is the opposite of reduction.

Finally, notice that there is no basis for deciding whether the difference in form exhibited by the article when it combines with the following noun is reduction or epenthesis. That is to say, we have a choice of saying that the *z* of *az*, 'the,' drops whenever *az* combines with a noun beginning with a consonant (i.e. that the pattern is reduction) or, alternatively, that the *z* is added whenever *a* combines with a noun beginning with a vowel (i.e. that the pattern is epenthesis).

3.3 SOLUTIONS

SOLUTION 1: MAYA

1. $W \rightarrow (Afn)Ns$
2. $Afn \rightarrow$ *ʔiN*
3. $Ns \rightarrow$ *cʔon, siʔ, kʔab, bat, pal, kab*
4. Tob (regressive) assimilation

$$N \begin{bmatrix} C_1 \\ C_2 \\ C_3 \end{bmatrix} \Rightarrow \begin{bmatrix} m \\ n \\ \eta \end{bmatrix} \begin{bmatrix} C_1 \\ C_2 \\ C_3 \end{bmatrix}$$

C_1 = any bilabial consonant
C_2 = any dental consonant
C_3 = any velar consonant

SOLUTION 2: MODERN GREEK

1. $NP \rightarrow (Det)N$
2. $Det \rightarrow$ *tin*
3. $N \rightarrow$ *pandofla, porta, tanalja, taverna, kiria, kori*
4. Topt (progressive) assimilation

$$n + \begin{bmatrix} p \\ t \\ k \end{bmatrix} \Rightarrow n + \begin{bmatrix} b \\ d \\ g \end{bmatrix}$$

SOLUTION 3: INDONESIAN

1. $W \rightarrow N(Pl)$
2. $N \rightarrow$ *kursi, lalat, ibu, gadzah, rumah, medzah*
3. Tob complete reduplication
   $N + Pl \Rightarrow N + N$

SOLUTION 4: TAGALOG

1. $W \rightarrow (Afv)Vs$
2. $Vs \rightarrow$ *bili, inom, sulat, layas, kain, ibig, pasok*

3. Tob partial reduplication

$$Afv\begin{bmatrix} Vw_1 \\ CVw_1 \end{bmatrix} \Rightarrow \begin{bmatrix} Vw_1 \\ C_1Vw_1 \end{bmatrix} + \begin{bmatrix} Vw_1 \\ C_1Vw_1 \end{bmatrix}$$

or, preferably,

$$Afv(C_1)Vw_1 \Rightarrow (C_1)Vw_1 + (C_1)Vw_1$$

SOLUTION 5: TURKISH

Solution A

1. $W \rightarrow Ns(Afn)$
2. $Afn \rightarrow lAr$
3. $Ns \rightarrow$ *diš, çocuk, asker, kedi, maca, gece, baba, kuš*
4. Tob vowel harmony

$$\begin{bmatrix} Vw_1 \\ Vw_2 \end{bmatrix}(C) + lA \Rightarrow \begin{bmatrix} Vw_1 \\ Vw_2 \end{bmatrix}(C) + l\begin{bmatrix} e \\ a \end{bmatrix}$$

$Vw_1 =$ any front vowel
$Vw_2 =$ any back vowel

Solution B (Objectionable)

1. $W \rightarrow Ns(Afn)$
2. $Afn \rightarrow lar$
3. Same as in Solution 5A
4. Tob

$$Vw(C) + la \Rightarrow Vw(C) + le$$

$Vw =$ any front vowel

SOLUTION 6: MODERN GREEK

1. $VP \rightarrow Prt + Vb$
2. $Vb \rightarrow Vs + Afv$
3. $Afv \rightarrow (Aspe)T$
4. $Aspe \rightarrow s$
5. $T \rightarrow o$
6. $Prt \rightarrow \theta a$
7. $Vs \rightarrow$ *γraf, ðjavaz, kapniz, lin, aniγ, trex, sfig, rav*

8. Tob dissimilation + assimilation, reduction

$$X \begin{bmatrix} C_1 \\ C_2 \\ C_3 \end{bmatrix} Aspe \Rightarrow \begin{bmatrix} Xp \\ X \\ Xk \end{bmatrix} Aspe$$

$$C_1 = f,\ v$$
$$C_2 = z,\ n$$
$$C_3 = \gamma,\ x,\ g$$

or, preferably,

$$\begin{bmatrix} C_1 \\ C_2 \\ C_3 \end{bmatrix} Aspe \Rightarrow \begin{bmatrix} p \\ \emptyset \\ k \end{bmatrix} Aspe$$

C_1, C_2, C_3 = same as above

SOLUTION 7: AMHARIC

1. $W \rightarrow Vs + Afv$
2. $Afv \rightarrow T\,(Pl)$
3. $T \rightarrow Pres,\ Pas$
4. $Pl \rightarrow u$
5. $Vs \rightarrow$ *gwd, wsd, mgb, kfl, dgm*
6. Tob

   $CCC + Pas \Rightarrow$ *CəCəCə*
7. Tob

   $CCC + Pres \Rightarrow$ *jiCəCiCəal*
8. Tob reduction

$$ə \begin{bmatrix} u \\ a \end{bmatrix} \Rightarrow \begin{bmatrix} u \\ a \end{bmatrix}$$

or, preferably,

$$ə + Vw \Rightarrow Vw$$

SOLUTION 8: KOREAN

1. $W \rightarrow Vs + Afv$
2. $Afv \rightarrow$ *ʉn, ta, kesso*
3. $Vs \rightarrow$ *joh, manh, jak, jop, talh*

4. Tob metathesis

$$h + C \Rightarrow Ch$$
$$C = t, k$$

SOLUTION 9: SAMOAN

1. $W \rightarrow Vs(Afv)$
2. $Vs \rightarrow$ *mate, nofo, galue, tanu, leo, alofa, taoto, atamaʔi*
3. Tob infixation

$$X(C_1)Vw_1(C)Vw + Afv \Rightarrow X(C_1)Vw_1(C)Vw_1(C)Vw$$

SOLUTION 10: MODERN GREEK

1. $Vb \rightarrow Vs + Afv$
2. $Afv \rightarrow \begin{Bmatrix} Aspe + Impe \\ Pres \end{Bmatrix}$
3. $Pres \rightarrow o$
4. $Aspe \rightarrow s$
5. $Impe \rightarrow e$
6. $Vs \rightarrow$ *plek, afin, aku, tro, spa, piγen*
7. Tob suppletion

$$\begin{bmatrix} afin \\ tro \\ pi\gamma en \end{bmatrix} Aspe \Rightarrow \begin{bmatrix} as \\ fa \\ am \end{bmatrix}$$

SOLUTION 11: HUNGARIAN

Solution A

1. $NP \rightarrow Det + N$
2. $N \rightarrow Ns(Afn)$
3. $Det \rightarrow aZ$
4. $Ns \rightarrow$ *cipøø, saboo, tyy, eke, fiuu, liba, haaz, tyyz, cukor, ember, kanaal, køteel, tej, vaj, ees, køññ, aall, aaǰ, kereek*
5. Tob epenthesis

$$\begin{bmatrix} Vw_1 \\ Vw_1Vw_1 \\ C_1 \\ C_1C_1 \end{bmatrix} Afn \Rightarrow \begin{bmatrix} Vw_1 \\ Vw_1Vw_1 \\ C_1 \\ C_1C_1 \end{bmatrix} \begin{bmatrix} Vw_1vAl \\ vAl \\ C_1Al \\ Al \end{bmatrix}$$

6. Tob vowel harmony

$$\begin{bmatrix} Vw_1 \\ Vw_2 \end{bmatrix} X + YA \Rightarrow \begin{bmatrix} Vw_1 \\ Vw_2 \end{bmatrix} X + Y \begin{bmatrix} a \\ e \end{bmatrix}$$

X = any or no string of consonants
Vw_1 = any back vowel
Vw_2 = any front vowel

7. Tob

$$z \begin{bmatrix} C \\ Vw \end{bmatrix} \Rightarrow \begin{bmatrix} \emptyset \\ z \end{bmatrix} \begin{bmatrix} C \\ Vw \end{bmatrix}$$

Solution B

1–3. Same as in Solution 11A
4. $Afn \rightarrow vAl$
5. Same as rule (4) of Solution 11A
6. Tob epenthesis

$$XY + Afn \Rightarrow XYY + Afn$$

$X \neq Y$
X = any vowel or consonant
Y = any vowel or consonant

7. Tob reduction

$$C_1C_1 + vAl \Rightarrow C_1C_1 + Al$$

8–9. Same as rules (6)–(7) of Solution 11A

3.4 DISCUSSION OF SOLUTIONS

3.4.1 The specification of morphophonemic patterns

The solutions just given, although different in detail, are, in fact, essentially the same in that:

(1) The first rule specifies the general structure of the words or phrases in the data: for example, rule (1) in Solution 4 (Tagalog) states that the structure of the words given is an optional prefix *(Afv)* followed by an obligatory verb stem *(Vs)*. Subsequent rules list the constituents (morphemes) of the various constituent-types and specify pronunciation changes at morpheme boundaries.

(2) One of the rules is always an obligatory or optional morphophonemic rule. This rule states what is to be changed (the left-hand side of the rule) and just what the change is (the right-hand side of the rule).

(3) Only those constituents that are involved in or are necessary for specifying a morphophonemic pattern are used in the rule; phonological classes are symbolized with the cover symbols, *C* and *Vw*. Unless explicitly defined otherwise, *C* means "any consonant" and *Vw* means "any vowel" which the grammar permits to occupy the position indicated by the cover symbol.

(4) The symbols *C* and *Vw* are used to indicate those classes that are *directly* pertinent to the postulated pattern; thus, in Solution 1 (Maya), only the final consonant of the prefix and the initial consonant of the stem are symbolized in the morphophonemic rule, since the preceding segments of the prefix and the remaining segments of the stem are not pertinent to the change.

(5) The cover symbols *X* and *Y* are used in two circumstances. First, they are used to abbreviate strings that are directly pertinent to the morphophonemic change, as, for example, in rule (6) of Solution 11B (Hungarian). Second, they are used to make clear the position of the consonants and vowels involved in the change. For example, in Solution 9 (Samoan), *X* is used to indicate the position of the consonants and vowels within a word, i.e. that part of the domain of the rule is the last two syllables of the verb stem. Similarly, in rule (6) of Solution 11A (Hungarian), *X* and *Y* are used to make it clear that it is the last vowel of the noun stem and a particular vowel of the suffix, respectively, that are involved in the change specified by that rule.

(6) Whether or not square brackets are used in a morphophonemic rule reflects not a different handling of the process in question but primarily whether or not the postulated morphophonemic patterns are uniform for all the elements involved.

Whenever square brackets are used in a morphophonemic rule, the patterns postulated for a set of elements are not uniform throughout the set. That is to say, the elements included in the square brackets on the left-hand side of the rule undergo a change which is unique to these elements (and thus constitute a subclass), or each element in the brackets undergoes a different change (and thus each constitutes a class or subclass), or both. For examples, see rule (7) of Solution 10 (Modern Greek) and rule (4) of Solution 5A (Turkish). (Notice that, in general, when square brackets are used in a rule, elements which are mutually exclusive are involved.)

Whenever square brackets are not used in a morphophonemic rule, this generally means that the morphophonemic patterns postulated are uniform throughout the set (for example, see rule [6] of Solution 7 [Amharic]), or that, although they are not uniform, (a) the rules specifying the changes must be ordered (see, for example, rules [6] and [7] for Solution 11B [Hungarian]) or (b) they simply cannot be used because only one pair would be necessary, and, as stated in Chapter 1, a single set of square brackets cannot be used in a rule. Since the preceding problems do not provide us with a situation for which such a rule might be possible, the following example may help make this point clear. In Modern Greek the particle *θa* combines with verbs to indicate the future tense. Under certain conditions, when *θa* combines with a verb beginning with a vowel, that vowel drops. This may be specified by a rule such as $a + Vw \Rightarrow a$ but not by a rule such as

$$a + \begin{bmatrix} a \\ o \\ u \\ i \\ e \end{bmatrix} \Rightarrow a.$$

3.4.2 Conventions

There are a number of conventions followed in the preceding solutions which shall now be discussed.

(1) **Convention of the theory.** The following convention is part of transformational theory and does not depend on the personal preference of any one person as do those conventions discussed in (2) below.

The symbol Ø 'zero' (not to be confused with the front rounded vowel ø appearing in Problem 11) means "no phonetic value"; i.e. whenever a rule replaces a symbol with a *zero*, this means that the replaced symbol has no phonetic value (or representation) in the position specified by the rule. For example, in the alternative rule (8) of Solution 6 (Modern Greek), the Ø indicates that *z* and *n* (i.e. C_2) have no phonetic value before *Aspe* or, in other words, that *z* and *n* do not appear in that position in the words generated by the solution.

In the long run, the use of the *zero* yields simpler rules than do the various ways that can be devised to avoid using it. For example, in Solution 6, the alternative for rule (8) is preferable precisely because it is the simpler of the two; that is, to avoid a rule in which the *zero* is used, not only did we have to write a rule which uses the cover symbol *X* (which is not necessary to make the domain of the rule clear), but in addition we had to use *X* four times, thus writing a rule with three symbols more than the rule written with the *zero*.

(2) **Notational conventions.** (a) Whenever the cover symbols for vowels and consonants have identical subscripts in any rule (but these cover symbols are not defined), this indicates that the value of these symbols must be the same each time they have the same subscript. For

example, rule (5) of Solution 11A (Hungarian) specifies that whichever vowel is the first *Vw* of the second line is also the second *Vw* of that line in the structural description and structural change of the rule. This convention enables us to specify the repetition of identical consonants and vowels.

(b) It should be noted that the initial string is omitted from the solutions to the preceding problems. This was done simply for the sake of convenience. This practice will be followed throughout the remainder of the book with the understanding that the double cross can be used whenever necessary; i.e. we will operate as if the initial string has been written in.

3.5 NOTES

1. Morphological variations sometimes occur only at morpheme boundaries but not within morphemes. In the morphophonemic rules of this book, the plus is therefore used to indicate morpheme boundaries. Strictly speaking, the plus thus is not a concatenating symbol but a vocabulary symbol in these rules; even though this is the case, the practice of omitting the pluses whenever morpheme boundaries are already marked by an abbreviator is followed, as long as there is no possibility that the omission of the pluses will result in a misinterpretation of a rule. It should be noted that the use of the plus in morphophonemic rules is tentative, for while it is clear that some kinds of symbols are necessary to indicate various phonological boundaries, it is not clear how these symbols are to be incorporated in a grammar.

2. The terminal symbols *Pl, Afv, Pres* and *Pas, Afv,* and *Afn* in Solutions 3 (Indonesian), 4 (Tagalog), 7 (Amharic), 9 (Samoan), and 11A (Hungarian), respectively, are what we called "grammatical" morphemes in Chapter 1; i.e. they are morphemes whose phonological representation is provided not by the first set of phonological rules but by the morphophonemic rules themselves. That is to say, the morpheme *Pas,* unlike the morpheme *wsd,* in Solution 7, for example, is not given a phonological representation by the set of rules that map *wsd* into *w–s–d*; instead, *Pas* is mapped into *ə–ə–ə* by rule (6).

3. Notice that in Solutions 4 (Tagalog) and 7 (Amharic) there are alternative rules for rules (3) and (8), respectively. These alternatives are preferable since they are simpler. Furthermore, the preferred rule of Solution 7 is more general than its alternative.

4. In rule (8) of Solution 6 and rule (7) of Solution 10 (both

Modern Greek), the non-terminal symbol *Aspe* is used to specify the pattern in question. We could have used the terminal symbol *s* instead of *Aspe* to postulate this change, but for these two solutions, which symbol is used is arbitrary. The decision as to whether *Aspe* or *s* should be used depends on the answer to two questions: (1) Does the pattern in question apply only to verbs? and (2) Are there other changes at morpheme boundaries involving an *s*? If the answer to both these questions is "yes," then *Aspe* should be used; otherwise either alternative may be used. If *s* is chosen, however, one must be on the alert for other boundary complications. The point, however, is that any symbol of the grammar which would facilitate the writing of such a rule may be used for this purpose.

5. The discussion of Problem 11 (Hungarian) pointed out that it is possible to have two interpretations concerning the patterning of *az* and *a* 'the.' The solution for this problem reflects this possibility; it specifies that a morpheme *aZ* is realized as *az* before a morpheme beginning with a vowel and as *a* before a morpheme beginning with a consonant. The alternative to this specification is to treat one of the forms of the article as the base form and derive the other form from it. This alternative is not appealing, however, since there is no non-arbitrary way to decide whether *az* or *a* should be selected as the base form.

The same is true of the treatment of the plural suffix in Solution 5B (Turkish). Even though Solution 5B is shorter than Solution 5A, it is nevertheless objectionable, not only because the selection of *lar* rather than *ler* as the base form for the plural morpheme is arbitrary, but because there is evidence that the vowel of the suffix is determined by the vowel of the stem.

Whenever the data are such that whether a difference in the form of one morpheme whenever it combines with another is due to one type of process rather than another is a matter of interpretation, this "ambiguity," so to speak, should be reflected in a solution, unless, that is, there is a good (i.e. non-arbitrary) reason for selecting one form as basic and deriving the other from it.

6. Solution 11B (Hungarian) is given to point out the possibility of a different interpretation of the data than the one given in Solution 11A. Solution 11B differs from 11A mainly in that the following two assumptions are made: (a) a stem ending in two different elements, say *X* and *Y*, changes to *XYY* whenever it combines with an affix and (b) the first consonant of the affix drops whenever it combines with a stem ending in two identical consonants; i.e. in this language a consonant cluster consisting of two identical consonants followed by the consonant *v* is not tolerated at morpheme boundaries.

7. In a number of solutions a general rule was written to specify a morphophonemic pattern even though the data did not indicate such a generalization. In the solution for Problem 4 (Tagalog), for example, *Vw* is used in the morphophonemic rule even though only the vowel *i* occurs initially. Similarly, in Solution 7 (Amharic) the preferred alternative of rule (8) makes the generalization that the vowel ə drops before all vowels.

3.6 SET II

In the following problems length is indicated by a raised dot after a vowel *(Vw·)*, stress by a stress mark over a vowel *(V́w)*, and tone by either acute or grave accents or a hyphen over a vowel *(V́w, V̀w, V̄w)* or by numeral superscripts after a vowel or consonant (Vw^1, Vw^2, C^{23}, etc.). An acute accent indicates a high tone, a grave accent indicates a low tone, and either a hyphen over a vowel or no mark indicates a mid tone; the lack of a mark over a vowel should be interpreted as its having a mid tone only when the other vowels in the data are marked with tones. Unless stated otherwise, the numeral 1 indicates a low tone, and each successively higher numeral indicates a successively higher tone. Two or more numerals after a vowel or consonant indicate glides and are to be treated as a single tone.

3.7 DATA

PROBLEM 12: TOSK ALBANIAN

1.	trim	*hero*	1a.	trimi	*the hero*
2.	mik	*friend*	2a.	miku	*the friend*
3.	djalë	*boy*	3a.	djali	*the boy*
4.	spital	*hospital*	4a.	spitali	*the hospital*
5.	vajzë	*girl*	5a.	vajza	*the girl*
6.	ši	*rain*	6a.	šiu	*the rain*
7.	liri	*freedom*	7a.	liria	*the freedom*
8.	ah	*oak*	8a.	ahu	*the oak*
9.	breg	*shore*	9a.	bregu	*the shore*

The forms in the second column end in a vowel, while those in the first end sometimes in a vowel and sometimes in a consonant. Notice, however, that even though we have no way of knowing which particular vowel will occur at the end of the forms in the second column, words 1a, 3a, and 4a end in *i*, 2a, 6a, 8a, and 9a end in *u*, and the remainder end in *a*.

PROBLEM 13: ENGLISH

1. fórmal	1a. formálity
2. bánal	2a. banálity
3. májor	3a. majórity
4. mínor	4a. minórity
5. nórmal	5a. normálity
6. légal	6a. legálity
7. équal	7a. equálity

Notice that the words in the second column differ from those in the first in that they (1) end with the suffix *ity* and (2) are stressed on the second rather than the first syllable. Stress in these data is regular, since it occurs always on the first syllable of a word when the word has no suffix, and always on the second syllable when it does have a suffix.

PROBLEM 14: MODERN GREEK

1. peðí	*child*	1a. peðáki	*diminutive of child*
2. arní	*lamb*	2a. arnáki	*diminutive of lamb*
3. γatí	*cat*	3a. γatáki	*diminutive of cat*
4. máti	*eye*	4a. matáki	*diminutive of eye*
5. psári	*fish*	5a. psaráki	*diminutive of fish*
6. xéri	*hand*	6a. xeráki	*diminutive of hand*

Notice that the words in the first column are stressed either on the first or on the second syllable, while those in the second column are stressed always on the second syllable. In addition, the words in the second column have an affix which may be considered to be either a single suffix *(aki)* or a diminutive suffix *(ak)* followed by a gender suffix *(i)*. Stress is irregular on words in the first column but regular on those in the second, since when a word is suffixless, stress occurs sometimes on the first syllable and sometimes on the last, but when a word has a suffix, stress occurs always on the second syllable.

PROBLEM 15: FANTI, a language of Ghana

1. kásá	*language*	1a. míkàsá	*my language*
2. síkán	*knife*	2a. násìkán	*his knife*
3. dénkém	*crocodile*	3a. hóndènkém	*their crocodile*
4. sídà	*shilling*	4a. násìdà	*his shilling*
5. wúrà	*master*	5a. hénwùrà	*our master*

Notice that the possessive forms differ from the non-possessive in that (1) they have a prefix with a high tone and (2) the second vowel has a low tone. Tone is regular on the first vowel of a word in both columns (it is always high) and on the second vowel of a word in the second (it is always low). Tone is irregular on the last vowel of words in both columns, however, since there it is sometimes high and sometimes low.

PROBLEM 16: MAYA

1. bát	*ax*	1a. ʔimbàt	*my ax*
2. lák	*bowl*	2a. ʔinlàk	*my bowl*
3. címin	*horse*	3a. ʔincìmin	*my horse*
4. mák	*man*	4a. ʔimmák	*my man*
5. kéh	*deer*	5a. ʔiŋkéh	*my deer*
6. léč	*trap*	6a. ʔinléč	*my trap*
7. kòl	*field*	7a. ʔiŋkòl	*my field*

As we saw in Problem 1, possession is indicated in Maya by a prefix, which we now see has a mid tone. The tone of the words in both columns is irregular since sometimes it is high and sometimes low. Notice, however, that words 4, 5, 6, and 7 have the same tone whether they are prefixed or not, while words 1, 2, and 3 have a high tone when they are not prefixed and low when they are.

PROBLEM 17: SIERRA POPOLUCA

1. pet	*sweep*	1a. pe·tʌ	*sweep!*
2. wan	*sing*	2a. wa·nʌ	*sing!*
3. poy	*run*	3a. po·yʌ	*run!*
4. nʌk	*go*	4a. nʌ·kʌ	*go!*
5. moh	*begin*	5a. mo·hʌ	*begin!*
6. miñ	*come*	6a. mi·ñʌ	*come!*

Notice that the words in the second column differ from those in the first in that (1) they end in ʌ and (2) the first vowel is lengthened. Length in these data is regular, since the first vowel of a word is always lengthened when the suffix ʌ is present.

PROBLEM 18: HUNGARIAN

1.	ha·z	*house*	1a.	ha·zak	*houses*
2.	ke·p	*picture*	2a.	ke·pek	*pictures*
3.	ke·s	*knife*	3a.	ke·sek	*knives*
4.	e·v	*year*	4a.	e·vek	*years*
5.	ke·z	*hand*	5a.	kezek	*hands*
6.	nya·r	*summer*	6a.	nyarak	*summers*
7.	ne·v	*name*	7a.	nevek	*names*
8.	u·t	*road*	8a.	utak	*roads*

Notice that one difference between the plural and the singular of the above words is that the plural words end in either *ek* or *ak*: the vowel of this suffix is *e* after front vowels and *a* after back vowels (i.e. we have an instance of vowel harmony). Another difference is that although the first vowel of a word is always lengthened in the singular, it is not always lengthened in the plural; i.e. length is regular in singular words but not in plural words.

PROBLEM 19: LALANA CHINANTEC[3]

1.	gwɨn^{12}ną^{23}	*I sleep.*
2.	gwɨn^{12}nɨ̨^{3}	*You sleep.*
3.	gwɨn^{12}	*He sleeps.*
4.	gwɨn^{12}ną^{2}	*We* (incl.) *sleep.*
5.	gwɨn^{12}nąˀ^{31}	*We* (excl.) *sleep.*
6.	gwɨn^{12}nąˀ^{3}	*You* (pl.) *sleep.*
7.	baˀn^{23}	*I hit it.*
8.	baˀn^{23}	*You hit it.*
9.	baˀ^{23}	*He hits it.*
10.	baˀ^{23}ra^{2}	*We* (incl.) *hit it.*

[3] A shortened version of Problem 44 in W. R. Merrifield, C. M. Naish, C. R. Rensch, and G. Story, *Laboratory Manual for Morphology and Syntax,* 2d ed., Summer Institute of Linguistics, Santa Ana, Calif., 1962.

11. baˀ^{23}raˀ^{31}	*We* (excl.) *hit it.*
12. baˀ^{23}raˀ^{3}	*You* (pl.) *hit it.*
13. hen^{31}ną^{1}	*I live.*
14. hen^{31}nɨ̨^{3}	*You live.*
15. hen^{31}	*He lives.*
16. hen^{31}ną^{2}	*We* (incl.) *live.*
17. hen^{31}nąˀ^{31}	*We* (excl.) *live.*
18. hen^{31}nąˀ^{3}	*You* (pl.) *live.*
19. ka·n^{23}	*I play.*
20. ka·n^{23}	*You play.*
21. ka·^{23}	*He plays.*
22. ka·^{23}ra^{2}	*We* (incl.) *play.*
23. ka·^{23}raˀ^{31}	*We* (excl.) *play.*
24. ka·^{23}raˀ^{3}	*You* (pl.) *play.*
25. heˀn^{23}ną^{23}	*I get rid of it.*
26. heˀn^{23}nɨ̨^{3}	*You get rid of it.*
27. heˀn^{23}	*He gets rid of it.*
28. heˀn^{23}ną^{2}	*We* (incl.) *get rid of it.*
29. heˀn^{23}nąˀ^{31}	*We* (excl.) *get rid of it.*
30. heˀn^{23}nąˀ^{3}	*You* (pl.) *get rid of it.*

There are five verbs in these data, each of which has a number of forms differing in person and number. Except for the third person singular, which has no such indicator, person and number are indicated by a suffix. Every suffix and the majority of stems have a tone, which is indicated by a numerical superscript. Tone is irregular for both the stems and suffixes.

The stems *baˀ*^{23} 'hit' and *ka·*^{23} 'play' have no tone when they occur with the suffixes *n*^{23} 'I' and *n*^{23} 'you,' but do have a tone when they occur with the other suffixes: *ra*^{2} 'we (incl.),' *raˀ*^{31} 'we (excl.),' and *raˀ*^{3} 'you (pl.).' The stems *gwɨn*^{12} 'sleep' and *heˀn*^{23} 'get rid of' have the suffixes *ną*^{23} 'I,' *nɨ̨*^{3} 'you,' *ną*^{2} 'we (incl.),' *nąˀ*^{31} 'we (excl.),' and *nąˀ*^{3} 'you (pl.),' while the stem *hen*^{31} 'live' has, with one exception, the same suffixes as *gwɨn*^{12} and *heˀn*^{23}; the exception is in the first person singular, where *hen*^{31} has the suffix *ną*^{1}, while the other two stems have *ną*^{23}. (Notice that whenever a vowel follows *n*, it is nasalized.) We can therefore say that, in general, three of the stems have the same set of suffixes, while two of the stems have a different, but related, set of suffixes. The difference between the two sets of suffixes can be explained in two ways. We can say that the difference is simply due to the fact that we have two subclasses of verbs, or, alternatively, that the difference is due to the final consonant of the verb stem; i.e. we have one set of suffixes when the stem ends in *n* and a different set of suffixes when the stem ends in any other consonant or vowel.

3.8 SOLUTIONS

SOLUTION 12: TOSK ALBANIAN

1. $W \rightarrow Ns(Afn)$
2. $Ns \rightarrow Ns_1, Ns_2, Ns_3$
3. $Ns_1 \rightarrow$ *trim, djalë, spital*
4. $Ns_2 \rightarrow$ *mik, ah, ši, breg*
5. $Ns_3 \rightarrow$ *vajzë, liri*
6. Tob

$$\begin{bmatrix} Ns_1 \\ Ns_2 \\ Ns_3 \end{bmatrix} Afn \Rightarrow \begin{bmatrix} Ns_1 \\ Ns_2 \\ Ns_3 \end{bmatrix} \begin{bmatrix} i \\ u \\ a \end{bmatrix}$$

7. Tob

$$Vw_1 + Vw_2 \Rightarrow Vw_2$$
$$Vw_1 \neq i$$

SOLUTION 13: ENGLISH

1. $W \rightarrow As(Afa)$
2. $As \rightarrow$ *formal, banal, major, minor, legal, equal, normal*
3. $Afa \rightarrow$ *ity*
4. Tob

$$\#(C)Vw \Rightarrow \#(C)\acute{V}w$$

5. Tob

$$'XVwC + Afa \Rightarrow X\acute{V}wC + Afa$$

SOLUTION 14: MODERN GREEK

Solution A (If affix is considered to be a single suffix)

1. $W \rightarrow Ns(Afn)$
2. $Ns \rightarrow$ *peðí, arní, γatí, máti, psári, xéri*
3. $Afn \rightarrow$ *aki*

4. Tob
   $\acute{V}wX + aki \Rightarrow VwX + \acute{a}ki$
5. Tob
   $i + \acute{a} \Rightarrow \acute{a}$

Solution B (If affix is considered to be two suffixes)

1. $W \rightarrow Ns + Afn$
2. $Afn \rightarrow (Dim)G$
3. $Ns \rightarrow$ *peð, arn, γat, mát, psár, xér*
4. $Dim \rightarrow ak$
5. $G \rightarrow i$
6. Tob
   $\begin{bmatrix} \acute{V}w \\ Vw \end{bmatrix} X + ak \Rightarrow \begin{bmatrix} Vw \\ Vw \end{bmatrix} X + \acute{a}k$
   X = any string of consonants
7. Tob
   $VwX + i \Rightarrow VwX + \acute{i}$
   X = any string of consonants

SOLUTION 15: FANTI

1. $W \rightarrow (Afn)Ns$
2. $Ns \rightarrow$ *kasá, sikán, denkém, sidà, wurà*
3. $Afn \rightarrow$ *mi, na, hon, hen*
4. Tob
   $Afn + CVw \Rightarrow Afn + C\grave{V}w$
5. Tob
   $\#CVw \Rightarrow \#C\acute{V}w$

SOLUTION 16: MAYA

1. $W \rightarrow (Afn)Ns$
2. $Afn \rightarrow$ *ʔiŊ*
3. $Ns \rightarrow$ *bat, lak, cimin, kòl, mák, kéh, léč*
4. Tob
   $Afn + CVw \Rightarrow Afn + C\grave{V}w$
5. Tob
   $\#CVwX \Rightarrow \#C\acute{V}wX$
   $X \neq Ŋ + W$

6. Tob

$$N\begin{bmatrix} C_1 \\ C_2 \\ C_3 \end{bmatrix} \Rightarrow \begin{bmatrix} m \\ n \\ \eta \end{bmatrix}\begin{bmatrix} C_1 \\ C_2 \\ C_3 \end{bmatrix}$$

C_1 = any labial consonant
C_2 = any dental consonant
C_3 = any velar consonant

SOLUTION 17: SIERRA POPOLUCA

1. $W \rightarrow Vs(Afv)$
2. $Vs \rightarrow$ *pet, wan, poy, nʌk, moh, miñ*
3. $Afv \rightarrow$ ʌ
4. Tob
   $VwC + Afv \Rightarrow Vw{\cdot}C + Afv$

SOLUTION 18: HUNGARIAN

1. $W \rightarrow Ns(Afn)$
2. $Ns \rightarrow$ *ha·z, ke·p, ke·s, e·v, kez, nyar, nev, ut*
3. $Afn \rightarrow Ak$
4. Tob
   $\#XVw(C)\# \Rightarrow \#XVw{\cdot}(C)\#$
   X = any or no string of consonants
5. Tob

$$\begin{bmatrix} Vw_1 \\ Vw_2 \end{bmatrix} C + A \Rightarrow \begin{bmatrix} Vw_1 \\ Vw_2 \end{bmatrix} C + \begin{bmatrix} e \\ a \end{bmatrix}$$

Vw_1 = any front vowel
Vw_2 = any back vowel

SOLUTION 19: LALANA CHINANTEC

Solution A (If difference of suffixes is due to subclasses of verbs)

1. $Vb \rightarrow Vs(Afv)$
2. $Afv \rightarrow$ *na*^{23}, *nɨ*^{3}, *na*^{2}, *na*^{ʔ31}, *na*^{ʔ3}
3. $Vs \rightarrow$ *gwɨn*^{12}, *hen*^{31}, *heʔn*^{23}, *ba*^{ʔ23}, *ka·*^{23}

4. Tob

$$Vs^{23}\begin{Bmatrix} na^{23} \\ n\dot{\imath}^{3} \end{Bmatrix} \Rightarrow Vs + n^{23}$$

$$Vs = ba^{?},\ ka\cdot$$

5. Tob

$$Vs^{23}\begin{bmatrix} na^{2} \\ na^{?31} \\ na^{?3} \end{bmatrix} \Rightarrow Vs^{23}\begin{bmatrix} ra^{2} \\ ra^{?31} \\ ra^{?3} \end{bmatrix}$$

$$Vs = ba^{?},\ ka\cdot$$

6. Tob

$$hen^{31} + na^{23} \Rightarrow hen^{31} + na^{1}$$

7. Tob

$$n^{X} + nVw \Rightarrow n^{X} + n\not{V}w$$

Solution B (If difference of suffixes is due to final consonant of stem)

1–3. Same as in Solution 19A

4. Tob

$$Vw(C)^{23}\begin{Bmatrix} na^{23} \\ n\dot{\imath}^{3} \end{Bmatrix} \Rightarrow Vw(C) + n^{23}$$

$$C \neq n$$

5. Tob

$$Vw(C)^{23}\begin{bmatrix} na^{2} \\ na^{?31} \\ na^{?3} \end{bmatrix} \Rightarrow Vw(C)^{23}\begin{bmatrix} ra^{2} \\ ra^{?31} \\ ra^{?3} \end{bmatrix}$$

$$C \neq n$$

6–7. Same as in Solution 19A

3.9 DISCUSSION OF SOLUTIONS

Whatever was said in the discussion of the solutions for the first set of problems is also true for this set; and whatever is said of the solutions of this set is true also for the preceding set of problems.

3.9.1 The specification of regular and irregular morphophonemic patterns

Whatever pattern is called "regular" in the discussions of the preceding problems is postulated by a morphophonemic rule in the solutions.

Since this rule specifies what the pattern is, we say that the rule **predicts** the pattern and that the pattern itself is **predictable.**

Whatever pattern is called "irregular" in the discussions of the problems is listed by a P-rule in the solutions. These patterns are called **unpredictable** because the conditions under which they are realized cannot be specified.

In Solution 13 (English), for example, rule (2) lists morphemes without stress, rule (4) places stress on the first syllable of these morphemes, and rule (5) specifies that the stress shift from the first to the second syllable whenever a suffix is present. This means that stress is predictable for both types of words in the data. In Solution 14A (Modern Greek), however, we find that in rule (2) the members of *Ns* are listed with their respective stresses, while rule (4) specifies that the stress shifts from the first to the second syllable whenever a suffix is present. This means that stress is unpredictable for singular words but predictable for plural words. Finally, notice that in Solution 15 (Fanti) the members of *Ns* are listed in rule (2) with a tone on the second but not the first vowel, rule (4) places a low tone on any vowel without tone whenever a prefix is present, and rule (5) then places a high tone on any first vowel of a string which has no tone. This means that the tone on the second vowel of a stem is unpredictable for both possessive and non-possessive words but predictable for the first vowel of a word in both types.

3.9.2 The specification of partially regular morphophonemic patterns

Although stress, tone, or length may be irregular in the data as a whole, it is possible at times to find small groups of words that under certain conditions behave regularly with regard to the element in question. This is the case in Problems 16 (Maya) and 19 (Lalana Chinantec). In Problem 16, for example, although the occurrence of a high or low tone on a vowel is irregular throughout the data, the first three words have a low tone when they have a prefix but a high tone when they do not, while the tone on the last four words remains the same whether they are prefixed or not. Now, in the solution for this problem, some of the members of *Ns* are listed in rule (3) with tone (the last four) and some without (the first three), and rules (4) and (5) place a tone on the toneless members of *Ns*. This means that, although tone is unpredictable for the problem as a whole, it is predictable for the first three words.

Solution 12 (Albanian) illustrates that whatever was just said about stress, tone, and length applies equally well to affixes (and stems). This solution specifies that, given *any* noun, it is impossible to predict the vowel of the suffix but, given a noun and its particular subclass, prediction of the vowel suffix is possible. Rule (2) specifies three subclasses of nouns, and rule (6) then predicts the vowel suffixes for each subclass: noun stems of subclass one take the suffix *i*, noun stems of subclass two take the suffix *u*, and noun stems of subclass three take the suffix *a*.

Two questions may now be asked. First: Why isn't the regularity of the last four words in rule (3) of Solution 16, for example, postulated in the grammar by one or more morphophonemic rules, since they, too, behave regularly with respect to tone under certain circumstances? Second: Since both subclasses behave in a predictable way with respect to tone, what is the basis for choosing to predict the one rather than the other? The answer to the first question is "Because we cannot predict the unpredictable; i.e. it simply cannot be done." The answer to the second question is "We choose that class to predict which requires the least number of symbols to do so." In Solution 16, for example, fewer symbols are required to predict the tone of the first three words than the last four.

3.9.3 Ordering morphophonemic rules

Notice that whenever two rules are used to predict the placement of stress, tone, or length, these rules are sometimes written in such a way that the product, or output, of the first rule serves as an input of the second. In Solution 13 (English), for example, the output of rule (4) is used as an input of rule (5). Similarly, the output of rule (4) of Solution 15 (Fanti) serves as an input of rule (5). The reader is encouraged to write rules ordered in this way whenever possible, since the result usually is a more economical solution. This can be seen by comparing, for example, the following two possible sets of morphophonemic rules for Solution 13. Set (a) are those rules that appear in Solution 13, while the rules of Set (b) are so written that the output of the first rule cannot serve as the input of the second.

Set (a):

4. Tob

$$\#(C)Vw \Rightarrow \#(C)\acute{V}w$$

5. Tob

$$'XVwC + Afa \Rightarrow X\acute{V}wC + Afa$$

Set (b):

4. Tob

$$\#(C)VwXVwC\# \Rightarrow \#(C)\acute{V}wXVwC\#$$

X = any string of consonants

5. Tob

$$XVwC + Afa \Rightarrow X\acute{V}wC + Afa$$

It should be noted that we cannot both reverse the order of rules (4) and (5) of Solution 13 *and* allow the output of the new rule (4) to serve as the input of the new rule (5).

3.10 NOTE

An alternative way of handling the suffixes in Problem 19 (Lalana Chinantec) is to consider the difference in form of the initial consonants as progressive assimilation; i.e. a suffix beginning with *r* changes to a suffix beginning with *n* whenever it follows a verb stem ending in *n*. The result of this interpretation, as we can see in the modification of Solution 19A below, is a simpler solution. (Solution 19B can be similarly modified and thereby simplified.)

SOLUTION 19A′

1. Same as in Solution 19A
2. *Afv* → *na*²³, *nɨ*³, *ra*², *ra*ˀ³¹, *ra*ˀ³
3–4. Same as in Solution 19A
5. Same as rule (6) of Solution 19A
6. Tob

    $n + r \Rightarrow n + n$
7. Tob

    nVw ⇒ *nV̦w*

3.11 COLLATERAL READING

Koutsoudas, Andreas: The Handling of Morphophonemic Processes in Transformational Grammars, in *Papers in Memory of G. C. Pappageotes,* Special Publication 5, *Word,* pp. 28–42, 1964.

3.12 EXERCISES

Assume that each of the following problems is the entire language (i.e. no forms and pronunciation patterns are possible other than those shown by the data) and write a solution for each.

1. BULGARIAN

1.	ezik	*language*	1a. ezici	*languages*
2.	vnuk	*grandson*	2a. vnuci	*grandsons*
3.	rak	*crab*	3a. raci	*crabs*
4.	očerk	*sketch*	4a. očerci	*sketches*
5.	vəlk	*wolf*	5a. vəlci	*wolves*
6.	vipusk	*grad*	6a. vipusk'i	*grads*
7.	obisk	*search*	7a. obisk'i	*searches*
8.	stav	*joint*	8a. stavi	*joints*
9.	trup	*trunk*	9a. trupi	*trunks*

2. PERSIAN

1.	daræm	*I have*	1a. daštæm	*I had*
2.	dari	*you* (sg.) *have*	2a. dašti	*you* (sg.) *had*
3.	daræd	*he has*	3a. dašt	*he had*
4.	darim	*we have*	4a. daštim	*we had*
5.	darid	*you* (pl.) *have*	5a. daštid	*you* (pl.) *had*
6.	darænd	*they have*	6a. daštænd	*they had*

3. KAROK, a language of California

1.	ta·t	*mother*	1a. mutta·t	*his mother*
2.	mah	*to see*	2a. ʔummah	*he sees*
3.	paθ	*to throw*	3a. ʔuppaθ	*he throws*
4.	sara	*bread*	4a. mussara	*his bread*
5.	xaviš	*wood*	5a. muxxaviš	*his wood*
6.	ke·na	*pants*	6a. mukke·na	*his pants*
7.	ča·s	*brother*	7a. muča·s	*his brother*
8.	apsih	*leg*	8a. mupsih	*his leg*
9.	axpih	*nail*	9a. muxpih	*his nail*

4. MAORI, a language of New Zealand

1.	kimo	*blink*	1a. kikimo	*blink hard*
2.	patu	*hit*	2a. papatu	*hit hard*
3.	moe	*sleep*	3a. momoe	*sleep deeply*

4.	paa	*touch*	4a.	papaa	*touch hard*
5.	rere	*fly*	5a.	rerere	*fly vigorously*
6.	meke	*punch*	6a.	memeke	*punch hard*
7.	puhi	*blow*	7a.	pupuhi	*blow hard*
8.	toro	*stretch*	8a.	totoro	*stretch vigorously*

1b.	kimokimo	*blink repeatedly*
2b.	patupatu	*hit repeatedly*
3b.	moemoe	*keep sleeping*
4b.	paapaa	*touch repeatedly*
5b.	rererere	*keep flying*
6b.	mekemeke	*keep punching*
7b.	puhipuhi	*keep blowing*
8b.	torotoro	*stretch repeatedly*

5. ZAPOTEC, a language of Mexico

1.	yèn	*neck*	1a.	yēnbōˀ	*his neck*
2.	ẓèž	*fiber*	2a.	ẓēžbōˀ	*his fiber*
3.	lòẓ	*beard*	3a.	lōẓbōˀ	*his beard*
4.	ẓsà	*bean*	4a.	ẓsàbōˀ	*his bean*
5.	ẓél	*sandal*	5a.	ẓélbōˀ	*his sandal*
6.	lčōˀ	*chest*	6a.	lčōˀōbōˀ	*his chest*

6. RUSSIAN

1.	lúk	*onion*	1a.	luká	*onions*
2.	sn'ék	*snow*	2a.	sn'igá	*snows*
3.	l'és	*forest*	3a.	l'isá	*forests*
4.	glás	*eye*	4a.	glazá	*eyes*
5.	górat	*town*	5a.	garadá	*towns*
6.	óstraf	*island*	6a.	astravá	*islands*
7.	pógr'ip	*vault*	7a.	pagr'ibá	*vaults*

7. JAVANESE

1.	pačol	*hoe*	1a.	mačol	*to hoe*
2.	tambaˀ	*dike*	2a.	nambaˀ	*to dike*
3.	čučoˀ	*bill*	3a.	ñučoˀ	*to peck*

4.	kuñči	*lock*	4a. ŋuñči	*to lock*
5.	bubor	*porridge*	5a. mbubor	*to make porridge*
6.	doŋɛŋ	*story*	6a. ndoŋɛŋ	*to tell a story*
7.	ǰɔrɔ	*drill*	7a. ñǰɔrɔ	*to drill*
8.	gunteŋ	*scissors*	8a. ŋgunteŋ	*to make scissors*
9.	maleŋ	*thief*	9a. maleŋ	*to steal*
10.	niyat	*intention*	10a. niyat	*to intend*
11.	ñari	*a measure*	11a. ñari	*to measure*
12.	ŋabar	*fragrance*	12a. ŋabar	*to be fragrant*
13.	sikat	*brush*	13a. ñikat	*to brush*
14.	waŋon	*form*	14a. maŋon	*to form*
15.	laras	*harmony*	15a. ŋlaras	*to harmonize*
16.	rɔtɔ	*even*	16a. ŋrɔtɔ	*to even up*
17.	yiyet	*liquid*	17a. ŋyiyet	*to liquefy*
18.	iǰo	*green*	18a. ŋiǰo	*to make green*
19.	ačar	*pickle*	19a. ŋačar	*to pickle*
20.	ombaˀ	*wave*	20a. ŋombaˀ	*to wave*

8. RUSSIAN

1.	straná	*country*	1a. stráni	*countries*
2.	galavá	*head*	2a. gólavi	*heads*
3.	z'iml'á	*land*	3a. z'éml'i	*lands*
4.	širatá	*width*	4a. široti	*widths*
5.	ruká	*arm*	5a. rúk'i	*arms*
6.	nagá	*foot*	6a. nag'í	*feet*
7.	múxa	*fly*	7a. múx'i	*flies*

9. JAVANESE

1.	bali	*return*	1a. bolabali	*keep returning*
2.	sileh	*different*	2a. silahsileh	*very different*
3.	perɔt	*squeeze*	3a. peratperɔt	*keep squeezing*
4.	kesɔt	*scoot*	4a. kesatkesɔt	*keep scooting*
5.	buŋah	*please*	5a. buŋahbuŋɛh	*keep pleasing*
6.	kuraŋ	*less*	6a. kuraŋkurɛŋ	*less and less*
7.	maŋan	*eat*	7a. moŋanmɛŋɛn	*eat a lot*
8.	z'arak	*distant*	8a. z'orakz'ɛrɛk	*very far*

10. BURIAT MONGOLIAN

1. axa	*brother*	1a. axaar	*by the brother*
2. hono	*fly*	2a. honoor	*by the fly*
3. hojoo	*tooth*	3a. hojoogoor	*by the tooth*
4. noxoi	*dog*	4a. noxoigoor	*by the dog*
5. hurguuli	*school*	5a. hurguulaar	*by the school*
6. byd	*cotton*	6a. bydøør	*by cotton*
7. yder	*day*	7a. yderøør	*by day*

Additional information:
The type of vowel(s) in the suffix is the same as that of the first vowel in the stem; e.g. in 7a they are both front.

11. MAYA

1. winik	*man*	1a. winkoob	*men*
2. kˀekˀen	*pig*	2a. kˀeˀnoob	*pigs*
3. ˀahaw	*king*	3a. ˀahwoob	*kings*
4. ˀakˀab	*night*	4a. ˀaˀboob	*nights*
5. ˀotoč	*house*	5a. ˀohčoob	*houses*
6. šanab	*shoe*	6a. šamboob	*shoes*
7. kan	*snake*	7a. kanoob	*snakes*
8. čeˀ	*tree*	8a. čeˀob	*trees*
9. tuˀ	*smell*	9a. tuˀob	*smells*

Additional information:
The fact that disyllabic words have identical vowels in the singular is accidental.

12. YORUBA, a language of Nigeria

1. mō bī ɔ́	*I asked you.*		
2. mō bī í	*I asked him.*		
3. mō rí ī	*I saw him.*		
4. mō pè ē	*I called him.*	4a. mō pè é	*I called him.*
5. ó wò ō	*He watched him.*	5a. ó wō ó	*He watched him.*
6. ó bī í	*He asked him.*		
7. ó bī mí	*He asked me.*		
8. ó pè mī	*He called me.*	8a. ó pè mí	*He called me.*
9. ó rí mī	*He saw me.*		

13. MAORI

1.	waru	*peel*	1a.	waruhia	*be peeled*
2.	amo	*carry*	2a.	amohia	*be carried*
3.	unu	*remove*	3a.	unuhia	*be removed*
4.	afi	*embrace*	4a.	afitia	*be embraced*
5.	piki	*climb*	5a.	pikitia	*be climbed*
6.	tuutaki	*meet*	6a.	tuutakitia	*be met*
7.	tui	*sew*	7a.	tuia	*be sewn*
8.	hoe	*paddle*	8a.	hoea	*be paddled*
9.	heu	*shave*	9a.	heua	*be shaved*
10.	ŋau	*bite*	10a.	ŋaua	*be bitten*
11.	paa	*touch*	11a.	paania	*be touched*
12.	tuu	*stand*	12a.	tuunia	*be stood*
13.	poo	*darken*	13a.	poonia	*be darkened*
14.	epa	*throw*	14a.	epaina	*be thrown*
15.	kata	*laugh*	15a.	kataina	*be laughed (about)*
16.	tua	*chop*	16a.	tuaina	*be chopped*
17.	tia	*steer*	17a.	tiaina	*be steered*
18.	paŋa	*throw*	18a.	paŋaa	*be thrown*
19.	haŋa	*construct*	19a.	haŋaa	*be constructed*
20.	kaŋa	*curse*	20a.	kaŋaa	*be cursed*

Additional information:

The form of the suffix depends on the very last or last two elements of the stem.

14. FINNISH

	Partitive Singular		*Partitive Plural*
1.	taloa	*house*	taloja
2.	sanaa	*word*	sanoja
3.	tietä	*road*	teita
4.	puuta	*tree*	puita
5.	maata	*land*	maita
6.	päätä	*head*	päitä
7.	työtä	*work*	töitä
8.	laskua	*count*	laskuja
9.	lakkoa	*strike*	lakkoja
10.	loppua	*end*	loppuja

11. kattoa *roof* kattoja
12. apua *aid* apuja
13. satoa *harvest* satoja
14. pukua *suit* pukuja
15. rantaa *shore* rantoja
16. iltaa *evening* iltoja
17. virtaa *stream* virtoja
18. sampoa *instrument* sampoja
19. pöllöä *owl* pöllöjä

Additional information:

The partitive suffix is *a* or *ta*, while the plural suffix is *j* or *i*.

15. COLLOQUIAL IRAQIAN ARABIC

Singular			*Plural*
1.	kámla	*louse*	1a. kámal
2.	síǰra	*tree*	2a. síǰar
3.	wórḳa	*leaf*	3a. wóraḳ
4.	láhma	*flesh*	4a. láham
5.	xášim	*rose*	5a. xšúm
6.	ǰélid	*skin*	6a. ǰlúd
7.	ḥálig	*mouth*	7a. ḥlúg
8.	gáran	*horn*	8a. grún
9.	rás	*head*	9a. rús
10.	ḍél	*tail*	10a. ḍúl
11.	ǰíbal	*mountain*	11a. ǰbál
12.	čélib	*dog*	12a. čláb

chapter four

CO-OCCURRENCE RELATIONS

INTRODUCTION

There are a number of grammatical relations which can be considered co-occurrence relations and which can be conveniently grouped into three basic types. These relations hold, in general, between two or more classes that occur in some well-specifiable position (or positions) in a given set of sentences, i.e. between classes that form what is traditionally called a constitute. Clearly, then, the simplest form any of these relations may take is between two classes.

The first type of co-occurrence relation is a **simple** (or unidirectional) **dependence** between two or more classes. Specifically, in some well-specifiable position(s) within a given set of sentences, the occurrence of one class requires the occurrence of the other(s) but not vice versa. For example, in English sentences such as *he flew over the mountains, he runs quickly, he told him a story yesterday, he walked* *slowly into the house,* and *he sang a song in the garden,* the occurrence of an adverb or prepositional phrase in the predicate requires the occurrence of a verb, but the occurrence of a verb does not require that of an adverb or prepositional phrase; put differently, the occurrence of the adverb and prepositional phrase in the predicate is optional. Witness, for example, *he flew, he runs, he told him a story, he walked into the house, he sang a song,* but not **he over the mountains, *he quickly, *he him a story yesterday, *he slowly into the house, *he a song in the garden.* In its simplest form a simple dependency relation can be specified in a grammar by a P-rule such as $A \rightarrow B(C)$.

The second type of co-occurrence relation is a **mutual** (or bidirectional) **dependence** between two or more classes. Specifically, in some well-specifiable position(s) within a given set of sentences, one class always occurs with the other(s) and vice versa. For example, in English sentences such as the ones given above, the subject pronoun and the verb always co-occur; that is to say, for these sentences to be grammatical, the occurrence of both these classes is obligatory. Thus, we have *he flew over the mountains* and *he told him a story* but not **flew over the mountains, *told him a story,* or **he.* In its simplest form this relation can be specified in a grammar by a P-rule such as $A \rightarrow B + C$.

The third type of co-occurrence relation is a **mutually exclusive** relation between (a) two or more classes or (b) some members of one class with certain members of another class. Specifically, within a given set of sentences (a) two or more classes, and the members of these classes, never co-occur in some well-specifiable position(s), or (b) some members of one class never co-occur with certain members of another class. An example of (a) is English sentences which have a simple subject and a predicate and in which pronouns and nouns never co-occur in subject position, nor do two pronouns or two nouns; witness *he arrived early* and *John runs* but not **he John arrived early, *he John runs* (although some dialects do have *John he runs*), **he I runs,* and **John Mary runs.* An example of (b) is English sentences in which certain nouns cannot be the object of certain verbs; witness *John runs a race* and *John walks a dog* but not **John runs a roll* and **John walks (a) truth.* In its simplest form a mutually exclusive relation of type (a) can be specified in a grammar by a P-rule such as $A \rightarrow \begin{Bmatrix} B \\ C \end{Bmatrix}$ or, equivalently, such as $A \rightarrow B,\ C$, while a mutually exclusive relation of type (b) can be specified by a P-rule such as $A \rightarrow \begin{Bmatrix} B_1 \ / \ X\_\_C \\ B_2 \end{Bmatrix}$.

The grammatical relations traditionally called **government** and **agreement** (or **concord**) are special cases of co-occurrence relations. They are distinguished from other co-occurrence relations in that they involve classes that are traditionally called "grammatical categories" (e.g. number, person, gender, case, etc.).[1] Government and agreement can be considered to differ from each other in that the grammatical category is considered to be a property of *all* the classes involved in agreement, while in government, there is always one class of which the grammatical category is not considered a property; i.e. the grammatical category is not considered a property of the class which governs (or requires) the occurrence of that category with the other class (or classes).[2] Whenever a co-occurrence relation is considered to be government, the category it requires is usually case.

To say that *X* **governs** (a *Y* in) *Z* is to say that a member *Y* of a grammatical category *C* must occur in *Z* whenever *Z* occurs with *X*. For example, in the Modern Greek sentences *o γjatros rotise to γjatro,* 'the doctor asked the doctor,' and *o γjatros milise tu γjatru,* 'the doctor talked to the doctor,' in which *o γjatros* is the subject, *rotise* and *milise* transitive verbs, and *to γjatro* and *tu γjatru* the object, the suffixes *s*, *zero* (or absence of *s*), and *u* mark the function of the noun in the sentence and therefore are said to represent case: *s* indicates the nominative case and that the noun is a subject, and *zero* and *u* indicate the accusative and genitive cases, respectively, and that the noun is an object. Whether the accusative or genitive case will occur with the object noun depends on the particular subclass of the verb in the sentence. Thus we say that a transitive verb in Modern Greek "governs (a noun in) the genitive or accusative case."

To say that *X* **agrees** with *Y* is to say that whichever grammatical category (or categories) is a property of *Y* is also a property of *X* whenever *X* occurs with *Y*. For example, in the English sentences *the girl wants roses* and *the girls want roses* not only do subject nouns and verbs co-occur, but both are inflected for number; i.e. they "agree" in num-

[1] In this book we shall use the term "grammatical category" or simply "category" in the discussions of the data and in the discussions of solutions. It should be remembered, however, that in a *grammar* a generic category (e.g. number or gender) is always a constituent-type in the same sense that *N*, *Vb*, and *Pron* are constituent-types, while a specific grammatical category or subcategory (e.g. masculine, feminine, singular, or plural) is usually a morpheme.

[2] It is conceivable that this distinction between government and agreement, in some instances, may not be meaningful; that is to say, government can be reduced to agreement by saying, for example, that a transitive verb is in fact a transitive verb and case.

ber; therefore sentences like **the girl want roses* and **the girls wants roses* are ungrammatical.

In the preceding examples of co-occurrence relations, the classes in question are contiguous; that is, in the English sentence *he sang a song,* for example, the subject pronoun precedes the verb, which in turn precedes the object noun, and each class member occurs in this sequence. Clearly, however, co-occurrence relations also hold between classes (and members of the same class) that are non-contiguous as well. For example, in the English sentences *is he smoking cigars, he called her up,* and *John looked him over,* the verbs *is smoking, called up,* and *looked over* are discontinuous in that they are separated by the occurrence of the subject and object pronouns. Similarly, in the English sentences *what party did you go to* and *who did you show the book to,* not only are the verbs *did go* and *did show* interrupted by the occurrence of the subject pronoun *you,* but the preposition *to* is separated from its object *what party* and *who,* respectively. (Compare these sentences with *to what party did you go* and *to whom did you show the book.*) In other words, co-occurrence relations hold between classes that are both contiguous and non-contiguous.

The problems in this chapter illustrate co-occurrence relations that are specified only by phrase structure rules (i.e. they illustrate co-occurrence relations other than agreement), while the problems of the next chapter illustrate co-occurrence relations that are specified primarily by syntactic transformations (i.e. they illustrate agreement).

4.1 DATA

PROBLEM 20: MAYA

1.	hun túl wínik	*one man*
2.	hun túl címin	*one horse*
3.	hun túl č^{ʔ}íč^{ʔ}	*one bird*
4.	ka^{ʔ}a túl címin	*two horses*
5.	ka^{ʔ}a túl wínik	*two men*
6.	hun wál lè^{ʔ}	*one leaf*
7.	hun wál wàh	*one tortilla*
8.	hun wál hú^{ʔ}un	*one sheet of paper*
9.	ka^{ʔ}a wál lè^{ʔ}	*two leaves*
10.	hun c^{ʔ}ít kìb	*one candle*
11.	ka^{ʔ}a c^{ʔ}ít há^{ʔ}as	*two bananas*

12. hun cʔít nàl — *one ear of corn*
13. kaʔa cʔít òk — *two legs*
14. hun kúl čèʔ — *one tree*
15. hun kúl nàl — *one cornstalk*
16. kaʔa kúl ròsa — *two rose plants*
17. hum pʔél lìbro — *one book*
18. hum pʔél ávion — *one airplane*
19. kaʔa pʔél tùkul — *two thoughts*
20. kaʔa pʔél wínik — *two men*
21. hum pʔél kìb — *one candle*
22. hum pʔél nàl — *one cornstalk*
23. kaʔa pʔél wàh — *two tortillas*

But not:

*hun túl čèʔ
*hun kúl wínik
*hun cʔít wàh
*hun túl tùkul

Since the numeral, noun classifier, and noun always co-occur in the above phrases, there is a mutual dependence between these three elements. In addition, there is a mutually exclusive relation between some nouns and some classifiers; e.g. *wínik* occurs with *túl* but not with *kúl.* Consider the *pʔél* which occurs before any noun a different element from the *pʔél* which occurs only before *lìbro* 'book,' *ávion* 'airplane,' and *tùkul* 'thought'; otherwise we cannot account for the latter restriction. Notice (1) that tone is regular for classifiers and for two subclasses of nouns (those occurring after the classifiers *túl* and *kúl*) and (2) that a nasal at word boundaries assimilates in point of articulation to the following bilabial stop.

PROBLEM 21: ENGLISH

1. the boy likes a girl
2. a boy terrifies the girl
3. John likes George
4. George sleeps
5. the girl terrifies John
6. John snores
7. George terrifies the boy
8. the boy sleeps
9. a boy terrifies a girl
10. a girl snores
11. John likes a boy
12. the boy likes the girl

But not:

*the John snores
*the boy snores the girl
*the boy terrifies
*likes the girl
*John likes a George
*boy likes girl
*the girl likes

We have two types of sentences in these data: (1) transitive, i.e. sentences with transitive verbs, and (2) intransitive, i.e. sentences with intransitive verbs. Both have a subject and a predicate, but (by definition) only the first type has an object. Transitive and intransitive verbs are not mutually substitutable in the predicate (and as such are mutually exclusive) and neither are proper and common nouns with respect to a determiner in the subject position. That is, while both types of nouns occur as subjects or objects, only common nouns occur after a determiner, which is in a mutual dependency relation with the following noun.

PROBLEM 22: ENGLISH

1. the mother admires the child
2. the child acknowledges the mother
3. a mother praises the boy
4. this deed pleases the boss
5. a book astonishes the boy
6. this flight terrifies a mother
7. a child admires this book
8. a boy acknowledges a deed
9. a child praises the flight
10. the boss pleases the child
11. the mother terrifies the man
12. a man astonishes this child

But not:

*the book admires the child
*this flight acknowledges the boy
*the deed praises the mother
*a man terrifies the book
*this boss pleases the flight
*the boy astonishes a deed

In the above transitive sentences there is a mutual dependence between (1) subject nouns and verbs, (2) verbs and object nouns, and (3) determiners and nouns. Notice that the verbs *admires, acknowledges, praises* occur with only animate subject nouns but with either animate or inanimate object nouns, while the verbs *pleases, astonishes, terrifies* occur with only animate object nouns but with either animate or inanimate subject nouns. In other words, some nouns are in a mutually exclusive relation with some verbs.

PROBLEM 23: THAI

1.	dìchǎn lég	*I am small.* (f. speaker)
2.	phǒm lég	*I am small.* (m. speaker)
3.	khǎw lég	*They are small.*
4.	dìchǎn lég mǎj	*Am I small?* (f. speaker)
5.	phǒm lég mǎj	*Am I small?* (m. speaker)
6.	khǎw lég mǎj	*Are they small?*
7.	phǒm lég khráb	*I am small.* (m. speaker)
8.	dìchǎn lég khâˀ	*I am small.* (f. speaker)
9.	khǎw lég khráb	*They are small.* (m. speaker)
10.	khǎw lég khâˀ	*They are small.* (f. speaker)
11.	phǒm lég mǎj khráb	*Am I small?* (m. speaker)
12.	khǎw lég mǎj kháˀ	*Are they small?* (f. speaker)
13.	phû·cha·j lég	*The man is small.*
14.	dèg lég	*The child is small.*
15.	phû·cha·j lég mǎj	*Is the man small?*
16.	dèg lég mǎj	*Is the child small?*
17.	dèg lég mǎj kháˀ	*Is the child small?* (f. speaker)
18.	phû·cha·j khon nán lég	*That man is small.*
19.	dèg khon nán lég	*That child is small.*
20.	phû·cha·j khon nán lég mǎj khráb	*Is that man small?* (m. speaker)
21.	phû·cha·j khon ní· lég khâˀ	*This man is small.* (f. speaker)
22.	dèg khon ní· lég mǎj	*Is this child small?*
23.	tóˀ jàj	*The table is big.*
24.	tóˀ tua nán jàj	*That table is big.*
25.	tóˀ tua ní· jàj	*This table is big.*
26.	phû·cha·j jàj	*The man is big.*
27.	tóˀ jàj mǎj	*Is the table big?*
28.	tóˀ tua nán jàj mǎj khráb	*Is that table big?* (m. speaker)

29. kàj jàj — *The chicken is big.*
30. kàj tua nán jàj — *That chicken is big.*
31. kàj tua ní· jàj — *This chicken is big.*
32. kàj jàj mǎj — *Is the chicken big?*
33. kàj tua ní· jàj mǎj kháʔ — *Is this chicken big?* (f. speaker)

But not:

*p̀hǒm lég khâʔ
*dìchǎn lég khráb
*tóʔ nán jàj
*dèg tua nán lég
*dìchǎn dèg lég

In the above sentences the subject and the predicate are always expressed at least by a noun and (verbal) adjective, respectively; therefore nouns and adjectives are in a mutual dependency relation; i.e. the occurrence of both is obligatory. A polite form is, in turn, in a simple dependency relation with both the subject and the (verbal) adjective. Now observe the following other co-occurrence relations: (1) within the sentence the polite forms *khâʔ* (and *kháʔ*) and *khráb* are mutually exclusive with certain subject pronouns; e.g. *khâʔ* does not occur with *phǒm*; (2) within the subject (a) pronouns and nouns are mutually exclusive, (b) classifiers and determiners are mutually dependent and are (c) in a simple dependency relation with the noun (i.e. they are optional), but (d) each classifier occurs only with certain nouns; i.e. some classifiers are mutually exclusive with some nouns; and (3) in the predicate (a) the occurrence of *mǎj* is optional, as is (b) the occurrence of the polite forms. Finally, notice that the tone of *khâʔ* changes to *kháʔ* whenever *mǎj* is present and that the tone of determiners is regular; i.e. it is always high.

PROBLEM 24: RUMANIAN

1. un copil e cu un cal mic — *A child is with a small horse.*
2. copilul e cu calul mic — *The child is with the small horse.*
3. un cal e pentru copil — *A horse is for the child.*
4. un cal e pentru copilul bun — *A horse is for the good child.*
5. calul e cu copilul — *The horse is with the child.*
6. un copil e lîngă cal — *A child is near the horse.*
7. copilul bun e lîngă calul bun — *The good child is near the good horse.*

8. copilul e lîngă un cal bun	*The child is near a good horse.*
9. copilul e lîngă un cal	*The child is near a horse.*
10. un cal e în oraș	*A horse is in town.*
11. calul bun e în orasul mic	*The good horse is in the small town.*
12. calul e într un oraș	*The horse is in a town.*
13. calul e într un oraș mic	*The horse is in a small town.*
14. un cal e cu un copil	*A horse is with a child.*
15. un cal e cu copilul	*A horse is with the child.*
16. un copil e cu un cal	*A child is with a horse.*
17. un cal bun e lîngă copil	*A good horse is near the child.*
18. orașul e pentru un cal	*The town is for a horse.*
19. orașul e pentru un cal bun	*The town is for a good horse.*

But not:

*un copilul e cu copil
*un copil e în oraș mic
*cal e cu copilul
*un cal e pentru copilul
*un cal e pentru copil bun
*copilul e cu cal

In all the above sentences the subject noun, the verb, the preposition and the noun which follows the preposition are in a mutual dependency relation, while an adjective following a noun is in a simple dependency relation with that noun. The determiner *un* that may precede a noun is mutually exclusive with the noun suffix *ul.* In addition, nouns ending in *ul* do not occur after any preposition except *cu* unless they are followed by an adjective. The presence of the ending *ul* indicates that a noun is definite, and the absence of this ending indicates that a noun is indefinite. Finally, notice that the preposition translated as 'in' is *într* before *un* and *în* otherwise.

PROBLEM 25: HUNGARIAN

1. a huusst laatom	*I see the meat.*
2. a huuss it van	*The meat is here.*
3. a huusst esem	*I eat the meat.*
4. a huuss ot van	*The meat is there.*
5. az astalt laatom	*I see the table.*
6. az astal ot van	*The table is there.*

7. a huusst hozom	*I bring the meat.*
8. az astalt hozom	*I bring the table.*
9. a šør it van	*The beer is here.*
10. a šørt hozom	*I bring the beer.*
11. az eke it van	*The plow is here.*
12. a libat laatom	*I see the goose.*

But not:

*a šørt it van
*a huuss hozom
*az huuss it van

There are two types of sentences in these data: (1) transitive and (2) intransitive. Transitive sentences have no subject (or, alternatively, have an "understood" subject) but have a predicate consisting of three mutually dependent and obligatory elements, namely, a determiner and a noun (which together constitute the object) and a verb. Intransitive sentences consist obligatorily of a subject, always expressed by a determiner and noun, and a predicate, always expressed by a verb and an adverb. In a transitive sentence the noun ends in *t* (i.e. it is in the accusative case), while in an intransitive sentence it does not have this ending (i.e. it is in the nominative case). This formal difference marks the function of the noun in the sentence: it is an object when it ends in *t* and a subject otherwise. A transitive verb in Hungarian is therefore said to govern a noun in the accusative case. Finally, notice the following morphophonemic change (which was illustrated in Problem 11 of Chapter 3): if the noun following the determiner begins with a consonant, the determiner is *a*, but if it begins with a vowel, the determiner is *az*.

PROBLEM 26: LATIN

1. puer virum videt	*The boy sees the man.*
2. vir puerum videt	*The man sees the boy.*
3. puer virum defendit	*The boy defends the man.*
4. vir puero nocet	*The man harms the boy.*
5. puer viro nocet	*The boy harms the man.*
6. puer viro subvenit	*The boy helps the man.*
7. puer viri meminit	*The boy remembers the man.*
8. puer viro meminit	*The boy remembers the man.*

But not:

*vir puer videt
*vir puerum nocet
*puer viro defendit
*puer vir meminit
*vir pueri nocet

There are three obligatory elements in the above sentences, namely, a subject noun, an object noun, and a verb. The suffixes *i*, *o*, and *um* of the object nouns signal the genitive, dative, and accusative cases, respectively. A verb is said to govern nouns in one of these cases: the verb *meminit* 'remembers' governs the genitive and dative cases, the verbs *nocet* 'harms' and *subvenit* 'helps' govern the dative case, and the verbs *videt* 'sees' and *defendit* 'defends' govern the accusative case. Subject nouns have no suffix and are in the nominative case.

PROBLEM 27: RUSSIAN

1.	eta p'erit praf'esaram	*This is before the professor.*
2.	eta p'erit stud'entam	*This is before the student.*
3.	eta p'erit praf'esarami	*This is before the professors.*
4.	eta za stud'entam	*This is behind the student.*
5.	eta za stud'entami	*This is behind the students.*
6.	eta s praf'esaram	*This is with the professor.*
7.	eta s praf'esarami	*This is with the professors.*
8.	eta sa stud'entami	*This is with the students.*
9.	eta s praf'esara	*This is from the professor.*
10.	eta s praf'esaraf	*This is from the professors.*
11.	eta sa stud'entaf	*This is from the students.*
12.	eta u stud'enta	*This is at the student.*
13.	eta u stud'entaf	*This is at the students.*
14.	eta d'l'a praf'esara	*This is for the professor.*
15.	eta d'l'a praf'esaraf	*This is for the professors.*

But not:

*eta p'erit praf'esara
*eta za stud'entaf
*eta u stud'entam
*eta d'l'a stud'entami

In the sentences in Problem 27 a preposition is said to govern the case of a noun: *p'erit, za,* and *s (sa)* govern the instrumental case, and *s (sa), u,* and *d'l'a* govern the genitive case. The affix which signals case also signals the category number; thus *am* and *ami* signal instrumental singular and plural, respectively, and *a* and *af* signal genitive singular and plural, respectively. Despite the double function of these affixes, however, we do not say that a preposition governs the number of nouns, since the singular and plural distinctions are not mutually exclusive with any preposition in the data. Notice the morphophonemic change between the preposition translated as 'with' and 'from' and the following noun: this preposition is *s* when the following noun begins with a stop, and *sa* otherwise.

PROBLEM 28: GERMAN

1. er zi·t den berg	*He sees the mountain.*
2. er zi·t den val	*He sees the wall.*
3. er zi·t den tiš	*He sees the table.*
4. er zi·t den va·gən	*He sees the car.*
5. er zi·t den markt	*He sees the market.*
6. er zi·t den plats	*He sees the square.*
7. er ist auf dem berg	*He is on the mountain.*
8. er ist hintər dem val	*He is behind the wall.*
9. er ist untər dem tiš	*He is under the table.*
10. er ist nebən dem va·gən	*He is by the car.*
11. er ist ybər dem plats	*He is over the square.*
12. er ge·t auf den berg	*He walks on the mountain.*
13. er ge·t hintər den val	*He walks behind the wall.*
14. er ge·t untər den tiš	*He walks under the table.*
15. er ge·t nebən den va·gən	*He walks by the car.*
16. er ge·t ybər den markt	*He walks over the market.*
17. der val ist gro·s	*The wall is big.*
18. der berg ist klain	*The mountain is small.*
19. de markt ist šøn	*The market is beautiful.*
20. der plats ist klain	*The square is small.*
21. der tiš ist gro·s	*The table is tall.*
22. der va·gən ist šøn	*The car is beautiful.*
23. er šte·t auf dem berg	*He stands on the mountain.*
24. er loift untər den val	*He runs under the wall.*
25. er loift ybər den plats	*He runs over the square.*

26. er ist gro·s — *He is tall.*
27. er ist klain — *He is short.*

But not:

*er ist auf den berg
*er ge·t auf dem val
*den val ist klain
*dem va·gən ist šøn
*er zi·t dem tiš
*er zi·t gro·s
*er ge·t klain

There are three types of sentences in these data: (1) transitive, (2) intransitive, and (3) copulative (i.e. sentences with predicate adjectives [or nouns]). The subject of a copulative sentence is either a determiner followed by a noun or simply a pronoun, while the predicate is the verb *ist* 'is' followed by a predicate adjective; the determiner *(der)* in these sentences is said to be in the nominative case. In transitive sentences the subject is a pronoun, and the predicate is a verb, a determiner in the accusative case (which is governed by the verb) and a noun. In intransitive sentences the subject is a pronoun, and the predicate is a verb and a prepositional phrase. The verb in these sentences governs a determiner in either the accusative *(den)* or dative *(dem)* case, regardless of which preposition introduces the phrase. Which case is selected depends on the particular subtype of intransitive verbs: a "verb of motion" such as *ge·t* or *loift* governs the accusative and any other verb governs the dative case.

PROBLEM 29: RUSSIAN

1. yil'éna v'íd'it ivána — *Elaine sees Ivan.*
2. iván v'íd'it yil'énu — *Ivan sees Elaine.*
3. ánna n'i v'íd'it ivána — *Anna doesn't see Ivan.*
4. st'ipán n'i v'íd'it ánni — *Steven doesn't see Anna.*
5. iván n'i v'íd'it yil'éni — *Ivan doesn't see Elaine.*
6. iván n'i v'íd'it st'ipána — *Ivan doesn't see Steven.*
7. iván v'íd'it stól — *Ivan sees the table.*
8. iván n'i v'íd'it stalá — *Ivan doesn't see the table.*
9. iván v'íd'it kn'ígu — *Ivan sees the book.*
10. iván n'i v'íd'it kn'íg'i — *Ivan doesn't see the book.*

But not:

*yil'éna v'íd'it iván
*iván v'íd'it yil'éna/kn'íga
*iván n'i v'íd'it st'ipán
*iván n'i v'íd'it yil'énu/kn'ígu
*iván n'i v'íd'it stól
*iván n'i v'íd'it kn'íga

Additional information:

The nominative of 'book' is *kn'íga* and that of 'table' is *stól.*
Subject nouns ending in *a* are feminine, and those ending in a consonant are masculine.

Although the sentences in these data are all transitive, notice that some are positive and others are negative. In negative sentences the verb governs nouns in the genitive case, regardless of whether the noun is animate or inanimate: *a* is the masculine and *i* the feminine genitive suffix. In positive sentences, however, the verb governs nouns in the genitive and the accusative cases: if the following noun is masculine animate, the verb governs the genitive case (i.e. the object noun ends in *a*); otherwise it governs the accusative case (i.e. the object noun ends in *zero*—or has no ending—if it is masculine inanimate and in *u* if it is feminine animate or inanimate). Notice, finally, that in negative sentences the stress on masculine inanimate nouns shifts from the stem to the suffix and, consequently, an unstressed *o* becomes *a*, and that the last consonant in *kn'íga* 'book' palatalizes before the suffix *i*: *kn'íg'i.*

4.2 SOLUTIONS

SOLUTION 20: MAYA

1. $NP \rightarrow Det + N$
2. $Det \rightarrow D + Cl$
3. $Cl \rightarrow Cl_1, Cl_2$
4. $N \rightarrow N_1, N_2, N_3, N_4, N_5$
5. $Cl_2 \rightarrow \left\{ \begin{array}{l} tul \ / \ \_\_ N_1 \\ wal \ / \ \_\_ N_2 \\ c^{?}it \ / \ \_\_ N_3 \\ kul \ / \ \_\_ N_4 \\ p^{?}el \end{array} \right\}$
6. $D \rightarrow$ *huŊ, kaˀa*

7. $Cl_1 \rightarrow$ *pʔel*
8. $N_1 \rightarrow$ *winik, cimin, čʔičʔ*
9. $N_2 \rightarrow$ *lèʔ, wàh, húʔun*
10. $N_3 \rightarrow$ *kìb, háʔas, nàl, òk*
11. $N_4 \rightarrow$ *čeʔ, nal, rosa*
12. $N_5 \rightarrow$ *lìbro, ávion, tùkul*
13. Tob

$$\#CVw]_{N_4} \Rightarrow \#C\grave{V}w]_{N_4}$$

14. Tob

$$X + CVw \Rightarrow X + C\acute{V}w$$

15. Tob

$$N \begin{bmatrix} C_1 \\ C_2 \end{bmatrix} \Rightarrow \begin{bmatrix} m \\ n \end{bmatrix} \begin{bmatrix} C_1 \\ C_2 \end{bmatrix}$$

C_1 = any voiceless labial consonant
$C_2 \neq C_1$

SOLUTION 21: ENGLISH

1. $S \rightarrow NP + VP$
2. $VP \rightarrow \begin{Bmatrix} Vtr + NP \\ Vin \end{Bmatrix}$
3. $NP \rightarrow \begin{Bmatrix} Det + N \\ Name \end{Bmatrix}$
4. $Det \rightarrow$ *a, the*
5. $N \rightarrow$ *boy, girl*
6. $Name \rightarrow$ *John, George*
7. $Vtr \rightarrow$ *likes, terrifies*
8. $Vin \rightarrow$ *sleeps, snores*

SOLUTION 22: ENGLISH

1. $S \rightarrow NP + VP$
2. $VP \rightarrow V + NP$
3. $V \rightarrow V_1, V_2$
4. $NP \rightarrow Det + N$

5. $$N \rightarrow \left\{ \begin{array}{l} Nan \;/ \left\{ \begin{array}{l} \_\_V_1 \\ V_2 + Det\_\_ \end{array} \right\} \\ Nan \\ Nin \end{array} \right\}$$

6. $Det \rightarrow$ *a, the, this*
7. $Nan \rightarrow$ *boy, child, mother, boss, man*
8. $Nin \rightarrow$ *deed, book, flight*
9. $V_1 \rightarrow$ *admires, praises, acknowledges*
10. $V_2 \rightarrow$ *pleases, astonishes, terrifies*

SOLUTION 23: THAI

1. $S \rightarrow NP + VP(Prt)$
2. $VP \rightarrow Adj(QM)$
3. $$NP \rightarrow \left\{ \begin{array}{c} N(Det) \\ Pron \end{array} \right\}$$
4. $Det \rightarrow Cl + D$
5. $N \rightarrow N_1, N_2$
6. $$Cl \rightarrow \left\{ \begin{array}{l} khon \;/\; N_1 \_\_ \\ tua \end{array} \right\}$$
7. $Pron \rightarrow Pr_1, Pr_2, Pr_3$
8. $$Prt \rightarrow \left\{ \begin{array}{l} \begin{bmatrix} khr\acute{a}b \\ kh\hat{a}ʔ \end{bmatrix} / \begin{bmatrix} Pr_1 \\ Pr_2 \end{bmatrix} X \_\_ \# \\ khr\acute{a}b \\ kh\hat{a}ʔ \end{array} \right\}$$
9. $QM \rightarrow$ *mǎj*
10. $D \rightarrow$ *ni·, nan*
11. $N_1 \rightarrow$ *phû·cha·j, dèg*
12. $N_2 \rightarrow$ *tóʔ, kàj*
13. $Pr_1 \rightarrow$ *phǒm*
14. $Pr_2 \rightarrow$ *dìchǎn*
15. $Pr_3 \rightarrow$ *khǎw*
16. $Adj \rightarrow$ *lég, jàj*
17. Tob

    $QM + kh\hat{a}ʔ \Rightarrow QM + kh\acute{a}ʔ$
18. Tob

    $Vw]_D \Rightarrow \acute{V}w]_D$

SOLUTION 24: RUMANIAN

Solution A

1. $S \rightarrow NP + VP$
2. $VP \rightarrow V + PP$
3. $PP \rightarrow Prep + NP$
4. $Prep \rightarrow P_1, P_2$
5. $NP \rightarrow \begin{Bmatrix} Det + Ns \\ Ns + Afn \end{Bmatrix} (Adj)$
6. $Afn \rightarrow \begin{Bmatrix} \emptyset / P_2 + Ns \_\_ \# \\ ul \end{Bmatrix}$
7. $Det \rightarrow un$
8. $P_1 \rightarrow cu$
9. $P_2 \rightarrow$ *pentru, lîngă, IN*
10. $Adj \rightarrow$ *bun, mic*
11. $Ns \rightarrow$ *copil, cal, oraș*
12. $V \rightarrow e$
13. Tob

$$IN \begin{bmatrix} Det \\ Ns \end{bmatrix} \Rightarrow \begin{bmatrix} \hat{\imath}ntr \\ \hat{\imath}n \end{bmatrix} \begin{bmatrix} Det \\ Ns \end{bmatrix}$$

Solution B

1–4. Same as in Solution 24A
5. $NP \rightarrow N(Adj)$
6. $N \rightarrow Ns + Co$
7. $Co \rightarrow Def, Indef$
8. $Def \rightarrow \begin{Bmatrix} \emptyset / P_2 + Ns \_\_ \# \\ ul \end{Bmatrix}$
9. $Indef \rightarrow un$

10–14. Same as rules (8)–(12) of Solution 24A

15. Tob

$$X + Ns + Indef(Adj) \Rightarrow X + Indef + Ns(Adj)$$

16. Tob

$$IN \begin{bmatrix} Indef \\ Ns \end{bmatrix} \Rightarrow \begin{bmatrix} \hat{\imath}ntr \\ \hat{\imath}n \end{bmatrix} \begin{bmatrix} Indef \\ Ns \end{bmatrix}$$

SOLUTION 25: HUNGARIAN

Solution A

1. $S \rightarrow NP + VP$
2. $VP \rightarrow \begin{Bmatrix} Adv + Vin \\ Vtr \end{Bmatrix}$
3. $NP \rightarrow Det + N$
4. $N \rightarrow Ns + Afn$
5. $Afn \rightarrow \begin{Bmatrix} t \,/\, Ns \_\_ Vtr \\ \emptyset \end{Bmatrix}$
6. $Det \rightarrow aZ$
7. $Ns \rightarrow$ *huuss, astal, šør, eke, liba*
8. $Vin \rightarrow$ *van*
9. $Vtr \rightarrow$ *laatom, esem, hozom*
10. $Adv \rightarrow$ *it, ot*
11. Tob

$$Z\begin{bmatrix} C \\ Vw \end{bmatrix} \Rightarrow \begin{bmatrix} \emptyset \\ z \end{bmatrix}\begin{bmatrix} C \\ Vw \end{bmatrix}$$

Solution B

1–3. Same as in Solution 25A
4. $N \rightarrow Ns + Ca$
5. $Ca \rightarrow \begin{Bmatrix} Acc \,/\, Ns \_\_ Vtr \\ Nom \end{Bmatrix}$
6. $Acc \rightarrow t$
7. $Nom \rightarrow \emptyset$

8–13. Same as rules (6)–(11) of Solution 25A

SOLUTION 26: LATIN

Solution A

1. $S \rightarrow N + VP$
2. $VP \rightarrow N + V$
3. $V \rightarrow Vs + Afv$
4. $Vs \rightarrow Vs_1, Vs_2, Vs_3$
5. $N \rightarrow Ns + Afn$

$$6.\quad Afn \rightarrow \begin{Bmatrix} um \,/\, Ns \_\_ \, Vs_1 \\ o \,/\, Ns \_\_ \, Vs_2 \\ \begin{Bmatrix} i \\ o \end{Bmatrix} /\, Ns \_\_ \, Vs_3 \\ \emptyset \end{Bmatrix}$$

7. $Afv \rightarrow t$
8. $Ns \rightarrow$ *puer, vir*
9. $Vs_1 \rightarrow$ *vide, defendi*
10. $Vs_2 \rightarrow$ *noce, subveni*
11. $Vs_3 \rightarrow$ *memini*

Solution B

1–4. Same as in Solution 26A
5. $N \rightarrow Ns + Ca$

$$6.\quad Ca \rightarrow \begin{Bmatrix} Nom \,/\, \#Ns \_\_ \\ Acc \,/\, Ns \_\_ \, V_1 \\ Dat \,/\, Ns \_\_ \, V_2 \\ Gen \\ Dat \end{Bmatrix}$$

7–11. Same as in Solution 26A
12. Tob

$$\begin{bmatrix} Nom \\ Acc \\ Dat \\ Gen \end{bmatrix} \Rightarrow \begin{bmatrix} \emptyset \\ um \\ o \\ i \end{bmatrix}$$

SOLUTION 27: RUSSIAN

Solution A

1. $S \rightarrow A + PP$
2. $PP \rightarrow Prep + N$
3. $N \rightarrow Ns + Afn$
4. $Prep \rightarrow P_1, P_2$

$$5.\quad Afn \rightarrow \begin{Bmatrix} \begin{Bmatrix} ami \\ am \end{Bmatrix} /\, P_1 + Ns \_\_ \\ a \\ af \end{Bmatrix}$$

6. $P_1 \rightarrow$ *p'erit, za, F*
7. $P_2 \rightarrow$ *F, u, d'l'a*
8. $A \rightarrow$ *eta*
9. $Ns \rightarrow$ *praf'esar, stud'ent*
10. Tob

$$F \begin{bmatrix} C_1 \\ C_2 \end{bmatrix} \Rightarrow \begin{bmatrix} s \\ sa \end{bmatrix} \begin{bmatrix} C_1 \\ C_2 \end{bmatrix}$$

$C_1 =$ any stop
$C_2 \neq C_1$

Solution B

1–3. Same as in Solution 27A
4. $Afn \rightarrow Ca + Nu$
5. $Nu \rightarrow Sg, Pl$
6. $Prep \rightarrow P_1, P_2$
7. $Ca \rightarrow \begin{Bmatrix} Instr \; / \; P_1 + Ns \_\_ \\ Gen \end{Bmatrix}$

8–11. Same as rules (6)–(9) of Solution 27A
12. Tob

$$Instr \begin{bmatrix} Sg \\ Pl \end{bmatrix} \Rightarrow \begin{bmatrix} am \\ ami \end{bmatrix}$$

13. Tob

$$Gen \begin{bmatrix} Sg \\ Pl \end{bmatrix} \Rightarrow \begin{bmatrix} a \\ af \end{bmatrix}$$

14. Same as rule (10) of Solution 27A

SOLUTION 28: GERMAN

1. $S \rightarrow NP + VP$
2. $VP \rightarrow \begin{Bmatrix} Vcop + Pred \\ Vb \end{Bmatrix}$
3. $Vb \rightarrow \begin{Bmatrix} Vtr + NP \\ Vin + PP \end{Bmatrix}$
4. $PP \rightarrow Prep + NP$
5. $NP \rightarrow \begin{Bmatrix} \begin{Bmatrix} Det + N \\ Pron \end{Bmatrix} / \; \# \_\_ \\ Det + N \end{Bmatrix}$

6. $Vin \rightarrow V_1, V_2$
7. $Det \rightarrow D + Ca$

$$8.\quad Ca \rightarrow \begin{Bmatrix} Dat \;/\; V_1 + Prep + D \_\_ \\ Acc \;/ \begin{Bmatrix} Vtr + D \_\_ \\ V_2 + Prep + D \_\_ \end{Bmatrix} \\ Nom \end{Bmatrix}$$

9. $D \rightarrow$ *de*
10. $Prep \rightarrow$ *auf, hintər, untər, nebən, ybər*
11. $Pred \rightarrow$ *gro·s, klain, šøn*
12. $Vcop \rightarrow$ *ist*
13. $Vtr \rightarrow$ *zi·t*
14. $V_1 \rightarrow$ *ist, šte·t*
15. $V_2 \rightarrow$ *ge·t, loift*
16. $Pron \rightarrow$ *er*
17. $N \rightarrow$ *berg, val, tiš, va·gən, markt, plats*
18. Tob

$$\begin{bmatrix} Dat \\ Acc \\ Nom \end{bmatrix} \Rightarrow \begin{bmatrix} m \\ n \\ r \end{bmatrix}$$

SOLUTION 29: RUSSIAN

1. $S \rightarrow N + VP$
2. $VP \rightarrow Vb + N$
3. $Vb \rightarrow (Neg)V$
4. $N \rightarrow Ns + Afn$
5. $Ns \rightarrow Nsm, Nsf$
6. $Nsm \rightarrow Nman, Nmin$
7. $Afn \rightarrow G + Ca$

$$8.\quad Ca \rightarrow \begin{Bmatrix} Nom \;/\; G \_\_ (Neg)V \\ Gen \;/ \begin{Bmatrix} Neg + X \\ V + Nman \end{Bmatrix} G\_\_ \\ Acc \end{Bmatrix}$$

$$9.\quad G \rightarrow \begin{Bmatrix} F \;/\; Nsf \_\_ \\ M \end{Bmatrix}$$

10. $Neg \rightarrow$ *n'i*
11. $V \rightarrow$ *v'id'it*
12. $Nman \rightarrow$ *iván, st'ipán*

13. *Nmin* → *stól*
14. *Nsf* → *yil'én, ánn, kn'ig*
15. Tob

$$\begin{bmatrix} Nsf \\ Nsm \end{bmatrix} \begin{bmatrix} F \\ M \end{bmatrix} Nom \Rightarrow \begin{bmatrix} Nsf \\ Nsm \end{bmatrix} \begin{bmatrix} a \\ \emptyset \end{bmatrix}$$

16. Tob

$$Nsm + M \begin{bmatrix} Acc \\ Gen \end{bmatrix} \Rightarrow Nsm \begin{bmatrix} \emptyset \\ a \end{bmatrix}$$

17. Tob

$$F \begin{bmatrix} Acc \\ Gen \end{bmatrix} \Rightarrow \begin{bmatrix} u \\ i \end{bmatrix}$$

18. Tob
    $C + i \Rightarrow C' + i$
    C = any velar consonant
19. Tob
    $\acute{o}X + a \Rightarrow aX + \acute{a}$

4.3 DISCUSSION OF SOLUTIONS

4.3.1 Context-restricted rules

The following discussion concerns the specification of co-occurrence relations through the use of context-restricted rules.

(1) **When they are used.** Notice that a context-restricted rule is used in the preceding solutions whenever (1) some members of one class are said to be in a mutually exclusive relation with some members of another class, (2) some members of a single class are said to occur only in a particular position, or (3) both (1) and (2) are the case. For example, in Problem 29 (Russian), masculine and feminine noun stems are mutually exclusive with masculine and feminine gender, masculine nouns in the nominative case are mutually exclusive with masculine and feminine nouns in the accusative case (the former occur before and the latter after a verb), and so on. In Problem 20 (Maya), although classifiers and nouns co-occur within a given phrase, some classifiers are mutually exclusive with a set of nouns. In Problem 23 (Thai), although a polite form in the predicate has a simple dependency relation with a verb, the polite forms are mutually exclusive with certain subject pronouns whenever both occur within the same sentence. In Problem 28

(German), while a determiner and a noun can occur both as the subject and the object of transitive sentences, a pronoun can occur only as the subject of such sentences.

(2) **Deciding which class should be expanded by a context-restricted rule.** That class which is **conditioned** by another class or position is the class which is specified by a context-restricted rule.

(a) By **conditioned by another class** is meant "*X* always determines *Y* but never vice versa whenever both *X* and *Y* occur in a sentence"; *Y* is then said to be conditioned by *X*, or to be predictable. That is, if, given a set of sentences in which the classes *X* and *Y* both occur, and a set of alternative members for both *X* and *Y*, by knowing that a particular member of *X* has occurred, we know which member of *Y* will occur but, by knowing that a particular member of *Y* has occurred, we do not know which member of *X* will occur, we then say that *X* conditions *Y*. In Solution 20 (Maya), for example, classifiers are expanded by a context-restricted rule the environment of which is different types of nouns. This is because, given any noun, we can always determine which of the five possible classifiers will occur with it, but the reverse cannot be done; that is to say, given any classifier, we cannot predict which noun will occur with it. It is the nouns, therefore, that condition the classifiers. (Notice that there is no conclusive evidence in Problem 23 [Thai], however, to decide whether it is the pronoun which conditions the polite form or vice versa.)

(b) Position alone or both a class and a position may be the conditioning factor(s) of another class. For example, in Problem 22 (English) the environmental factors that condition the occurrence of certain nouns are a particular subclass of verbs and a specific position: animate nouns occur with one set of verbs in subject position but with another set of verbs in object position. In this case position and class are equally important as conditioning factors.

When the members of a single class are mutually exclusive with each other in well-specifiable positions within a given sentence, however, position is the sole conditioning factor. In Problem 29 (Russian), for example, position alone conditions the occurrence of the nominative case: the nominative occurs only when the noun precedes the verb. Whenever position is the sole conditioning factor of a class, subclassification of another class is not necessary, and there may or may not be a constituent-type (or types) in terms of which position is specified in the context-restricted rule. For example, in rule (8) of Solution 29 (Russian) *G* and *(Neg)V* are used to define the position of *Nom,* but in rule (5) of

Solution 28 (German) a constituent-type is not used to define the position in which *NP* may be expanded as either *Det* + *N* or *Pron* (instead, the sentence boundary symbol is used).

4.3.2 Inconsistencies in postulating constituents

As may have been noticed, there are a number of inconsistencies with respect to postulating certain types of constituents in the preceding solutions. These inconsistencies revolve around a subject which was briefly discussed in 2.3.1, namely, the justification for postulating constituents in the phrase structure grammar. Although this subject will be more fully discussed in Chapter 6, where we will have a better basis for doing so, let us see what the reasons are for the inconsistencies in the preceding solutions.

First, notice that in some solutions it is postulated that a verb has two constituents, a verb stem and an affix, but in others these constituents are not postulated even though there may be some reason in the data for suspecting that they should be. For example, in Solution 26 (Latin) it is postulated that a verb stem plus an affix are constituents of *V*, while in the solutions for Problems 21 and 22 (English) constituents of the types *Vs* and *Afv* are not postulated, even though there is reason to suspect, from the data given, that they should be; instead, only various types of verbs are postulated. Although our suspicions may be verified when we have additional data, postulating a verb stem and an affix cannot be justified in the latter two solutions, since the postulation of such constituents would not simplify any rules of the grammar.

A similar inconsistency may be observed with the two alternative solutions, A and B, given for Problems 24 to 27, which differ from each other in only one essential respect: a grammatical category is always postulated in Solution B but never in Solution A. In the solutions for Problem 24 (Rumanian), for example, the category concreteness is postulated in Solution B but not in A; similarly, the categories number and case are postulated in Solution B for Problem 27 (Russian) but not in A. If we are concerned only with the data given, Solutions A are preferable to B because the category (or categories) postulated in the latter solutions is not used in any other part of the grammar. If, however, some use could be found in the grammar for the categories, Solutions B would be preferable to A. This is the case when there is agreement: unless the grammatical categories gender, number, and case are postulated in a grammar of Latin and Russian, for example, there is no way to specify that an adjective agrees in these categories with a noun. Clearly, then, a B type of solution is preferable in such instances (see Chapter 5 for examples of such instances). The solutions given for Problems 28 (German) and 29 (Russian) are modeled after the B solutions on the grounds that there will definitely be a need for the grammatical categories postulated as soon as more data are introduced. But notice that in Solution 28, contrary to intuition (and, perhaps, our knowledge of German), case is postulated as a constituent of determiners and not as a constituent of nouns; given the way the problem is constructed, however, no other reasonable choice remains.

4.3.3 Grammatical subcategories as terminal and non-terminal symbols

In Solutions 26B, 27B, 28, and 29 the grammatical subcategories are terminal symbols (and therefore grammatical morphemes), while in Solutions B for Problems 24 and 25, they are non-terminal symbols. This difference in the treatment of subcategories reflects, in general, whether the category is overtly expressed in the data by a *distinct* affix, i.e. an affix which does not simultaneously express another grammatical subcategory (e.g. the plural suffix *s* in English *boys* and *girls*): if the subcategory in question is not expressed by a distinct affix, it is treated as a terminal symbol; if, however, the subcategory is expressed by a distinct affix, then whichever practice results in the simpler solution is adopted.

Whenever grammatical subcategories are terminal symbols (and thus grammatical morphemes), a set of morphophonemic rules must provide the correct morphophonemic representation of these subcategories. In Solution B for Problem 27 (Russian), for example, the subcategories *Gen, Instr, Sg,* and *Pl* are grammatical morphemes, and their morphophonemic representation is provided by rules (12) and (13).

4.3.4 Morphophonemic rules

(1) **Unambiguous environments.** Notice that environments that can be unambiguously determined are omitted from morphophonemic rules. In Solution 27B (Russian), for example, *Ns* is omitted in rules (12) and (13) because there is no ambiguity that *Ns* is the only environment to which these rules can refer. Similarly, in Solution 28 (German), *D* is omitted in rule (18), since *D* is the only possible environment to which this rule can refer. That is, since the only constituent-type of which *Ca* is a constituent is *Det,* and since rule (18) provides morphophonemic representations for *Ca, D* is omitted from this rule because there is no possibility that it will be misinterpreted, e.g. as applying to nouns or verbs rather than to determiners.

(2) **A new notational convention.** In Solution 20 (Maya) a new notational convention is introduced in (the morphophonemic) rule (13),

namely, $]_{N_4}$ at the end of a string. This notation is used whenever we wish to indicate that the change in question applies only to a certain constituent-type (that which is indicated by the subscript). An alternative notation that serves the same purpose is paired square brackets with a subscript, e.g. $_N[\ ]$ or $[\ ]_N$, around the string in question.

4.3.5 Grammaticality of novel sentences

The grammaticality of some of the novel sentences generated by the preceding solutions might be questioned because their translation seems semantically aberrant. The following are examples of such sentences:

(a) *From Solution 24 (Rumanian):*

orașul e într un copil	*The town is in a child.*
orașul e într un cal	*The town is in a horse.*

(b) *From Solution 28 (German):*

der tiš zi·t den berg	*The table sees the mountain.*
der tiš ge·t nebən dem markt	*The table goes by the market.*

(c) *From Solution 29 (Russian):*

kn'iga n'i v'id'it stalá	*The book doesn't see the table.*
stól v'id'it stól	*The table sees the table.*

We allow these and other such sentences to be generated by a grammar simply because we have no evidence that they are not grammatical. The ultimate criterion for deciding whether we should allow such sentences to be generated is whether they are judged grammatical by a native speaker of the language in question, and *not* whether they are considered meaningful. There are many sentences in English, for example, such as *my horse smokes a dozen telephones* and *the verbs are blue,* which although nonsensical are nevertheless judged as grammatical by native speakers of English and therefore are allowed to be generated by a grammar of English.[3] Admittedly, the question how one asks a native speaker whether a given sentence is grammatical is an extremely difficult one to answer; nevertheless, a native speaker's judgment is the

[3] In light of what was just said, the reader may wonder why the "*But not*" sentences of Problem 42 (English) were given as ungrammatical data. The reason is simply to restrict the data so that they can be used to illustrate how to write a solution for a particular situation.

For a more detailed discussion concerning the grammaticality of sentences, see N. Chomsky, *Syntactic Structures,* Mouton and Company, The Hague, 1957 (2d printing with additional bibliography, 1962), chap. 2, and his *Aspects of the Theory of Syntax,* The M.I.T. Press, Cambridge, Mass., 1965, Chap. 1.

criterion by which we ultimately accept or reject the sentences generated by a grammar.[4]

As stated in Chapter 2, whenever a native speaker is not available, a reasonable procedure is to generalize as much as possible (i.e. write rules with the least number of restrictions [preferably none] imposed on them) and then wait to see if the grammar thus written must be changed in light of new information or insights gained from some reliable source.

To go back to the questionable novel sentences, suppose we were to ask a native speaker of Rumanian, for example, whether sentences such as *orașul e într un cal* are grammatical and he says they are not, i.e. that this type of sentence is ungrammatical if the subject is inanimate. We would then have to go back and correct the solution as follows:

1. $S \rightarrow NP + VP$
2. $VP \rightarrow V + PP$
3. $PP \rightarrow Prep + NP$
4. $NP \rightarrow N(Adj)$
5. $N \rightarrow Ns + Co$
6. $Ns \rightarrow \begin{Bmatrix} Nan \ / \ \# \text{—} \\ Nan \\ Nin \end{Bmatrix}$
7. $Prep \rightarrow P_1, P_2$

The remaining rules would be the same as those of Solution B for Problem 23, with one exception: the rule *Ns* → *copil, cal, oraș* would be replaced by the two rules (a) *Nan* → *copil, cal* and (b) *Nin* → *oraș*.

4.4 NOTES

Notice that although rule (15) of Solution 24B (Rumanian) permutes only *Indef* of the category *Co,* the category is not lost in deriving Rumanian sentences with *un* 'a,' since, as was noted in 1.5.1, whenever we permute two adjacent constituents, we are allowed to carry intermediate structure (in this case, *Co*) as long as we do not destroy any other structure as a result; thus rule (15) assigns the following derived constituent structure for the Rumanian sentence *un cal e cu un copil:*

[4] For a discussion of this question, see H. A. Gleason, *An Introduction to Descriptive Linguistics,* rev. ed., Holt, Rinehart and Winston, Inc., New York, 1961, chap. 13.

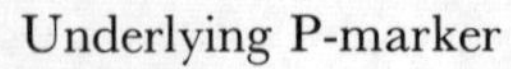

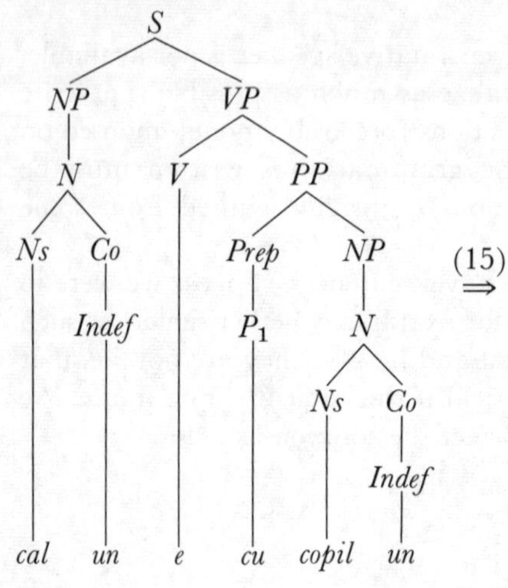

(15) ⇒

Derived P-marker

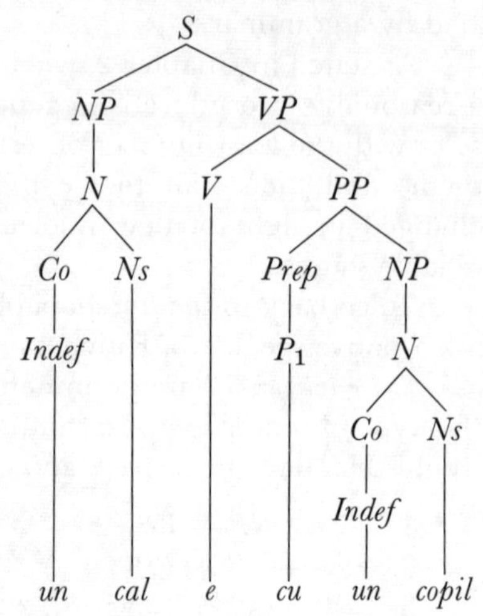

and not the following:

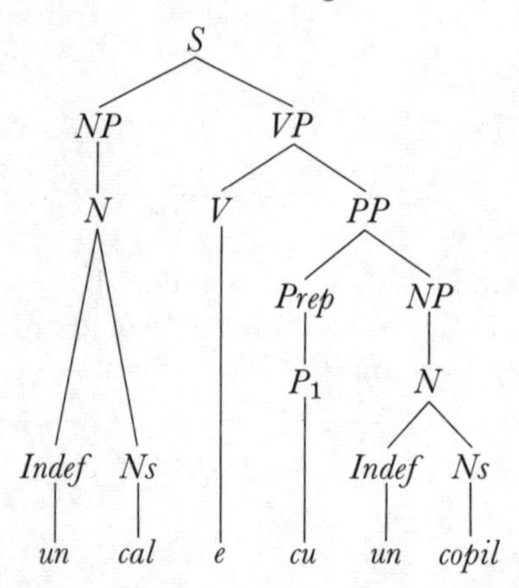

4.5 EXERCISES

1. INDONESIAN

1. kasim sakit — *Kasim is sick.*
2. samin bodoh — *Samin is stupid.*
3. ibu itu sakit — *The mother is sick.*
4. paman itu bodoh — *The uncle is stupid.*

5. kasim tidaˀ sakit — *Kasim is not sick.*
6. ibu itu tidaˀ bodoh — *The mother is not stupid.*
7. samin tidaˀ sakit — *Samin is not sick.*
8. paman itu tidaˀ bodoh — *The uncle is not stupid.*
9. kasim guru — *Kasim is a teacher.*
10. samin murit — *Samin is a pupil.*
11. ibu itu guru — *The mother is a teacher.*
12. paman itu murit — *The uncle is a pupil.*
13. kasim bukan guru — *Kasim is not a teacher.*
14. samin bukan murit — *Samin is not a pupil.*
15. paman itu bukan guru — *The uncle is not a teacher.*
16. ibu itu bukan murit — *The mother is not a pupil.*

But not:

*kasim itu sakit
*kasim bukan sakit
*kasim tidaˀ guru
*ibu sakit
*ibu guru itu

2. KOREAN

1. mojaka haŋkä issʉmnita — *There is a hat.*
2. sakwaka haŋkä issʉmnita — *There is an apple.*
3. soka hammali issʉmnita — *There is an ox.*
4. käka hammali issʉmnita — *There is a dog.*
5. mali hammali issʉmnita — *There is a horse.*
6. mojaka tukä issʉmnita — *There are two hats.*
7. sakwaka tukä issʉmnita — *There are two apples.*
8. soka tumali issʉmnita — *There are two oxen.*
9. käka tumali issʉmnita — *There are two dogs.*
10. mali tumali issʉmnita — *There are two horses.*
11. papi haŋkʉlʉl issʉmnita — *There is a bowl of rice.*
12. kuki haŋkʉlʉl issʉmnita — *There is a bowl of soup.*
13. papi tukʉlʉl issʉmnita — *There are two bowls of rice.*
14. kuki tukʉlʉl issʉmnita — *There are two bowls of soup.*
15. mojaka sekä issʉmnita — *There are three hats.*
16. sakwaka sekä issʉmnita — *There are three apples.*
17. soka semali issʉmnita — *There are three oxen.*
18. käka semali issʉmnita — *There are three dogs.*

19.	papi sekʉlʉl issʉmnita	*There are three bowls of rice.*
20.	kuki sekʉlʉl issʉmnita	*There are three bowls of soup.*
21.	mali semali issʉmnita	*There are three horses.*

But not:

*mojaka haŋmali issʉmnita
*soka haŋkä issʉmnita
*papi haŋkä issʉmnita
*soka tukʉlʉl issʉmnita
*papi semali issʉmnita

Additional information:

Each subject noun has a suffix subject marker; this suffix is *ka* after nouns ending in a vowel and *i* after nouns ending in a consonant, e.g. *moja-ka* versus *pap-i*.

3. INDONESIAN

1.	kami məliat dua ɛkɔr kuda	*We saw two horses.*
2.	kami məliat dua ɛkɔr ayam	*We saw two chickens.*
3.	mərɛka məliat dua ɛkɔr kuciŋ	*They saw two cats.*
4.	kami məliat dua buah surat	*We saw two letters.*
5.	mərɛka məliat dua buah buku	*They saw two books.*
6.	kami məliat dua buah maŋga	*We saw two mangoes.*
7.	mərɛka məliat dua ɔraŋ wanita	*They saw two women.*
8.	kami məliat dua ɔraŋ pəncuri	*We saw two thieves.*
9.	kami məliat dua ɔraŋ dɔktər	*We saw two doctors.*
10.	kami məliat dua litər miñaʔ	*We saw two liters of oil.*
11.	kami məliat dua gram əmas	*We saw two grams of gold.*
12.	kami məliat tiga buah buku	*We saw three books.*
13.	kami məliat əmpat ɔraŋ wanita	*We saw four women.*
14.	kami məliat əmpat gram əmas	*We saw four grams of gold.*
15.	mərɛka məliat lima ɛkɔr ayam	*They saw five chickens.*
16.	kami məliat lima buah surat	*We saw five letters.*
17.	kami məliat lima ɔraŋ pəncuri	*We saw five thieves.*
18.	mərɛka məliat lima litər miñaʔ	*They saw five liters of oil.*

But not:

*kami məliat dua buah kuda
*kami məliat tiga ɛkɔr wanita
*kami məliat dua litər maŋga

*kami məliat lima ɛkɔr buku
*kami məliat dua ɔraŋ ayam
*kami məliat tiga gram wanita

4. THAI

1.	khun pen khru·	*You are a teacher.*
2.	khun pen khru· mǎj	*Are you a teacher?*
3.	khun pen khru· rʏ̌·	*Are you a teacher?*
4.	khun mâj pen khru·	*You aren't a teacher.*
5.	khun mâj pen khru· rʏ̌·	*Aren't you a teacher?*
6.	khǎw pen tháhǎ·n	*He is a soldier.*
7.	khǎw pen tháhǎ·n mǎj	*Is he a soldier?*
8.	khǎw pen tháhǎ·n rʏ̌·	*Is he a soldier?*
9.	khǎw mâj pen tháhǎ·n	*He isn't a soldier.*
10.	khǎw mâj pen tháhǎ·n rʏ̌·	*Isn't he a soldier?*
11.	tháhǎ·n pen khru·	*The soldier is a teacher.*
12.	khru· pen tháhǎ·n mǎj	*Is the teacher a soldier?*
13.	tháhǎ·n pen khru· rʏ̌·	*Is the soldier a teacher?*
14.	tháhǎ·n mâj pen khru·	*The soldier isn't a teacher.*
15.	khru· mâj pen tháhǎ·n rʏ̌·	*Isn't the teacher a soldier?*
16.	khǎw di·	*He is good.*
17.	tháhǎ·n kèŋ	*The soldier is clever.*
18.	khun di· mǎj	*Are you good?*
19.	khru· di· rʏ̌·	*Is the teacher good?*
20.	khǎw mâj kèŋ	*He isn't clever.*
21.	khǎw mâj kèŋ rʏ̌·	*Isn't he clever?*
22.	tháhǎ·n mâj di· rʏ̌·	*Isn't the soldier good?*
23.	khun phû·d kàb khǎw	*You're speaking with him.*
24.	khǎw phû·d kàb khru·	*He's speaking with the teacher.*
25.	khru· paj kàb tháhǎ·n	*The teacher is going with the soldier.*
26.	tháhǎ·n paj kàb khun	*The soldier is going with you.*
27.	khru· phû·d kàb khǎw mǎj	*Is the teacher speaking with him?*
28.	khun paj kàb tháhǎ·n rʏ̌·	*Are you going with the soldier?*

29.	tháhǎ·n mâj phû·d kàb khru·	*The soldier isn't speaking with the teacher.*
30.	tháhǎ·n mâj phû·d kàb khru· rý·	*Isn't the soldier speaking with the teacher?*
31.	khǎw mâj paj kàb khun rý·	*Isn't he going with you?*
32.	khru· mâj paj kàb khǎw rý·	*Isn't the teacher going with him?*

But not:

*khun khru·
*khun pen di·
*khun mâj pen khru· mǎj
*khru· mâj di· mǎj
*khru· di· mǎj rý·
*khun phû·d khru·
*khun pen kàb khru·
*khun di· kàb khru·

5. LATIN

1.	oppidum kirkumda·bant	*They surrounded the town.*
2.	oppida kirkumda·bant	*They surrounded the towns.*
3.	agrum kirkumda·bant	*They surrounded the field.*
4.	agro·s kirkumda·bant	*They surrounded the fields.*
5.	eks oppido· in agrum migra·bant	*They migrated from the town to the field.*
6.	eks agro· in oppidum migra·bant	*They migrated from the field to the town.*
7.	eks oppidi·s in agrum migra·bant	*They migrated from the towns to the field.*
8.	eks agri·s in oppidum migra·bant	*They migrated from the fields to the town.*
9.	eks oppidi·s in agro·s migra·bant	*They migrated from the towns to the fields.*
10.	eks agri·s in oppida migra·bant	*They migrated from the fields to the towns.*

But not:

*oppido· kirkumda·bant
*eks oppidum in agrum migra·bant

*eks oppido· in agro· migra·bant
*agra kirkumda·bant
*eks oppido· kirkumda·bant
*oppidum migra·bant

6. TAIRORA, a language of New Guinea

1.	oriba biro	*Ori went.*
2.	aintaantaba biro	*The mother-in-law went.*
3.	bakaaba biro	*The elder brother went.*
4.	naaʔuba biro	*The grandfather went.*
5.	nahentibano biro	*The woman went.*
6.	baraatabano biro	*The girl went.*
7.	ʔatabano biro	*The younger brother went.*
8.	baintibano biro	*The man went.*
9.	bainti biro	*The man went.*
10.	nahenti biro	*The woman went.*
11.	baraata biro	*The girl went.*
12.	ʔata biro	*The younger brother went.*
13.	bakaaba ariro	*The elder brother hit (him/it).*
14.	bakaara ariro	*He hit the elder brother.*
15.	bakaara tabero	*He saw the elder brother.*
16.	ʔatabano ariro	*The younger brother hit (him/it).*
17.	ʔata ariro	*He hit the younger brother.*
18.	ʔata tabero	*He saw the younger brother.*
19.	orira ariro	*He hit Ori.*
20.	nahenti tabero	*He saw the woman.*
21.	oriba aniro	*Ori came.*
22.	baraatabano aniro	*The girl came.*
23.	baraata aniro	*The girl came.*

But not:

*naaʔu aniro
*baintiba aniro
*ori tabero
*bakaabano ariro
*ʔataba biro

7. GERMAN

1. der man ge·t	*The man is walking.*
2. der man arbaitet	*The man is working.*
3. der froint arbaitet	*The friend is working.*
4. der man arbaitet in dem la·den	*The man is working in the store.*
5. der man ge·t in dem la·den	*The man is walking in the store.*
6. der man ge·t in den la·den	*The man is walking into the store.*
7. der man ge·t um den la·den	*The man is walking around the store.*
8. der froint ge·t um den štu·l	*The friend is walking around the chair.*
9. der froint arbaitet mit dem man	*The friend is working with the man.*
10. der froint ge·t aus dem la·den	*The friend is walking out of the store.*
11. der man baut den la·den	*The man is building the store.*
12. der man maxt den štu·l	*The man is making the chair.*
13. der froint maxt den štu·l	*The friend is making the chair.*
14. der froint helft dem man	*The friend is helping the man.*
15. der man dankt dem froint	*The man is thanking the friend.*

But not:

*dem man ge·t
*der la·den ge·t
*der štu·l baut den la·den
*der froint helft dem štu·l
*der man baut den froint
*der la·den dankt dem man

8. FINNISH

1. äiti panee lusikan kuppiin	*The mother puts the spoon into the cup.*
2. äiti ottaa kupin kaapista	*The mother takes the cup from the cupboard.*

3. äiti panee maton lattialle — *The mother puts the carpet onto the floor.*
4. äiti ottaa maton lattialta — *The mother takes the carpet from the floor.*
5. äiti ottaa lusikan kupista — *The mother takes the spoon from the cup.*
6. äiti ottaa lusikan matolta — *The mother takes the spoon from the carpet.*
7. äiti panee maton kaappiin — *The mother is putting the carpet into the cupboard.*
8. äiti ei panel lusikkaa kuppiin — *The mother does not put the spoon into the cup.*
9. äiti ei otak kuppia kaapista — *The mother is not taking the cup from the cupboard.*
10. äiti ei otam mattoa lattialta — *The mother is not taking the carpet from the floor.*
11. äiti ei otal lusikkaa kupista — *The mother does not take the spoon from the cup.*
12. äiti ei panek kuppia lattialle — *The mother is not putting the cup onto the floor.*
13. äiti ei panem mattoa kaappiin — *The mother does not put the carpet into the cupboard.*

But not:

*äiti panee lusikan kupille
*äiti ottaa lusikan kupilta
*äiti ei panek kupin lattialle
*äiti ottaa kupin kaapilta
*äiti panee maton lattiaan
*äiti ottaa maton lattiasta
*äiti ottaa lusikkaa kupista

Additional information:

(1) In negative sentences the object takes the suffix *a*.
(2) The selection of classes of locational suffixes (i.e. *lta, sta* versus *in, lle*) is governed by the type of verb that occurs in the sentence; the selection of a particular suffix (i.e. *lta* versus *sta*) is governed by the noun.

chapter five

AGREEMENT

INTRODUCTION

In the introduction to Chapter 4 agreement was defined as a special kind of co-occurrence relation such that to say that "class *X* agrees with class *Y*" is to say that "whichever grammatical categories are a property of *Y* are also a property of *X* whenever *X* and *Y* occur in some well-specifiable positions within a given set of sentences." To this statement we now add that, while the postulation of agreement may be based on what we can directly observe in the data, agreement is actually a generalization concerning formal relations that may or may not be observable in the data (this is true also of government). That is to say, while there may be an overt difference in form that signals the presence of a grammatical category in the classes that are said to agree, there need not be any.

For example, in English sentences such as *the girl runs quickly, the girls run quickly, the boy is sick,* and *the boys are sick,* the presence or absence of *s* at the end of *girl* and *boy*, the presence or absence of *s* after *run*, and the change of *is* to *are* overtly signal the grammatical category number. In addition, we can observe a correspondence between verb forms and noun endings: *girl* and *boy* do not end in *s* when the verb is *is* or ends in *s* (i.e. both the noun and the verb are singular), and *boy* and *girl* do end in *s* when the verb is *are* or does not end in *s* (i.e. the noun and the verb are plural). In sentences such as the following, however, there is no overt difference in form that signals number, and as a result we cannot observe any formal correspondence between the number of the subject noun and that of the verb: *the sheep is healthy, the sheep are healthy, the boy can do it, the boys can do it.* Nevertheless, on the basis of sentences such as the preceding, i.e. those in which an overt formal difference between the classes that are said to agree is observed, we say that the subject noun and the verb in these sentences agree in number.

The problems in this chapter illustrate some of the more common types of agreement; any type not illustrated can be specified in essentially the same manner as that shown in the acceptable solutions.

It should be noticed that the following problems are discussed in such a way that, having pointed out that two or more classes agree in some grammatical category, the decision as to which class agrees with which (e.g. whether a subject noun agrees in number with the verb or vice versa) has already been made. This is done because, in general, there are not enough data to permit a non-arbitrary decision. (See 5.3.3, however, for the considerations involved in making this decision.)

5.1 DATA

PROBLEM 30: ENGLISH

1. this boy	1a. these boys
2. that boy	2a. those boys
3. this house	3a. these houses
4. that house	4a. those houses
5. this girl	5a. these girls
6. that girl	6a. those girls
7. this table	7a. these tables
8. that table	8a. those tables
9. this dog	9a. these dogs
10. that dog	10a. those dogs

But not:

*this boys
*these girl
*that tables
*those table

Notice that although the words in the second column differ from those in the first in that the noun ends in *s* and the determiner is either *these* or *those,* there is the following definite formal correspondence between the words in each column: the determiner and the noun are either both singular (the words in the first column) or both plural (the words in the second column), but never is one singular and the other plural (we do not get, for example, **these boy* or **that boys*). Thus we can say that the determiner agrees with the noun in the grammatical category called **number.**

PROBLEM 31: RUSSIAN

1.	ya čitayu	*I read*	7.	ya rabotayu	*I work*
2.	ti čitayiš	*you read*	8.	ti rabotayiš	*you work*
3.	on čitayit	*he reads*	9.	on rabotayit	*he works*
4.	ya znayu	*I know*	10.	ya igrayu	*I play*
5.	ti znayiš	*you know*	11.	ti igrayiš	*you play*
6.	on znayit	*he knows*	12.	on igrayit	*he plays*

But not:

*ya znayiš
*ti čitayu
*on čitayiš
*ti znayit
*on znayu
*ya čitayit

There are three different pronominal forms in this problem. This difference in the pronominal forms marks the grammatical category called **person** (number is irrelevant here since we do not have the distinction of singular and plural pronouns): *ya* is first, *ti* second, and *on* third person. Notice that whenever the pronoun is first person, the ending of the verb is *u*; whenever it is second person, the ending of the verb is *iš*; and whenever it is third person, the ending of the verb is *it*; thus we have an instance of agreement in which the verb agrees in person with the pronoun.

PROBLEM 32: SPANISH

1. mučačo	*boy*	1a. el mučačo	*the boy*
2. mučača	*girl*	2a. la mučača	*the girl*
3. tio	*uncle*	3a. el tio	*the uncle*
4. tia	*aunt*	4a. la tia	*the aunt*
5. gato	*cat* (masc.)	5a. el gato	*the cat* (masc.)
6. gata	*cat* (fem.)	6a. la gata	*the cat* (fem.)
7. palo	*stick*	7a. el palo	*the stick*
8. pala	*shovel*	8a. la pala	*the shovel*

But not:

*el mučača
*la mučačo

Notice first that nouns end in either *o* or *a*, and any given noun has the same ending in both columns above. This difference in the form of the ending of the nouns marks the grammatical category called **gender.** In Spanish, most nouns ending in *o* are said to be masculine and most nouns ending in *a* are said to be feminine. Now notice that *el* occurs only before masculine nouns and *la* occurs only before feminine nouns; we therefore say that articles agree in gender with the nouns that follow them.

PROBLEM 33: SWEDISH

1. et nyt hüs	*a new house*
2. et sturt barn	*a big child*
3. et elakt glin	*a naughty brat*
4. et nyt rüm	*a new room*
5. et sturt burd	*a big table*
6. et elakt brev	*a wicked letter*
1a. det nya hüset	*the new house*
2a. det stura barnet	*the big child*
3a. det elaka glinet	*the naughty brat*
4a. det nya rümet	*the new room*
5a. det stura burdet	*the big table*
6a. det elaka brevet	*the wicked letter*

But not:

*et nyt hüset
*et nya hüs
*det nya hüs
*det nyt hüs
*et nya hüset
*det nya burd
*det nyt burdet
*et nya burdet

The only difference between the nouns in the above two columns is that those in the second column end in *et*. This difference in form marks the grammatical category called **concreteness** (or **definiteness**). In Swedish, nouns ending in *et* are said to be definite, while those without this ending are said to be indefinite. Now notice that adjectives end in *t* before indefinite but in *a* before definite nouns; the article *et* occurs only before indefinite nouns and *det* only before definite nouns. We therefore say that both the adjective and the article agree in concreteness with the noun.

PROBLEM 34: MODERN GREEK

1. o γjatros vlepi ton anθropo	*The doctor sees the man.*
2. o anθropos prosexi ton γjatro	*The man watches the doctor.*
3. o stratiotis prosexi ton γalata	*The soldier watches the milkman.*
4. o γalatas kseri ton stratioti	*The milkman knows the soldier.*
5. o maθitis vlepi ton andra	*The student sees the man.*
6. o andras kseri ton maθiti	*The man knows the student.*
7. o exθros prosexi ton exmaloto	*The enemy watches the prisoner.*
8. o exmalotos vlepi ton exθro	*The prisoner sees the enemy.*

But not:

*ton γjatros vlepi ton andra
*o γjatros kseri o maθitis
*o andra kseri ton γalata
*o exθros kseri ton andras

The nouns in these sentences have two forms: one that ends in *s* and one that may be said to have no ending. This difference in form corresponds to whether a noun is the subject (when it ends in *s*) or the object (when it has no final *s*) and marks the grammatical category called **case.** In this problem a noun is said to be in the nominative case when it ends in *s* and in the accusative case whenever it does not have this ending. Now notice that the article agrees in case with the noun that it precedes: the article is *o* whenever the noun is in the nominative case and *ton* whenever the noun is in the accusative case.

PROBLEM 35: SWEDISH

	Singular			Plural
1.	et nyt hüs	*a new house*	1a.	nya hüs
2.	det nya hüset	*the new house*	2a.	de nya hüsen
3.	et sturt barn	*a big child*	3a.	stura barn
4.	det stura barnet	*the big child*	4a.	de stura barnen
5.	et elakt glin	*a naughty brat*	5a.	elaka glin
6.	det elaka glinet	*the naughty brat*	6a.	de elaka glinen
7.	et sturt burd	*a big table*	7a.	stura burd
8.	det stura burdet	*the big table*	8a.	de stura burden
9.	et elakt brev	*a wicked letter*	9a.	elaka brev
10.	det elaka brevet	*the wicked letter*	10a.	de elaka breven

But not:

*et elaka glin
*et elakt glinet
*det elakt brevet
*det elaka brev
*nyt hüs
*de stura barn
*de stura barnet

This problem is an extension of Problem 33 in that we now have the plural of definite and indefinite forms in addition to the singular. Notice that singular and plural definite nouns end in *et* and *en,* respectively, and that singular and plural indefinite nouns have no ending. The articles *det* and *de* occur before definite singular and plural nouns, respectively; *et* occurs before indefinite singular nouns; and there is no article before indefinite plural nouns. Adjectives end in *t* before singular indefinite nouns but in *a* before any other noun. Articles and adjectives, therefore, agree not only in concreteness but also in number with the noun.

PROBLEM 36: RUSSIAN

1. ya čitayu	*I read*	7. ya dumayu	*I think*
2. ti čitayiš	*you read*	8. ti dumayiš	*you think*
3. on čitayit	*he reads*	9. on dumayit	*he thinks*
4. mi čitayim	*we read*	10. mi dumayim	*we think*
5. vi čitayit'i	*you read*	11. vi dumayit'i	*you think*
6. on'i čitayut	*they read*	12. on'i dumayut	*they think*

But not:

*ya dumayiš
*ti dumayut
*on čitayim
*mi čitayiš
*vi dumayit
*on'i dumayu

By extending Problem 31, we now have the plural of pronouns and verbs in addition to the singular. Notice in particular that whenever the pronoun is first, second, or third person singular, the ending of the verb is *u*, *iš*, or *it*, respectively, and that whenever the pronoun is first, second, or third person plural, the ending of the verb is *im*, *it'i*, or *ut*, respectively. In this problem, then, the verb agrees in both person and number with the subject pronoun. (It should be noted that the above set of forms justifies only one grammatical category with six subcategories and not a 2 × 3 system; therefore "number" is derived from a wider knowledge of Russian and not just from the above data.)

PROBLEM 37: SPANISH

1. el granxero	*the farmer* (masc.)
2. la granxera	*the farmer* (fem.)
3. el ermano	*the brother*
4. la ermana	*the sister*
5. el ixo	*the son*
6. la ixa	*the daughter*
7. el granxero simpatiko	*the nice farmer* (masc.)
8. la granxera simpatika	*the nice farmer* (fem.)
9. el ermano bueno	*the good brother*
10. la ermana buena	*the good sister*
11. el ixo pekeño	*the little son*
12. la ixa pekeña	*the little daughter*

1a.	los granxeros	*the farmers* (masc.)
2a.	las granxeras	*the farmers* (fem.)
3a.	los ermanos	*the brothers*
4a.	las ermanas	*the sisters*
5a.	los ixos	*the sons*
6a.	las ixas	*the daughters*
7a.	los granxeros simpatikos	*the nice farmers* (masc.)
8a.	las granxeras simpatikas	*the nice farmers* (fem.)
9a.	los ermanos buenos	*the good brothers*
10a.	las ermanas buenas	*the good sisters*
11a.	los ixos pekeños	*the little sons*
12a.	las ixas pekeñas	*the little daughters*

But not:

*los ixas
*la ixo
*el ermano buena
*el ermano buenos
*el ermanos bueno
*el ermana(s) buena(s)

By extending Problem 32, we now have the singular and plural of masculine and feminine forms. Notice that masculine nouns end in *o* in the singular and *os* in the plural, while feminine nouns end in *a* in the singular and *as* in the plural, and that both the article and the adjective can be said to agree with the noun in gender and number: the article is *el* before masculine singular and *los* before masculine plural nouns, and *la* before feminine singular and *las* before feminine plural nouns; the adjective, which is optional, occurs after the noun and takes the same ending as the noun it follows.

PROBLEM 38: MODERN GREEK

1.	o γítonas periméni tin mitéra	*The neighbor waits for the mother.*
2.	i γinéka proséxi ton γítona	*The woman watches the neighbor.*
3.	i mitéra pléni tin aðelfí	*The mother washes the daughter.*
4.	i aðelfí pirázi tin γinéka	*The sister annoys the woman.*
5.	o ándras pliróni ton erγáti	*The man pays the worker.*

6.	o erγátis fonázi ton ándra	*The worker calls the man.*
7.	i γítones periménun tiz mitéres	*The neighbors await the mothers.*
8.	i γinékes proséxun tuz γítones	*The women watch the neighbors.*
9.	i mitéres plénun tis aðelfés	*The mothers wash the sisters.*
10.	i aðelfés pirázun tiz γinékes	*The sisters annoy the women.*
11.	i ándres plirónun tus erγátes	*The men pay the workers.*
12.	i erγátes fonázun tus ándres	*The workers call the men.*
13.	i aðelfí pliróni tus erγátes	*The sister pays the workers.*
14.	i γítones pirázun tin γinéka	*The neighbors annoy the woman.*
15.	i mitéres fonázun ton ándra	*The mothers call the man.*
16.	o ándras pléni tis aðelfés	*The man washes the sisters.*
17.	to peðí vlépi to korítsi	*The child sees the girl.*
18.	to korítsi fonázi to peðí	*The girl calls the child.*
19.	ta peðjá periménun ta korítsja	*The children await the girls.*
20.	ta korítsja vlépun ta peðjá	*The girls see the children.*
21.	to peðí pirázi ta korítsja	*The child annoys the girls.*
22.	ta korítsja periménun to peðí	*The girls await the child.*
23.	o γítonas íne kalós	*The neighbor is good.*
24.	i γinéka íne kalí	*The woman is kind.*
25.	to peðí íne kaló	*The child is good.*
26.	i ándres íne kalí	*The men are kind.*
27.	i mitéres íne kalés	*The mothers are kind.*
28.	ta korítsja íne kalá	*The girls are good.*
29.	i mitéra íne aγaθí	*The mother is meek.*
30.	ta peðjá íne ómorfa	*The children are handsome.*
31.	o ándras íne afstirós	*The man is strict.*

But not:

*o mitéra pléni ton ándra
*i mitéra plénun ton ándra
*tin mitéra pléni ton ándra
*i mitéra pléni o ándras
*o ándras plénun tin mitéra
*o ándras pléni tiz mitéra
*o ándras íne kalí
*o ándras íne kaló

This problem is an extension of Problem 34 and illustrates three types of agreement: agreement in gender, case, and number between (1) an article and the following noun, (2) a predicate adjective and the preceding subject noun, and (3) agreement in number between the verb and the subject.

Notice that nouns in Modern Greek have three grammatical categories; namely, gender, case, and number: in the nominative case (i.e. when subjects) masculine nouns end in *s* in the singular and *es* in the plural, while feminine and neuter (a third gender) nouns have no ending in the singular but end in *es* and *a*, respectively, in the plural; in the accusative case (i.e. when objects) nouns of all three genders have no ending in the singular, but masculine and feminine nouns end in *es* and neuter nouns in *a* in the plural.

Notice further that the article in the nominative singular is *o*, *i*, *to* before masculine, feminine, and neuter nouns, respectively, while in the nominative plural the article is *i* before masculine and feminine nouns and *ta* before neuter nouns. In the accusative singular the article is *ton, tin, to* before masculine, feminine, and neuter nouns, respectively, while in the accusative plural the article is *tus, tis, ta* before masculine, feminine, and neuter nouns, respectively. Thus the article agrees in gender, case, and number with the noun.

Predicate adjectives agree in gender, case, and number with subject nouns: the adjective ends in *s*, *i*, or *zero* when the subject noun is singular and masculine, feminine, or neuter, respectively, while the adjective ends in *i*, *es*, or *a* when the subject noun is plural and masculine, feminine, or neuter, respectively.

Now notice that whenever the subject is singular, a transitive verb ends in *i*, while whenever it is plural, a transitive verb ends in *un*; thus a transitive verb agrees in number with the subject. The verb *ine* 'is, are' also agrees in number with the subject, but number in this verb is "neutralized"; i.e. it has the same ending in both the singular and the plural.

Finally, notice that (1) in the accusative plural the final consonant of the article assimilates in voice to the following vowel or consonant, i.e. it is *z* before voiced consonants and *s* before any vowel or voiceless consonant; (2) the stem of neuter nouns ends in *i* in the singular, but in *j* in the plural, e.g. *peðí* 'the child' but *peðjá* 'the children'; and (3) stress is regular for verbs (i.e. it occurs always on the next to the last vowel) but irregular for the remaining classes.

PROBLEM 39: SPANISH

1. el bjéxo trabáxa múčo	*The old man works a lot.*
2. la bjéxa ríka trabáxa	*The rich old woman works.*

3. los bjéxos simpátikos trabáxan	*The nice old men work.*
4. las bjéxas trabáxan	*The old women work.*
5. jo trabáxo siémpre	*I always work.*
6. un mučáčo simpátiko estúdja	*A nice boy studies.*
7. úna mučáča estúdja	*A girl studies.*
8. únos mučáčos ríkos estúdjan	*Rich boys study.*
9. únas mučáčas ríkas estúdjan	*Rich girls study.*
10. estúdjo múčo	*I study very much.*
11. el pádre deskánsa	*The father rests.*
12. la mádre simpátika deskánsa	*The nice mother rests.*
13. los pádres buénos deskánsan	*The good fathers rest.*
14. las mádres deskánsan tempráno	*The mothers rest early.*
15. tu deskánsas	*You* (sg.) *rest.*
16. un ómbre ríko bjáxa siémpre	*A rich man always travels.*
17. úna mujér buéna bjáxa múčo	*A good woman travels a lot.*
18. únos ómbres bjáxan	*Men travel.*
19. únas mujéres simpátikas bjáxan	*Nice women travel.*
20. bjáxas	*You* (sg.) *travel.*
21. un bjéxo buéno estúdja	*A good old man studies.*
22. la mučáča trabáxa tempráno	*The girl works early.*
23. únos pádres bjáxan	*Fathers travel.*
24. las mučáčas buénas deskánsan	*The good girls rest.*
25. nosótros deskansámos	*We rest.*
26. trabaxámos	*We work.*
27. úna bjéxa estúdja	*An old woman studies.*
28. bosótros estudjáis	*You* (pl.) *study.*
29. el ómbre trabáxa	*The man works.*
30. bjaxáis siémpre	*You* (pl.) *always travel.*
31. las mujéres deskánsan	*The women rest.*
32. tu estúdjas	*You* (sg.) *study.*
33. el trabáxa múčo	*He works a lot.*
34. éyos deskánsan	*They* (masc.) *rest.*
35. bjáxa	*He* (or *she*) *travels.*
36. estúdjan tempráno	*They* (masc. or fem.) *study early.*
37. éya bjáxa	*She travels.*
38. éyas deskánsan	*They* (fem.) *rest.*

But not:

*el bjéxa trabáxa
*úna bjéxo trabáxa
*únos bjéxas trabáxan

*las bjéxos trabáxan
*jo trabáxa
*tu deskansáis
*bosótros bjáxas
*éyas deskánsa
*nosótros bjáxo
*el estúdjan

This problem is an extension of Problem 37 and illustrates the following types of agreement: (1) agreement between an article, adjective, and noun in gender and number and (2) agreement between the verb and subject in person and number. The subject is overtly expressed by a determiner and a noun (which may be followed by an adjective), a pronoun, or simply by a verb ending; therefore, although a noun phrase and a pronoun are mutually exclusive in subject position, the occurrence of either as the subject is optional. The predicate is expressed by a verb or a verb and an adverb; the occurrence of an adverb, therefore, is optional.

Nouns in the above data have two grammatical categories, namely, gender and number: nouns are masculine or feminine and singular or plural. Most masculine nouns end in *o* in the singular and *os* in the plural, and most feminine nouns end in *a* in the singular and *as* in the plural.

Both the article and the adjective in a noun phrase agree in gender and number with the noun: the articles *el, un* and *los, únos* occur before masculine singular and plural nouns, respectively, and *la úna* and *las, únas* occur before feminine singular and plural nouns, respectively; the adjective takes the same ending as the noun it follows.

The pronoun has several forms which mark the grammatical categories of person and number: *jo* is first person singular, *tu* is second person singular, *nosótros* is first person plural, *bosótros* is second person plural. The forms of third person pronouns also have gender: *el* and *éya* are third person singular masculine and feminine, respectively, and *éyos* and *éyas* are third person plural masculine and feminine, respectively.

The verb agrees with the subject in person and number: the verb ends in *o*, *as*, or *a* whenever it follows a first, second, or third person singular pronoun, respectively, and in *amos, ais,* or *an* whenever it follows a first, second, or third person plural pronoun, respectively; similarly, the verb ends in *a* when it follows a singular subject noun and in *an* when it follows a plural subject noun.

Finally, notice that stress is regular for verbs, adverbs, and polysyllabic pronouns and determiners: it always occurs on the penultimate (i.e. on the next to the last vowel) of each; monosyllabic pronouns and determiners have no stress.

5.2 SOLUTIONS

SOLUTION 30: ENGLISH

Solution A (Objectionable)

1. $NP \rightarrow Det + N$
2. $N \rightarrow Ns(Pl)$
3. $Pl \rightarrow s$
4. $Ns \rightarrow$ *boy, house, girl, table, dog*
5. $Det \rightarrow$ *this, that*
6. Tob

$$\begin{bmatrix} this \\ that \end{bmatrix} Ns + Pl \Rightarrow \begin{bmatrix} these \\ those \end{bmatrix} Ns + Pl$$

Solution B

1. $NP \rightarrow Det + N$
2. $Det \rightarrow D$
3. $D \rightarrow D_1, D_2$
4. $N \rightarrow Ns + Nu$
5. $Nu \rightarrow Sg, Pl$
6. $Ns \rightarrow$ *boy, house, girl, table, dog*
7. Tob agreement (in number)
   $D - Ns + Nu \Rightarrow D + Nu - Ns + Nu$
8. Tob

$$D_1 \begin{bmatrix} Sg \\ Pl \end{bmatrix} \Rightarrow \begin{bmatrix} this \\ these \end{bmatrix}$$

9. Tob

$$D_2 \begin{bmatrix} Sg \\ Pl \end{bmatrix} \Rightarrow \begin{bmatrix} that \\ those \end{bmatrix}$$

10. Tob

$$\begin{bmatrix} Sg \\ Pl \end{bmatrix} \Rightarrow \begin{bmatrix} \emptyset \\ s \end{bmatrix}$$

SOLUTION 31: RUSSIAN

Solution A (Objectionable)

1. $VP \rightarrow Pron + Vb$
2. $Vb \rightarrow Vs + Per$
3. $Per \rightarrow it$

4. $Vs \rightarrow$ *čitay, znay, rabotay, igray*
5. $Pron \rightarrow$ *on*
6. Topt

$$on + Vs + it \Rightarrow \begin{bmatrix} ya \\ ti \end{bmatrix} Vs \begin{bmatrix} u \\ i\check{s} \end{bmatrix}$$

Solution B

1. $VP \rightarrow Pron + Vb$
2. $Vb \rightarrow Vs$
3. $Pron \rightarrow Pr + Per$
4. $Per \rightarrow Fir, Sec, Thi$
5. $Vs \rightarrow$ *čitay, znay, rabotay, igray*
6. Tob agreement (in person)

$$Pr + Per + Vs \Rightarrow Pr + Per + Vs + Per$$

7. Tob

$$Pr \begin{bmatrix} Fir \\ Sec \\ Thi \end{bmatrix} \Rightarrow \begin{bmatrix} ya \\ ti \\ on \end{bmatrix}$$

8. Tob

$$\begin{bmatrix} Fir \\ Sec \\ Thi \end{bmatrix} \Rightarrow \begin{bmatrix} u \\ i\check{s} \\ it \end{bmatrix}$$

SOLUTION 32: SPANISH

Solution A (Objectionable)

1. $NP \rightarrow (Det)N$
2. $N \rightarrow Ns + G$
3. $G \rightarrow M, F$
4. $Det \rightarrow \begin{Bmatrix} el \;/\; \_\_ Ns + M \\ la \end{Bmatrix}$
5. $M \rightarrow o$
6. $F \rightarrow a$
7. $Ns \rightarrow$ *mučač, ti, gat, pal*

Solution B

1. $NP \rightarrow (Det)N$
2. $Det \rightarrow D$
3. $N \rightarrow Ns + G$

4. $G \rightarrow M, F$
5. $M \rightarrow o$
6. $F \rightarrow a$
7. $D \rightarrow l$
8. $Ns \rightarrow$ *mučač, ti, gat, pal*
9. Tob agreement (in gender)
   $D - Ns + G \Rightarrow D + G - Ns + G$
10. Tob
    $D + M \Rightarrow el$

SOLUTION 33: SWEDISH

1. $NP \rightarrow Det + Adj + N$
2. $Det \rightarrow D$
3. $Adj \rightarrow A$
4. $N \rightarrow Ns + Co$
5. $Co \rightarrow Def, Indef$
6. $Ns \rightarrow$ *hüs, barn, glin, rüm, burd, brev*
7. $A \rightarrow$ *ny, stur, elak*
8. Tob agreement (in concreteness)
   $D - A - Ns + Co \Rightarrow D + Co - A + Co - Ns + Co$
9. Tob
   $$D \begin{bmatrix} Def \\ Indef \end{bmatrix} \Rightarrow \begin{bmatrix} det \\ et \end{bmatrix}$$
10. Tob
    $$Ns \begin{bmatrix} Def \\ Indef \end{bmatrix} \Rightarrow Ns \begin{bmatrix} et \\ \emptyset \end{bmatrix}$$
11. Tob
    $$\begin{bmatrix} Def \\ Indef \end{bmatrix} \Rightarrow \begin{bmatrix} a \\ t \end{bmatrix}$$

SOLUTION 34: MODERN GREEK

1. $S \rightarrow NP + VP$
2. $VP \rightarrow V + NP$
3. $NP \rightarrow Det + N$
4. $Det \rightarrow D$

5. $N \rightarrow Ns + Ca$

6. $Ca \rightarrow \begin{Bmatrix} Acc / \_\_ \# \\ Nom \end{Bmatrix}$

7. $Ns \rightarrow$ *γjatro, anθropo, γalata, maθiti, andra, exθro, exmaloto, stratioti*

8. $V \rightarrow$ *vlepi, prosexi, kseri*

9. Tob agreement (in case)

$$D - Ns + Ca \Rightarrow D + Ca - Ns + Ca$$

10. Tob

$$D \begin{bmatrix} Nom \\ Acc \end{bmatrix} \Rightarrow \begin{bmatrix} o \\ ton \end{bmatrix}$$

11. Tob

$$\begin{bmatrix} Nom \\ Acc \end{bmatrix} \Rightarrow \begin{bmatrix} s \\ \emptyset \end{bmatrix}$$

SOLUTION 35: SWEDISH

Solution A (Objectionable)

1. $NP \rightarrow Det + Adj + N$
2. $Adj \rightarrow As + Afa$
3. $N \rightarrow Ns(Afn)$
4. $Afn \rightarrow Af_1, Af_2$
5. $Det \rightarrow \begin{Bmatrix} det / \_\_ X + Af_1 \\ de / \_\_ X + Af_2 \\ et \end{Bmatrix}$
6. $Afa \rightarrow \begin{Bmatrix} t / et + As \_\_ Ns \\ a \end{Bmatrix}$
7. $Af_1 \rightarrow et$
8. $Af_2 \rightarrow en$
9. $Ns \rightarrow$ *hüs, barn, glin, burd, brev*
10. $As \rightarrow$ *ny, stur, elak*
11. Topt

$$et + As + t + Ns \Rightarrow As + a + Ns$$

Solution B

1. $NP \rightarrow Det + Adj + N$
2. $Det \rightarrow D$
3. $Adj \rightarrow A$

4. $N \rightarrow Ns + Afn$
5. $Afn \rightarrow Co + Nu$
6. $Co \rightarrow Def, Indef$
7. $Nu \rightarrow Sg, Pl$
8. $Ns \rightarrow$ *hüs, barn, glin, burd, brev*
9. $A \rightarrow$ *ny, stur, elak*
10. Tob agreement (in concreteness and number)
    $D - A - Ns + Afn \Rightarrow D + Afn - A + Afn - Ns + Afn$
11. Tob
    $$D + Def\begin{bmatrix} Sg \\ Pl \end{bmatrix} \Rightarrow \begin{bmatrix} det \\ de \end{bmatrix}$$
12. Tob
    $$D + Indef\begin{bmatrix} Sg \\ Pl \end{bmatrix} \Rightarrow \begin{bmatrix} et \\ \emptyset \end{bmatrix}$$
13. Tob
    $$Ns + Def\begin{bmatrix} Sg \\ Pl \end{bmatrix} \Rightarrow \begin{bmatrix} et \\ en \end{bmatrix}$$
14. Tob
    $Ns + Indef + Nu \Rightarrow Ns$
15. Tob
    $Indef + Sg \Rightarrow t$
16. Tob
    $Co + Nu \Rightarrow a$

SOLUTION 36: RUSSIAN

Solution A (Objectionable)

1. $VP \rightarrow Pron + Vb$
2. $Vb \rightarrow Vs + Afv$
3. $Pron \rightarrow Fir, Sec, Thi$
4. $$Afv \rightarrow \begin{Bmatrix} u \ / \ Fir + Vs \_\_ \\ i\check{s} \ / \ Sec + Vs \_\_ \\ it \end{Bmatrix}$$
5. $Fir \rightarrow$ *ya*
6. $Sec \rightarrow$ *ti*
7. $Thi \rightarrow$ *on*
8. $Vs \rightarrow$ *čitay, dumay*

9. Topt

$$\begin{bmatrix} ya \\ ti \\ on \end{bmatrix} Vs \begin{bmatrix} u \\ i\check{s} \\ it \end{bmatrix} \Rightarrow \begin{bmatrix} mi \\ vi \\ on'i \end{bmatrix} Vs \begin{bmatrix} im \\ it'i \\ ut \end{bmatrix}$$

Solution B

1. $VP \rightarrow Pron + Vb$
2. $Vb \rightarrow Vs$
3. $Pron \rightarrow Pr + Afp$
4. $Afp \rightarrow Per + Nu$
5. $Per \rightarrow Fir, Sec, Thi$
6. $Nu \rightarrow Sg, Pl$
7. $Vs \rightarrow$ *čitay, dumay*
8. Tob agreement (in person and number)
   $Pr + Afp + Vs \Rightarrow Pr + Afp + Vs + Afp$
9. Tob

$$Pr \begin{bmatrix} Fir \\ Sec \\ Thi \end{bmatrix} Sg \Rightarrow \begin{bmatrix} ya \\ ti \\ on \end{bmatrix}$$

10. Tob

$$Pr \begin{bmatrix} Fir \\ Sec \\ Thi \end{bmatrix} Pl \Rightarrow \begin{bmatrix} mi \\ vi \\ on'i \end{bmatrix}$$

11. Tob

$$\begin{bmatrix} Fir \\ Sec \\ Thi \end{bmatrix} Sg \Rightarrow \begin{bmatrix} u \\ i\check{s} \\ it \end{bmatrix}$$

12. Tob

$$\begin{bmatrix} Fir \\ Sec \\ Thi \end{bmatrix} Pl \Rightarrow \begin{bmatrix} im \\ it'i \\ ut \end{bmatrix}$$

SOLUTION 37: SPANISH

1. $NP \rightarrow Det + N(Adj)$
2. $Det \rightarrow D$
3. $Adj \rightarrow A$

4. $N \rightarrow Ns + Afn$
5. $Afn \rightarrow G(Pl)$
6. $G \rightarrow M, F$
7. $M \rightarrow o$
8. $F \rightarrow a$
9. $Pl \rightarrow s$
10. $D \rightarrow l$
11. $Ns \rightarrow$ *granxer, ix, erman*
12. $A \rightarrow$ *simpatik, buen, pekeñ*
13. Tob agreement (in gender and number)
    $D - Ns + Afn(A) \Rightarrow D + Afn - Ns + Afn(A + Afn)$
14. Tob
    $D + M + X \Rightarrow el + X$
    $X \neq Pl + W$

SOLUTION 38: MODERN GREEK

1. $S \rightarrow NP + VP$
2. $VP \rightarrow \begin{Bmatrix} Vtr + NP \\ Vcop + Adj \end{Bmatrix}$
3. $Adj \rightarrow A$
4. $Vtr \rightarrow Vst + Afv$
5. $Vcop \rightarrow Vsc + Afv$
6. $Afv \rightarrow Pres$
7. $NP \rightarrow Det + N$
8. $Det \rightarrow D$
9. $N \rightarrow Ns + Afn$
10. $Ns \rightarrow Nsm, Nsf, Nsn$
11. $Afn \rightarrow G + Ca + Nu$
12. $G \rightarrow \begin{Bmatrix} M \,/\, Nsm\_\_ \\ F \,/\, Nsf\_\_ \\ Neu \end{Bmatrix}$
13. $Ca \rightarrow \begin{Bmatrix} Acc \,/\, \_\_Nu\# \\ Nom \end{Bmatrix}$
14. $Nu \rightarrow Sg, Pl$
15. $A \rightarrow$ *kaló, aγaθó, ómorfo, afstiró*
16. $Nsm \rightarrow$ *γítona, ándra, erγáti*
17. $Nsf \rightarrow$ *γinéka, mitéra, aδelfí*

18. $Nsn \rightarrow$ *peði, koritsi*
19. $Vst \rightarrow$ *perimen, prosex, plen, piraz, pliron, fonaz, vlep*
20. $Vsc \rightarrow$ *in*
21. Tob agreement (in gender, case, and number)
$$D - Ns + Afn \Rightarrow D + Afn - Ns + Afn$$
22. Tob agreement (in gender, case, and number)
$$Ns + Afn + Vcop + A \Rightarrow Ns + Afn + Vcop + A + Afn$$
23. Tob agreement (in number)
$$Ns + X + Nu + Y + Pres \Rightarrow Ns + X + Nu + Y + Pres + Nu$$
24. Tob
$$D + Neu + Ca \begin{bmatrix} Sg \\ Pl \end{bmatrix} \Rightarrow \begin{bmatrix} to \\ ta \end{bmatrix}$$
25. Tob
$$D \begin{bmatrix} M \\ F \end{bmatrix} Nom + Sg \Rightarrow \begin{bmatrix} o \\ i \end{bmatrix}$$
26. Tob
$$D \begin{bmatrix} M \\ F \end{bmatrix} Acc + Sg \Rightarrow \begin{bmatrix} ton \\ tin \end{bmatrix}$$
27. Tob
$$D \begin{bmatrix} M \\ F \end{bmatrix} Acc + Pl \Rightarrow \begin{bmatrix} tuZ \\ tiZ \end{bmatrix}$$
28. Tob
$$D \begin{Bmatrix} M \\ F \end{Bmatrix} Nom + Pl \Rightarrow i$$

or, equivalently,

$$D + G + Nom + Pl \Rightarrow i$$

or, equivalently and preferably,

$$D + Afn \Rightarrow i$$

29. Tob
$$A \begin{bmatrix} F \\ M \end{bmatrix} Ca \begin{bmatrix} Sg \\ Pl \end{bmatrix} \Rightarrow A + i$$
30. Tob
$$Neu + Ca + Pl \Rightarrow a$$
31. Tob
$$G + Ca + Pl \Rightarrow es$$

32. Tob

$$M + Nom + Sg \Rightarrow s$$

33. Tob

$$\begin{bmatrix} Ns \\ A \end{bmatrix} \left\{ \begin{matrix} \left\{ \begin{matrix} Neu \\ F \end{matrix} \right\} Ca \\ M + Acc \end{matrix} \right\} Sg \Rightarrow \begin{bmatrix} Ns \\ A \end{bmatrix}$$

or, equivalently and preferably,

$$Afn \Rightarrow \emptyset$$

34. Tob

$$VwC + Pres \Rightarrow \acute{V}wC + Pres$$

35. Tob

$$Vsc + Afv \Rightarrow Vsc + e$$

36. Tob

$$Pres \begin{bmatrix} Sg \\ Pl \end{bmatrix} \Rightarrow \begin{bmatrix} i \\ un \end{bmatrix}$$

37. Tob

$$\begin{bmatrix} i \\ \acute{i} \end{bmatrix}_{Nsn} + a \Rightarrow j]_{Nsn} + \begin{bmatrix} a \\ \acute{a} \end{bmatrix}$$

38. Tob

$$X \begin{bmatrix} Vw_1 \\ \acute{V}w_1 \end{bmatrix}_{Ns,\, A} + Vw_2 \Rightarrow X]_{Ns,\, A} + \begin{bmatrix} Vw_2 \\ \acute{V}w_2 \end{bmatrix}$$

$$Vw_1 = a,\ o,\ i$$
$$Vw_2 = e,\ i,\ a$$

39. Tob

$$z \begin{bmatrix} C \\ X \end{bmatrix} \Rightarrow \begin{bmatrix} z \\ s \end{bmatrix} \begin{bmatrix} C \\ X \end{bmatrix}$$

C = any voiced consonant
X = any vowel or voiceless consonant

SOLUTION 39: SPANISH

1. $S \rightarrow NP + VP$
2. $VP \rightarrow Vb(Adv)$
3. $Vb \rightarrow Vs + Afv$
4. $Afv \rightarrow Pres$
5. $NP \rightarrow \left\{ \begin{matrix} Det + N(Adj) \\ Pron \end{matrix} \right\}$

6. $Det \rightarrow D$
7. $Adj \rightarrow A$
8. $Pron \rightarrow Pr + Af + Per$
9. $N \rightarrow Ns + Af + Per$

10. $$Per \rightarrow \begin{Bmatrix} Thi \ / \ Ns + Af\_\_ \\ Fir \\ Sec \\ Thi \end{Bmatrix}$$

11. $Af \rightarrow G(Pl)$
12. $Ns \rightarrow Nsm, Nsf$

13. $$G \rightarrow \begin{Bmatrix} M \ / \ Nsm\_\_ \\ F \ / \ Nsf\_\_ \\ M \\ F \end{Bmatrix}$$

14. *M → o*
15. *F → a*
16. *Pl → s*
17. *D → l, un*
18. *A → rík, simpátik, buén*
19. *Adv → mučo, siempre, temprano*
20. *Nsm → pádre, ómbre, bjéx, mučáč*
21. *Nsf → mádre, mujér, bjéx, mučáč*
22. *Vs → trabax, estudj, deskans, bjax*
23. Tob agreement (in person and number)
    $X(Pl)Per + Vs + Pres \Rightarrow X(Pl)Per + Vs + Pres(Pl)Per$
24. Tob agreement (in gender and number)
    $D - Ns + Af + Per(A) \Rightarrow$
    $D + Af - Ns + Af + Per(A + Af)$
25. Topt
    $Pron + VP \Rightarrow VP$
26. Tob
    $$\begin{bmatrix} l \\ un \end{bmatrix} M + X \Rightarrow \begin{bmatrix} el \\ un \end{bmatrix} + X$$
    $$X \neq Pl + W$$
27. Tob
    mujér + F + Pl + Per ⇒ mujére + Pl
28. Tob
    mujér + F + Per ⇒ mujér

29. Tob

$$\begin{bmatrix} pádre \\ mádre \\ ómbre \end{bmatrix} G(Pl)Per \Rightarrow \begin{bmatrix} pádre \\ mádre \\ ómbre \end{bmatrix} (Pl)$$

30. Tob

$$Pr \begin{bmatrix} M \\ F \end{bmatrix} Pl + Thi \Rightarrow \begin{bmatrix} eyos \\ eyas \end{bmatrix}$$

31. Tob

$$Pr \begin{bmatrix} M \\ F \end{bmatrix} Thi \Rightarrow \begin{bmatrix} el \\ eya \end{bmatrix}$$

32. Tob

$$Pr + G + Pl \begin{bmatrix} Fir \\ Sec \end{bmatrix} \Rightarrow \begin{bmatrix} nosotros \\ bosotros \end{bmatrix}$$

33. Tob

$$Pr + G \begin{bmatrix} Fir \\ Sec \end{bmatrix} \Rightarrow \begin{bmatrix} jo \\ tu \end{bmatrix}$$

34. Tob

$$Pres + Pl \begin{bmatrix} Fir \\ Sec \\ Thi \end{bmatrix} \Rightarrow \begin{bmatrix} amos \\ ais \\ an \end{bmatrix}$$

35. Tob

$$Pres \begin{bmatrix} Fir \\ Sec \\ Thi \end{bmatrix} \Rightarrow \begin{bmatrix} o \\ as \\ a \end{bmatrix}$$

36. Tob

$$Per \Rightarrow \emptyset$$

37. Tob

$$VwXVwX\#]_{Vb,\ Adv,\ Pron,\ Det} \Rightarrow \acute{V}wXVwX\#]_{Vb,\ Adv,\ Pron,\ Det}$$

X = any or no string of consonants

5.3 DISCUSSION OF SOLUTIONS

5.3.1 Objectionable solutions

The "objectionable" solutions for Problems 30 to 32 and 35 to 36 are given because, in general, they (a) work, (b) contain a fewer number of symbols than the corresponding acceptable solutions, and (c) may, therefore, be the type of solutions one would write. These solutions are objectionable, however, primarily because they fail to specify that the *same* grammatical category (or categories) occurs in all the classes which are said to agree; that is to say, they fail to specify agreement.

Solution 31A (Russian), for example, is objectionable first because it introduces the category person as a constituent of verbs and thus contradicts the statement made in the discussion of this problem. Even if this objection is discounted, however, the following cannot be: the solution does not specify that the category person is a constituent of pronouns as well as of verbs and, therefore, it does not specify that there is any type of agreement between these two types of constituents. Now, we demand this information not so much because Problem 31 necessitates it, but because we know that when we introduce additional data, there will be more complicated types of agreement (and morphophonemic changes), such as agreement between subjects and predicate nominatives in copulative sentences, agreement between pronouns and verbs in compound sentences, etc. If we fail to specify that person is a constituent of both pronouns and verbs, it will be extremely difficult, if not impossible, to specify the additional agreement just mentioned.

Solution 35 A (Swedish), to take another example, is objectionable for several reasons. First, there is no justification for deriving definite from indefinite nouns. That is to say, rule (3) is arbitrary since there is no reason, other than the fact that it works (this type of criticism applies, in general, to all the A solutions), for postulating that indefinite nouns are basic and definite nouns are derived from them by adding *Afn* to indefinite nouns. Second, rule (11) is not only arbitrary but misleading since it hides the fact that the article *et* is chosen only when the following noun is indefinite and singular. Finally, and most important, Solution 35A is objectionable in that, by postulating both noun and adjective affixes (i.e. *Afn* and *Afa*, respectively) in the phrase structure grammar, it not only fails to specify agreement but it specifies that adjective affixes represent a different element of structure than noun affixes.

To summarize, the primary objections to the "objectionable" solutions is that they do not specify agreement, or they make erroneous structural claims, or both. Specifically, (1) by postulating that a category is a constituent of A and then expanding a non-terminal symbol B in the context of that category (or its subcategories), we are making the claim that the category in question is a constituent only of A and not of B; and (2) by using different symbols for the same grammatical category (or categories) with every type of constituent that is said to be involved in the agreement, the claim is being made that the gender of a determiner, for example, is not the same structural element as the gender of a noun; or, for another example, that the number of the verb in a sentence is a different structural element than the number of the subject pronoun or noun.

5.3.2 The proper specification of agreement

At this point we might well ask: "Just what is the proper specification of agreement?" or, more precisely: "How can we specify agreement without making any erroneous structural claims about the grammatical categories classes are said to agree in?" The answer to this question is: the grammatical categories in which two or more classes are said to be in agreement are introduced as constituents of *one* constituent-type in the phrase structure grammar, and these categories are then postulated to be constituents of other constituent-types through an adjunction transformation (see note 6 of 5.4, however). For example, in Solution 30B (English) number is introduced as a constituent of *N* by rule (4), and *Det* acquires number as a constituent through the application of rule (7), which is an adjunction transformation.

Clearly, by introducing grammatical categories as constituents of one constituent-type in the phrase structure grammar, we simplify that part of the grammar, and by postulating that these categories are constituents of other constituent-types through an adjunction transformation, we are postulating that the categories the two or more types of constituents are said to agree in are the *same* structural elements.

5.3.3 Considerations for specifying agreement

Specifying agreement in the manner just described requires making two major decisions: (1) with which constituent-type to introduce the categories and (2) how the categories should be introduced with that constituent-type.

(1) **Deciding with which constituent-type to introduce the categories.** There are two criteria that help us decide, when confronted with two or more alternatives, which choice will result in the simpler solution: (a) conditioning and (b) economy.

(a) *Conditioning.* If the postulation of a category *C* as a constituent of *A* enables us to predict which subcategory of *C* a constituent of type *B* will have when both *A* and *B* co-occur in a given sentence, but the reverse is not possible, we should postulate the category to be a constituent of *A* in the phrase structure grammar.

For example, given English sentences such as *the girl writes, the girls write a letter, the boy travels abroad,* and *the boys travel abroad,* it is impossible to determine whether it is the verb which agrees in number with the noun or vice versa, since we have no evidence that by knowing the number of the noun we can predict the number of the verb and not vice versa. Given additional English sentences, such as *the girl and boy write a letter, the girls and the boy write a letter, the girl and the boys write a letter,* however, in which the verb is always plural, the two subject nouns are either both singular or one plural and the other singular, and the fact that the reverse of this pattern does not exist in English (i.e. sentences in which the predicate is two singular verbs, or one plural and one singular verb, while the subject noun is always plural), it is clear that number must be considered a constituent of nouns. That is to say, since (a) if we know the number of the subject noun(s), we also know the number of the verb but not vice versa, and (b) should number, therefore, be considered a constituent of verbs, we could not write a solution that would properly specify agreement between subject nouns and verbs in English, number must be considered a constituent of nouns and not of verbs.

(b) *Economy.* If we cannot use the criterion of conditioning to decide with which constituent-type to introduce the categories, our decision must be based on which alternative would result in the most economical solution.[1] For an example let us turn again to English and the question of whether number should be postulated to be a constituent of nouns or of verbs. This time, however, let us consider sentences in which there is no evidence that, by knowing the number of the subject pronoun, we can predict the number of the verb but not vice versa, but in which it can be seen that the number of object nouns is independent of the number of subject nouns and verbs: *the girl writes a letter, the girls write letters, the boys and the girls write a letter.* If, on the basis of these sentences alone, we were to introduce number as a constituent of verbs in the phrase structure grammar: (1) one T-rule would be needed to establish number agreement between verbs and subject nouns, which is not objectionable, but (2) another T-rule would have to be written to specify that non-subject nouns also may be singular or plural independently of the subject noun and verb, and the only way that this could be done would be to add not the category number but the subcategories of

[1] It is very unlikely that when writing a grammar of a language there will not be clear-cut cases of conditioning. The discussion of economy above is given, nevertheless, to help the reader understand how he can use the criterion of economy for making this decision when writing a solution for limited data.

number to object nouns by a rule such as

$$X + Vs + Y + N \Rightarrow X + Vs + Y + N\begin{Bmatrix} Sg \\ Pl \end{Bmatrix}$$

and this is objectionable because we would thus be postulating that the category number is a constituent of subject nouns but not of non-subject nouns. If, however, we were to introduce number as a constituent of nouns in the phrase structure grammar, we would be postulating that number is a constituent of *all* nouns and only one T-rule would be necessary, i.e. that which would establish number agreement between subject nouns and verbs. The obvious conclusion, therefore, is that number should be introduced as a constituent of nouns.

For a final example let us take Problem 39 (Spanish) and use the criteria of conditioning and economy to decide whether we should postulate that the verb agrees in person with the pronoun or vice versa. Given just the data of Problem 39, this decision is arbitrary; i.e. neither the criterion of conditioning nor that of economy can help us reach a decision. Let us assume, therefore, that we have added sentences in which there are object pronouns as well as subject pronouns. As long as the subject is a single pronoun, whether person should be postulated to be a constituent of the pronoun or the verb cannot be decided on the basis of conditioning, since there is no basis for deciding whether it is the person of the pronoun that determines the person of the verb but not vice versa. We can make a decision on the basis of economy, however: since an object pronoun can be in any person regardless of the person of the subject pronoun, it would be more economical to introduce person with pronouns rather than with verbs (for the same reasons we saw illustrated with the English example above). If we extend the data to include sentences in which there are compound subjects, however, we can use the criterion of conditioning. If the subject consists of two (or more) pronouns, it is clear that if we know the person of the subject pronouns, we can predict the person of the verb but not vice versa. For example, given *tu i jo bjaxámos* 'you and I travel,' *tu i el bjaxáis* 'you and he travel,' *el i éya bjáxan* 'he and she travel,' *jo trabáxo i bjáxo* 'I work and travel,' *nosótros deskansámos i estudjámos* 'we rest and study,' we know that (a) if any of the subject pronouns is first person, the verb is also first person, (b) if no first person pronoun is present but a second person pronoun is, the verb is second person also, (c) if both pronouns are third person, the verb is third person also; but, by knowing the person of the verb, we cannot predict the person of the subject pronouns. Clearly, then, person should be postulated to be a constituent of pronouns.

(2) **Deciding how to introduce grammatical categories.** Two decisions are involved in this question: (a) whether the categories should be introduced as one constituent-type, e.g. as *Afn* or as *Afv*, or as a sequence of different constituent-types, e.g. as *G* + *Ca* + *Nu* and *G* + *Nu*; and (b) whether, once this decision is made, the constituents should be postulated as obligatory or optional, e.g. as *Ns* + *Afn* or as *Ns* + *G(Pl)*.

(a) When only one grammatical category must be postulated, clearly there is no problem concerning its introduction: the category is introduced as one constituent-type, and the symbol representing it is then expanded into as many subcategories the category has. For example, in Solution 30B (English) there is but one category in question, i.e. number, that has two subcategories, singular and plural. Number *(Nu)* is introduced by rule (4) as a constituent of *N* and is expanded by rule (5) into *Sg* and *Pl.* Person, which has three subcategories, is treated in the same way in Solution 31B (Russian); and the same is true of the categories in Solutions 32B (Spanish), 33 (Swedish), and 34 (Modern Greek).

When there is more than one category that must be introduced, whether a sequence of these categories should be postulated to be a constituent-type depends on whether doing so will simplify the T-rule(s) specifying agreement. Clearly, our grammar will be simplified if a sequence of categories is postulated to be a constituent-type which can be used in the transformation specifying agreement. For example, in Solution 38 (Modern Greek), by postulating that gender, case, and number are the constituents of *Afn*, we simplify the statement of two agreement rules in that *Afn* rather than *G* + *Ca* + *Nu* is used in them (see rules [21] and [22]). (Notice, however, that in rule [23] only *Nu* is used, since a verb agrees with a subject noun only in number and not in the other categories.)

In Solution 39 (Spanish), however, a sequence of three categories (i.e. gender, number, and person) is not postulated to be an *Afn*, since *Afn* cannot be used in any of the agreement rules in this solution. That is, since all the classes that are involved in agreement do not agree in all three categories (i.e. verbs agree with subject nouns and pronouns only in person and number, while determiners and adjectives agree with nouns only in gender and number), we cannot simplify the statement of any T-rules by postulating an *Afn* constituent-type. An *Af* constituent-type is postulated because it can be used in one of the agreement rules. The postulation that *G(Pl)* is an *Af* is arbitrary, however, for we could have postulated that *(Pl)Per* is an *Af* and thereby simplified rule (23) rather than rule (24).

(b) In the preceding solutions all the categories except number were postulated to be obligatory. Number was sometimes postulated as obligatory (and each subcategory was symbolized; e.g. see Solution 30B [English]) and sometimes as optional (and only the subcategory "plural" was symbolized; e.g. see rule [5] of Solution 37 [Spanish]). The criterion for deciding whether a category should be postulated to be optional or obligatory is simplicity; i.e. that alternative should be chosen which will yield the simplest grammar. The following may serve as a good rule of thumb to follow in making this decision:

> A grammatical category should be postulated to be obligatory *unless* (a) only two subcategories are apparent in the data (e.g. definite and indefinite concreteness) and (b) only *one* of these subcategories is expressed by a *distinct* affix (defined in 4.3.3). If both conditions are apparent in the data, the category in question may be postulated either as optional or as obligatory, depending on which choice results in the simpler grammar.

In both English and Spanish, for example, there are two subcategories of number, singular and plural, which in most nouns are marked by the absence or presence of *s*, respectively. Number may therefore be postulated as obligatory in a grammar of English, since, as a result, the rules for subject and verb agreement are simplified, while in a grammar of Spanish, the plural morpheme may be postulated as optional, since, as a result, the morphophonemic rules are simplified.

5.3.4 Inherent gender

If the solutions for the Spanish problems (32, 37, and 39) are compared, it will be seen that a distinction between masculine and feminine noun stems is made in the last solution but not in the first two. The reason for this is that while in Problems 32 and 37 *all* nouns have a gender suffix, in Problem 39 there are some nouns which do not. Despite the fact that they do not have a gender suffix, however, these nouns pattern or behave either like feminine or like masculine nouns but never like both. For example, although *padre* does not have the masculine gender suffix *o*, and *madre* does not have the feminine gender suffix *a*, *padre* patterns always as a masculine noun in that the preceding article is always *el, los, un,* or *unos* and any following adjective always has the masculine gender endings *o* or *os*; and *madre* patterns as a feminine noun in that the accompanying articles and adjectives are feminine in gender. These nouns (and all nouns which behave in such a manner) are said to have an **inherent gender.**

Given such situations, some means must be found to keep track of the appropriate gender of each noun so that the proper agreement can later be established between any such noun and a preceding article, for example. The simplest way to do this is to subdivide noun stems into masculine and feminine, despite the fact that, as a result, all noun stems having gender suffixes must be listed twice in the lexicon. For example, in the solution for Problem 39 both *bjex* and *mučač* are listed once as masculine noun stems and again as feminine noun stems, by rules (20) and (21), respectively.

Notice that inherent gender is also attributed to every noun in Modern Greek, since, although there never is an instance of a gender suffix marker for nouns, they nevertheless pattern either as masculine, feminine, or neuter, but never as combinations of these.

5.3.5 Specifying sentences without an overt subject

Rule (25) of Solution 39 postulates that Spanish sentences without a nominal subject are derived from sentences having a pronoun as the subject by deleting this pronoun. Since the reason for specifying these sentences in this way may not be immediately apparent, let us examine alternative ways of specifying them.

It would seem that we could generate the sentences in question by: (a) making *NP* in the first rule an optional choice; i.e. omit rule (25) and change rule (1) to

$S \rightarrow (NP)\,VP$

(b) optionally deleting the entire noun phrase; i.e. change rule (25) to

Topt
$NP + VP \Rightarrow VP$

(c) optionally deleting *Det* + *N* of *NP*; i.e. change rule (25) to

Topt
$Det + N + VP \Rightarrow VP$

Alternative (a) must be rejected because the sentences in question would not be generated; that is, there would be no way to specify the proper endings for the verbs in these sentences since agreement in person (and number) can be specified only for P-markers in which *NP* appears.

Alternative (b) must be rejected because it deletes too much; that is, this alternative introduces a redundancy, since by deleting both *Det* + *N* and *Pron,* we delete third person (and number) as many times as there are *Det* + *N*'s and third person pronouns. In other words, deletion of one will accomplish what we want. The question, then, is: Do we delete *Pron,* as is done in rule (25), or *Det* + *N?* The latter is alternative (c).

Alternative (c) must be rejected because sentences without a nominal subject with verbs in the first and second person will not be generated if we adopt it. That is to say, since the only person in which verbs agree with a noun is the third, when we delete *Det* + *N* to derive #*VP*#, the verbs in #*VP*# can only be in the third person.

The only remaining alternative that meets all the objections raised by the other alternatives without raising any of its own is the one adopted in rule (25), namely, to delete *Pron.*

5.3.6 Non-terminal symbols that are expanded into a single non-terminal symbol

In the preceding solutions some symbols are expanded into a single non-terminal symbol, which, in turn, is expanded into other non-terminal or terminal symbols, even though there is no motivation apparent in the data for doing so. For example, in Solution 31B (Russian) *Vb* is expanded only into *Vs*, which is, in turn, expanded as a list of morphemes, and in Solution 32B (Spanish) *Det* is expanded only into *D*, which is, in turn, expanded into a lexical morpheme. This may raise the question: Why not expand *Vb* directly into a list of morphemes and *Det* directly into a lexical morpheme instead of introducing what seems to be an extra non-terminal symbol? The answer is simple: The "extra" non-terminal symbol is required by the solutions for these problems. If *Vb* were not first expanded into *Vs* in Solution 31B, for example, there would be no way to include *Per* as a constituent of *Vb* through rule (6). In other words, a rule of the form $A \rightarrow B$, where both A and B are non-terminal symbols, is justified in a grammar if there is at least one T-rule in the grammar which adjoins at least one symbol to B (under A).

5.4 NOTES

1. Although agreement rules may be written with the highest ordered symbol dominating the grammatical categories, there is no possibility that, because of this, agreement has not been established. That is, it should not be forgotten that a T-rule operates on P-markers provided by the P-rules (and other T-rules); thus, when a transformation specifies that a C which is a constituent of B in an underlying P-marker

is adjoined to *A*, the entire structure of *C* is adjoined to *A* in every P-marker that meets the structural description of the rule. By writing the agreement rule with the highest ordered symbol that dominates the categories, then, we always adjoin not only that symbol but everything it dominates in any given underlying P-marker the rule applies to. For example, in Solution 33 (Swedish) *Co* is postulated to be a constituent of nouns in the phrase structure grammar and is expanded into two (mutually exclusive) subcategories, *Def* and *Indef;* thus, in some underlying P-markers, *Def* will be attached to *Co* and in others *Indef* will be attached to *Co.* The agreement rule then adjoins *Co* with *Def* to the *D* under *Det* in the former P-markers and *Co* with *Indef* to the *D* under *Det* in the latter P-markers to form the derived P-markers.

2. Notice that in some of the preceding solutions we used a notational convention discussed in 1.5.1; namely, a hyphen is used between symbols to be considered as a group and a plus is used between symbols in a group when it might be ambiguous whether a given symbol is being adjoined to the left of one symbol or to the right of another. In Solution 38 (Modern Greek), for example, this notation is used in rule (21), i.e. $D - Ns + Afn \Rightarrow D + Afn - Ns + Afn$, since otherwise we would not know whether *Afn* should be adjoined to the right of *D* or to the left of *Ns*. It is not used in rule (22) of the same solution, i.e. $Ns + Afn + Vcop + A \Rightarrow Ns + Afn + Vcop + A + Afn$, however, because *A* is the last symbol in the string; therefore there is no doubt that *Afn* should be adjoined to the right of *A* and attached to *Adj*. From the rules mentioned and the convention for attachment given in 1.5.1, we get, for example, the following derived P-marker (which, it should be noticed, is not completed):

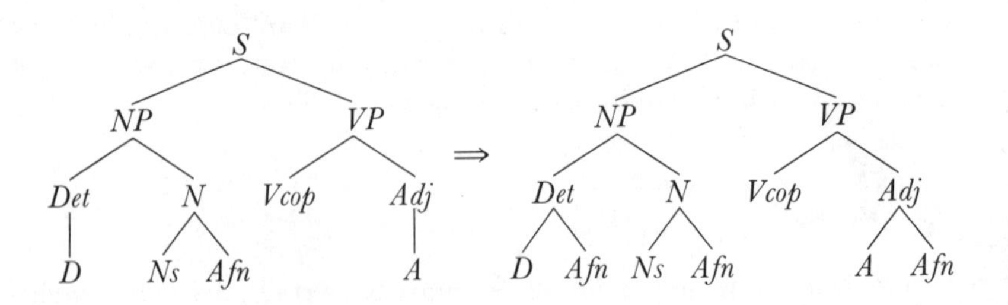

3. By taking advantage of the fact that the rules of a grammar are ordered, we were able to simplify several of the preceding solutions in that we were able to simplify one or more morphophonemic rules. For example, in Solution 38 (Modern Greek) the shorter and therefore pref-

erable alternatives to rules (28) and (33), $D + Afn \Rightarrow i$ and $Afn \Rightarrow \emptyset$, respectively, are possible because the rules are ordered. That is, since the rules are ordered and since rule (28) follows four rules which specify phonological representations for constituents of the type *Afn* when they follow *D*, rule (28) can apply only to those constituents of the type *Afn* which have *not* appeared in the preceding rules. Similarly, since the rules are ordered and since rule (33) follows a number of rules which specify a phonological representation of various constituents of the type *Afn* when they follow *Ns* and *A*, rule (33) can apply only to those constituents of the type *Afn* which have not appeared in the preceding rules. Rule (16) of Solution 35B (Swedish) and rule (36) of Solution 39 (Spanish) simplify the solutions for the same reason.

4. An alternative way to handle the suffixes of Spanish verbs in Problem 39, which may turn out to be better in the long run than the one given, is to adjust rules (34) and (35) of the solution so that *mos, is, n* instead of *amos, ais, an,* and *s* instead of *as* are generated; we would then write an additional morphophonemic rule which would either reduce certain vowel clusters (if stems are listed with a final *a*) or add the vowel *a* (if stems are listed without a final *a*) under certain conditions.

It should also be noted that there are several other ways to handle the suffixes of nouns and adjectives in Modern Greek; the treatment given in this chapter reflects the author's personal preference.

5. Following the practice adopted in the previous chapter, environments that can be unambiguously determined are omitted from morphophonemic rules. For example, in Solution 35B (Swedish) *A* is omitted in rules (15) and (16) because all other environments in which $Def \begin{bmatrix} Sg \\ Pl \end{bmatrix}$ occurs have been specified (i.e. in rules [11] to [14]), and we know unambiguously that *A* is the only environment to which the rules can refer. Similarly, in Solution 36B (Russian) *Vs* is omitted in rules (11) and (12) because all other environments in which person and number may occur have been specified (i.e. in rules [9] and [10]); thus we know that the only remaining environment these categories may occur in is *Vs*.

6. In Solution 39 (Spanish), contrary to what was said in 5.3.2, the grammatical categories are postulated to be constituents of two constituent-types in the phrase structure grammar rather than, as is desirable, of only one; i.e. *Af* and *Per* are postulated to be constituents of both *N* and *Pron* (see rules [8] and [9]) instead, as would be desirable, of *NP*. This was done simply because, given the position of *Adj* in relation to *N*, it was simpler to introduce this redundancy in the phrase structure grammar than to write the complicated agreement rules that

would be necessary if we had attempted to postulate that *Af* + *Per* is a constituent of *NP*. In a more comprehensive grammar of Spanish this problem would not arise, since the adjective would be made a constituent of a noun phrase through an embedding transformation (see 8.3.6).

A similar redundancy appears in rules (4) and (5) of Solution 38 (Modern Greek); i.e. *Afv* is postulated to be a constituent of *Vst* and of *Vsc*. See Solution 44B (in Chapter 6) for the proper introduction of *Afv*.

5.5 COLLATERAL READING

Postal, Paul M.: *Constituent Structure: a Study of Contemporary Models of Syntactic Description,* Indiana University Research Center in Anthropology, Folklore, and Linguistics, Publication 30, pp. 43–50 (*International Journal of American Linguistics,* vol. 30, no. 1, pt. 3, 1964).

5.6 EXERCISES

1. MUNDURUKU, a language of Brazil

1.	hũn horaoberedn	*I am tall.*
2.	hẽn heraoberedn	*You are tall.*
3.	ˀiteˀ taoberedn	*He is tall.*
4.	hũn horeˀuˀ	*I smell good.*
5.	hẽn hereˀuˀ	*You smell good.*
6.	ˀiteˀ teˀuˀ	*He smells good.*
7.	hũn horirebm	*I am wet.*
8.	hẽn herirebm	*You are wet.*
9.	ˀiteˀ tirebm	*He is wet.*
10.	hũn horatšep	*I am swollen.*
11.	hẽn heratšep	*You are swollen.*
12.	ˀiteˀ tatšep	*He is swollen.*

But not:

*hẽn horaoberedn
*ˀiteˀ herirebm
*hũn tirebm

2. RUSSIAN

1. stud'ent bil tut *The student was here.*
2. stud'entka bila tut *The coed was here.*
3. stud'ent bil tam *The student was there.*
4. stud'entka bila tam *The coed was there.*
5. stud'enti bil'i tam *The students were there.*
6. stud'entk'i bil'i tut *The coeds were here.*
7. may stud'ent žil tam *My student lived there.*
8. maya stud'entka žila tam *My coed lived there.*
9. mayi stud'enti žil'i tam *My students lived there.*
10. mayi stud'entk'i žil'i tut *My coeds lived here.*

But not:

*stud'ent bila tam
*stud'entka bil tam
*maya stud'ent bil tam
*may stud'entka bila tam

3. SPANISH

1. el gáto es pekéño *The cat* (masc.) *is small.*
2. la gáta es pekéña *The cat* (fem.) *is small.*
3. el pálo es pekéño *The stick is small.*
4. la pála es pekéña *The shovel is small.*
5. un gáto es gránde *A cat* (masc.) *is large.*
6. una gáta es gránde *A cat* (fem.) *is large.*
7. el pálo es gránde *The stick is large.*
8. la pála es gránde *The shovel is large.*
9. una máno es pekéña *A hand is small.*
10. la máno es gránde *The hand is large.*
11. el mápa es pekéño *The map is small.*
12. un mápa es gránde *A map is large.*
13. el mápa es útil *The map is useful.*
14. una pála es útil *A shovel is useful.*
15. la kapitál es arxentína *The capital city is Argentinian.*
16. el kapitál es arxentíno *The capital is Argentinian.*
17. el profesór es distraído *The teacher* (masc.) *is absent-minded.*

18. la profesóra es distraída	*The teacher* (fem.) *is absent-minded.*
19. un profesór es arxentíno	*A teacher* (masc.) *is Argentinian.*
20. una profesóra es arxentína	*A teacher* (fem.) *is Argentinian.*
21. el arxentíno es superiór	*The Argentinian* (masc.) *is superior.*
22. la arxentína es superiór	*The Argentinian* (fem.) *is superior.*
23. el profesór es superiór	*The teacher* (masc.) *is superior.*

But not:

*el gáto es grándo
*una gáta es gránda
*la máno es pekéño
*el profesór es distraída
*la arxentína es superióra

4. BRAZILIAN PORTUGUESE

1. eli esta kõ fomi	*He is hungry.*
2. ɛla esta kõ fomi	*She is hungry.*
3. eu estou kõ fomi	*I am hungry.*
4. eli esta kõ sonu	*He is sleepy.*
5. ɛla esta kõ sonu	*She is sleepy.*
6. eu estou kõ sonu	*I am sleepy.*
7. eli esta kãsadu	*He is tired.*
8. ɛla esta kãsada	*She is tired.*
9. eu estou kãsadu	*I* (masc.) *am tired.*
10. eu estou kãsada	*I* (fem.) *am tired.*
11. eli esta enɛxžiku	*He is strict.*
12. ɛla esta enɛxžika	*She is strict.*
13. eu estou enɛxžiku	*I* (masc.) *am strict.*
14. eu estou enɛxžika	*I* (fem.) *am strict.*
15. eli ɛ baianu	*He is Baian.*
16. ɛla ɛ baiana	*She is Baian.*
17. eu sou baiana	*I* (fem.) *am Baian.*
18. eu sou baianu	*I* (masc.) *am Baian.*
19. eli ɛ ũgaru	*He is Hungarian.*
20. ɛla ɛ ũgara	*She is Hungarian.*
21. eu sou ũgaru	*I* (masc.) *am Hungarian.*
22. eu sou ũgara	*I* (fem.) *am Hungarian.*

23. eu sou alto — *I* (masc.) *am tall.*
24. eu sou alta — *I* (fem.) *am tall.*
25. eli ɛ alto — *He is tall.*
26. ɛla ɛ alta — *She is tall.*

But not:

*eli esta kõ altu
*ɛla ɛ kãsada
*eli esta kãsada
*ɛla esta kãsadu
*ɛla sou alta

5. TOSK ALBANIAN

1. vajza është e bukur — *The girl is pretty.*
2. dhoma është e mirë — *The room is good.*
3. hoteli është i mirë — *The hotel is good.*
4. burri është i nalt — *The man is tall.*
5. vajza s është e nalt — *The girl isn't tall.*
6. burri s është i bukur — *The man isn't pretty.*
7. një hotel s është i mirë — *A hotel isn't good.*
8. një vajzë s është e nalt — *A girl isn't tall.*
9. një burr është i nalt — *A man is tall.*
10. një dhom është e mirë — *A room is good.*
11. një pesk është i mirë — *A fish is good.*
12. pesku është i nalt — *The fish is tall.*
13. miku s është i nalt — *The friend isn't tall.*
14. një mik është i mirë — *A friend is good.*
15. vajza është e mire — *The girl is good.*
16. miku është një burr — *The friend is a man.*
17. një mik është një burr — *A friend is a man.*
18. vajza s është një burr — *The girl isn't a man.*
19. një vajzë është miku — *A girl is the friend.*

But not:

*një vajza është e bukur
*hotel është i mirë
*vajza është i bukur
*hoteli është e mirë

6. FRENCH

1.	mõ pti frɛr e mešã	*My little brother is naughty.*
2.	ma ptit sœr e mešãt	*My little sister is naughty.*
3.	sõ frɛr e grã	*His brother is tall.*
4.	sa sœr e grãd	*His sister is tall.*
5.	la grãd pɔrt e blãš	*The big door is white.*
6.	lø pti livr e blã	*The little book is white.*
7.	sa sœr e frãsɛz	*His sister is French.*
8.	sõ frɛr e frãse	*Her brother is French.*
9.	ta sœr e brijãt	*Your sister is brilliant.*
10.	tõ grã frɛr e brijã	*Your big brother is brilliant.*
11.	l elɛv e ptit	*The coed is small.*
12.	l elɛv e pti	*The student is small.*
13.	la grãd sœr e movɛz	*The big sister is bad.*
14.	lø grã livr e move	*The big book is bad.*
15.	ma grɔs šat e blãš	*My big cat* (fem.) *is white.*
16.	mõ gro ša e blã	*My big cat* (masc.) *is white.*

But not:

*ma pti frɛr e move
*ma pti sœr e movɛz
*ma sœr e frãse
*mõ blã šat e gro
*la ptit elɛv e move

7. YIDDISH

1.	ix ze di šeine froi	*I see the pretty woman.*
2.	ix ze di šeine štul	*I see the pretty chair.*
3.	ix ze dem šeinem man	*I see the handsome man.*
4.	ix ze dem šeinem tiš	*I see the pretty table.*
5.	ix ze dos šeine meidl	*I see the pretty maiden.*
6.	er zet di froi	*He sees the woman.*
7.	er zet di šeine bild	*He sees the pretty picture.*
8.	er zet di bild	*He sees the picture.*
9.	di šeine froi molt a bild	*The pretty woman paints a picture.*
10.	di froi molt a šeine bild	*The woman paints a pretty picture.*

11. der šeiner man molt a bild — *The handsome man paints a picture.*
12. der man molt dos meidl — *The man paints (a picture of) the maiden.*
13. dos šeine meidl molt a bild — *The pretty maiden paints a picture.*
14. der šeiner man zet a šeinem tiš — *The handsome man sees a pretty table.*
15. ix ze a štul — *I see a chair.*
16. ix ze a šeine štul — *I see a pretty chair.*
17. er zet a man — *He sees a man.*
18. er zet a šeinem man — *He sees a handsome man.*
19. ix mole di štul — *I paint (a picture of) a chair.*
20. ix mole di šeine štul — *I paint (a picture of) a pretty chair.*
21. er molt a tiš — *He paints (a picture of) a table.*
22. er molt a šeinem tiš — *He paints (a picture of) a pretty table.*

But not:

*er zet dem šeiner man
*ix ze di šeinem man
*er zet dem šeinem froi
*er ze di bild
*dem šeiner man molt a bild
*ix zet a štul

8. RUSSIAN

1. iván v'id'it ad'in nóvij stól — *Ivan sees one new table.*
2. iván v'id'it dva nóvava staló — *Ivan sees two new tables.*
3. iván v'id'it t'r'i nóvava staló — *Ivan sees three new tables.*
4. jósif xóčit p'at' nóvix stalóf — *Joseph wants five new tables.*
5. iván xóčit s'em' nóvix stalóf — *Ivan wants seven new tables.*
6. jósif xóčit mnóga nóvix stalóf — *Joseph wants many new tables.*
7. iván v'id'it adnavó stárava atcá — *Ivan sees one old father.*
8. iván xóčit adnavó nóvava atcá — *Ivan wants one new father.*
9. iván xóčit dvux nóvix atcóf — *Ivan wants two new fathers.*
10. jósif xóčit dvux stárix atcóf — *Joseph wants two old fathers.*

11. jósif v’íd’it t’r’ox stárix atcóf	*Joseph sees three old fathers.*
12. jósif v’íd’it t’r’ox nóvix atcóf	*Joseph sees three new fathers.*
13. jósif xóčit mnóga stárix atcóf	*Joseph wants many old fathers.*
14. iván xóčit mnóga nóvix atcóf	*Ivan wants many new fathers.*
15. iván v’íd’it p’at’ stárix atcóf	*Ivan sees five old fathers.*
16. jósif v’íd’it p’at’ nóvix atcóf	*Joseph sees five new fathers.*
17. iván v’íd’it s’em’ stárix atcóf	*Ivan sees seven old fathers.*
18. iván xóčit s’em’ nóvix atcóf	*Ivan wants seven new fathers.*

But not:

*iván xóčit adnavó nóvij stól
*iván xóčit ad’in stárava atcá
*iván xóčit ad’in nóvij stalá
*iván xóčit adnavó stárij atcá
*iván v’íd’it p’at’ nóvix stalá
*iván v’íd’it s’em’ nóvava stalóf
*iván v’íd’it p’at’ stárix atcá
*iván xóčit s’em’ stárava atcóf

Additional information:

(1) The cardinal numbers in sentences 1 to 6 are in the accusative case; the nominative forms of these numbers are the same as the accusative.

(2) The nominative forms of ‘new,’ ‘old,’ ‘table,’ and ‘father’ are *nóvij, stárij, stól,* and *at’éc,* respectively.

9. SWAHILI

1. kisu kidogo kimoja kilitoša	*One small knife sufficed.*
2. visu vidogo vitatu vilitoša	*Three small knives sufficed.*
3. kikapu kikubwa kile kitatoša	*That big basket will suffice.*
4. vikapu vikubwa vile vitatoša	*Those big baskets will suffice.*
5. vikapu vizuri vile vitatoša	*Those good baskets will suffice.*
6. mtoto mzuri mmoja atatoša	*One good boy will suffice.*
7. watoto wazuri watatu watatoša	*Three good boys will suffice.*
8. mtu mrefu yule alitoša	*That tall man sufficed.*
9. watu warefu wale walitoša	*Those tall men sufficed.*
10. mtu mzuri mmoja atatoša	*One good man will suffice.*
11. mkate mzuri ule utatoša	*That good loaf of bread will suffice.*

12.	mikate mizuri ile itatoša	*Those good loaves of bread will suffice.*
13.	mzizi mrefu ule utatoša	*That long root will suffice.*
14.	mizizi mirefu ile itatoša	*Those long roots will suffice.*
15.	mizizi midogo itatu itatoša	*Three small roots will suffice.*
16.	yai kubwa lile lilitoša	*That large egg sufficed.*
17.	mayai makubwa yale yalitoša	*Those large eggs sufficed.*
18.	cungwa dogo litatoša	*The small orange will suffice.*
19.	macungwa madogo yatatoša	*The small oranges will suffice.*

But not:

*kisu kidogo kimoja vilitoša
*visu vidogo vimoja kilitoša
*kisu vidogo vimoja kilitoša
*visu kidogo kidogo vilitoša
*kisu madogo yalitoša
*mayai yikubwa yalitoša
*wasu wadogo wamoja walitoša

10. SWEDISH, as written in Finland

1.	en čuv slog ett barn	*A thief hit a child.*
2.	ett glin slog en yŋliŋ	*A brat hit a youngster.*
3.	yŋliŋen slog glinet	*The youngster hit the brat.*
4.	barnet slog čuven	*The child hit the thief.*
5.	en fet čuv slog en klok yŋliŋ	*A fat thief hit a wise youngster.*
6.	ett klokt glin slog en stor čuv	*A wise brat hit a big thief.*
7.	en elak yŋliŋ slog ett fett barn	*A wicked youngster hit a fat child.*
8.	den elaka čuven slog ett stort barn	*The wicked thief hit a big child.*
9.	det feta glinet slog den kloka yŋliŋen	*The fat brat hit the wise youngster.*
10.	den kloka yŋliŋen slog den feta čuven	*The wise youngster hit the fat thief.*
11.	yŋliŋar slog glin	*Youngsters hit brats.*
12.	barn slog čuvar	*Children hit thieves.*

13. glin slog barn	*Brats hit children.*
14. čuvarna slog barnen	*The thieves hit the children.*
15. glinen slog yŋliŋarna	*The brats hit the youngsters.*
16. čuvarna slog yŋliŋarna	*The thieves hit the youngsters.*
17. feta yŋliŋar slog stora čuvar	*Fat youngsters hit big thieves.*
18. stora barn slog feta barn	*Big children hit fat children.*
19. kloka yŋliŋar slog elaka glin	*Wise youngsters hit wicked brats.*
20. de elaka čuvarna slog de feta barnen	*The wicked thieves hit the fat children.*
21. de stora glinen slog de kloka yŋliŋarna	*The big brats hit the wise youngsters.*
22. de feta yŋliŋarna slog de stora čuvarna	*The fat youngsters hit the big thieves.*
23. čuven slog de feta barnen	*The thief hit the fat children.*
24. de stora čuvarna slog ett barn	*The big thieves hit a child.*
25. glin slog elaka barn	*Brats hit wicked children.*
26. den kloka yŋliŋen slog čuvar	*The wise youngster hit thieves.*
27. ett elakt glin slog yŋliŋarna	*A wicked brat hit the youngsters.*

But not:

*ett čuv slog en barn
*en elakt yŋliŋ slog ett klok barn
*yŋliŋet slog ett fet glin
*de feta čuven slog den fett barnet
*ett elaka barn slog čuv
*den klok yŋliŋen slog det fet barnet
*en slog barnet den kloka čuven
*barnet det slog klokt glin
*stora yŋliŋen slog čuvar
*stor barn slog kloka yŋliŋar

chapter six

PERMUTATION

INTRODUCTION

The problems in this chapter contain sentences that differ from each other primarily in that the order of the words in them varies. As a result, some of these sentences can be derived from others by permutation rules. In other words, the problems contain sentences which can be said to be related in that they have the same underlying P-marker but different derived P-markers, some of which are derived by the application of at least one optional transformation that permutes (or rearranges) a constituent (or constituents) in the underlying P-marker. The primary purpose of this chapter thus is to illustrate the writing of permutation rules.

Since this is the first chapter to contain any number of related sentences, we now have a basis for a more detailed discussion of the fundamental question: How do we decide what constituent structure to assign to kernel sentences? or put differently: What is the justification for the constituent-types postulated in the phrase structure grammar? A secondary purpose of this chapter is, therefore, to provide some answers to this question.

6.1 DATA

PROBLEM 40: ROGLAI, a language of South Vietnam

1. ñu naw	*He goes.*	7. ñu pə suka	*He flies fast.*
2. naw ñu	*He goes!*	8. pə suka ñu	*He flies fast!*
3. ñu naw ata	*He goes far.*	9. ñu naw suka	*He goes fast.*
4. naw ata ñu	*He goes far!*	10. naw suka ñu	*He goes fast!*
5. ñu pə	*He flies.*	11. ñu pə ata	*He flies far.*
6. pə ñu	*He flies!*	12. pə ata ñu	*He flies far!*

But not:

*ata naw ñu
*suka pə ñu
*ata ñu naw

The above intransitive sentences are either declarative or exclamatory. The declarative sentences consist of a subject, which is expressed by a pronoun, followed by a predicate, which is expressed by either a verb alone or a verb followed by an adverb. The exclamatory sentences differ from the declarative only in that their predicate precedes the subject; that is, while in declarative sentences the order of subject and predicate is subject first and predicate second, in exclamatory sentences the order is predicate first and subject second.

PROBLEM 41: FRENCH

1. žø pus	*I push.*
2. ty pus	*You are pushing.*
3. pjɛr pus	*Peter pushes.*
4. žø n pus pa	*I am not pushing.*
5. ty n pus pa	*You don't push.*
6. mari n pus pa	*Mary is not pushing.*
7. žø parl	*I am speaking.*
8. ty parl	*You speak.*
9. mari parl	*Mary speaks.*
10. žø n parl pa	*I don't speak.*
11. ty n parl pa	*You are not speaking.*
12. mari n parl pa	*Mary doesn't speak.*

But not:

*mari n pa parl
*n mari pa pus
*n ty parl pa

The above intransitive sentences are either affirmative or negative. Affirmative sentences consist of a subject, which is expressed by a noun or pronoun, and a predicate, which is expressed by a verb. Negative sentences differ from affirmative sentences only in that their predicate includes a pair of negative particles. In addition to being simply dependent on the verb, the negative particles are in a mutual dependency relation with each other and their occurrence is discontinuous: *n* occurs before and *pa* after the verb.

PROBLEM 42: ENGLISH

1. the policeman brought the thief
2. the policeman brought in the thief
3. the policeman brought the thief in
4. the policeman brought him in
5. he brought him
6. he brought him in
7. he took the thief
8. he took him
9. the lawyer took him
10. the lawyer took him out
11. the lawyer took out the thief
12. the lawyer took the thief out
13. he took him out
14. he looked at the policeman
15. the policeman looked at him
16. the thief talked about the lawyer
17. the thief talked about him
18. he talked about him
19. the thief hurt the lawyer
20. he hurt him

But not:

*the policeman brought in him
*he talked the policeman
*he talked the lawyer about
*the thief hurt about the lawyer

*he took out him
*he talked him about
*he hurt him in

In the above transitive sentences the subject is expressed by a pronoun or by a determiner followed by a noun, and the predicate is expressed by a verb, which is either simple (one word) or complex (i.e. a main verb followed by one of the particles *in, at, out,* or *about*), and a direct object, which is either a pronoun or a determiner and a noun.

The subject, verb, and object occur in that order except when the verb is either *brought in* or *took out,* in which case the direct object must occur between the main verb and the particle if it is a pronoun, but it may or may not occur between the main verb and the particle if it is a determiner and a noun.

PROBLEM 43: INDONESIAN

1. guru itu makan səmaŋka
   teacher the eat watermelon
   The teacher is eating watermelon.
2. guru itu rupaña makan səmaŋka
   The teacher is apparently eating watermelon.
3. rupaña guru itu makan səmaŋka
   The teacher is apparently eating watermelon.
4. guru itu makan səmaŋka rupaña
   The teacher is apparently eating watermelon.
5. guru itu disini kamarin makan səmaŋka
   teacher the here yesterday eat watermelon
   The teacher ate watermelon here yesterday.
6. disini kamarin guru itu makan səmaŋka
   The teacher ate watermelon here yesterday.
7. guru itu makan səmaŋka disini kamarin
   The teacher ate watermelon here yesterday.
8. makan səmaŋka guru itu
   The teacher is eating watermelon.
9. rupaña makan səmaŋka guru itu
   Apparently the teacher is eating watermelon.
10. makan səmaŋka guru itu rupaña
    The teacher is eating watermelon apparently.
11. makan səmaŋka rupaña guru itu
    The teacher apparently is eating watermelon.

12. disini kamarin makan səmaŋka guru itu
    The teacher ate watermelon here yesterday.
13. makan səmaŋka guru itu disini kamarin
    The teacher ate watermelon here yesterday.
14. makan səmaŋka disini kamarin guru itu
    The teacher ate watermelon here yesterday.

But not:

*səmaŋka itu makan guru
*guru itu makan səmaŋka itu
*guru itu makan rupaña səmaŋka
*makan guru itu səmaŋka
*makan disini kamarin səmaŋka guru itu

In the above transitive sentences the subject and predicate are both obligatory, but the adverbs are optional. The subject is expressed by a noun phrase consisting of an animate noun followed by a determiner, and the predicate is expressed by a verb followed by an inanimate noun. The adverb *rupaña* 'apparently' is mutually exclusive with the two mutually dependent adverbs *disini* 'here' and *kamarin* 'yesterday'; the latter two adverbs always occur in that order.

The subject either precedes or follows the predicate, and the adverbs occur in a number of positions: (1) before everything else in a sentence, (2) after everything else in a sentence, or (3) between the subject and the predicate regardless of their order. In other words, except for the restriction on the order of *disini* and *kamarin*, the subject, predicate, and adverb(s) occur in any order with respect to each other.

PROBLEM 44: MODERN GREEK

The data of Problem 38 and the following:

32. periméni tin mitéra o γítonas	*Is the neighbor waiting for the mother?*
33. tin mitéra periméni o γítonas	*Is it the mother the neighbor is waiting for?*
34. fonázun ton ándra i mitéres	*Are the mothers calling the man?*
35. ton ándra fonázun i mitéres	*Is it the man the mothers are calling?*
36. proséxun tiz mitéres ta peðjá	*Are the boys watching the mothers?*

37. tiz mitéres proséxun ta peðjá	*Is it the mothers the boys are watching?*
38. íne kalós o γítonas	*Is the neighbor good?*
39. kalós íne o γítonas	*Is the neighbor good?*
40. íne ómorfa ta peðjá	*Are the children beautiful?*
41. ómorfa íne ta peðjá	*Are the children beautiful?*

But not:

*o γítonas tin mitéra periméni
*periméni o γítonas tin mitéra
*tin mitéra o γítonas periméni
*ómorfa ta peðjá íne
*ta peðjá ómorfa íne

Sentences 1 to 31 (i.e. Problem 38) are either transitive or copulative declarative sentences, and the order of the functional groupings in them is subject – verb – complement. Sentences 32 to 41 above are also either transitive or copulative, but differ from sentences 1 to 31 in that they are either interrogative or interrogative-emphatic. The order of the functional groupings in interrogative sentences is verb – complement – subject, and in interrogative-emphatic sentences it is complement – verb – subject. The complement in all transitive sentences is a noun phrase, while the complement in copulative sentences is a predicate adjective.

PROBLEM 45: SWEDISH

1. jag kan gɔ	*I can go.*
2. jag kan gɔ nu	*I can go now.*
3. nu kan jag gɔ	*I can go now.*
4. jag kan inte gɔ	*I can't go.*
5. kan jag gɔ	*Can I go?*
6. nar kan jag gɔ	*When can I go?*
7. kan jag gɔ nu	*Can I go now?*
8. kan jag inte gɔ nu	*Can't I go now?*
9. nar kan jag inte gɔ	*When can't I go?*
10. jag kan gɔ imorgon	*I can go tomorrow.*
11. imorgon kan jag gɔ	*I can go tomorrow.*
12. jag kan inte gɔ imorgon	*I cannot go tomorrow.*
13. imorgon kan jag inte gɔ	*I cannot go tomorrow.*
14. kan jag inte gɔ imorgon	*Can't I go tomorrow?*
15. vart kan jag gɔ nu	*Where can I go now?*

16. jag kan gɔ hem — *I can go home.*
17. hem kan jag gɔ — *I can go home.*
18. jag kan inte gɔ hem nu — *I can't go home now.*
19. kan jag gɔ hem — *Can I go home?*
20. kan jag inte gɔ hem nu — *Can't I go home now?*
21. imorgon kan jag gɔ hem — *I can go home tomorrow.*
22. hem kan jag gɔ imorgon — *I can go home tomorrow.*
23. jag kan gɔ hem imorgon — *I can go home tomorrow.*
24. nar kan jag inte gɔ hem — *When can't I go home?*

But not:

*nar kan jag gɔ nu
*nar kan jag gɔ imorgon
*nar vart kan jag gɔ
*nu nar kan jag gɔ
*imorgon vart kan jag gɔ
*hem imorgon kan jag gɔ

The above intransitive sentences are either affirmative, negative, interrogative, or negative-interrogative, and consist always of a subject pronoun and an auxiliary and a main verb; the occurrence of a time adverb, a location adverb, or both, is optional. Interrogative sentences are marked by the occurrence of one of the two interrogative adverbs, while negative sentences are marked by the occurrence of the negative particle.

In both affirmative and negative sentences, the subject pronoun may occur in either of two positions: (1) before both the auxiliary and main verb or (2) between the auxiliary and main verb; in interrogative and negative-interrogative sentences, the subject pronoun occurs only between the auxiliary and main verb. Whenever the pronoun precedes both the auxiliary and main verb, the positions of the optional elements are: negative particle before *gɔ* and either a location or a time adverb after the auxiliary and main verb. Whenever the pronoun occurs between the auxiliary and main verb, the positions of the optional elements are: interrogative abverb before everything else; negative particle before *gɔ*; location and time adverbs: (1) any one either before *kan* or after *gɔ* and (2) either one before *kan* and the other after *gɔ*.

Whenever the adverbs of location and time occur in sequence, the location always precedes the time adverb. Although an interrogative adverb is never immediately followed by another adverb, either a time or a location adverb can occur at the end of the same sentence; *nar,* however, does not co-occur with time adverbs, and *vart* does not co-occur with a location adverb.

PROBLEM 46: PALANTLA CHINANTEC[1]

1. kazyéw za	*Someone arrived.*
2. hní kalóˀ haná	*I bathed there.*
3. za kazyéw hayó zyéw	*Someone arrived way over there yesterday.*
4. hala kaŋì za ho	*Someone walked here day before yesterday.*
5. hní kaŋì hala	*I walked here.*
6. hayó kaŋì hní	*I walked way over there.*
7. zyéw kalóˀ hní	*Yesterday I bathed.*
8. ho kazyéw za haná	*Day before yesterday someone arrived there.*
9. za kalóˀ	*Someone bathed.*
10. kazyéw hní hayó ho	*I arrived way over there day before yesterday.*
11. zyéw hní kalóˀ	*Yesterday I bathed.*
12. zyéw haná hní kaŋì	*Yesterday I walked there.*
13. haná za kalóˀ zyéw	*Someone bathed there yesterday.*

But not:

*kazyéw haná za
*za kazyéw zyéw hayó
*hní hala kaŋì
*haná zyéw hní kaŋì

The above sentences are intransitive and either declarative or emphatic, with the subject expressed by a pronoun and the predicate by a verb alone or a verb and one or more adverbs. In declarative sentences the verb precedes the pronoun (and the adverbs follow it); the order of the various elements in emphatic sentences depends on what is being emphasized.

Notice that, except for the following two restrictions, the pronoun, verb, and adverb(s) occur in any order:

(1) The pronoun and verb are always contiguous; i.e. adverbs do not occur between the pronoun and verb regardless of whether the pronoun precedes or follows the verb.

(2) A time adverb precedes a location adverb whenever both occur before the verb, but whenever both occur after the verb, a time adverb follows a location adverb.

[1] A modified version of Problem 93 in W. R. Merrifield, C. M. Naish, C. R. Rensch, and G. Story, *Laboratory Manual for Morphology and Syntax,* Summer Institute of Linguistics, Santa Ana, Calif., 1962.

PROBLEM 47: HUNGARIAN

1. ez az uuj cipøø	*This is the new pair of shoes.*
2. ez a cipøø uuj	*This pair of shoes is new.*
3. ezek az uuj cipøøk	*These are the new pairs of shoes.*
4. ezek a cipøøk uujok	*These pairs of shoes are new.*
5. az az uuj bøørønd	*That is the new suitcase.*
6. az a bøørønd uuj	*That suitcase is new.*
7. azok az uuj bøøröndøk	*Those are the new suitcases.*
8. azok a bøøröndøk uujok	*Those suitcases are new.*
9. ez naǰ soba	*This is a large room.*
10. azok naǰ sobaak	*Those are large rooms.*
11. az uuj kefe	*That is a new brush.*
12. ezek uuj kefeek	*These are new brushes.*
13. a naǰ haaz	*The house is big.*
14. a haaz naǰ	*The house is big.*
15. a naǰ haazok	*The houses are big.*
16. a haazok naǰok	*The houses are big.*
17. az a naǰ haaz	*That is the big house.*
18. az a haaz naǰ	*That house is big.*
19. azok a naǰ haazok	*Those are the big houses.*
20. azok a haazok naǰok	*Those houses are big.*
21. ez a seep keep	*This is the pretty picture.*
22. ez a keep seep	*This picture is pretty.*
23. ezek a seep keepek	*These are the pretty pictures.*
24. ezek a keepek seepek	*These pictures are pretty.*

But not:

*ezek azok seep keepek
*ez a seep keepek
*ezek a seepek keepek
*naǰ a haaz
*haaz a naǰ

The above sentences are copulative and consist of a demonstrative pronoun, which can be said to express the subject; a definite article, which could belong to either the subject or the predicate; and a noun and adjective, which together express the predicate. Although the occurrence of both the demonstrative pronoun and the article is optional, one of them must always occur in a sentence.

A demonstrative pronoun always precedes the other elements in a sentence; the article follows the demonstrative and precedes the noun and adjective, which, in turn, may occur in any order with respect to each other.

Notice that the demonstrative pronoun and the adjective agree in number with the noun but that plurality is overtly expressed in an adjective only when it follows a noun.

Finally, notice the following morphophonemic patterns: (1) the plural suffix is *k* after a stem ending in two (identical) vowels and vowel + *k* otherwise; (2) vowel harmony; and (3) the definite article is *az* before words beginning with a vowel and *a* otherwise.

PROBLEM 48: FRENCH

1. pus ɛž	*Do I push?*
2. ɛskø ž pus	*Do I push?*
3. ɛskø pjɛr pus	*Is Peter pushing?*
4. žø pus	*I push.*
5. ty pus	*You are pushing.*
6. pjɛr pus	*Peter pushes.*
7. ɛskø ty pus	*Are you pushing?*
8. pus ty	*Are you pushing?*
9. ɛsk il pus	*Does he push?*
10. pust il	*Does he push?*
11. žø n pus pa	*I am not pushing.*
12. ty n pus žame	*You never push.*
13. il nø pus pa	*He is not pushing.*
14. ž e puse	*I pushed.*
15. ty a puse	*You pushed.*
16. pjɛr a puse	*Peter pushed.*
17. ɛsk il a puse	*Did he push?*
18. žø n e žame puse	*I never pushed.*
19. ɛž puse	*Did I push?*
20. a ty puse	*Did you push?*
21. at il puse	*Did he push?*
22. žø ve puse	*I'm going to push.*
23. ɛskø ž ve puse	*Am I going to push?*
24. v ɛž puse	*Am I going to push?*
25. žø n ve pa puse	*I am not going to push.*
26. ty va puse	*You are going to push.*
27. ɛskø ty va puse	*Are you going to push?*
28. va ty puse	*Are you going to push?*

29. ty n va pa puse — *You are not going to push.*
30. il va puse — *He is going to push.*
31. vat il puse — *Is he going to push?*
32. ɛsk il va puse — *Is he going to push?*
33. il nø va žame puse — *He is never going to push.*
34. ɛskø ž nø pus pa — *Am I not pushing?*
35. nø pus ɛž pa — *Am I not pushing?*
36. ɛskø ž n e pa puse — *Didn't I push?*
37. n ɛž pa puse — *Didn't I push?*
38. ɛskø ž nø ve žame puse — *Am I never going to push?*
39. nø v ɛž pa puse — *Am I not going to push?*
40. ɛskø ty n pus pas — *Don't you push?*
41. nø pus ty pa — *Don't you push?*
42. ɛskø ty n a pa puse — *Didn't you push?*
43. n a ty žame puse — *Didn't you ever push?*
44. ɛskø ty n va pa puse — *Are you not going to push?*
45. nø va ty pa puse — *Are you not going to push?*
46. ɛsk il nø pus pa — *Isn't he pushing?*
47. nø pust il pa — *Isn't he pushing?*
48. ɛsk il n a pa puse — *Didn't he push?*
49. n at il žame puse — *Didn't he ever push?*
50. ɛsk il nø va pa puse — *Isn't he going to push?*
51. nø vat il pa puse — *Isn't he going to push?*
52. ɛskø pjɛr nø pus pa — *Isn't Peter pushing?*
53. ɛskø pjɛr n a pa puse — *Didn't Peter push?*
54. ɛskø pjɛr nø va pa puse — *Isn't Peter going to push?*

But not:

*pus pjɛr
*a pjɛr pus
*ɛskø nø pus ty pa
*ɛskø pjɛr il nø pus pa
*ɛskø pjɛr nø pust il pa
*nø pus pjɛr pa
*nø pus pa ty
*n a žame ty puse

The above sentences are, like those in Problem 41, intransitive and consist of a subject, expressed by a proper noun or pronoun, and a predicate, expressed by a main verb which, in contrast to Problem 41, is sometimes preceded by an auxiliary verb. The verb may be either present (as in the other French problem), past, or future: the past and future tenses are expressed by the present tense of the auxiliary verbs 'to have' and 'to go,' respectively, followed by the past participle of the main verb (which always ends in *e*); the present tense is expressed by the main verb alone and has no overt affixes signaling either person or tense. The auxiliary verb agrees in person with the subject.

In addition to being intransitive, the above sentences are also either affirmative, negative, interrogative, or negative-interrogative.

In affirmative and negative sentences, as we saw in Problem 41, the subject precedes the predicate, and negative sentences differ from the affirmative only in that they contain the negative particles *nø* ... *pa* or *nø* ... *žame*. When the verb is in the present tense, *nø* occurs before and *pa* or *žame* after the main verb, and in the other two tenses, *nø* occurs before and *pa* or *žame* after the auxiliary verb.

Interrogative sentences are signaled in one of two ways: (1) simply by adding *ɛskø* at the beginning of a sentence or (2) by reversing the order of the subject and predicate; i.e. instead of subject – predicate, the order is predicate – subject, with the subject between the auxiliary and main verb whenever both occur in a sentence.[2] Notice that *ɛskø* occurs in sentences in which the subject is either a noun or pronoun, while the subject – predicate order is reversed only whenever the subject is a pronoun.

The negative-interrogative sentences are signaled in two ways: either (1) by beginning a negative sentence with *ɛskø* or (2) by the following order of elements: either *nø* – main verb – subject – *pa* (or *žame*) or *nø* – auxiliary verb – subject – *pa* (or *žame*) – main verb. As in interrogative sentences, we have (2) only when a pronoun is the subject and (1) when either a name or a pronoun is the subject.

Finally, notice the following morphophonemic patterns:

(1) A sequence of two vowels at morpheme boundaries reduces to the second vowel when the first vowel is any vowel other than *y*, e.g. *ɛž* of sentences 19 and 24.

(2) Whenever the vowel *ø* occurs *after* either (a) any consonant followed by a vowel which is followed by a consonant or (b) a sentence-initial vowel followed by a consonant, the *ø* drops.

(3) The first person pronoun is *ɛž* whenever it is preceded by a consonant or the vowel *e*, but *žø* otherwise.

[2] *ɛskø* is considered a question marker here only for the sake of convenience; in a more comprehensive grammar of French, it might be treated differently (see Solution 67 in Chapter 8). Similarly, the verb 'to go' is considered an auxiliary and the *e* in forms like *puse* 'push' is considered a past participle marker simply for the sake of convenience.

(4) A verb acquires a word-final epenthetic *t* whenever it is followed by the pronoun *il*.

PROBLEM 49: SPANISH

1. yo regalo el libro a el	*I give him the book.*
2. el regala la karta a mi	*He gives me the letter.*
3. yo se lo regalo	*I give it* (masc.) *to him (her).*
4. la mučača me la regala	*The girl gives it* (fem.) *to me.*
5. el le regala el libro	*He gives him (her) the book.*
6. yo me regalo la karta	*I give me the letter.*
7. yo regalo el libro a la mučača	*I give the book to the girl.*
8. el mučačo le regala el libro	*The boy gives her (him) the book.*
9. el lo regala a eya	*He gives it* (masc.) *to her.*
10. el se lo regala	*He gives it* (masc.) *to her (him).*
11. yo le regalo la karta	*I give her (him) the letter.*
12. yo se la regalo	*I give it* (fem.) *to her (him).*
13. el mučačo lo regala a eya	*The boy gives it* (masc.) *to her.*
14. el se lo regala	*He gives it* (masc.) *to him (her).*
15. yo la regalo a el	*I give it* (fem.) *to him.*
16. eya regala el mučačo a la mučača	*She gives the boy to the girl.*
17. el lo regala a mi	*He gives it* (masc.) *to me.*

But not:

*yo lo regalo se
*yo se regalo lo
*el se regala el libro
*el se lo regalo
*yo regalo el libro a le
*yo se el libro regalo
*yo regalo mi a la karta
*el libro regala la karta a mi

These sentences are transitive, with the subject expressed by a pronoun or by a determiner followed by a noun, and the predicate expressed by a verb, a direct object, and an indirect object. Both these types of objects are expressed by either a pronoun or a determiner and a noun, but the subject and indirect object nouns are always animate. The verb agrees in person with the subject; the determiner, which precedes a noun, agrees in gender with it.

Notice that the subject always precedes the predicate, while the order of the objects with regard to the verb varies; i.e. they may occur as follows:

(1) both after the verb in the order direct – indirect;
(2) both before the verb in the order indirect – direct;
(3) direct object before and indirect object after the verb or vice versa.

In (1) above, the direct object is a determiner and a noun, and the indirect object, which is preceded by the animate object marker *a*, is either a pronoun or a determiner and a noun; in (2) both objects are pronouns; and in (3) whichever object precedes the verb is a pronoun, and the one following it is a pronoun if it is the indirect object, but a determiner and a noun if it is the direct object.

Finally, notice the following morphophonemic patterns: (1) the first person pronoun is *yo* whenever it is the subject, *mi* whenever it is an indirect object and occurs immediately after an animate object marker, but *me* when it occurs elsewhere; and (2) the third person pronoun is *el* (masc.) or *eya* (fem.) whenever it is the subject, *se* (masc. and fem.) whenever it is an indirect object and immediately precedes a direct object, but *le* (masc. and fem.) when it occurs elsewhere.

PROBLEM 50: NORTHERN TEPEHUAN[3]

1. koiñši anʌ	*I slept?*
2. koipʌši api	*You slept?*
3. sobiñši anʌ	*I spied?*

[3] A modified version of Problem 95 in W. R. Merrifield, C. M. Naish, C. R. Rensch, and G. Story, *Laboratory Manual for Morphology and Syntax*, Summer Institute of Linguistics, Santa Ana, Calif., 1962.

4. sobipʌši api	*You spied?*
5. maikoipʌši api	*You didn't sleep?*
6. maisobipʌši api	*You didn't spy?*
7. apipʌši koi	*You slept?*
8. apipʌši sobi	*You spied?*
9. apipʌši maikoi	*You didn't sleep?*
10. apipʌši maisobi	*You didn't spy?*
11. maitapʌši koi api	*You didn't sleep?*
12. maitapʌši sobi api	*You didn't spy?*

But not:

*koiñši api
*koipʌši anʌ
*koiñši
*pʌši koi
*api pʌši
*mai pʌši koi api

Additional information:
ñ and *pʌ* are person markers; *ši* is a question marker.

The above sentences are interrogative; some, in addition, are either negative or emphatic, or negative – emphatic. The obligatory elements in these sentences are a subject pronoun, a verb stem, a person marker, and a question marker *(ši)*, while the optional elements are a negative particle *(mai)* and a "verb emphasizer" *(ta)*.

In interrogative and negative-interrogative sentences, the verb precedes the subject and the order of the elements is: *(mai)* – verb stem – person marker – *ši* – pronoun (with a word division between *ši* and the pronoun).

In both emphatic and negative-emphatic sentences, when the subject is emphasized, the verb follows the subject and the order of elements is: pronoun – person marker – *ši* – *(mai)* – verb stem (with a word division between *ši* and *mai*, or between *ši* and verb stem if *mai* does not occur). When the verb is emphasized, the order of elements is: *mai* – *ta* – person marker – *ši* – verb stem – pronoun (with word divisions between *ši* and the verb stem and between the verb stem and pronoun).

Finally, notice that whether the person marker should be considered an affix of the pronoun or of the verb cannot be determined from the data.

6.2 SOLUTIONS[4]

SOLUTION 40: ROGLAI

1. $S \rightarrow Pron + VP$
2. $VP \rightarrow V(Adv)$
3. $Pron \rightarrow$ *ñu*
4. $V \rightarrow$ *naw, pə*
5. $Adv \rightarrow$ *ata, suka*
6. Topt exclamation

$$Pron + VP \Rightarrow VP + Pron$$

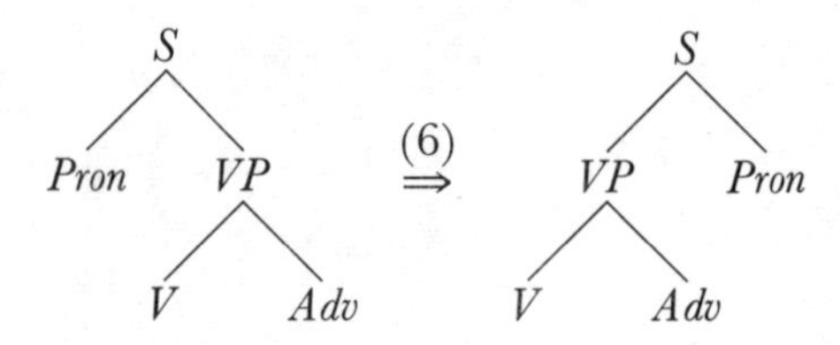

SOLUTION 41: FRENCH

Solution A (Objectionable)

1. $S \rightarrow NP + VP$
2. $NP \rightarrow Name, Pron$
3. $VP \rightarrow (Neg)V$
4. $Neg \rightarrow Ng + Prt$
5. $Ng \rightarrow n$
6. $Prt \rightarrow$ *pa*
7. $V \rightarrow$ *pus, parl*
8. $Name \rightarrow$ *pjɛr, mari*
9. $Pron \rightarrow$ *žø, ty*
10. Tob

$$X + Prt + V \Rightarrow X + V + Prt$$

[4] In this and the following chapters, one or more P-markers accompany some of the solutions. In general, only as much of a P-marker is given as is necessary to illustrate the transformations in question. The number in parentheses above the arrow indicates the rule applied to derive the following P-marker; the head of the arrow indicates that the following P-marker is derived from the P-marker that precedes the tail of the arrow.

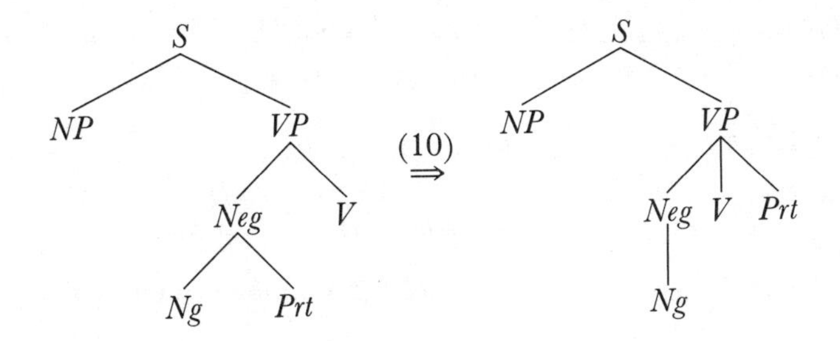

Solution B

1–2. Same as in Solution 41A
3. $VP \rightarrow (Neg + Prt)V$
4. $Neg \rightarrow n$
5. $Prt \rightarrow pa$
6–8. Same as rules (7)–(9) of Solution 41A
9. Tob
$$X + Prt + V \Rightarrow X + V + Prt$$

S
NP VP
Neg Prt V
(9) ⇒
S
NP VP
Neg V Prt

SOLUTION 42: ENGLISH

1. $S \rightarrow NP + VP$
2. $VP \rightarrow Vb + NP$
3. $Vb \rightarrow \begin{Bmatrix} Vtc + Prt \\ Vtr \end{Bmatrix}$
4. $NP \rightarrow \begin{Bmatrix} Det + N \\ Pron \end{Bmatrix}$
5. $Pron \rightarrow \begin{Bmatrix} he \;/\; \#\text{—} \\ him \end{Bmatrix}$
6. $Det \rightarrow$ *the*
7. $N \rightarrow$ *policeman, thief, lawyer*
8. $Vtc \rightarrow$ *brought, took*

9. $Prt \rightarrow$ *in, out*
10. $Vtr \rightarrow$ *brought, took, hurt, looked at, talked about*
11. Tob
    $Vtc + Prt + Pron \Rightarrow Vtc + Pron + Prt$
12. Topt
    $Vtc + Prt + Det + N \Rightarrow Vtc + Det + N + Prt$

or, preferably, rules (11) and (12) can be combined as follows:

11′. T
    $Vtc + Prt + NP \Rightarrow Vtc + NP + Prt$
    obligatory if *NP* is *Pron* and optional otherwise

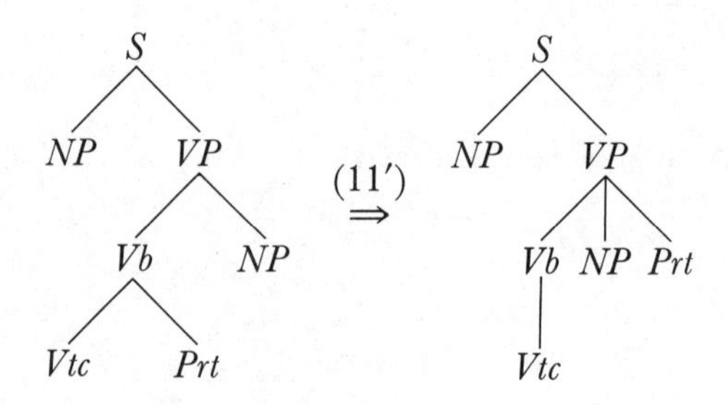

SOLUTION 43: INDONESIAN

1. $S \rightarrow NP + VP(Adv)$
2. $Adv \rightarrow \begin{Bmatrix} Loc + Tm \\ Ad \end{Bmatrix}$
3. $VP \rightarrow V + NP$
4. $NP \rightarrow \begin{Bmatrix} N + Det \,/\, \_V \\ N \end{Bmatrix}$
5. $N \rightarrow \begin{Bmatrix} Nan \,/\, \_Det \\ Nin \end{Bmatrix}$
6. $Det \rightarrow$ *itu*
7. $Nan \rightarrow$ *guru*
8. $Nin \rightarrow$ *səmaŋka*
9. $V \rightarrow$ *makan*
10. $Loc \rightarrow$ *disini*
11. $Tm \rightarrow$ *kamarin*
12. $Ad \rightarrow$ *rupaña*

13. Topt

$$NP + VP(Adv) \Rightarrow VP + NP(Adv)$$

14. Topt

$$X + Y + Adv \Rightarrow \begin{Bmatrix} Adv + X + Y \\ X + Adv + Y \end{Bmatrix}$$

$X = NP$ or VP; $Y = NP$ or VP

or, preferably, rules (13) and (14) may be combined as follows:

13′. Topt

$$W + X + Y + Z \Rightarrow W + Y + X + Z$$

$X = N + Det$ or VP or Adv; $Y = N + Det$ or VP or Adv

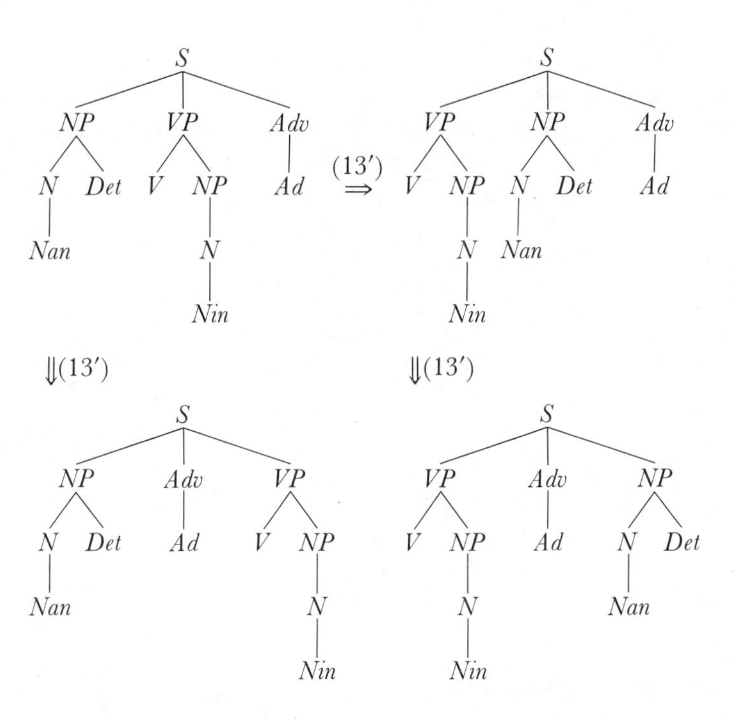

SOLUTION 44: MODERN GREEK

Solution A

Add to Solution 38 the following two rules *after* rule (23) (i.e. after the agreement rule), and then renumber the remaining rules:

(new) 24. Topt question

$$NP + VP \Rightarrow VP + NP$$

(new) 25. Topt emphatic question

$$\begin{bmatrix} Vtr \\ Vcop \end{bmatrix} X + NP \Rightarrow X \begin{bmatrix} Vtr \\ Vcop \end{bmatrix} NP$$

Solution B

(a) Replace the first five rules of Solution 38 with the following:

1. $S \rightarrow NP + VP$
2. $VP \rightarrow Vb + Pred$
3. $Vb \rightarrow \begin{Bmatrix} Vcop \\ Vtr \end{Bmatrix} Afv$
4. $Pred \rightarrow \begin{Bmatrix} Adj \;/\; Vcop + Afv\_\_ \\ NP \end{Bmatrix}$
5. $Adj \rightarrow A$

(b) Add to the solution thus modified the following two rules *after* rule (23) and renumber the rules:

(new) 24. Topt question

$$NP + VP \Rightarrow VP + NP$$

(new) 25. Topt emphatic question

$$Vb + Pred + NP \Rightarrow Pred + Vb + NP$$

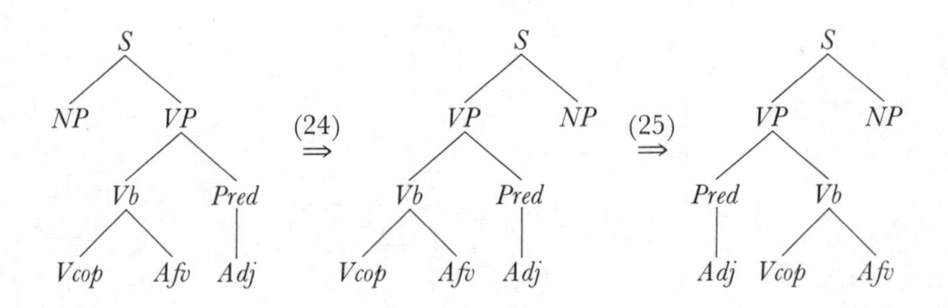

SOLUTION 45: SWEDISH

Solution A (Objectionable)

(a)
1. $S \rightarrow Pron + VP$
2. $VP \rightarrow Vb(Adv)$
3. $Adv \rightarrow (Loc)(Tm)$
4. $Vb \rightarrow Aux(Neg)V$

. . .

(b) 1. $S \rightarrow S_1(Adv)$
2. $S_1 \rightarrow Pron + VP$
3. $VP \rightarrow Aux + Vb$
4. $Vb \rightarrow (Neg)V$

. . .

(c) 1. $S \rightarrow Pron + VP(Adv)$
2. $VP \rightarrow Aux + Vb$
3. $Vb \rightarrow (Neg)V$

. . .

Solution B

1. $S \rightarrow Pron + VP(Loc)(Tm)$
2. $VP \rightarrow Aux(Neg)V$
3. $Pron \rightarrow$ *jag*
4. $Aux \rightarrow$ *kan*
5. $Neg \rightarrow$ *inte*
6. $V \rightarrow$ *gɔ*
7. $Loc \rightarrow$ *hem*
8. $Tm \rightarrow$ *imorgon, nu*
9. Topt
$$X + Aux + Y \Rightarrow Aux + X + Y$$
10. Topt
$$\#Aux + X\begin{bmatrix} Tm \\ Loc \end{bmatrix}Y \Rightarrow \#\begin{bmatrix} Tm \\ Loc \end{bmatrix}Aux + X + Y$$
11. Topt
$$\begin{bmatrix} Loc \\ Tm \end{bmatrix}Aux + X \Rightarrow \begin{bmatrix} vart \\ nar \end{bmatrix}Aux + X$$

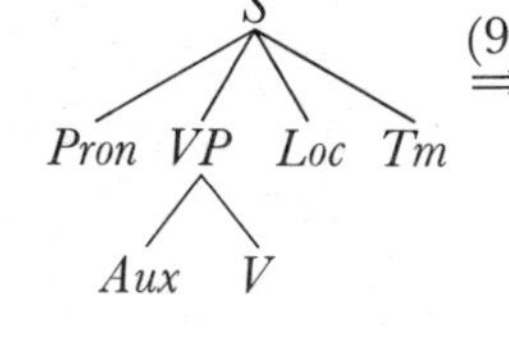
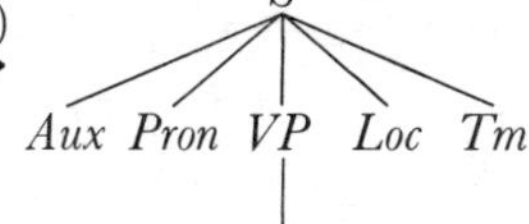
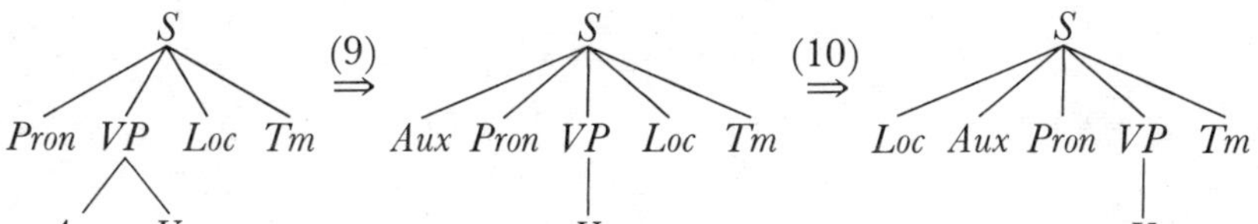

⇓(10)

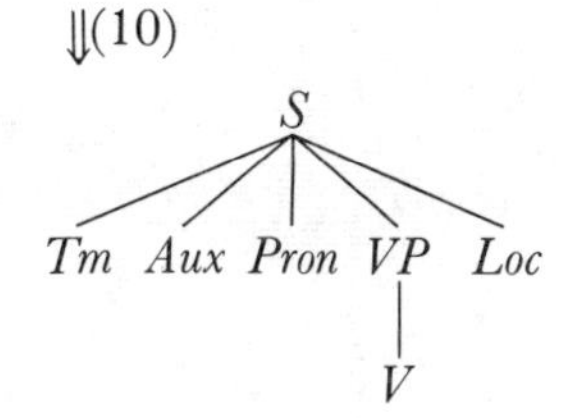

Solution C

1–6. Same as in Solution 45B

7. $Tm \rightarrow imorgon, nu, nar$

8. $Loc \rightarrow \begin{Bmatrix} hem\ /\ \_\_nar \\ hem \\ vart \end{Bmatrix}$

9. T question

$$Pron + Aux + X \Rightarrow Aux + Pron + X$$

obligatory if $X = W \begin{Bmatrix} vart \\ nar \end{Bmatrix} Y$ and optional otherwise

10. T

$$X \begin{bmatrix} Tm \\ Loc \end{bmatrix} Y \Rightarrow \begin{bmatrix} Tm \\ Loc \end{bmatrix} X + Y$$

obligatory if $X = \#Aux + W$ and $Tm = nar$ or $Loc = vart$

optional if $X \neq \#Aux + W$ and $Tm \neq nar$ or $Loc \neq vart$

11. Tob

$$X + Y + Aux + Z \Rightarrow X + Aux + Y + Z$$

$$X \text{ and } Y \neq null$$

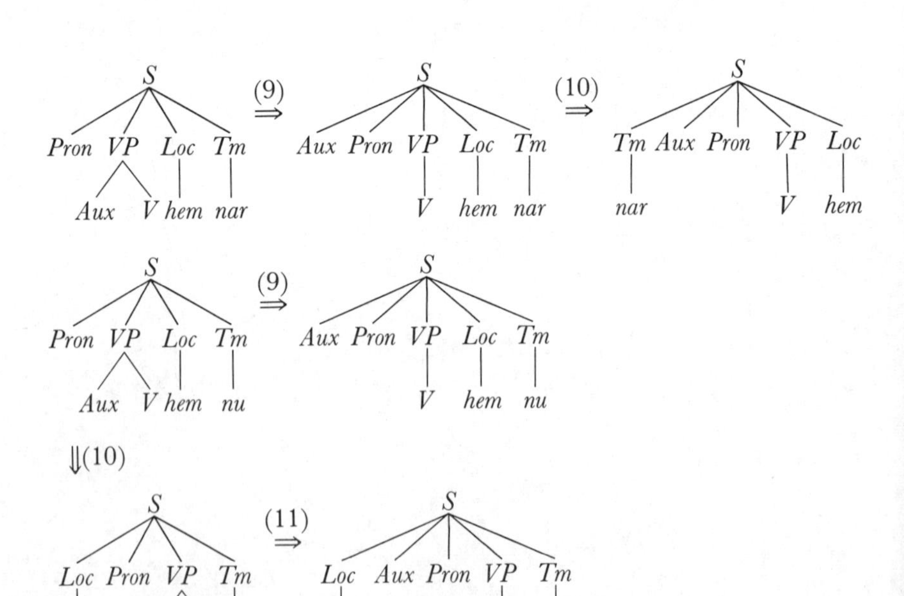

SOLUTION 46: PALANTLA CHINANTEC

1. $S \rightarrow V + Pron(Loc)(Tm)$
2. $Tm \rightarrow$ *zyéw, ho*
3. $Loc \rightarrow$ *haná, hayó, hala*
4. $V \rightarrow$ *kazyéw, kalóˀ, kaŋì*
5. $Pron \rightarrow$ *za, hní*
6. Topt subject emphasis
   $V + Pron + X \Rightarrow Pron + V + X$
7. Topt location emphasis
   $X + Loc + Y \Rightarrow Loc + X + Y$
8. Topt time emphasis
   $X + Tm \Rightarrow Tm + X$

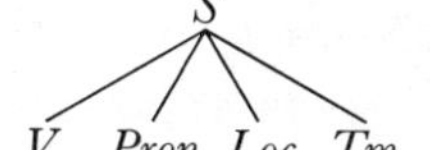

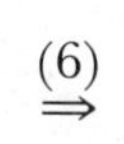

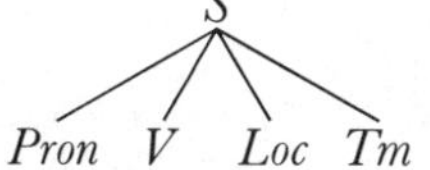

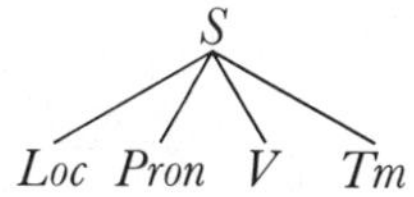

⇓(8)

S
Tm V Pron Loc

⇓(8)

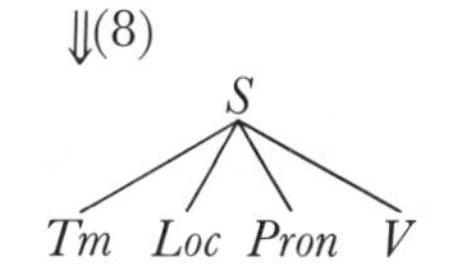

SOLUTION 47: HUNGARIAN[5]

1. $S \rightarrow Pron + Pred$
2. $Pred \rightarrow (Det)NP$
3. $NP \rightarrow N + Adj$
4. $N \rightarrow Ns(Pl)$
5. $Pron \rightarrow Pr$
6. $Adj \rightarrow A$
7. $Ns \rightarrow$ *cipøø, bøørønd, soba, haaz, keep, kefe*
8. $A \rightarrow$ *uuj, naǰ, seep*
9. $Pr \rightarrow$ *ez, az*
10. $Det \rightarrow$ *aZ*
11. $Pl \rightarrow$ *k*
12. Tob agreement
    $Pr - X - Ns + Pl + A \Rightarrow$
    $Pr + Pl - X - Ns + Pl + A + Pl$

[5] Compare the morphophonemic rules of this solution with those of Solution 11 in 3.3.

13. Topt
$$X + N + A(Pl) \Rightarrow X + A + N$$
14. Topt
$$Pron + Det + NP \Rightarrow Det + NP$$
15. Tob
$$\begin{bmatrix} Vw_1(C) \\ Vw_2C \\ CVw_3 \end{bmatrix} k \Rightarrow \begin{bmatrix} Vw_1(C)Vw_1 \\ Vw_2Co \\ CVw_3Vw_3 \end{bmatrix} k$$
Vw_1 = any front vowel; Vw_2 = any central or back vowel
Vw_3 = any central vowel; C = any consonant or string of consonants

16. Tob
$$Z\begin{bmatrix} C \\ Vw \end{bmatrix} \Rightarrow \begin{bmatrix} \emptyset \\ z \end{bmatrix}\begin{bmatrix} C \\ Vw \end{bmatrix}$$
17. Tob
$$Vw_1Vw_1Vw_1 \Rightarrow Vw_1Vw_1$$

SOLUTION 48: FRENCH

1. $S \rightarrow (QM)NP + VP$
2. $NP \rightarrow \begin{Bmatrix} Name \\ Pron \end{Bmatrix} Per$
3. $Per \rightarrow \begin{Bmatrix} Non\text{-}Fir \;/\; Name\_\_ \\ Fir \\ Non\text{-}Fir \end{Bmatrix}$
4. $VP \rightarrow (Neg + Prt)(Aux)V$
5. $Aux \rightarrow M + e$
6. $M \rightarrow$ *al, av*
7. $QM \rightarrow$ *ɛskø*
8. $Name \rightarrow$ *pjɛr*
9. $Neg \rightarrow$ *nø*
10. $Prt \rightarrow$ *pa, žame*
11. $V \rightarrow$ *pus*
12. Tob agreement
$$X + Per - Y - M \Rightarrow X + Per - Y - Per + M$$
13. Tob
$$Neg + Prt\begin{bmatrix} V \\ Aux \end{bmatrix}X \Rightarrow Neg\begin{bmatrix} V \\ Aux \end{bmatrix}Prt + X$$

14. Topt question

$$QM + Pron + Per + X \begin{bmatrix} V \\ Aux \end{bmatrix} Y \Rightarrow X \begin{bmatrix} V \\ Aux \end{bmatrix} Pron + Per + Y$$

$$X \neq Aux$$

15. Tob

$$Xe]_{Aux} + Y + V \Rightarrow X]_{Aux} + Y + V + e$$

16. Tob

$$Pron \begin{bmatrix} Fir \\ Non\text{-}Fir \end{bmatrix} \Rightarrow \begin{bmatrix} \check{z}ø \\ \begin{Bmatrix} ty \\ il \end{Bmatrix} \end{bmatrix}$$

17. Tob

$$\begin{bmatrix} Fir \\ Non\text{-}Fir \end{bmatrix} al \Rightarrow v \begin{bmatrix} e \\ a \end{bmatrix}$$

18. Tob

$$\begin{bmatrix} Fir \\ Non\text{-}Fir \end{bmatrix} av \Rightarrow \begin{bmatrix} e \\ a \end{bmatrix}$$

19. Tob

$$Per \Rightarrow \emptyset$$

20. Tob

$$X]_{Aux,V} + il \Rightarrow Xt]_{Aux,V} + il$$

21. Tob

$$CVwCø \Rightarrow CVwC$$

22. Tob

$$\begin{bmatrix} C \\ e \end{bmatrix} + \check{z}ø \Rightarrow \begin{bmatrix} C \\ e \end{bmatrix} + \varepsilon\check{z}$$

23. Tob

$$Vw_1 + Vw_2 \Rightarrow Vw_2$$
$$Vw_1 \neq y$$

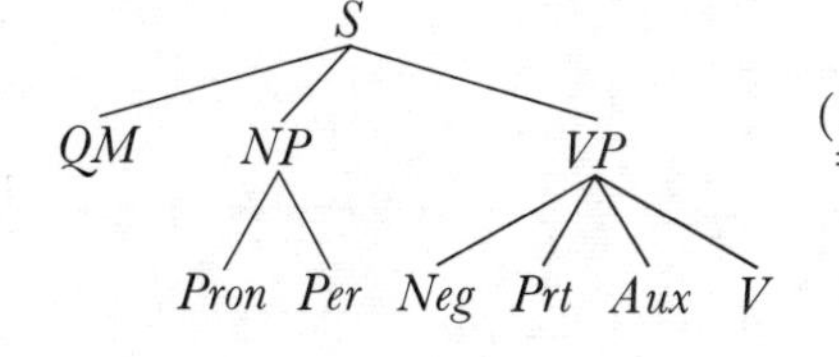

(13) ⇒

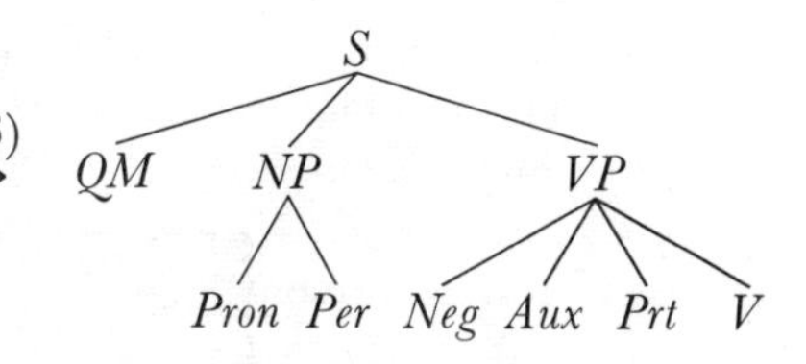

⇓(14)

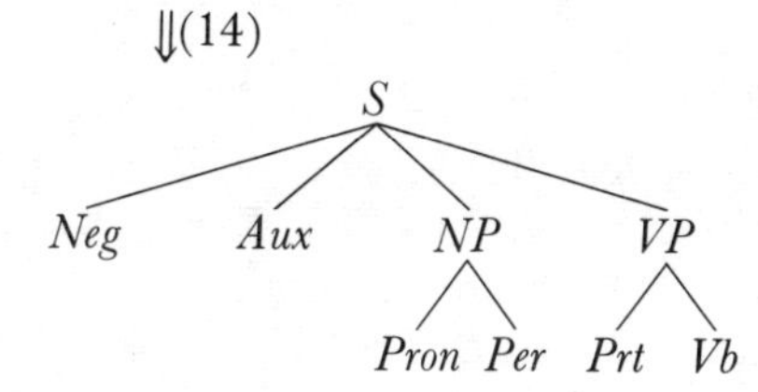

SOLUTION 49: SPANISH

1. $S \rightarrow NP + VP$
2. $VP \rightarrow V + NP + IO$
3. $V \rightarrow Vs$
4. $IO \rightarrow Prep + NP$
5. $NP \rightarrow \begin{Bmatrix} Det + N \\ Pron \end{Bmatrix}$
6. $Det \rightarrow D$
7. $N \rightarrow Ns + G + Per$
8. $Pron \rightarrow Pr + G + Per$
9. $Per \rightarrow \begin{Bmatrix} Thi \,/ \begin{Bmatrix} Ns + G\_\_ \\ Vs + Pr + G\_\_ \end{Bmatrix} \\ Fir \\ Thi \end{Bmatrix}$
10. $Ns \rightarrow \begin{Bmatrix} Nan \,/ \begin{Bmatrix} \#D\_\_ \\ Prep + D\_\_ \end{Bmatrix} \\ Nan \\ Nin \end{Bmatrix}$
11. $G \rightarrow M, F$
12. $Nan \rightarrow \begin{Bmatrix} Nman \,/ \,\_\_M \\ Nfan \end{Bmatrix}$
13. $Nin \rightarrow \begin{Bmatrix} Nmin \,/ \,\_\_M \\ Nfin \end{Bmatrix}$
14. $M \rightarrow o$
15. $F \rightarrow a$
16. $D \rightarrow l$
17. $Prep \rightarrow a$
18. $Nman \rightarrow mučač$
19. $Nmin \rightarrow libr$
20. $Nfan \rightarrow mučač$
21. $Nfin \rightarrow kart$
22. $Vs \rightarrow regal$
23. Tob agreement
    $X - D - Ns + G - Y \Rightarrow X - D + G - Ns + G - Y$
24. Tob agreement
    $X + Per - Vs - Y \Rightarrow X + Per - Vs + Per - Y$
25. Topt
    $X - V + NP + Prep + Pron \Rightarrow X - K + Pron + V + NP$
26. Tob
    $X - V + Pron + Y \Rightarrow X - R + Pron + V + Y$
27. Tob
    $D + M \Rightarrow el$

28. Tob

$$Vs\begin{bmatrix}Fir\\Thi\end{bmatrix} \Rightarrow Vs\begin{bmatrix}o\\a\end{bmatrix}$$

29. Tob

$$K + Pr + G + Thi \Rightarrow \begin{Bmatrix}se\ /\ \_\_R\\le\end{Bmatrix}$$

30. Tob

$$K + Pr + G + Fir \Rightarrow me$$

31. Tob

$$R + Pr\begin{bmatrix}M\\F\end{bmatrix}Thi \Rightarrow \begin{bmatrix}lo\\la\end{bmatrix}$$

32. Tob

$$Pr\begin{bmatrix}M\\F\end{bmatrix}Thi \Rightarrow \begin{bmatrix}el\\eya\end{bmatrix}$$

33. Tob

$$Pr + G + Fir \Rightarrow \begin{Bmatrix}mi\ /\ Prep\_\_\\yo\end{Bmatrix}$$

34. Tob

$$Per \Rightarrow \emptyset$$

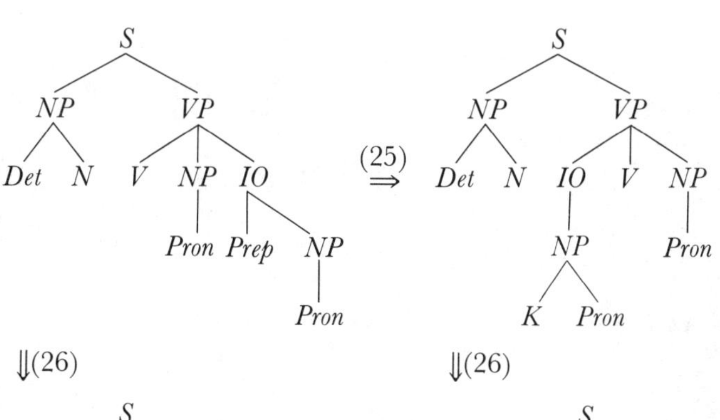

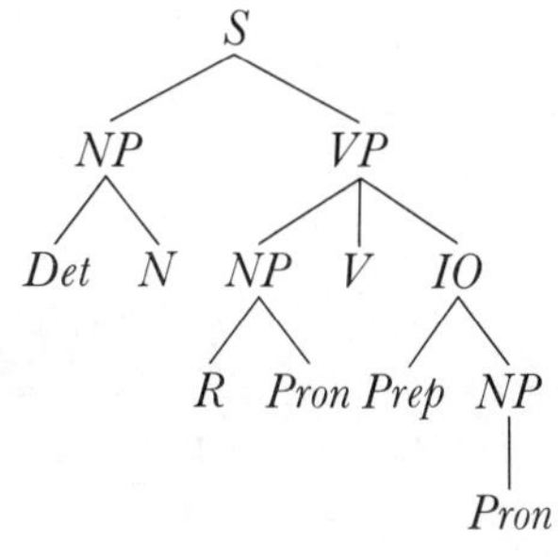

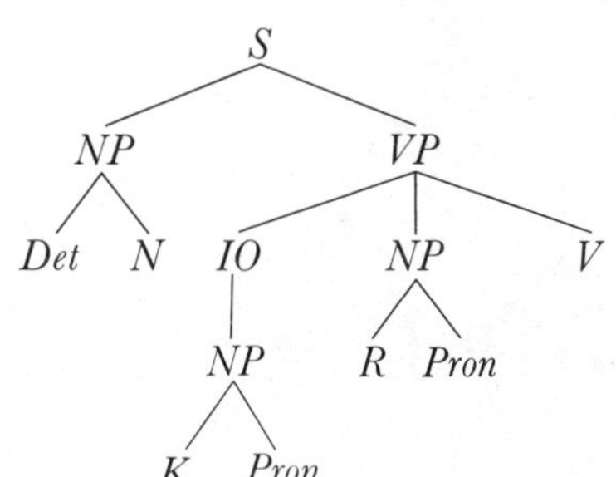

SOLUTION 50: NORTHERN TEPEHUAN

Solution A (Objectionable)

1. $S \rightarrow NP + Vb$
2. $NP \rightarrow Pron + QM$

   or, alternatively,

   (a) 1′. $S \rightarrow VP + Pron$
   2′. $VP \rightarrow Vb + QM$
   (b) 1″. $S \rightarrow NP + VP$
   2″. $VP \rightarrow QM + Vb$
3. $Vb \rightarrow (Neg)V$
4. $Pron \rightarrow Pr + PM$
5. $PM \rightarrow$ *ñ, pʌ*
6. $Pr \rightarrow \left\{\begin{array}{l} an\Lambda \;/\; \_\tilde{n} \\ api \end{array}\right\}$
7. $QM \rightarrow$ *ši*
8. $Neg \rightarrow$ *mai*
9. $V \rightarrow$ *koi, sobi*
10. Topt
    $Pr + X + Vb \Rightarrow Vb + X + Pr$
11. Topt
    $mai - V + PM + QM + Pr \Rightarrow$
    $maita - PM + QM + V + Pr$

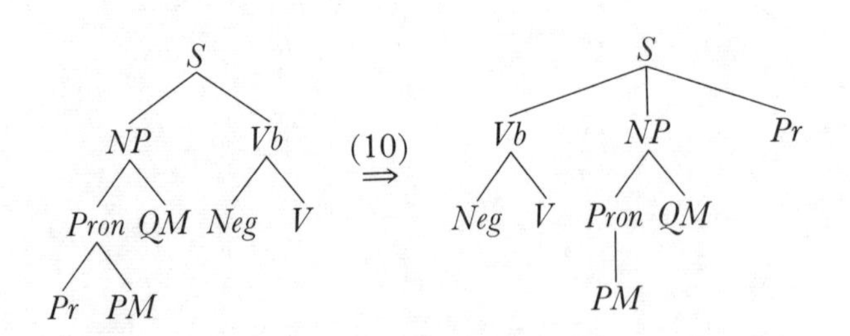

Solution B

1. $S \rightarrow Pron + PM + QM + Vb$

   or, alternatively,

   1′. $S \rightarrow Pron + Nuc + Vb$
   2′. $Nuc \rightarrow PM + QM$

2. $Vb \rightarrow (Neg)V$

3–7. Same as rules (5)–(9) of Solution 50A, except that rule (4) should expand *Pron* and not *Pr.*

8. Topt

$$X + Vb \Rightarrow Vb + X$$

9. Topt

$$X + Neg + Y \Rightarrow Neg + X + Y$$

10. Tob

$$X + Pron + Y \Rightarrow X + Y + Pron \quad X \neq null$$

11. Tob

$$mai + PM + X \Rightarrow maita + PM + X$$

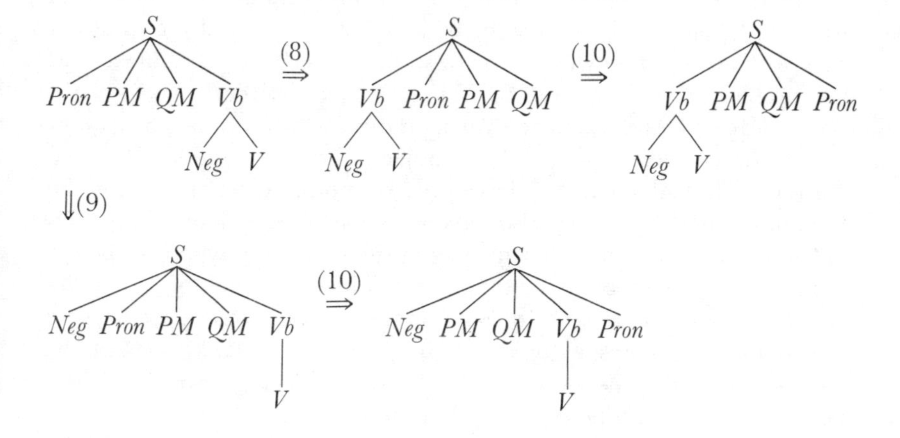

6.3 DISCUSSION OF SOLUTIONS

6.3.1 Deciding which sentences to postulate as kernels

Since each problem in this chapter contains sentences that are related to each other, the first decision to be made is which sentences to consider kernel and which to consider derived. The two criteria for making this decision, as stated in 2.4, are: (1) those sentences which cannot be derived from another sentence are considered kernels while those sentences that can be derived from another sentence are considered derived and (2) if two or more sentences can be derived from each other, that sentence is postulated as kernel which will yield the simpler solution.

Because the problems in this chapter are restricted, there are few examples of the first criterion and even fewer of the second; i.e. for the most part, the resulting solutions were equally simple regardless of which sentences were postulated as kernel. However, let us go over those solutions in which these criteria determined which sentences to consider kernel and which to consider derived.

(1) **At least one sentence cannot be derived from the other(s).** This is clearly the case only in Problems 48 (French) and 49 (Spanish). In Problem 48 affirmative sentences and interrogative sentences which have a pronoun as subject and a reversal of the "affirmative order" are related.[6] Since the affirmative sentences may have either a pronoun or a noun as the subject, while the type of interrogatives in question may have only a pronoun as the subject, the former must be considered kernel; otherwise affirmative sentences with a noun as subject would not be generated.

In Problem 49 there are four types of sentences that can be said to be related; they are based on the order of the functional groupings in them and are the following: type *a*: subject – verb – direct object – indirect object; type *b*: subject – indirect object – direct object – verb; type *c*: subject – direct object – verb – indirect object; and type *d*: subject – indirect object – verb – direct object. Type *b* sentences cannot be considered kernel since they have only pronouns as objects, while the remaining three types may also have nouns as objects. Thus, if type *b* is postulated as kernel, not all sentences of the remaining types can be derived from it. Types *c* and *d* cannot be considered kernel for essentially the same reason: type *c* has only animate nouns as objects and type *d* only inanimate nouns as objects, while type *a* has both; not all the sentences of type *a*, therefore, can be derived from either *c* or *d*. Clearly, then, only type *a* can be considered kernel sentences.

(2) **Simplicity.** The only clear-cut case where simplicity is the decisive factor in determining which sentences to postulate as kernel is in the solution for Problem 47 (Hungarian). In this problem those sentences in which the adjective precedes the noun can be derived from those in which it follows the noun, and vice versa. The latter sentences are postulated as kernel on the basis of economy: this alternative requires one less rule than the other, namely, that which would otherwise be necessary to delete the plural morpheme whenever the adjective precedes the noun.

6.3.2 Objectionable solutions

The primary reason the "objectionable" solutions for Problems 41 (French), 45 (Swedish), and 50 (Tepehuan) are rejected is that they fail

[6] *ɛskø*-type interrogative sentences are not included in this consideration since they have the same underlying structure as the affirmative sentences.

to meet one of the basic requirements of a grammar; namely, they fail to assign, on the basis of the data given, a reasonable structure to the sentences they generate. More specifically, the constituent structure assigned to sentences by the P-rules in these solutions is unreasonable (and, consequently, so is that assigned by the T-rules). What in particular is unreasonable about them will now be pointed out, while what is considered reasonable, and why, is discussed in 6.3.3.

Solution 41A is objectionable because it postulates that the sequence of the two negative particles is a *Neg,* but *Neg* is not used in any other rule of the solution and is thus superfluous.

P-rules (a) of Solution 45A are objectionable because they postulate an unreasonable analysis for both the adverbs and the auxiliary: not only is the constituent-type *Adv* superfluous but, in addition, it is postulated to be a constituent of *VP* instead of *S*; and the auxiliary is postulated to be a constituent of *Vb* instead of *VP*. P-rules (b) overcome the latter objection but still are objectionable, because like (a) they postulate the superfluous *Adv;* and in addition they postulate two other superfluous constituent-types, namely, S_1 and *Vb*. Although P-rules (c) do not postulate that the sequence *Pron* + *VP* is a constituent-type, they are objectionable because, like P-rules (a) and (b), they postulate a superfluous *Adv* and a superfluous *Vb*.

Solution 50A is objectionable because the question and person markers in all the alternatives for the first two rules are not postulated to be constituents of *S*; consequently the permutation rules in this solution will assign an unreasonable derived constituent structure, e.g. rules (10) and (11).

6.3.3 Justifications for postulating constituent-types

A legitimate question at this point is: How do we know what is a reasonable constituent structure to postulate for kernel sentences? Put differently, we may ask: Just what is the justification for the constituent-types (nodes in the P-markers) postulated by our P-rules? This question has been raised several times and the answer given was, in brief: Any constituent-type is postulated that will result in a simplification of the grammar. We shall now see that by this we mean the transformational part of the grammar.

With regard to lower order constituent-types, or what are traditionally called "morpheme classes," the particular consideration is whether or not the postulation of a constituent-type will simplify the T-rules (and the morphophonemic rules) of the grammar. For example, one consequence of not postulating lower order constituent-types (such as *N*, *V*, and *Nu*) in a grammar is that in order to specify agreement in number between a morpheme that may function as the subject and any morpheme that may function as the verb of a sentence, we would have to write as many T-rules as there are such morphemes. In other words, there would be no way to make the generalization that subject nouns and verbs agree in number.

With regard to higher order constituent-types, or what are traditionally called "constitutes," the particular consideration is again whether or not the postulation of a constituent-type will simplify the transformational part of the grammar. For example, the reason given in point (2) of 5.3.3 for postulating in Solution 38 (Modern Greek) that the sequence of categories gender, case, and number is an *Afn* is that the two agreement rules were thus simplified; i.e. *Afn* rather than $G + Ca + Nu$ is used in them. Similarly, a reason for postulating in a grammar of English that a sequence of a determiner plus a noun is an *NP* is that some T-rules are simplified by postulating this constituent-type, e.g. the rule which shifts a determiner and (object) noun to sentence-initial position to form passives. In addition, by postulating that *Pron* also is an *NP*, we further simplify the grammar in that these T-rules thus refer to both $Det + N$ and *Pron*; i.e. the grammar is simplified in that (a) each change that applies to both $Det + N$ and *Pron* is specified in the simplest way, i.e. with *NP* instead of $\left\{\begin{matrix} Det + N \\ Pron \end{matrix}\right\}$, and (b) we are thereby making the generalization that a pronoun and a sequence of a determiner plus a noun behave alike in a number of circumstances.

Whether or not the postulation of a lower order constituent-type will simplify a grammar (i.e. whether it will be "useful") usually is more obvious than whether or not we should postulate a higher order constituent-type; that is, it is easier to decide, in general, whether, for example, *N* should be postulated in a grammar than to decide whether the sequence $Neg + V$ should be postulated to be a *VP*. Therefore, in our discussion of the solutions in this chapter, we shall be primarily concerned with why a sequence of two or more lower order constituents is postulated to be a higher order constituent-type, or, in traditional terminology, we shall be concerned with the justification for making one immediate constituent cut rather than another.

As was mentioned in 2.4, the most profitable way to find clues concerning what constituent structure to postulate for kernel sentences is to study how kernels behave under transformation. The most relevant data for the problems in this chapter were the permutation patterns of related sentences. It must be remembered, however, that any decisions made on the basis of permutation alone are tentative and should be supported (or may even be changed) when we observe how kernels behave under various other transformations.

A sequence of two or more constituents may be postulated to be a constituent-type if there are a number of grammatical situations in which it behaves as a group. The following may serve as a good rule of thumb for deciding what constitutes behaving as a group *under permutation*: two or more constituents can be considered to "behave as a group" if they are shifted together to precede or follow other constituent-types, e.g. the noun phrases in Problem 43 (Indonesian).

In the preceding solutions, whenever a sequence of two or more constituents *always* behaved as a group under permutation, it was postulated to be a constituent-type, say *A*, since we then knew that *A* could be used to simplify the transformational part of the grammar. Whenever a sequence of constituents *sometimes* behaved as a group under permutation, whether or not it was postulated to be a constituent-type, say *B*, was determined on the basis of whether postulating *B* would be useful in the transformational part of the grammar. Now for some examples.

First, even from data as restricted as Problems 40 (Roglai) and 41 (French), we have grounds for deciding whether or not to postulate certain constituent-types in the solutions for these problems. That is, we have grounds for deciding why a sequence of a verb and an adverb should be postulated to be a constituent-type *(VP)* in Solution 40, and why a sequence of the negative particles should not be postulated as a constituent-type *(Neg)* in Solution 41A. These grounds are that: (1) in the Roglai problem the verb and adverb always either both precede or both follow the pronoun; and (2) in the French problem, while (a) there is no evidence that the negative particles ever function as a group, (b) there is some evidence that they do not, namely, one particle always remains constant while the other is shifted; thus rule (6) of Solution 40 is simplified by the use of *VP*, but there is no use for *Neg* in Solution 41A.

In the solution for Problem 43 (Indonesian) six types of lower order constituents are postulated: *N* (a subject or object noun), *Det, V, Loc, Tm,* and *Ad* (the last three are adverbs). Notice that it is because the sequence of a determiner and a noun on the one hand, and the verb and its object on the other, behave, respectively, as a group under a permutation transformation that this solution can be simplified by postulating that they are constituents of the types *NP* and *VP* respectively. That is to say, the number of symbols in the permutation rules thus are fewer than if we did not postulate *NP* and *VP*. As for the adverbs, since two (mutually dependent) adverbs are mutually exclusive with the third, and the adverbs occur in various positions within a sentence, we immediately know that it will simplify our solution to have an *Adv* constituent-type.

We now ask whether there are any other relationships we can postulate between any of the three types of constituents we have thus far decided to postulate: *NP, VP,* and *Adv*. Note that there are only two possibilities, namely, either that all three constituent-types function independently with respect to each other or that two of them function as a group with respect to the third. The fact that any one of the three can be permuted with either of the other two constituent-types clearly establishes that no two function as a group with respect to the third and that there is no need for the introduction of another constituent-type. We therefore postulate that $NP + VP + Adv$ is an *S*. In other words, on the basis of permutational evidence alone, there is no justification for any further grouping among the constituents $NP + VP + Adv$. It should be noted, however, that there might be good evidence on other grounds for postulating, for example, that $NP + VP$ is an S_1 constituent-type and then that S_1 and *Adv* are the constituents of *S*. The data given also do not provide any insights as to what the position of *Adv* should be relative to the other constituents of *S* in the phrase structure grammar, nor would any position postulated affect the simplicity of the grammar in any way; therefore, whichever position is postulated is equally acceptable.

In Solution 46 (Palantla Chinantec) four types of constituents are postulated, *Pron, V, Loc,* and *Tm*. In view of the fact that in Solution 43 (Indonesian) the adverbs were postulated to be constituents of the type *Adv,* one may wonder why the adverbs are not treated similarly in this solution. The reason for this is that no use can be made of such a constituent-type in this solution. Notice that unlike the adverbs in the Indonesian problem, the two types of adverbs in Problem 46 co-occur. This means that we do not automatically know whether any rules will be simplified by postulating an *Adv* constituent-type. The decisive factor is how *Tm* and *Loc* behave under permutation: because either type of adverb can be shifted under any circumstances without the other, these adverbs do not behave as a group under permutation. Since this is the case, *Adv* could not be used to simplify any transformations and therefore is not postulated in the phrase structure part of the grammar. Consequently the occurrence of both types of adverbs together at the beginning or end of a sentence is interpreted as an accident resulting from an almost absolute freedom of word order and not as an indication that the adverbs are functioning as a group.

The fact that *Loc* and *Tm* do not themselves behave as a group does not, however, preclude the possibility that either or both of them behave(s) as a group with *Pron* and/or *V*. Turning again to what happens under transformation, we note that whether alone or together, neither type of adverb behaves as a group with either or both *Pron* and *V*. Since, in addition, the fact that *V* may precede or follow *Pron* is not an indication that *V* and *Pron* are behaving as a group, we conclude that there is no need for postulating any other constituent-types and therefore that *V* + *Pron(Loc)(Tm)* are the constituents of *S*.

Problem 50 (Tepehuan) presents what seems to be a situation similar to the problem just discussed, in that its sentences also have a pronoun *(Pron)* and verb *(V)* but, instead of adverbs, there is a person marker *(PM)* and a question marker *(QM)*, and in addition there is a negative *(Neg)*. Assuming that each of the preceding is a type of constituent, the crucial questions for this problem are: (1) What is the relation of *PM* and *QM* to each other and to the other constituent-types? and (2) What is the relation of the negative to the verb?

Since *PM* and *QM* themselves never shift but other constituent-types are shifted to precede and follow them (without ever separating them), it is questionable whether they should be postulated to be a constituent-type, as they are in rule (2′) of Solution B. The postulation that *PM* + *QM* is a *Nuc* is particularly questionable because there is reason to suspect that the person marker is either a pronoun or a verb affix and not a particle. If the person marker is an affix and not a particle, probably *PM* and *QM* should be said to be constituents of different constituent-types, for, usually, question markers and affixes are not the same type of constituents. Since there is not enough evidence to make a decision, this indeterminacy concerning the relation of *PM* and *QM* to each other is reflected in the two alternatives for rule (1) of Solution 50B.

Now, notice that although under one transformation the negative and verb can be shifted to precede all other constituent-types, under another only the negative is shifted.[7] In other words, the negative and verb behave like the adverbs in Problem 46 in that they both may be shifted to precede all other constituents, but the negative and verb also behave unlike these adverbs in that neither can be shifted independently of the other. The question, then, is whether we should say that *Neg* is a constituent of the verb, in which case we should have a con-

[7] Alternatively, we may think of the verb as shifting while the negative remains constant, although this interpretation is discouraged (see point [2] of 6.3.5 for the reason). Whichever interpretation is chosen, however, the fact remains that one constituent always remains constant while the other is shifted.

stituent of the type *Vb* in the solution, or whether we should say that the negative and verb both are constituents of *S*. Since the postulation of *Vb* would simplify the solution in that there is at least one T-rule in which it could be used, it was decided that *Vb* is a constituent-type whose constituents are sometimes adjacent and sometimes non-adjacent. Thus, unlike the similar situation in Problem 46, the fact that the same two constituents (in this case the negative and the verb) may occur in a sequence at the beginning or end of a sentence is not interpreted as accidental.

For a last example let us examine Solution 47 (Hungarian). Unlike the higher order constituents of a sentence postulated in the other solutions, those postulated in this one are unjustifiable; i.e. none of the reasons for postulating the constituent-types *Pred* and *NP* can be supported on the basis of any simplification of the transformational part of the grammar. One major reason for this is that there is not one single instance in which two (or more) constituent-types are shifted as a group. Nevertheless, let us see what justifications can be given for postulating *NP* and *Pred.*

The first decision made after the four types of constituents *Pron, Det, N,* and *Adj* were postulated was that the sequence of a demonstrative plus an article is not a constituent-type. The reason for this is that the demonstrative is the only constituent-type that always agrees in number with the noun, and therefore it was considered a subject pronoun (as *this* and *that* are subject pronouns in English sentences like *this is a hat* and *those are hats*), while the determiner (which never shows agreement) was considered part of the predicate. Now, since (1) under a permutation transformation the noun and adjective are the only constituents that shift, and (2) the adjective agrees in number with the noun at least part of the time, it was decided that *N* and *Adj* function as a group and the sequence *N Adj* should be postulated to be an *NP.*

The next decision concerned the assignment of *Det;* i.e. whether, (1) because it always precedes *NP,* it should be considered to function as a group with it, and we should therefore postulate that the sequence *Det NP* is a *Pred,* or (2) because *Det* never agrees with the noun, it should be considered a constituent of *S.* This question is not answerable on the basis of the data; therefore the decision to postulate that the sequence *Det NP* is a *Pred* is (like the decisions just discussed) arbitrary.

6.3.4 Permutation rules

Up to this point we have been using the term "permutation rule" to refer to any transformation that rearranges the order of constituents.

Technically, however, not all such rules are permutation transformations. That is, the operation performed by a T-rule is considered a permutation *only* if *two adjacent constituents,* which may or may not be attached to the same node, are rearranged; otherwise a transformation that rearranges constituents is made up of two operations: deletion and adjunction. The following illustration may be helpful for understanding what is meant by "two adjacent constituents":

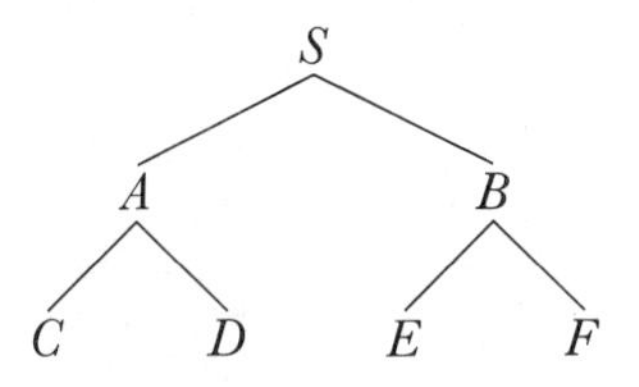

Examples of *two* strings that are *adjacent* but *not constituents* in the above P-marker are: (1) *C D E* and *F,* (2) *C* and *D E F,* and (3) *D E* and *F*; while *two* strings which are *constituents* but *not adjacent* are: (1) *C* and *E F,* (2) *F* and *C D,* (3) *D* and *F,* and (4) *A* and *F.* A rule which rearranges any one of the preceding strings, therefore, is not a permutation transformation, but a transformation which deletes one of the strings and adjoins this same string to (the right or the left of) the other. In contrast, examples of strings which are *adjacent and constituents* in the above P-marker are: (1) *A* and *B,* (2) *C D* and *E,* (3) *D* and *E F,* and (4) *D* and *E.* A rule which rearranges any one of the latter two strings, therefore, is considered a permutation transformation.

Most of the permutation rules in the preceding solutions are, strictly speaking, permutation transformations. For example, rule (6) of Solution 40 (Roglai) is a permutation transformation since *Pron* and *VP* are two adjacent constituents and the rule simply changes their position with respect to each other. Similarly, rule (11′) of Solution 42 (English) is a permutation transformation since *Prt* and *NP* (although not attached to the same node) are adjacent constituents, and the rule specifies that their position with respect to each other be reversed.

On the other hand, rule (10) of Solution 45C (Swedish) is a transformation made up of deletion and adjunction, since, as we can see from the P-markers below the solution, although *Aux* and *Tm* both are constituents, they are not adjacent; the same is true of rule (10) of Solution 45B. In Solution 48 (French) rule (13) is a permutation transformation, while rule (14) is a deletion and adjunction transformation.

Similarly, in Solution 49 (Spanish) rule (25) is a deletion and adjunction transformation, while rule (26) is a permutation transformation. Rule (25) of Solution 49 (Spanish) is not a permutation transformation because, although *Pron* and the *NP* in question are constituents, they are not adjacent.

An example of a rule that rearranges strings that are adjacent but not constituents is in Solution 50A (Tepehuan): the *X* in rule (10) represents the string *PM* + *QM*, which, although adjacent to *Vb*, is not a constituent. Rule (10) therefore is a transformation made up of deletion and adjunction.

The reason we want to distinguish between permutation transformations on the one hand and deletion plus adjunction transformations on the other is that each transformation assigns a different derived constituent structure. That is (as stated in 1.5.1), the convention for constructing a P-marker derived by permutation is that the elements to be permuted are detached, permuted, and reattached to the lowest node that dominated both in the source P-marker (and any intermediate structure that does not destroy other structure can be carried), while the convention for adjunction is such that a constituent is adjoined to the right or left of a given constituent and attached to the lowest node that dominates it. If the distinction between these two types of transformation were not maintained, these conventions would no longer have any significance, and consequently we would not be able to write a rule that assigns the first derived P-marker (adjunction) rather than the second (permutation), or vice versa:

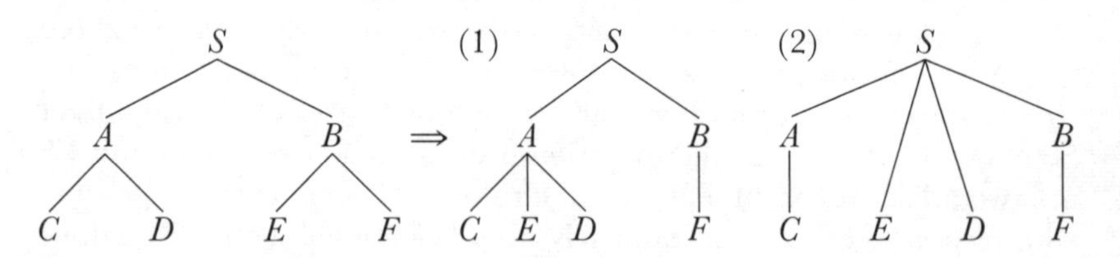

In other words, although in order to effect a permutation transformation adjacent constituents must be involved, it is not the case that whenever adjacent constituents are involved, a permutation must be effected; one may choose to effect a transformation made up of deletion and adjunction even if the strings in question are two adjacent constituents.

We shall continue to use the term "permutation rule" to refer to both types of transformations, however, whenever a distinction between them is not pertinent to any discussion, but will use the more precise "permutation transformation" and "deletion plus adjunction transformation" when it is pertinent.

6.3.5 Considerations for writing permutation rules

The following closely related considerations are the most important for writing permutation rules that generate derived sentences.

(1) **Structural description of the rule.** Usually there is no question as to what the structural description of a permutation rule should be. For example, that of rule (11′) in Solution 42 (English) must be *Vtc* + *Prt* + *NP*, since it is the only possible underlying structure from which *Vtc* + *NP* + *Prt* can be derived. Occasionally, however, this may not be the case. In writing Solution 48 (French), for example, it is not obvious whether we should derive interrogative sentences with the predicate preceding the subject pronoun from sentences with the underlying structure *QM* + *NP* + *VP* or *NP* + *VP*, i.e. whether the structural description should begin with *QM* + *Pron* or #*Pron*. Whenever more than one structural description may be specified for a given permutation rule, this means that more than one structural claim can be made concerning the relationship between the underlying and derived sentences in question. Since each of these claims will have different implications, the reader should carefully consider the alternatives and choose accordingly. Thus the decision to consider the type of interrogative sentences mentioned above to be derived from *ɛskø*-type interrogatives (i.e. *QM* + *Pron*) rests on the desire to reveal a relationship that otherwise would be obscured, namely, that sentences having the underlying structure *QM* + *Pron* + *VP* and those having the (derived) structure *VP* + *Pron* are both questions.

(2) **Derived constituent structure.** As stated in 1.7, transformations gradually destroy constituent structure; i.e. the constituent structure postulated by the P-rules is changed every time a transformation is applied. The more transformations applied to generate a given sentence, then, the more different the final derived P-marker will be from the underlying P-marker. This difference is that a number of relationships postulated by the P-rules no longer exist after the application of T-rules. This is evidenced in P-markers derived through permutation transformations by the fact that there is *less* subbranching in these P-markers than in the P-markers from which they are derived. Compare, for example, the two P-markers below, which are assigned by the rules of Solution 42 (English):

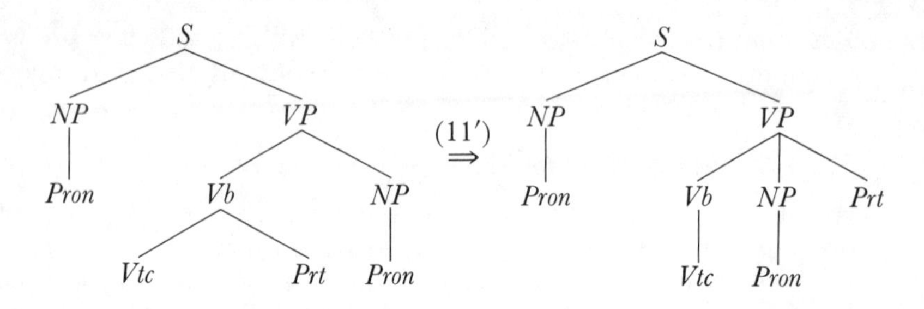

Notice that in the underlying or source P-marker (on the left) there is one more relationship postulated than in the derived; i.e. in the underlying P-marker it is postulated that *Vtc* and *Prt* are constituents of *Vb,* while in the derived P-marker this relationship between *Vtc* and *Prt* no longer exists.

To say that there is one more relationship in a P-marker, then, means that there is one more node which has at least two branches; thus the more nodes that have at least two branches (i.e. the more subbranching) in a P-marker, the more relationships we are postulating. Conversely, to say that *Vtc* and *Prt* above no longer are constituents of *Vb* is another way of saying that the relation "*Vtc* + *Prt* is a *Vb*" is destroyed by a permutation. The less subbranching in a derived P-marker as compared with its underlying (or source) P-marker, therefore, the more relationships (i.e. structure) we have destroyed. Notice that the relationship between *Vb, NP,* and *Prt,* i.e. that they are constituents of *VP* (or, in other words, "*Vb* + *NP* + *Prt* is a *VP*"), obtained after a permutation transformation is new but the *VP* type of constituent is not, nor does *VP* have a different relationship to the other types of constituents in the P-marker than it had previously.

From the above discussion it should be clear that an important consideration in specifying derived sentences is the derived constituent structure that the optional transformations will postulate as underlying them. Just as the structure postulated as underlying kernel sentences must be reasonable, so must that of derived sentences. The primary criterion for judging what is a reasonable derived constituent structure is the usefulness of constituents for later transformations, i.e. whether they will, in general, simplify the transformations that will follow. Specifically, the transformations written to generate derived sentences should, whenever possible, assign derived P-markers that include only those types of constituents which will be used later on in the grammar.

For example, suppose that we were to replace rules (8), (9), and (10) of Solution 50B (Tepehuan) with the following:

8′. Topt
Pron + *X* + *Vb* ⇒ *Vb* + *X* + *Pron*

9′. Topt
Neg + *V* + *X* + *Pron* ⇒ *Neg* + *X* + *V* + *Pron*

At first glance, these rules seem perfectly acceptable since not only do they generate the desired sentences, but they do so with fewer rules than in Solution 50B; look at the P-markers they assign, however:

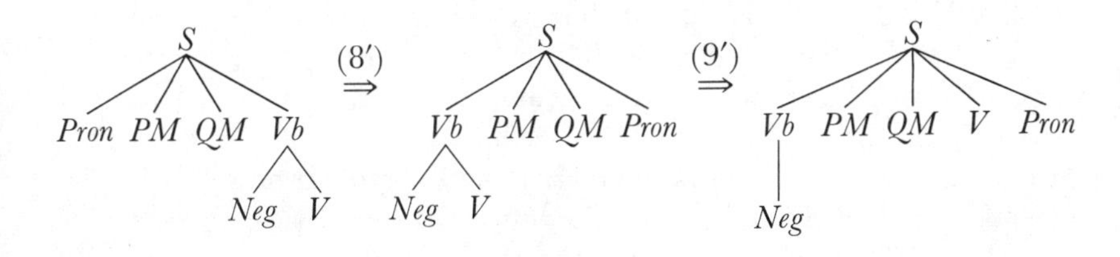

Although, clearly, the constituent structure assigned by rule (8′) is not unreasonable, that assigned by rule (9′) is. The latter P-marker is unreasonable primarily because the node dominating *Neg* is useless. If this node is to be retained at all after a transformation, it should be dominating *V*, not *Neg*. This is because, while there is a possibility that a T-rule might be needed later on in the grammar, for which *Vb* dominating *V* might be required as part of the domain of the rule, no such possibility is likely for *Vb* dominating *Neg*. The assignment of this unreasonable constituency is due to (1) choosing to write the rule for the shifting of *Pron* first, leaving no alternative but to specify the remaining permutations in one rule, (9′), with the result that (2) we have no choice but to say that *V* (and not *Neg*) shifts (or, alternatively, it can be said to be due to attempting too much with too few rules).

It should be noted that it is still unsettled whether any node, such as *Vb* above, which in an underlying (or source) P-marker dominates two or more symbols but in a derived P-marker dominates only one, should be retained in the derived P-marker. A number of linguists, the author included, feel that since a constituent-type is introduced in a grammar to postulate a relationship between two or more constituents, once this relationship is destroyed by a transformation, the constituent-type in question should automatically i.e. by convention) be eliminated.

6.3.6 The order of transformations

As we saw from the example in (2) above, it may sometimes be necessary to write a carefully ordered series of transformations (as in Solution 50B) in order to ensure that a reasonable constituent structure is assigned to derived sentences. The way transformations are ordered may also reveal that various derived sentences are of the same type, may simplify a solution, or sometimes both.

By writing optional T-rules so that the product of one serves as the only domain of another, we are postulating that all the sentences generated through the application of the rules thus ordered, by virtue of the fact that they have undergone the same optional transformation, are sentences of the same type, but that those generated by applying only the first rule are one subtype of that type and those generated by applying both rules are another subtype. In Solution 44B (Modern Greek), for example, by writing the two optional permutation rules, (24) and (25), in such a way that rule (25) can be applied only if rule (24) has been applied (i.e. by having the output of rule [24] serve as the input of rule [25]), we are postulating that the sentences generated by these two rules are all questions, but different subtypes. If we were to rewrite our rules in such a way as to destroy this dependency, e.g. by combining them into a rule

$$NP + Vb + Pred \Rightarrow \begin{Bmatrix} Vb + Pred + NP \\ Pred + Vb + NP \end{Bmatrix}$$

we would be stating that the sentences this rule generates have the same underlying structure, but we have no way of knowing whether they are the same or different types of sentences or whether they are stylistic variants of the same type of sentence. The implication of this rule therefore is that a native speaker of Modern Greek would not recognize that both *íne kalí i γinéka* 'is the woman kind?' and *kalí íne i γinéka* 'is the woman <u>kind</u>?' are questions, and that the latter sentence, although a question, is different from the former in that it has emphasis. Solution 44B therefore is preferable to a solution which would contain the above rule, despite the fact that if it were modified to contain this rule, the solution would be shorter, precisely because it formally characterizes the difference between these two types of questions.

By comparing the acceptable solutions for Problem 45 (Swedish), we can see even more vividly how crucial the order in which transformations are stated is to the claims that we are making about the sentences of a language. Although Solution B is shorter than Solution C, the latter is preferable and the former is, in fact, objectionable, because of the different claims each solution makes about the sentences of Swedish. Specifically, notice that in Solution B fronted-adverb assertive sentences are derived (through rule [10]) from questions (which are generated through rule [9]), and then question-word questions (i.e. those beginning with *vart* or *nar*) are derived from fronted-adverb assertions (through rule [11]). In other words, we are claiming that stylistic variants of statements are derived from questions, and question-word questions are derived from stylistic variants of statements. Thus, not only is it not revealed that the sentences generated by rules (9) and (11) are questions, but there is no formal characterization of questions at all in the grammar. In contrast, Solution C, although not as simple as Solution B, makes much more reasonable claims about Swedish and, in addition, formally characterizes questions. Notice that: (a) rule (9), which is optional for all underlying P-markers other than those whose terminal nodes include *vart* or *nar,* postulates that statements are all questioned in the same way; (b) rule (10), which may operate on the output of rule (9), then postulates that the adverb shift to sentence-initial position is obligatory for *vart* and *nar* (thus formally indicating that question-word questions are a type of question) but optional otherwise; and (c) rule (11) then postulates that the auxiliary is always the second constituent of a sentence except in yes-no questions (i.e. since the output of rule [9] cannot serve as an input of this rule).[8]

It should be noticed that if the two permutation rules given in Solution 48 (French) had been given in the reverse order, another rule would have been needed to reverse the order of the pronoun and particle (to ensure the generation of negative-interrogative sentences).

Finally, the agreement rules in Solutions 44 (Modern Greek) and 49 (Spanish) precede the permutation rules because the reverse order would require a more complicated specification of agreement.

6.3.7 Discontinuous constituents

Certain elements that are always or sometimes discontinuous in the data are treated as contiguous in the phrase structure part of the grammar, and their correct order is then provided by a transformation later on in the grammar. Thus the negative particles (which are always discontinuous) in Problems 41 and 48 (French) and the complex verbs (sometimes

[8] It should be noted that Solution C may very well be objectionable in the long run because it fails to make all possible generalizations regarding questions and the shift of the auxiliary in Swedish.

discontinuous) in Problem 42 (English) are introduced as contiguous, i.e. as *Neg* + *Prt* and as *Vtc* + *Prt,* respectively, in the phrase structure grammar, and later on a transformation shifts the particles to the proper position. It should be noted that if, in the French solutions, *Neg* and *Prt* were not introduced as contiguous constituents, it would be extremely complicated, if not impossible, to write rules specifying the various positions they may have in sentences (see also note 3 of 6.4).

6.3.8 Notational conventions

Certain notational conventions adopted in some of the preceding solutions will now be discussed.

(1) The convention of adding restrictions (or conditions) or giving additional information concerning a rule below the structural description and change of this rule is used in some of the preceding solutions because it enables us to make generalizations we could not make otherwise. In Solution 42 (English), for example, rules (11) and (12) specify exactly the same changes as rule (11′). This convention, used in rule (11′), however, enables us to make the generalization, hidden by rules (11) and (12), that any noun phrase can be shifted; and the information below the structural description and change of this rule tells us that the shift is obligatory under certain conditions and optional otherwise. Similarly, in rule (13′) of Solution 43 (Indonesian) the use of cover symbols which are defined in terms of specific constituents enables us to write a more general rule than we could otherwise.

(2) In Problem 49 (Spanish) certain morphophonemic changes are specified in a notation heretofore reserved for context-restricted P-rules. This notation has been extended to morphophonemic rules simply because it is the simplest notation for specifying certain changes. For example, of the three alternatives for writing the changes specified by rule (33) in Solution 49, alternative (c) is the shortest:

(a) $$\begin{bmatrix} Prep \\ X \end{bmatrix} Pr + G + Fir \Rightarrow \begin{bmatrix} Prep \\ X \end{bmatrix} \begin{bmatrix} mi \\ yo \end{bmatrix}$$

$$X \neq Prep$$

(b) $$Prep + Pr + G + Fir \Rightarrow Prep + mi$$
$$X + Pr + G + Fir \Rightarrow X + yo$$

(c) $$Pr + G + Fir \Rightarrow \begin{Bmatrix} mi \;/\; Prep \text{\_\_} \\ yo \end{Bmatrix}$$

6.4 NOTES

1. A number of rules in the preceding solutions provide us with good examples for a reminder that cover symbols represent *any* strings the grammar permits to occupy a position, i.e. any strings generated by the T-rules as well as the P-rules of a grammar. For example, since the *X* in rule (10) of Solution 50B (Tepehuan) represents any string the P-rules and T-rules permit in that position, it is restricted to be "not null" so that the rule will apply only to P-markers generated by rule (8) or rule (9) but not to underlying P-markers.

2. The main difference between Solutions A and B for Problem 44 (Modern Greek) is that a relationship is postulated between verbs and their mutually dependent complements in B that is not postulated in A. More specifically, in Solution B verbs and complements are each said to be constituents of the types *Vb* and *Pred*, respectively (and *Vb* + *Pred* is, in turn, then postulated to be a *VP*), while in A, a constituent of the type *Pred* is not postulated. The postulation of *Vb* and *Pred* results in a simpler solution, however (compare rules [25] of Solutions 44A and 44B); Solution B, therefore, must be considered preferable to A.

Although Solution A is objectionable in the light of the above discussion, it is not labeled as such because it is quite conceivable that, given additional data, Solution A (with the proper modifications) would be preferable to B. That is, new data might reveal that the relationship postulated between verbs and complements in Solution B is too restricted to merit such a generalization.

3. (a) The decision to postulate that the past participle suffix of French verbs is a constituent of an auxiliary verb and then have a T-rule shift the participle to follow the main verb is completely arbitrary as far as the solution for these data is concerned. Alternatively (and just as correctly), the past participle suffix can be handled as a morphophonemic change; that is, we can modify Solution 48 so that this suffix is not introduced at all in the phrase structure part of the grammar but is added by a morphophonemic rule to a verb whenever an auxiliary is chosen.

The treatment of person (by agreement) as a constituent of *Aux* instead of *V* is not arbitrary, however. It is based primarily on the fact that, for the data given, it is in the auxiliary verb (and never in the main verb) that we can observe variations of person.

(b) Although the order of the French negative particles is given as *nø* + *pa* in Solution 48, judging from the data given, there is no reason for preferring that order to the order *pa* + *nø;* therefore whichever order is postulated is equally acceptable. Once sentences like *il prome dø n pa parle* 'he promises not to speak' are included in the data, however, this no longer is true. The order of these particles must be *nø* + *pa* since the reverse order would require an extra rule to generate sentences such as that above.

Sentences like the one above also provide an independent reason for introducing the negative particles as contiguous in the phrase structure grammar. In 6.3.7 the reason given for introducing the particles as contiguous was that otherwise a solution would be too complicated, if not impossible, to write. Assuming, however, that we succeeded in writing a solution in which the particles were introduced as non-adjacent constituents, an extra rule would be required to permute the particles *pa* and *žame* in such a way that sentences like the above would be generated, whereas if the particles are introduced as contiguous, such a rule is not necessary.

4. Notice that the various changes that the object pronouns in Problem 49 (Spanish) undergo are specified in the solution in two steps: (1) the object morphemes *K* and *R* are added to pronouns whenever the latter are permuted to precede the verb (rules [25] and [26]), and then (2) a number of morphophonemic rules are given which effect different changes, depending on whether pronouns have object morphemes.

An alternative solution in which the various forms of the object pronouns are specified by introducing the grammatical category of case, which would then be expanded by a set of context-restricted rules, was considered and was rejected for two main reasons. First, because it is suspected that, in general, the position of the object plays no role in determining the particular shape these pronouns may have. If, as it is suspected, in longer sentences, object pronouns should occupy several positions with respect to verbs, the task of writing context-restricted rules for all these positions becomes hopeless. Second, and irrespective of the first objection, the introduction of case in the solution is highly questionable, primarily because, in languages for which it is usually postulated, both nouns and pronouns can be considered to have case, and there is no evidence in the data given that this is true in Spanish.

5. The decision to divide Spanish nouns first into animate and inanimate and then into masculine and feminine (see rules [11] to [13] of Solution 49), rather than vice versa, rested on the fact that a more complex environment would be needed for the former expansion if we did the reverse, or, in brief, because it simplifies the solution.

While there was a basis for making this decision in Solution 49, decisions involving overlapping subclasses are usually arbitrary. Unlike so many other previously discussed arbitrary decisions, however, these will not be resolved with the addition of new data, because in this case the arbitrariness is due to the inadequacy of our theoretical tools and not to the fact that the data are limited.[9]

6.5 COLLATERAL READING

Bach, Emmon: "The Order of Elements in a Transformational Grammar of German," *Language,* vol. 38, no. 3, pt. 1, pp. 263–269, 1962.

6.6 EXERCISES

1. ROGLAI

1. ñu naw	*He goes.*
2. ñu naw ata	*He goes far.*
3. ñu naw luˀ	*Does he go?*
4. ñu naw ata luˀ	*Does he go far?*
5. ñu naw ata čeˀ	*How far does he go?*
6. ñu naw suka	*He goes fast.*
7. ñu naw suka čeˀ	*How fast does he go?*
8. ñu naw suka luˀ	*Does he go far?*
9. ñu pə ata	*He flies far.*
10. ñu pə suka luˀ	*Does he fly fast?*
11. ñu pə ata čeˀ	*How far does he fly?*
12. ñu pə suka čeˀ	*How fast does he fly?*
13. hayəw ñu naw	*How does he go?*
14. hayəw ñu pə ata	*How does he fly far?*
15. hayəw ñu naw suka	*How does he go fast?*
16. naw ñu	*He goes!*
17. pə ata ñu	*He flies far!*
18. naw suka ñu	*He goes fast!*

[9] Some of the changes in transformational theory discussed by Chomsky in *Aspects of the Theory of Syntax* (*op. cit.,* 1965) are proposed to obviate the problem of subclassification. These modifications have not been sufficiently developed, however, to be incorporated in this book.

But not:

*ñu naw čeʔ
*luʔ ñu naw
*ñu pə hayəw
*hayəw ñu naw luʔ
*hayəw ñu naw ata čeʔ
*naw ñu luʔ
*naw luʔ ñu
*suka naw ñu

2. VIETNAMESE

1.	añ di ŋay čuəñɨt	*You went (will go) on Sunday.*
2.	añ den ŋay thɨha·y	*You came (will come) on Tuesday.*
3.	añ den thaŋ ča·p	*You came (will come) in December.*
4.	añ di thaŋ ziəŋ	*You went (will go) in January.*
5.	añ di ŋay na·w	*What day did you go?*
6.	añ den ŋay na·w	*What day did you come?*
7.	añ di thaŋ na·w	*What month did you go?*
8.	thaŋ na·w añ di	*What month will you go?*
9.	ŋay na·w añ den	*What day will you come?*
10.	thaŋ na·w añ den	*What month will you come?*
11.	thaŋ ziəŋ añ di	*You went (will go) in January.*
12.	ŋay čuəñɨt añ den	*You came (will come) on Sunday.*
13.	thaŋ ča·p añ den	*You came (will come) in December.*
14.	ŋay thɨha·y añ di	*You went (will go) on Tuesday.*

But not:

*di añ ŋay čuəñɨt
*di añ ŋay na·w
*ŋay na·w den añ

3. FRENCH

1.	il parl a mari	*He is talking to Mary.*
2.	il lyi parl	*He is talking to her.*
3.	žø parl a pɔl	*I am talking to Paul.*

4. žø lyi parl	*I am talking to him.*
5. mari parl a pɔl	*Mary is talking to Paul.*
6. ɛl lyi parl	*She is talking to him.*
7. pɔl obei a mari	*Paul obeys Mary.*
8. pɔl lyi obei	*Paul obeys her.*
9. il m obei	*He obeys me.*
10. ɛl mø parl	*She is talking to me.*
11. mari m obei	*Mary obeys me.*
12. pɔl pãs a mari	*Paul is thinking of Mary.*
13. il pãs a ɛl	*He is thinking of her.*
14. mari pãs a pɔl	*Mary is thinking of Paul.*
15. ɛl pãs a lyi	*She is thinking of him.*
16. mari pãs a mwa	*Mary is thinking of me.*
17. ɛl sõž a mwa	*She is dreaming of me.*
18. pɔl sõž a ɛl	*Paul is dreaming of her.*
19. il sõž a mari	*He is dreaming of Mary.*
20. žø sõž a lyi	*I am dreaming of him.*
21. pɔl sõž a mari	*Paul is dreaming of Mary.*

But not:

*žø parl a lyi
*il obei a ɛl
*žø lyi pãs
*il pãs a mø
*il mø sõž

4. ENGLISH

1. the book will be there
2. will the book be there
3. it will be there
4. will it be there
5. there it will be
6. the paper should be here
7. should the paper be here
8. it should be here
9. should it be here
10. here it should be
11. the book should be here
12. the paper will be there
13. will the paper be there
14. the paper will be bad
15. will the paper be bad
16. it will be bad
17. will it be bad
18. the book should be good
19. should the book be good
20. should the paper be bad
21. it should be good
22. should it be good

But not:

*there the book will be
*here the paper should be
*bad should be the book
*bad the book should be
*bad should be it
*bad it should be

5. KRIO, a language of Sierra Leone

1.	i bay binč	*He bought beans.*
2.	a bay rɛs	*I bought rice.*
3.	i go it banana	*He will eat bananas.*
4.	a go bay tamatis na di makit	*I will buy tomatoes at the market.*
5.	i go it rɛs na di kičin	*He will eat rice in the kitchen.*
6.	i bay tamatis na salon	*He bought tomatoes in Sierra Leone.*
7.	na banana i bay	*He bought bananas.*
8.	na binč a go it	*I will eat beans.*
9.	na tamatis i go bay na fritɔŋ	*He will buy tomatoes in Freetown.*
10.	na di kičin i it binč	*He ate beans in the kitchen.*
11.	na di makit a go it banana	*I will eat bananas at the market.*
12.	na di makit a bay tamatis	*I bought tomatoes at the market.*
13.	na salon i go it rɛs	*He will eat rice in Sierra Leone.*
14.	na ĩ go it rɛs	*He will eat rice.*
15.	na mi bay binč na fritɔŋ	*I bought beans in Freetown.*
16.	na ĩ it binč na di kičin	*He ate beans in the kitchen.*
17.	na mi go it tamatis	*I will eat tomatoes.*

But not:

*i bay na binč
*na i bay binč
*binč i bay
*na na di kičin i it rɛs

6. VIETNAMESE

1.	hwa di	*Hoa's going.*
2.	toy den	*I'm coming.*
3.	hwa den khoŋ	*Is Hoa coming?*
4.	hwa khoŋ den	*Hoa isn't coming?*

5. toy khoŋ di	*I'm not going.*
6. toy di khoŋ	*Am I going?*
7. toy den cɨə	*Am I coming yet?*
8. toy cɨə den	*I'm not coming yet.*
9. hwa cɨə di	*Hoa's not going yet.*
10. hwa den cɨə	*Is Hoa coming yet?*
11. hwa di dɨək	*Hoa can go.*
12. hwa dɨək den	*Hoa has the privilege of coming.*
13. hwa den dɨək khoŋ	*Can Hoa come?*
14. hwa khoŋ den dɨək	*Hoa can't come.*
15. toy dɨək di khoŋ	*Do I have the privilege of going?*
16. toy khoŋ dɨək di	*I don't have the privilege of going?*
17. toy den dɨək cɨə	*Can I come yet?*
18. toy cɨə den dɨək	*I can't come yet.*
19. toy cɨə dɨək den	*I don't have the privilege yet of coming.*
20. hwa dɨək den cɨə	*Does Hoa have the privilege yet of coming?*
21. toy di cɨə dɨək	*I can't go yet.*
22. hwa den khoŋ dɨək	*Hoa can't come.*

But not:

*khoŋ hwa di
*khoŋ den hwa
*toy dɨək cɨə den

7. HUNGARIAN

1. jaanoš el ment	*John went away.*
2. jaanoš ki ment	*John went out.*
3. ø ki ment	*He went out.*
4. ki ment el	*Who went away?*
5. ki ment ki	*Who went out?*
6. jaanoš ment ki	*John went out.*
7. ø ment el	*He went away.*
8. jaanoš ki akar menni	*John wants to go out!*
9. ø akar ki menni	*He wants to go out.*
10. ø el akar menni	*He wants to go away!*
11. ki akar ki menni	*Who wants to go out?*
12. ki akar el menni	*Who wants to go away?*
13. ki ment jaanoš	*Did John go out?*
14. el ment ø	*Did he go away?*
15. akar el menni jaanoš	*Does John want to go away?*

But not:

*jaanoš el menni
*jaanoš ki akar ment
*ki jaanoš ment el
*ø akar menni ki
*akar menni el

8. KOREAN

1.	haksängi jøki kamnita	*A student goes there (in sight).*
2.	haksängi kamnita jøki	*A student goes there.*
3.	jøki haksängi kamnita	*A student goes there.*
4.	jøki kamnita haksängi	*A student goes there.*
5.	salami jøki kamnita	*A man goes there.*
6.	salami samnita jøki	*A man lives there.*
7.	yøki salami samnita	*A man lives here.*
8.	yøki omnita salami	*A man comes here.*
9.	jø salami jøki kamnita	*That man (in sight) goes there.*
10.	i haksängi omnita jøki	*This student comes there.*
11.	yøki jø haksängi kamnita	*That student goes here.*
12.	yøki samnita i salami	*This man lives here.*
13.	i salami kamnita køki	*This man goes there (out of sight).*
14.	yøki kʉ salami omnita	*That man (out of sight) comes here.*
15.	køki samnita jø haksängi	*That student lives there.*
16.	kʉ haksängi køki kamnita	*That student goes there.*

But not:

*kamnita haksängi jøki
*samnita yøki salami
*i køki salami kamnita

9. INDONESIAN

1.	ɔraŋ itu makan kacaŋ kamarin	*The man ate peanuts yesterday.*
2.	ɔraŋ itu kamarin makan kacaŋ	*The man ate peanuts yesterday.*

3. kamarin ɔraŋ itu makan kacaŋ	*The man ate peanuts yesterday.*
4. kamarin makan kacaŋ ɔraŋ itu	*The man ate peanuts yesterday.*
5. makan kacaŋ kamarin ɔraŋ itu	*The man ate peanuts yesterday.*
6. makan kacaŋ ɔraŋ itu kamarin	*The man ate peanuts yesterday.*
7. anaʔ itu makan kacaŋ kamarin	*The child ate peanuts yesterday.*
8. anaʔ itu kamarin məmbəli kacaŋ	*The child bought peanuts yesterday.*
9. kamarin guru itu məmbəli kacaŋ	*The teacher bought peanuts yesterday.*
10. kamarin məmbəli kuwe guru itu	*The teacher bought cookies yesterday.*
11. məmbəli kuwe ɔraŋ itu kamarin	*The man bought cookies yesterday.*
12. makan kacaŋ kamarin anaʔ itu	*The child ate peanuts yesterday.*
13. kapan ɔraŋ itu makan kuwe	*When did the man eat cookies?*
14. kapan məmbəli kuwe anaʔ itu	*When did the child buy cookies?*
15. guru itu kapan makan kacaŋ	*When did the teacher eat peanuts?*
16. məmbəli kacaŋ kapan ɔraŋ itu	*When did the man buy peanuts?*
17. məmbəli kuwe anaʔ itu kapan	*When did the child buy cookies?*
18. guru itu makan kuwe kapan	*When did the teacher eat cookies?*
19. siapa makan kacaŋ kamarin	*Who ate peanuts yesterday?*
20. siapa kamarin makan kuwe	*Who ate cookies yesterday?*
21. kamarin siapa məmbəli kuwe	*Who bought cookies yesterday?*
22. yaŋ kamarin məmbəli kacaŋ siapa	*Who bought peanuts yesterday?*
23. yaŋ makan kacaŋ siapa kamarin	*Who ate peanuts yesterday?*
24. yaŋ məmbəli kuwe kamarin siapa	*Who bought cookies yesterday?*

But not:

*kamarin məmbəli kacaŋ siapa
*makan kacaŋ siapa kamarin
*məmbəli kuwe kamarin siapa
*itu anaˀ makan kacaŋ kamarin
*guru itu kuwe məmbəli kamarin

10. SPANISH

1. yo regalo los libros a el	*I give the books to him.*
2. el regala las kartas a mi	*He gives the books to me.*
3. yo se las regalo	*I give them* (fem.) *to him (her).*
4. el me las regala	*He gives them* (fem.) *to me.*
5. yo se los regalo	*I give them* (masc.) *to him (her).*
6. el se las regala	*He gives them* (masc.) *to me.*
7. yo me los regalo	*I give them* (masc.) *to me.*
8. el se las regala	*He gives them* (fem.) *to him (her).*
9. yo le regalo las kartas	*I give him (her) the letters.*
10. el me regala los libros	*He gives me the books.*
11. yo me regalo los kartas	*I give me the letters.*
12. el le regala los libros	*He gives him (her) the books.*
13. yo kiero regalar le los libros	*I want to give him (her) the books.*
14. yo kiero regalar se los	*I want to give them* (masc.) *to him (her).*
15. yo kiero regalar le las kartas	*I want to give him (her) the letters.*
16. yo kiero regalar se las	*I want to give them* (fem.) *to him (her).*
17. el kiere regalar le los libros	*He wants to give him (her) the books.*
18. el kiere regalar le los	*He wants to give them* (masc.) *to him (her).*
19. el kiere regalar le las kartas	*He wants to give him (her) the letters.*
20. el kiere regalar se las	*He wants to give them* (fem.) *to him (her).*
21. el kiere regalar me los libros	*He wants to give me the books.*
22. el kiere regalar me los	*He wants to give them* (masc.) *to me.*
23. yo kiero regalar me las kartas	*I want to give the letters to me.*
24. yo kiero regalar me las	*I want to give them* (fem.) *to me.*

But not:

*yo kiero regalar los libros a el
*yo se regalo las
*yo se regalo las kartas
*yo kiero regalar se los libros
*yo kiero regalar le los

11. GERMAN

1.	der man li·bt di frau	*The man loves the woman.*
2.	li·bt der man di frau	*Does the man love the woman?*
3.	di frau li·bt den man	*The woman loves the man.*
4.	li·bt di frau den man	*Does the woman love the man?*
5.	das kint le·rt di frau	*The child teaches the woman.*
6.	le·rt der man das kint	*Does the man teach the child?*
7.	das mɛdxən hat das kint gəli·bt	*The girl loved the child.*
8.	hat das mɛdxən das kint gəli·bt	*Did the girl love the child?*
9.	di švestər hat den brudər gəle·rt	*The sister taught the brother.*
10.	der brudər hat das mɛdxən gəli·bt	*The brother loved the girl.*
11.	hat di švestər di frau gəle·rt	*Did the sister teach the woman?*
12.	di frau virt den man li·bən	*The woman will love the man.*
13.	virt di frau den man li·ben	*Will the woman love the man?*
14.	das kint virt di švestər le·rən	*The child will teach the sister.*
15.	virt der brudər das mɛdxən le·rən	*Will the brother teach the girl?*
16.	der man zol das kint le·rən	*The man should teach the child.*
17.	zol das mɛdxən den brudər li·bən	*Should the girl love the man?*
18.	di švestər vil das kint li·bən	*The sister wants to love the child.*

19.	vil der man di frau le·rən	*Does the man want to teach the woman?*
20.	der man li·bt	*The man loves.*
21.	das mɛdxən hat gəli·bt	*The girl loved.*
22.	di švestər virt li·bən	*The sister will love.*
23.	di frau le·rt	*The woman teaches.*
24.	das kint hat gəle·rt	*The child taught.*
25.	der brudər zol le·rən	*The brother should teach.*

But not:

*der man di frau li·bt
*der frau li·bt den man
*den brudər li·bt di frau
*li·bt den man di frau
*der man hat gəli·bt di frau
*der man hat di frau li·bən
*der man virt di frau gəli·bt
*der man di frau virt li·bən

12. FINNISH

1.	minä olen sotilas	*I'm a soldier.*
2.	olen sotilas	*I'm a soldier.*
3.	olenko minä sotilas	*Am I a soldier?*
4.	olenko sotilas	*Am I a soldier?*
5.	sinä et ole sotilas	*You are not a soldier.*
6.	et sinä ole sotilas	*You are not a soldier.*
7.	et ole sotilas	*You are not a soldier.*
8.	etkö sinä ole mestari	*Are you not a master?*
9.	etkö ole mestari	*Are you not a master?*
10.	enkö minä ole mestari	*Am I not a master?*
11.	enkö ole sotilas	*Am I not a soldier?*
12.	minä en ole räätäli	*I'm not a tailor.*
13.	en minä ole räätäli	*I'm not a tailor.*
14.	en ole sotilas	*I'm not a soldier.*
15.	sinä olet mestari	*You are a master.*
16.	olet räätäli	*You are a tailor.*
17.	etkö sinä ole mestari	*Are you not a master?*
18.	etkö ole sotilas	*Are you not a soldier?*
19.	olen minä sotilas	*I am a soldier.*

20. räätäli minä olen *I am a tailor.*
21. mestariko olet sinä *Are you a master?*
22. mestariko olen *Am I a master?*
23. sotilasko sinä olet *A soldier are you?*
24. mestariko olet *A master are you?*
25. minäkö olen sotilas *Am I a soldier?*
26. sinäkö sotilas olet *Are you a soldier?*
27. räätäli minä en ole *A tailor I am not.*
28. sotilas et ole *A soldier you are not.*
29. mestari et sinä ole *A master you are not.*
30. sotilas en ole *A soldier I am not.*

But not:

*enkö minä oleko sotilas
*räätäli ole en minä
*mestari ole minä en
*ko olet sotilas
*olen minä sotilas

Additional information:

The question marker has two variants: *ko* after a stem containing at least one back vowel (that is, *u*, *o*, *a*) and *kö* after any other stem.

chapter seven

CONJOINING

INTRODUCTION

All the syntatic transformations used in the preceding chapters convert a representation of a sentence from one form to another. To do this, they operate on *one* P-marker at a time and, therefore, are called **single-base,** or **singulary,** transformations.

The derived sentences generated by single-base transformations are, accordingly, said to be derived from one sentence. There are, however, other sentences that can be said to be derived from *two* sentences. More precisely, there are sentences that can be said to be derived from the structure underlying two (source) sentences. The purpose of this and the following chapter is to illustrate the specification of relatively simple examples of such sentences.

The transformations that specify these derived sentences operate simultaneously on *two* P-markers and therefore are called **double-base,** or **generalized,** transformations.

They can be thought of as those rules of a grammar that convert representations of two sentences into that of a third sentence.

In addition to the fact that they operate simultaneously on two P-markers, double-base transformations differ from single-base transformations in that, given our restrictions on the order in which rules may be applied, they provide the recursive power of a grammar. That is, double-base transformations can operate on their own product in such a way that they will produce an infinite number of different P-markers, each representing a longer sentence. Specifically, the output of a double-base transformation may be used as part of the input of this same transformation, and then the resulting output may be used as part of the input of the same transformation, *ad infinitum.* Thus, the more times the same double-base transformation is applied in generating a sentence, the longer the sentence will be.

In terms of their derivation, there are two types of sentences that are said to be derived simultaneously from two sentences: (a) those derived by **conjoining** two sentences (i.e. by adding one sentence to another) and (b) those derived by **embedding** (i.e. inserting) one sentence within another. The rules that specify these sentences are, accordingly, referred to as conjoining and embedding rules, respectively. The problems in this chapter illustrate conjoining, and those of the next chapter illustrate embedding. In both these chapters we shall refer to sentences with neither conjoined nor embedded elements as **simple sentences,** to sentences with conjoining (but no embedding) as **compound sentences,** and to sentences with embedded elements (whether the embedded elements are simple or compound) as **complex sentences.**

It should be noted that the data in the first three of the following problems are restricted in a way that the data in the last three are not; e.g. sentences with compounded elements that are lexically identical are given as ungrammatical data in the first three problems but not in the last three. This was done not to focus on any particular pattern, but to be able to illustrate the use of certain notational devices for imposing restrictions on double-base transformations.

7.1 DATA

PROBLEM 51: MANDARIN CHINESE

1. ta chyù	*He is going.*
2. ta lái	*He is coming.*
3. nǐ chyù	*You are going.*

4. ta chyù nǐ chyù — *Is he going or are you going?*
5. ta chyù ta lái — *Is he going or is he coming?*
6. ta chyù shr nǐ chyù — *Is he going or are you going?*
7. ta chyù háishr nǐ chyù — *Is he going or are you going?*
8. shr ta chyù shr nǐ chyù — *Is he going or are you going?*
9. shr ta chyù háishr nǐ chyù — *Is he going or are you going?*
10. háishr ta chyù háishr nǐ chyù — *Is he going or are you going?*
11. háishr ta chyù háishr ta lái — *Is he going or is he coming?*

But not:

*háishr ta chyù nǐ chyù
*shr ta chyù nǐ chyù
*háishr ta chyù shr nǐ chyù
*ta chyù ta chyù

The above sentences are either simple or compound. The simple sentences are intransitive and consist of a subject pronoun followed by a verb. The compound sentences are interrogative and differ from the simple sentences in that they consist of two simple, but different, sentences; i.e. they are two (lexically different) sentences compounded. The sentences are compounded in four ways: either (1) one sentence is simply added to the other (i.e. there is no conjunctive particle) or (2) they are joined by conjunctive particles in one of the following three ways: (a) *shr* precedes the first sentence and either *shr* or *háishr* joins it to the second sentence, (b) *háishr* precedes the first sentence and is repeated before the second sentence, or (c) no particle precedes the first sentence and either *shr* or *háishr* precedes the second sentence. The restrictions on compound sentences thus are that (1) a sentence-initial conjunctive particle may not be the only such particle, (2) if the sentence-initial particle is *háishr,* the second conjunctive particle must also be *háishr,* and (3) the simple sentences that are compounded must be lexically different.

PROBLEM 52: THAI

1. khǎw kin khâ·w — *He eats rice.*
   he eat rice
2. khǎw ság sŷaphâ· — *He washes clothes.*
   he wash clothes
3. khǎw kin khâ·w lέʔ ság sŷaphâ· — *He eats rice and washes clothes.*
4. phǒm phû·d — *I speak.*

5. phǒm kin khâ·w	*I eat rice.*
6. phǒm phû·d lɛ́ʔ kin khâ·w	*I speak and eat rice.*
7. phǒm phû·d lɛ́ʔ ság sŷaphâ	*I speak and wash clothes.*
8. khun ság sŷaphâ·	*You wash clothes.*
9. khun phû·d	*You speak.*
10. khun ság sŷaphâ· lɛ́ʔ phû·d	*You wash clothes and speak.*
11. khun phû·d lɛ́ʔ ság sŷaphâ·	*You speak and wash clothes.*
12. khǎw phû·d lɛ́ʔ ság sŷaphâ·	*He speaks and washes clothes.*
13. khǎw kin khâ·w lɛ́ʔ phû·d	*He eats rice and speaks.*

But not:

*khun ság kin
*khun kin sŷaphâ·
*khun phû·d lɛ́ʔ phû·d
*khun phû·d lɛ́ʔ sŷaphâ·
*khun kin khâ·w lɛ́ʔ kin khâ·w
*khun ság khâ·w

The above sentences are either simple or compound. The simple sentences are transitive or intransitive and consist of a subject pronoun followed by a predicate. The predicate of intransitive sentences is an intransitive verb, while that of transitive sentences is a transitive verb followed by an (object) noun, which must be *sŷaphâ·* 'clothes' if the verb is *ság* 'washes,' and *khâ·w* 'rice' if the verb is *kin* 'eats.' The compound sentences differ from the simple only in that their predicate consists of *two* different verbs (and objects, if either or both the verbs are transitive) joined by *lɛ́ʔ* 'and'; in other words, they differ only in that the predicate of compound sentences is compounded.

PROBLEM 53: KOREAN

1. yohani chäkʉl iknʉnta
   John book read
   John is reading a book.
2. mariaka chäkʉl iknʉnta
   Mary is reading a book.
3. yohan kwa mariaka chäkʉl iknʉnta
   John and Mary are reading a book.
4. maria wa yohani chäkʉl iknʉnta
   Mary and John are reading a book.

5. chølsuka nolälʉl pulʉnta
   Chul Soo song sing
   Chul Soo is singing a song.
6. yøŋsuni nolälʉl pulʉnta
   Young Soon is singing a song.
7. chølsu wa yøŋsuni nolälʉl pulʉnta
   Chul Soo and Young Soon are singing a song.
8. yohan kwa mariaka nolälʉl pulʉnta
   John and Mary are singing a song.
9. yohani koŋpulʉl hanta
   John lesson study
   John is studying a lesson.
10. mariaka koŋpulʉl hanta
    Mary is studying a lesson.
11. maria wa yohani koŋpulʉl hanta
    Mary and John are studying a lesson.
12. yøŋsun kwa chølsuka koŋpulʉl hanta
    Young Soon and Chul Soo are studying a lesson.
13. yohan kwa chølsuka koŋpulʉl hanta
    John and Chul Soo are studying a lesson.
14. maria wa yøŋsuni chäkʉl pulʉnta
    Mary and Young Soon are singing (from) a book.

But not:

*chølsuka yøŋsuni nolälʉl pulʉnta
*yøŋsun chølsuka chäkʉl iknʉnta
*yohan kwa yohani koŋpulʉl hanta
*yohan koŋpulʉl hanta

The above transitive sentences are either simple or compound. The simple sentences consist of a subject, which is expressed by a name, and a predicate, which is expressed by an object noun followed by a verb; the verb consists, in turn, of a stem followed by the present tense marker *n* and the sentence-final marker *ta*. A suffix is always attached to the name and marks it as the subject of the sentence; it is *i* after names ending in a consonant, and *ka* after names ending in a vowel. The compound sentences differ from the simple primarily in that the subject of the former sentences is the same as the subject of *two* simple sentences joined by a conjunction. Notice, however, that (1) compounded subjects must differ lexically and (2) only the second subject has the subject marker suffix. Finally, notice that the conjunction has two forms: *kwa* after a name ending in a consonant and *wa* after a name ending in a vowel.

PROBLEM 54: FRENCH

1. pjɛr ete agreabl
   Peter was pleasant.
2. žak ete agreabl
   Jack was pleasant.
3. pjɛr e žak ete agreabl
   Peter and Jack were pleasant.
4. žak ete sɛrjø
   Jack was serious.
5. žak e pjɛr ete sɛrjø
   Jack and Peter were serious.
6. žak ete sɛrjø e agreabl
   Jack was serious and pleasant.
7. pjɛr ete sɛrjø e agreabl
   Peter was serious and pleasant.
8. pjɛr ete sɛ̃patik
   Peter was likeable.
9. pjɛr ete agreabl e sɛ̃patik
   Peter was pleasant and likeable.
10. žak ete agreabl e sɛ̃patik
    Jack was pleasant and likeable.
11. pjɛr e žak ete sɛ̃patik
    Peter and Jack were likeable.
12. žak ete agreabl e sɛ̃patik e sɛrjø
    Jack was pleasant and likeable and serious.
13. pjɛr e žak ete sɛrjø e agreabl e sɛ̃patik
    Peter and Jack were serious and pleasant and likeable.
14. pjɛr travaje a la mezõ
    Peter used to work at the house.
15. žak travaje a la mezõ
    Jack used to work at the house.
16. žak e pjɛr travaje a la mezõ
    Jack and Peter used to work at the house.
17. žak ete a la plaž
    Jack was at the beach.
18. pjɛr ete a la plaž
    Peter was at the beach.
19. pjɛr e žak ete a la plaž
    Peter and Jack were at the beach.
20. pjɛr e žak travaje a la plaž
    Peter and Jack used to work at the beach.

21. žak e pjɛr ete a la mezõ
    Jack and Peter were at the house.
22. pjɛr ete a la mezõ e a la plaž
    Peter was at the house and at the beach.
23. žak ete a la mezõ e a la plaž
    Jack was at the house and at the beach.
24. pjɛr e žak ete a la mezõ e a la plaž
    Peter and Jack were at the house and at the beach.
25. pjɛr travaje a la mezõ e a la plaž
    Peter used to work at the house and at the beach.
26. žak e pjɛr travaje a la mezõ e a la plaž
    Jack and Peter used to work at the house and at the beach.
27. žak e pjɛr ete agreabl e sɛrjø
    Jack and Peter were pleasant and serious.
28. žak ete sɛrjø me pjɛr ete agreabl
    Jack was serious but Peter was pleasant.
29. žak ete sɛrjø e pjɛr ete agreabl
    Jack was serious and Peter was pleasant.
30. pjɛr ete sɛ̃patik me žak ete agreabl
    Peter was likeable but Jack was pleasant.
31. pjɛr ete sɛ̃patik e žak ete sɛrjø e agreabl
    Peter was likeable and Jack was serious and pleasant.
32. pjɛr travaje a la mezõ me žak travaje a la plaž
    Peter used to work at the house but Jack used to work at the beach.
33. pjɛr travaje a la mezõ e žak travaje a la plaž
    Peter used to work at the house and Jack used to work at the beach.
34. žak ete a la mezõ me pjɛr ete a la plaž
    Jack was at the house but Peter was at the beach.
35. žak ete a la mezõ e pjɛr ete a la plaž
    Jack was at the house and Peter was at the beach.

But not:

*pjer me žak ete a la plaž
*pjer ete sɛrjø me agreabl
*pjer ete a la mezõ me a la plaž

The simple sentences above are either copulative or intransitive. Both types of sentences have a name as the subject, while, as a predicate, copulative sentences have a copulative verb followed by an adjective, and intransitive sentences have an intransitive verb followed by a locative phrase (the locative phrase consists of a preposition, determiner, and a noun). The compound sentences differ from the simple in that either (1) they have subjects or predicates (or both) compounded by *e* 'and' or (2) they are two sentences (either or both of which are simple or compound), compounded by either *e* 'and' or *me* 'but.' Notice that *me* cannot be used to compound anything but sentences.

PROBLEM 55: MODERN GREEK

The data of Problem 44 and the following:

42. o γitonas ine kalós ke aγaθós
    The neighbor is kind and meek.
43. ine kalós ke aγaθós o γitonas
    Is the neighbor kind and meek?
44. i γinéka ine ómorfi ke kalí
    The woman is pretty and kind.
45. ine ómorfi ke kalí i γinéka
    Is the woman pretty and kind?
46. to korítsi ine ómorfo ke afstiró
    The girl is pretty and severe.
47. ine ómorfo ke afstiró to korítsi
    Is the girl pretty and severe?
48. i γitones ine kalí ke aγaθí
    The neighbors are kind and meek.
49. ine kalí ke aγaθí i γitones
    Are the neighbors kind and meek?
50. i γinékes ine kalés ke ómorfes
    The women are good and pretty.
51. ine kalés ke ómorfes i γinékes
    Are the women good and pretty?
52. ta korítsja ine afstirá ke ómorfa
    The girls are severe and pretty.
53. ine afstirá ke ómorfa ta korítsja
    Are the girls severe and pretty?

But not:
*ine ómorfo to korítsi ke afstiró
*ómorfo ine ke afstiró to korítsi

The additional data are compound sentences that have compounded complements, i.e. two adjectives that are joined by *ke* 'and.' Notice that just as predicates of simple sentences may occur at the beginning of sentences (i.e. subjects and predicates are permuted to form questions; see Solution 44), so may predicates of compound sentences.

PROBLEM 56: ENGLISH

1. who can clean the house
2. Betty can clean the house
3. Jane can clean the house
4. Jane and Betty can clean the house
5. can Jane clean the house
6. can Betty and Jane clean the house
7. what can Betty clean
8. what can Betty and Jane clean
9. who can sweep the house
10. Betty can sweep the house
11. Jane can sweep the house
12. Betty and Jane can sweep the house
13. can Betty sweep the house
14. can Jane and Betty sweep the house
15. what can Betty sweep
16. what can Betty and Jane sweep

But not:

*what can clean the house
*who can Betty clean
*can clean Jane the house

The above simple and compound sentences are transitive and either affirmative or interrogative; they differ from each other primarily in that the subject of the compound sentences is compounded, by *and.* Affirmative sentences, whether simple or compound, have a subject and a predicate (in that order); the subject is one name (if simple) or two names (if compounded), and the predicate is an auxiliary followed by a main verb which, in turn, are followed by a noun phrase (i.e. a determiner followed by a noun). Interrogative sentences, whether simple or compound, are of two types: the so-called yes-no questions and the wh-questions. In the yes-no type, the auxiliary precedes the subject (whether it is compounded or not) and the remaining elements occur in the same order as in affirmative sentences. In the wh-questions, the subject is *who* and the object is a noun phrase, or the subject is one or two names and the object is *what.* When *who* is the subject, it begins the sentence and the order of the remaining elements is auxiliary – main verb – object; when *what* is the object, it begins the sentence and the order of the remaining elements is auxiliary – subject – main verb.

7.2 SOLUTIONS

SOLUTION 51: MANDARIN CHINESE

1. $S \rightarrow Pron + V$
2. $Pron \rightarrow$ *ta, nǐ*
3. $V \rightarrow$ *chyù, lái*
4. Tconj

$$\left.\begin{matrix} S \\ S' \end{matrix}\right\} \Rightarrow S((\text{hái})\text{shr})S'$$

where $S \neq S'$

5. Topt

$$X(\text{hái})\text{shr} + Y \Rightarrow \text{shr} + X(\text{hái})\text{shr} + Y$$

6. Topt

$$\text{shr} + X + \text{hái} + \text{shr} + Y \Rightarrow \text{hái} + \text{shr} + X + \text{hái} + \text{shr} + Y$$

SOLUTION 52: THAI

1. $S \rightarrow NP + VP$
2. $VP \rightarrow \begin{Bmatrix} Vtr + NP \\ Vin \end{Bmatrix}$
3. $NP \rightarrow \begin{Bmatrix} Pron \; / \; \# \text{—} \\ N \end{Bmatrix}$
4. $Vtr \rightarrow Vt_1, Vt_2$
5. $N \rightarrow \begin{Bmatrix} N_1 \; / \; Vt_1\text{—} \\ N_2 \end{Bmatrix}$
6. $Pron \rightarrow$ *khǎw, phǒm, khun*
7. $N_1 \rightarrow$ *khâ·w*
8. $N_2 \rightarrow$ *syâphâ·*
9. $Vt_1 \rightarrow$ *kin*
10. $Vt_2 \rightarrow$ *ság*
11. $Vin \rightarrow$ *phû·d*

12. Tconj

$$\left.\begin{array}{l} NP - VP \\ NP' - VP' \end{array}\right\} \Rightarrow NP - VP + l\acute{\varepsilon}ʔ + VP'$$

where $NP = NP'$; $VP \neq VP'$

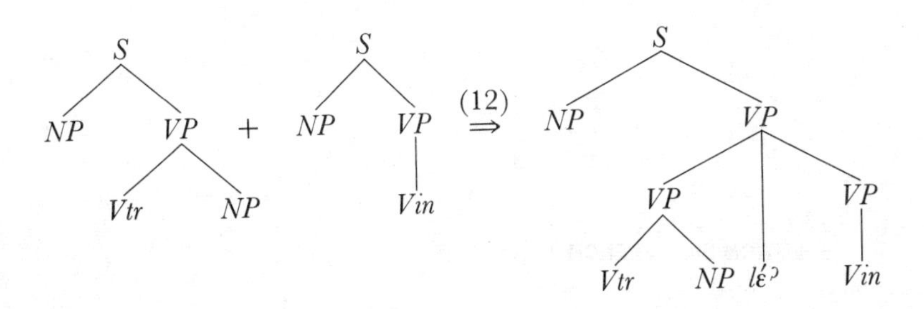

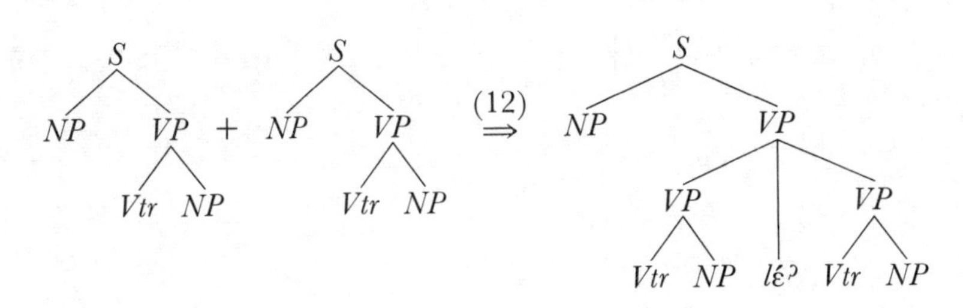

SOLUTION 53: KOREAN

1. $S \rightarrow NP + VP$
2. $VP \rightarrow NP + Vb$
3. $NP \rightarrow \left\{\begin{array}{l} Name \,/\, \#\text{—} \\ N \end{array}\right\}$
4. $Vb \rightarrow SM + V + Afv$
5. $Afv \rightarrow Pres + SFM$
6. $Pres \rightarrow n$
7. $SFM \rightarrow ta$
8. *V* → *iknɨ, pulɨ, ha*
9. *Name* → *yohan, maria, chølsu, yøŋsun*
10. *N* → *chäkɨl, nolälɨl, koŋpulɨl*
11. Tconj

$$\left.\begin{array}{l} NP - VP \\ NP' - VP' \end{array}\right\} \Rightarrow NP + WA + NP' - VP$$

where $NP \neq NP'$; $VP = VP'$

12. Tob

$$X - Name - N - SM - Y \Rightarrow X - Name + SM - N - Y$$

13. Tob

$$SM \Rightarrow \begin{Bmatrix} i \ / \ C\_\_ \\ ka \end{Bmatrix}$$

14. Tob

$$WA \Rightarrow \begin{Bmatrix} kwa \ / \ C\_\_ \\ wa \end{Bmatrix}$$

SOLUTION 54: FRENCH

1. $S \rightarrow NP + VP$
2. $VP \rightarrow Vb \begin{Bmatrix} Adj \\ Loc \end{Bmatrix}$
3. $Vb \rightarrow \begin{Bmatrix} Vcop \ / \ \_\_Adj \\ Vin \end{Bmatrix}$
4. $Loc \rightarrow Prep + NP$
5. $NP \rightarrow \begin{Bmatrix} Det + N \ / \ Prep\_\_ \\ Name \end{Bmatrix}$
6. $Prep \rightarrow$ *a*
7. $Det \rightarrow$ *la*
8. $N \rightarrow$ *mezõ, plaž*
9. $Name \rightarrow$ *pjɛr, žak*
10. $Vcop \rightarrow$ *ete*
11. $Vin \rightarrow$ *travaje, ete*
12. $Adj \rightarrow$ *agreabl, sɛrjø, sɛ̃patik*
13. Tconj

$$\left.\begin{matrix} X - Y - Z \\ X - W - Z \end{matrix}\right\} \Rightarrow X - Y + e + W - Z$$

where both Y and W are either:
(a) *Adj* or *Loc*, or
(b) *NP* if $X \neq Prep$, or
(c) S

14. Tconj

$$\left.\begin{matrix} S \\ S' \end{matrix}\right\} \Rightarrow S + me + S'$$

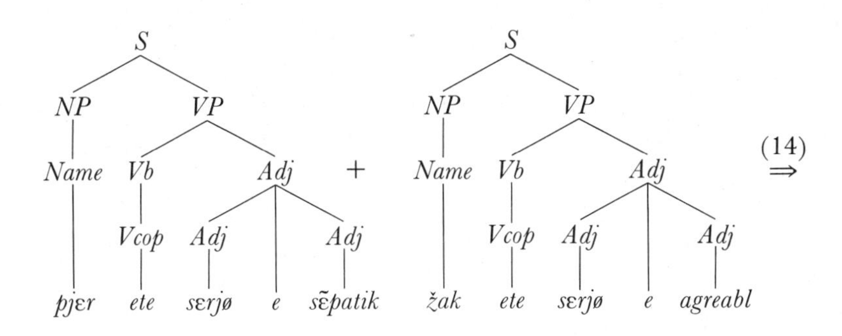

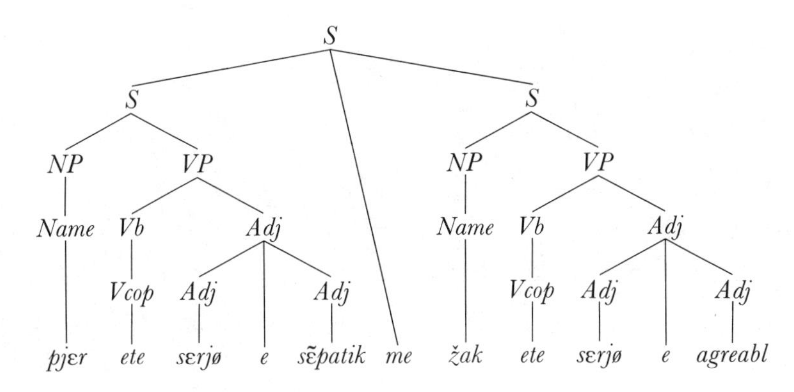

SOLUTION 55: MODERN GREEK

1–22. Same as in Solution 44B

23. Tconj

$$\left.\begin{array}{l} NP - Vcop - Pred \\ NP' - Vcop' - Pred' \end{array}\right\} \Rightarrow NP - Vcop - Pred + ke + Pred'$$

where $NP = NP'$; $Vcop = Vcop'$

24. Tob agreement

$$D - Ns + Afn \Rightarrow D + Afn - Ns + Afn$$

25. Tob agreement

$$Ns + Afn + X + A - Y \Rightarrow Ns + Afn + X + A + Afn - Y$$

26. Tob agreement

$$Ns + X + Nu + Y + Pres \Rightarrow Ns + X + Nu + Y + Pres + Nu$$

27. Topt question

$$NP + VP \Rightarrow VP + NP$$

28. Topt emphatic question
 $Vb + Pred + NP \Rightarrow Pred + Vb + NP$

29–44. Same as rules (26)–(41) of Solution 44B (which are the same as rules [24]–[39] of Solution 38)

SOLUTION 56: ENGLISH

1. $S \rightarrow NP + VP$
2. $VP \rightarrow Vb + NP$
3. $NP \rightarrow \begin{Bmatrix} Name \ / \ \#\text{—} \\ Det + N \end{Bmatrix}$
4. $Vb \rightarrow Aux + V$
5. $Aux \rightarrow can$
6. $V \rightarrow clean, sweep$
7. $Det \rightarrow the$
8. $N \rightarrow house$
9. $Name \rightarrow Betty, Jane$
10. Tconj

$$\left.\begin{matrix} NP - VP \\ NP' - VP' \end{matrix}\right\} \Rightarrow NP + and + NP' - VP$$

 where $VP = VP'$

11. Topt yes-no question
 $NP + Aux + X \Rightarrow Aux + NP + X$
12. Topt wh-question
 $Aux - X - NP - Y \Rightarrow WH + NP - Aux - X - Y$
13. Tob

$$WH \begin{bmatrix} Name(and + Name) \\ Det + N \end{bmatrix} \Rightarrow \begin{bmatrix} who \\ what \end{bmatrix}$$

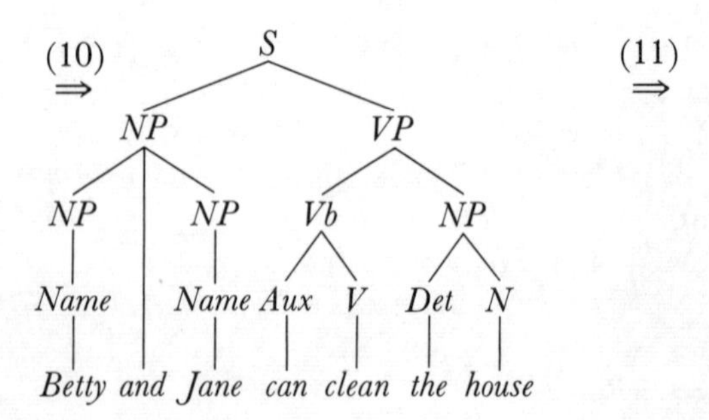

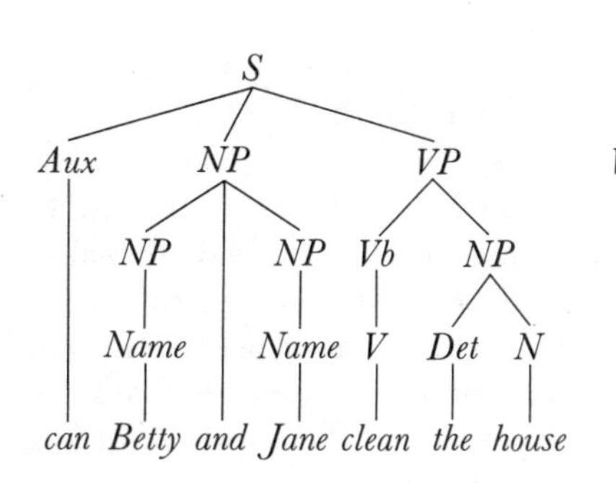

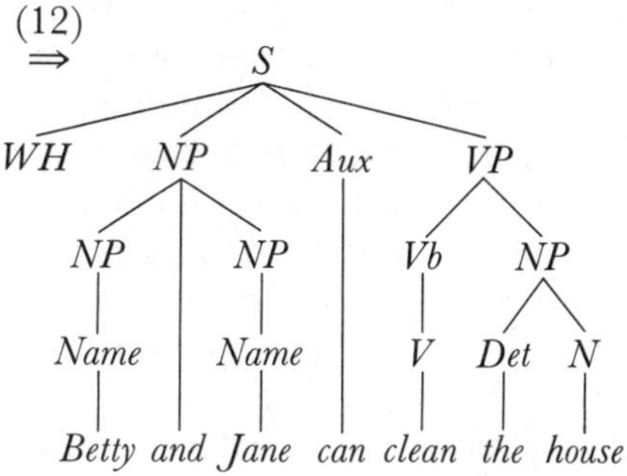

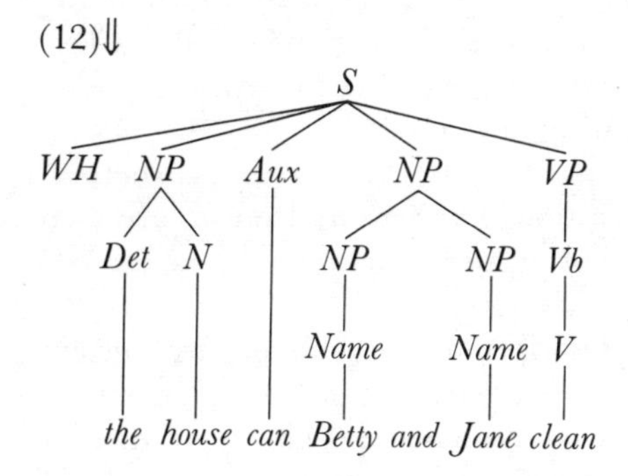

7.3 DISCUSSION OF SOLUTIONS

7.3.1 Format of conjoining rules

Essentially, there is only one notational convention adopted for stating conjoining rules, but since there is a slight difference between the notation used in rule (13) of Solution 54 (French) and that used in all the other conjoining rules, we shall discuss the latter rules first, using rule (12) of Solution 52 (Thai) as an example, and then we shall discuss how rule (13) of Solution 54 differs.

Rule (12) of Solution 52 (Thai):

12. Tconj

$$\left.\begin{array}{l} NP - VP \\ NP' - VP' \end{array}\right\} \Rightarrow NP - VP + l\acute{\varepsilon}ʔ + VP'$$

where $NP = NP'$; $VP \neq VP'$

(1) *Tconj* above and to the left of the structural description indicates that the rule is a conjoining rule. All conjoining rules are optional; therefore there is no need to indicate the optionality of these rules.[1]

(2) The *structural description* consists of two lines enclosed on the right by a single brace. Each line states the general form of a P-marker underlying a source sentence. Every constituent in the second line is marked with a single prime so that it will be completely unambiguous in the structural change from which source P-marker a particular constituent has been taken. The reader must remember, therefore, that since prime marks are simply a notational device, they do not represent bits of structure; consequently they do not appear in trees.

(3) The *right-hand single brace* enclosing the two lines of the structural description indicates that the rule operates on both P-markers simultaneously. (This symbol should not be confused with the paired braces, { }, which are an abbreviating device.)

(4) As in singulary transformations, the arrow and structural change follow the structural description; hyphens and pluses are used to indicate the grouping of symbols for proper attachment in the derived P-marker.

(5) Beneath the structural description and change are certain *conditions,* introduced by "where." These conditions, or restrictions, tell us precisely which P-markers can be conjoined (i.e. how two sentences must be the same and how they can differ); they specify in more detail what the constituent structure of two sentences must be in order for them to be conjoined. Since this is the case, these conditions, together with the structural description, define the domain of the rule.

In the notation used to state these conditions the equality sign and the inequality sign are of particular importance. Notice how each is read in our example "where $NP = NP'$; $VP \neq VP'$": "This rule applies to two P-markers with the general structure specified in the structural description that have **identical** noun phrases and **different** verb phrases."

By identical, expressed by the equality sign, is meant that the node in question dominates exactly the same set of strings, including the terminal, in both source P-markers.

[1] The distinction between the optional and obligatory application of transformations is not meaningful when speaking of double-base transformations, since calling conjoining (or embedding) rules obligatory would mean that the only grammatical sentences in a language are those that contain conjunctions (or embeddings). Furthermore, since these rules are recursive, to say that they are obligatory would mean that we could never get out of the grammar. For example, the only sentences Solution 52 (Thai) would specify would be those with infinitely long conjoined predicates, and these would never be generated.

By different, expressed by the inequality sign, is meant that in one source P-marker at least one string, including the terminal, dominated by the node in question is different from the strings dominated by the same node in the other source P-marker. For example, in the (partial) P-markers below, the strings dominated by *VP* in (1) and (2) are identical, while those in (3) and (4) are different from both (1) and (2) and from each other; (3) differs from the first two by the terminal string, while (4) differs from the other three P-markers by more than one string:

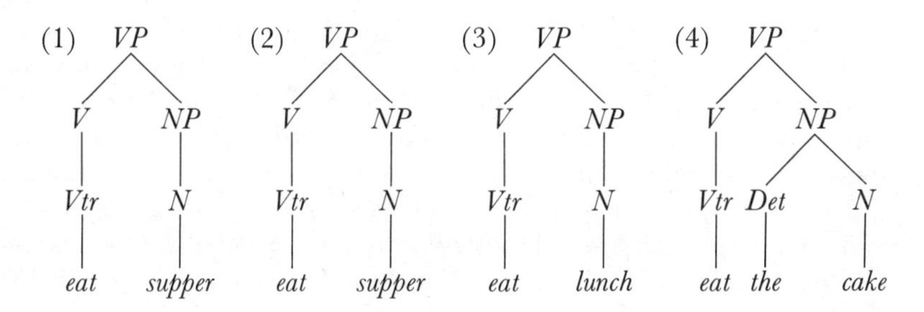

Whenever there are no conditions added below the structural description and structural change to restrict constituents conjoined by a rule, this means that the strings dominated by the node in question may be the *same or different* in both source P-markers. This is the case in rules (13) and (14) of Solution 54 (French), rule (23) of Solution 55 (Modern Greek), and rule (10) of Solution 56 (English).

Rule (13) of Solution 54 (French):

13. Tconj

$$\left.\begin{array}{l} X - Y - Z \\ X - W - Z \end{array}\right\} \Rightarrow X - Y + e + W - Z$$

where both Y and W are either:
(a) *Adj* or *Loc*, or
(b) *NP* if $X \neq Prep$, or
(c) S

The main notational difference between the above conjoining rule and a rule with the format of rule (12) of the Thai solution is that rule (13) is written in terms of cover symbols rather than class symbols and that prime marks are not used. The two dissimilar cover symbols, *Y* and *W*, represent the two constituents that are conjoined by the rule and thus have the same function in the structural change as the prime marks in rule (12) of the Thai solution. The fact that the other two cover symbols are identical in both lines indicates (as we saw in 1.2.1, point [2]) that they represent identical strings in the source P-markers. Thus, by taking advantage of the fact that identical cover symbols in a rule represent identical strings, we have obviated the necessity for using two distinct symbols, such as X and X' and adding the restriction $X = X'$, and have thereby simplified the statement of this rule.

As in rule (12) of Solution 52, given beneath the structural description of rule (13) are certain additional conditions imposed on the source P-markers. Unlike rule (12), however, there are three alternative conditions (indicated by *or*), which define the constituents conjoined by this rule and thereby also specify three different sets of P-markers to which rule (13) can apply. That is to say, since the structural description and the structural change of this rule are written (except for the conjunctive morpheme) entirely in terms of cover symbols, conditions (a), (b), and (c) tell us not only which constituents may be conjoined by this rule, but in so doing, precisely which P-markers this rule can be applied to. To determine these P-markers, we first note what constituent-types Y and W may represent and then use this information to determine which strings X and Z may represent. Since condition (a) above tells us that Y and W may be *Adj* or *Loc,* we know that one string that the grammar permits to precede *Adj,* for example, is $NP + Vcop$. One of the domains of rule (13) of Solution 54 thus is any two P-markers with the general structure $NP - Vcop - Adj$ and in which all strings dominated by NP and *Vcop* are identical. Similarly, condition (b) tells us that Y and W may be NP if X is not *Prep;* thus X may be *null* and Z may be VP (or X may be $NP + VP + e$ and Z may again be VP). Another domain of rule (13), then, is any two P-markers with the general structure $NP - VP$ and in which all strings dominated by VP are identical (or any two P-markers with the structure $NP + VP + e + NP' + VP'$ and in which the strings dominated by $NP + VP$ and by VP' are identical). Finally, condition (c) tells us that Y and W may be S, in which case X and Z are *null;* thus another domain of this rule is any two P-markers that have the structure S.

7.3.2 Considerations for writing conjoining rules

Regardless of whether we want to conjoin sentences or constituents of sentences, and whatever the conjoined constituents may be, the conjoining is always specified in the same way; i.e. by a rule that operates on two P-markers. Accordingly, the considerations for writing conjoining rules, regardless of whether we are conjoining constituents or sentences, are the same, namely, (1) the domain of the rule and (2) the derived constituent structure assigned.

(1) **Domain of the rule.** Although the domain is stated (or defined) in two parts—i.e. (1) the two lines enclosed on the right by a brace that specify the general structure of the P-markers to be conjoined and (2) the conditions beneath the structural description and change that impose further restrictions on these P-markers—both parts must be considered simultaneously and not separately. The following two closely related considerations are the most important for deciding how to write the domain of a conjoining rule.

(a) First, only constituents dominated by the same node can be conjoined; therefore the general structure of the source P-markers must be the same.[2] As can be seen in all the preceding solutions, both lines of the structural description must be identical (this is true even of rules written with cover instead of class symbols, as we saw in 7.3.1); for example, if the class symbols in the first line are $NP - VP$, those in the one below it must also be $NP - VP$.

(b) The motivation for adopting the convention of stating the domain in two parts is to make the conjoining rules as simple as possible but at the same time to impose the proper restrictions on them (see also 6.3.8). The reader should therefore take advantage of the fact that he can add restrictions to the P-markers defined in the structural description and state the latter in as general terms as possible.

The inequality sign helps us generalize in that if we define the structural description on very high order symbols and then add the condition that the strings dominated by one of these symbols in the source P-markers must differ by at least one string, we will have written a very general rule. For example, because we can use the inequality sign to impose the proper restriction on the verb phrases to be conjoined by rule (12) of Solution 52 (Thai), not only are we able to simplify the solution in that we do not need separate rules to conjoin the verb phrases of transitive and intransitive sentences, but we are also able to state the structure of the source P-markers in the most general way possible $\left(\text{i.e. as } NP - VP \text{ rather than as } NP - \begin{Bmatrix} Vtr + NP \\ Vin \end{Bmatrix}\right)$. In addition to reducing the number of symbols in the rule, we are also making the

[2] An additional way to generate compound sentences is to conjoin sentences and then delete identical constituents under certain conditions. We could thus generate sentences such as the following: *I gave the dog a bone and the cat a mouse* and *I floated and he swam across the lake.*

generalization that transitive and intransitive predicates are conjoined in the same way as two transitive predicates.

An even more powerful way of generalizing, however, is to state the structure of the source P-markers in terms of cover symbols (and then define the cover symbols below the structural description). For example, Solution 54 (French) would be much more complicated if we had not used cover symbols in the structural description of rule (13) to define the general structure of the P-markers and then defined the cover symbols below the structural description. That is to say, since sentences and parts of sentences can be conjoined in the same way, i.e. with *e* 'and,' the use of cover symbols in one rule obviates the necessity for writing a separate rule for each such constituent. If we had not used the cover symbols, not only would we have needed three rules to specify conjoining with *e* 'and' rather than one rule, but we would have hidden the generalization that the various constituent-types represented by the cover symbols *Y* and *W* are all conjoined in the same way.

(2) **Derived constituent structure.** Conjoining rules operate on two P-markers in one of two ways: either (1) they add one entire P-marker to another (with the proper conjunctive morpheme[s], if any), e.g. rule (4) of Solution 51 (Mandarin Chinese), or (2) they add a part of the second P-marker to the first (with the proper conjunctive morpheme[s]) and delete the remainder of the second P-marker, e.g. rule (23) of Solution 55 (Modern Greek) (the latter results in what is traditionally called a **coordinate construction**). Notice that the conjunctions are introduced as individual morphemes, and not as a constituent-type, by conjoining rules; otherwise we would be violating restriction 4 in 2.2.1, namely, that no non-terminal symbol which does not appear in some underlying P-marker can be used in a T-rule.

Since at least part of the first P-marker remains unchanged by a conjoining rule, the derived constituent structure assigned to that part is clear: the constituents not conjoined by the rule have the same relationships in the derived that they did in the source P-markers; i.e. the nodes and attachments remain the same. The attachment of the conjunctive morphemes is also clear: they are attached to the same node to which the conjoined constituents themselves are. But a question arises with regard to the derived constituent structure of the conjoined constituents themselves, namely: What type of constituent are the conjoined constituents? or, in other words: To what node do we attach conjoined constituents?

We want the answer to this question to be: Constituents conjoined by a transformation are constituents of the same type that each was in its respective source P-marker; e.g. we want *NP* + *conj* + *NP* and *NP* + *conj* + *NP* + *conj* + *NP*, etc., to be an (or to be attached to) *NP*, for the following reasons.

First, since, as we can see in Solutions 55 and 56 (Modern Greek and English, respectively), whatever grammatical relations hold for constituents when they are not conjoined also hold when they are, the transformational part of the grammar will be simplified if we consider the conjoined constituents to be the same type of constituent that each is in the source P-markers. That is, since in Problem 55 (Modern Greek), for example, predicates with either a simple or a compound predicate adjective can be permuted in the same way, the solution for this problem will be simplified if the permutation rule for shifting *Pred* to precede *Vb* applies to both types of predicates. The same is true of Solution 56 (English) with regard to the formation of yes-no and wh-questions: since both compound and simple subjects are permuted (and deleted) in the same way to form these questions, the specification of these sentences will be simplified if it can be done in terms of a constituent-type that includes both simple and compound noun phrases.

Second, by saying that the conjoined constituents are the same type of constituent which each is in the source P-markers, we can provide for the infinite conjoining of constituents in a finite way; i.e. we thus make these rules recursive. That is to say, we can now write one rule that will keep reapplying to its product, thereby producing P-markers with any number of conjoined constituents. For example, if we apply rule (11) of Solution 53 (Korean) once, we get the following derived P-marker:

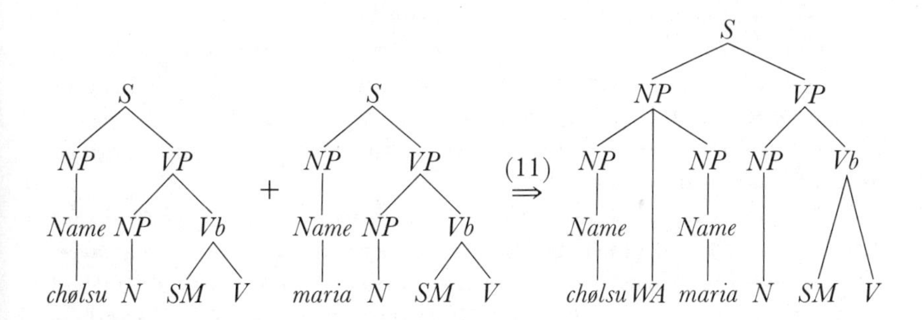

Since, as we can see above, sentences generated by applying this rule once also have the general structure *NP* — *VP*, it follows that, given any other P-marker having this same general structure, rule (11) can be reapplied to these two P-markers (as long as they satisfy all other necessary conditions) to form yet another:

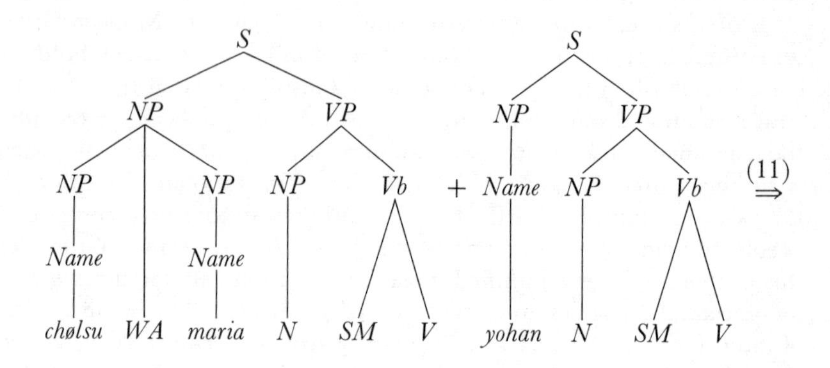

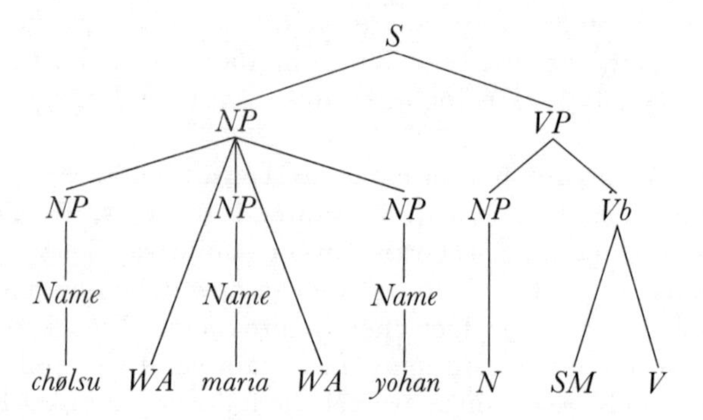

We could keep reapplying rule (11) in the same manner indefinitely. This rule thus is infinitely recursive despite the fact that the number of morphemes that can be involved in the conjoining are extremely limited, because each time the conjoining rule is applied, the *NP* in the newly derived P-marker will be different from any *NP* in previously derived (or any underlying) P-markers.

Although we have answered the question "To what node do we attach the conjoined constituents?" and given our reasons for the answer, we are now faced with the following problem: there is no established convention that will give the derived P-markers we want (i.e. P-markers such as those above).[3] That is to say, no provision has been made, as

[3] In one of the few published articles that discuss coordinate constructions and include P-markers in the discussion ("O Pereformulirivanij Transformacionnyx Grammatik" [On Reformulating Transformational Grammars], *Voprosy Jazykoznanija,* vol. 10, no. 6, pp. 41–50,

yet, within transformational theory for the introduction into a grammar of a constituent-type that dominates itself, e.g. for a constituent-type X that dominates $X + conj + X$ or $X + conj + X + conj + X$, etc. Since there is no convention that gives the proper derived P-markers, we shall tentatively adopt the following:[4]

> When two constituents are first conjoined by a transformation, they are attached to a node with the same label these constituents had in the source P-markers; i.e. a new node is created. After that, conjoined constituents are attached to the newly created node in accordance with the convention for attachment by adjunction (see 1.5.1).

7.3.3 Sentence relatedness

Since compound (and complex) sentences are postulated to be derived from *two* P-markers and since the definition of related sentences given in 1.7 covers only sentences which are postulated to be derived from one (underlying) P-marker, we must now adjust our definition of related sentences to include compound (and complex) sentences.

1960), R. B. Lees suggests that P-markers derived through conjoining can be constructed in accordance with the general convention for substitution. But after giving the following rule:

$$\left.\begin{matrix} X + A + Y \\ X + B + Y \end{matrix}\right\} \Rightarrow X + A + i + B + Y$$

he states that the rule assigns the following derived constituent structure:

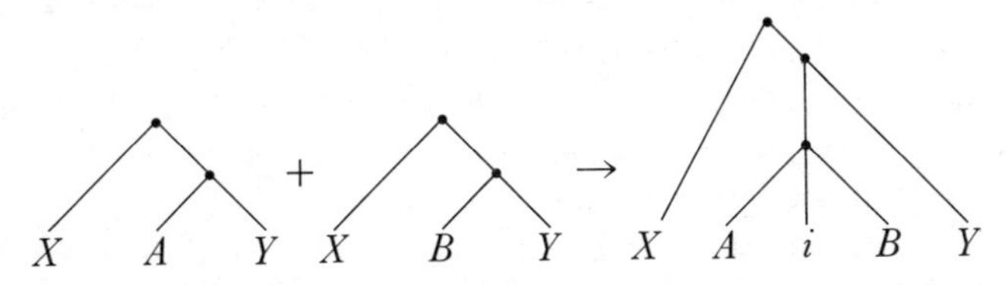

If the above derived P-marker is to be construed as one derived by substitution, it is substitution of a different character than that specified by single-base transformations (and embedding rules; see 8.3.1); that is, since the convention for constructing P-markers derived through substitution requires that replacing elements take on the structure of those they replace, A, i, and B above should be attached to the same node that Y is attached to. Instead, a new node has been created, and A, i, and B are attached to it.

[4] The adoption of this convention clearly must be considered tentative since it is not useful for every type of conjoining we will want to specify; i.e. it does not provide the correct derived constituent structure for sentences like *John and Mary, Roger and Helen, and Bill and June went to the show,* for example.

We say that two (or more) sentences are related to each other if their structural descriptions differ *only* in that one has undergone at least one *optional singulary* transformation which the other has not. By this definition, then, Solution 55 (Modern Greek) and Solution 56 (English) are the only solutions in this chapter which generate sentences that can be said to be related, since they are the only solutions that contain optional singulary transformations.

Specifically, from Solution 55, for example, we can say that *i γinéka íne kalí ke aγaθí* 'the woman is kind and meek,' *íne kalí ke aγaθí i γinéka* 'is the woman kind and meek?' *kalí ke aγaθí íne i γinéka* 'is the woman kind and meek?' are related to each other since their structural descriptions differ only in that the second sentence has undergone an optional singulary transformation that the first has not (i.e. rule [27]) and the third sentence has undergone an optional singulary transformation that the second has not (i.e. rule [28]) and two optional singulary transformations that the first sentence has not (i.e. rules [27] and [28]). In contrast, we do not say that *íne kalí ke aγaθí ke ómorfi i γinéka* 'is the woman kind and meek and beautiful?' is related to any of the above sentences, because it does not differ from any one of them *only* in that it has undergone at least one optional singulary transformation that the other sentences have not. Specifically, *íne kalí ke aγaθí ke ómorfi i γinéka* has an underlying P-marker in its structural description which none of the above sentences do, i.e. that underlying the sentence *i γinéka íne ómorfi* 'the woman is beautiful.' Notice, however, that while *i γinéka íne kalí ke aγaθí ke ómorfi* 'the woman is kind and meek and beautiful,' *íne kalí ke aγaθí ke ómorfi i γinéka* 'is the woman kind and meek and beautiful?' and *kalí ke aγaθí ke ómorfi íne i γinéka* 'is the woman kind and meek and beautiful?' are not related to the above set of sentences, they *are* related *to each other* since their structural descriptions differ only in that one sentence has undergone at least one optional singulary transformation that the other has not.

Similarly, from Solution 56 (English), we can say that *Betty can clean the house, can Betty clean the house, who can clean the house,* and *what can Betty clean* are related to each other since their structural descriptions differ only in that some of these sentences have undergone at least one optional singulary transformation that the others have not. For another example, we say that *Betty and Jane can clean the house, can Betty and Jane clean the house, what can Betty and Jane clean,* and *who can clean the house* are related to each other since their structural descriptions differ only in that some of these sentences have undergone at least one optional singulary transformation that the others have not. In contrast, we cannot say that *can Betty clean the house,* for example, is related to *Betty and Jane can clean the house* or to any of the questions that can be derived from the latter sentence. This is because *can Betty clean the house* is derived from the P-marker underlying *Betty can clean the house,* while *Betty and Jane can clean the house* (and the questions that can be derived from it) is derived from two P-markers, that underlying *Betty can clean the house* and that underlying *Jane can clean the house.* In brief, the structural descriptions of these sentences differ more than simply in the choice of optional singulary transformations applied to generate them.

7.3.4 Ordering transformations

Since in Solutions 51 (Mandarin Chinese), 52 (Thai), and 53 (Korean) the conjoining rule is the only syntactic transformation, ordering transformations is not a consideration in these solutions. While there is no other type of syntactic transformation in Solution 54 (French) either, there are two conjoining rules: the rule for conjoining with *e* 'and' precedes that for conjoining (sentences) with *me* 'but.' This order is completely arbitrary so far as this solution is concerned; i.e. the reverse order would be equally acceptable.

The only solutions in which there are both single-base and double-base transformations are, as said earlier, Solutions 55 and 56 (Modern Greek and English, respectively). In both these solutions the conjoining rule *precedes* the optional single-base transformations. The reason for this order is the same as that given in 6.3.6 for the order of permutation rules; i.e. it simplifies the grammar.

In Solution 56, for example, by having the conjoining rule precede all other T-rules, we have simplified the solution in that (1) no extra rules are needed to permute compound subjects and the auxiliary, (2) the rule for conjoining noun phrases is less complicated than it would be if it followed the permutation rule, and (3) since the output of the conjoining rule serves as the input of those rules by means of which both types of questions are generated, we are making the generalization that simple and compound sentences are questioned in the same way.[5]

In Solution 55 (Modern Greek), in addition to the two optional permutation rules that generate two types of interrogative sentences, there are obligatory transformations that establish agreement in case, gender, and number. The conjoining rule precedes the permutation rules for the same reasons that this order is given in Solution 56. The con-

[5] In the long run, however, because of contrasts such as *who is coming?* and **who are coming?,* and *what is coming?* and **what are coming?,* we may not want to make this generalization; i.e. we may want to derive wh-questions only from P-markers underlying simple sentences.

joining rule also precedes the agreement rules since not only (a) agreement does not affect the specification of conjoining in any way, but, more important, (b) we thus make the generalization that the agreement between two (or more) constituent-types is the same regardless of whether or not conjoining has taken place.

7.3.5 Assigning constituent structure

In 6.3.3 we saw that noting how kernel sentences behave under permutation can help us decide what constituent structure to assign to kernel sentences. The possibility of conjunction (i.e. how kernels behave under conjoining transformations) is another criterion for deciding what to postulate as the constituent structure of kernel sentences.

The fact, for example, that in Problem 53 (Thai) either two transitive predicates or a transitive and an intransitive predicate can be conjoined justifies the postulation of *VP*, since the solution for this problem is thereby simplified. Specifically, it is simplified in that by stating the conjoining transformation in terms of this constituent-type, we not only have fewer symbols in that rule but thereby make the generalization (which we otherwise would not) that any two predicates can be conjoined by *lέʔ*; i.e. two transitive verbs and their objects are, for example, conjoined (or function) in the same way as an intransitive verb and a transitive verb and its object.

Similarly, in Solution 54 (French) *Loc* is postulated to simplify the rule for conjoining locative phrases: *Y* and *W* are defined as *Loc* instead of *Prep* + *NP*.

7.4 NOTES

1. (a) An alternative way of handling the subject marker in Problem 53 (Korean) is to make it a constituent of *NP* and write a morphophonemic rule that would delete all but the last subject marker after the conjoining transformation has been applied. Specifically, we could omit *SM* from rule (4), add it after *Name* to rule (3), and replace rule (12) with the following:

12′. Tob

$$X + SM + Y + SM + Z \Rightarrow X + Y + SM + Z$$

Although there is nothing in the data to indicate that the above treatment is any more or less justifiable than that given in Solution 53, rule (12′) above is more general than rule (12) and therefore preferable.

(b) It may seem that rule (11) of Solution 53 is inconsistent with the statement that conjunctions are introduced as individual morphemes (see 7.3.2, [2]); i.e. it may appear in this rule that *WA* is a class symbol which is rewritten later on in the grammar, by rule (14), as the morphemes *kwa* and *wa*. That *WA* is not a class symbol, however, but a morpheme having two different pronunciations, is evidenced by the fact that the occurrence of *kwa* and *wa*, unlike, for example, that of *háishr* and *shr* in Mandarin Chinese, is phonologically conditioned: when conjoining subjects, the conjunction is *kwa* if the preceding noun ends in a consonant, and *wa* otherwise. In short, while we cannot predict when *háishr* or *shr* will be selected to conjoin sentences in Mandarin Chinese, we can always predict when *kwa* and *wa* will be selected in Korean. Since this is the case, the symbol *WA*, introduced by the conjoining rule, is a morpheme, and rule (14) is a morphophonemic rule which specifies its proper pronunciation.

2. By convention, rule (25) of Solution 55 (Modern Greek), which establishes agreement between a subject noun and one or more predicate adjectives, operates in such a way that *Afn* is adjoined to the right of each successively left-most occurrence of *A* until every *A* in the P-marker has *Afn* to the right of it (i.e. until the rule exhausts the string). Rule (12′) in note 1 above works in precisely the same manner; i.e. each successively left-most occurrence of *SM* (except the last) is deleted.

3. The replacement of noun phrases by *who* or *what* to form wh-questions in Solution 56 (English) is specified by the same technique used in Solution 49 (Spanish), namely, by (a) shifting noun phrases to sentence-initial position while simultaneously adding a *WH* morpheme and (b) giving a morphophonemic rule which effects changes which are dependent upon whether the following noun phrases are one or more names or a determiner and a noun.

7.5 EXERCISES

1. KOREAN

1. yohani papʉl møknʉnta
   John is eating (his) meal.
2. yohani kʉkʉl møknʉnta
   John is having soup.
3. yohani papkwa kʉkʉl møknʉnta
   John is having (his) meal and soup.
4. mariaka chäkʉl iknʉnta
   Mary is reading a book.

5. mariaka sinmunʉl iknʉnta
   Mary is reading a (news)paper.
6. mariaka chäkwa sinmunʉl iknʉnta
   Mary is reading a book and a paper.
7. chølsuka photojulʉl masinta
   Chul Soo is drinking wine.
8. chølsuka sojulʉl masinta
   Chul Soo is drinking liquor.
9. chølsuka photojuwa sojulʉl masinta
   Chul Soo is drinking wine and liquor.
10. yøŋsuni yaŋmalʉl ttunta
    Young Soon is knitting the socks.
11. yøŋsuni jaŋkapʉl ttunta
    Young Soon is knitting the gloves.
12. yøŋsuni yaŋmalkwa jaŋkapʉl ttunta
    Young Soon is knitting the socks and gloves.

But not:

*yohani papkwa papʉl møknʉnta
*mariaka chäkʉl sinmunʉl iknʉnta
*chølsulʉl photojuwa sojulkwa masinta
*mariaka chäkwa papʉl iknʉnta
*johani jaŋkapkwa masinta
*mariaka kʉkwa ttunta

2. BRAZILIAN PORTUGUESE

1. maria foi au teatru — *Maria went to the theater.*
2. maria foi au sinema — *Maria went to the show.*
3. maria foi au baili — *Maria went to the dance.*
4. alisia foi au mexkadu — *Alice went to the market.*
5. alisia foi au axmazẽ — *Alice went to the grocery store.*
6. alisia foi au xestaurãti — *Alice went to the restaurant.*
7. maria esta nu teatru — *Maria is in the theater.*
8. maria esta nu sinema — *Maria is at the show.*
9. maria esta nu mexkadu — *Maria is in the market.*
10. alisia esta nu baili — *Alice is at the dance.*
11. alisia esta nu axmazẽ — *Alice is in the grocery store.*
12. alisia esta nu xestaurãti — *Alice is in the restaurant.*
13. maria foi au teatru i alisia au mexkadu
    Maria went to the theater and Alice went to the market.

14. maria foi au sinema i alisia au xestaurãti
    Maria went to the show and Alice went to the restaurant.
15. alisia foi au axmazẽ i maria au baili
    Alice went to the grocery store and Maria went to the dance.
16. maria esta nu teatru i alisia nu xestaurãti
    Maria is in the theater and Alice is in the restaurant.
17. alisia esta nu axmazẽ i maria nu sinema
    Alice is in the grocery store and Maria is at the show.

But not:
*maria foi nu teatru
*maria esta au sinema
*maria foi au sinema i maria au xestaurãti
*maria foi au sinema i alisia au sinema
*alisia foi au axmazẽ i maria nu baili
*maria esta nu teatru i alisia au baili

3. JAPANESE

1. kore wa yasui
   This is cheap.
2. are wa takai
   That is expensive.
3. kore wa yasuku(te) are wa takai
   This is cheap and that is expensive.
4. kore wa široi
   This is white.
5. are wa kuroi
   That is black.
6. are wa kuroku(te) kore wa široi
   That is black and this is white.
7. are wa takaku(te) are wa yasui
   That is expensive and that is cheap.
8. kore wa kuroku(te) kore wa široi
   This is black and this is white.
9. kore wa yasuku(te) are wa kuroi
   This is cheap and that is black.
10. are wa kuroku(te) kore wa takai
    That is black and this is expensive.
11. kore wa široku(te) yasui
    This is white and cheap.

12. are wa kuroku(te) yasui
    That is black and cheap.
13. kore wa yasuku(te) kuroi
    This is cheap and black.
14. are wa široku(te) kuroi
    That is white and black.
15. are wa yasuku(te) takai
    That is cheap and expensive.

But not:

*kore wa yasui are wa takai
*kore wa yasuku(te) kore wa yasui
*are wa yasuku(te) are wa yasui

NOTE: The parentheses around *te* indicate that the conjunctive particle has two forms: *ku* and *kute.*

4. BRAZILIAN PORTUGUESE

1. loidi kõprou sebolaz
   Lois bought onions.
2. loidi kõprou alju
   Lois bought garlic.
3. loidi trousi kaxni
   Lois brought meat.
4. loidi trousi axoz
   Lois brought rice.
5. loidi kõprou feižau
   Lois bought beans.
6. loidi kõprou sebolaz alju kaxni axoz i feižau
   Lois bought onions, garlic, meat, rice, and beans.
7. loidi trousi sebolaz i alju
   Lois brought onions and garlic.
8. loidi trousi sebolaz alju i kaxni
   Lois brought onions, garlic, and meat.
9. loidi kõprou sebolaz alju kaxni i axoz
   Lois bought onions, garlic, meat, and rice.
10. loidi kõprou kaxni i trousi axoz
    Lois bought meat and brought rice.
11. loidi trousi sebolaz i feižau i kõprou alju
    Lois brought onions and beans and bought garlic.

12. loidi foi au mexkadu
    Lois went to the market.
13. loidi foi au axmazẽ
    Lois went to the grocery store.
14. loidi foi au mexkadu i kõprou sebolaz
    Lois went to the market and bought onions.
15. loidi foi au axmazẽ i trousi feižau axoz i sebolaz
    Lois went to the grocery store and brought beans, rice, and onions.
16. loidi trousi sebolaz i foi au axmazẽ
    Lois brought onions and went to the grocery store.
17. loidi kõprou axoz i sebolaz i foi au mexkadu
    Lois bought rice and onions and went to the market.
18. loidi foi au mexkadu i au axmazẽ
    Lois went to the market and the grocery store.

But not:

*loidi kõprou kaxni i loidi kõprou kaxni
*loidi kõprou kaxni i kõprou kaxni
*loidi foi au axmazẽ i loidi foi au axmazẽ
*loidi foi au mexkadu i foi au mexkadu
*loidi foi au mexkadu i au mexkadu

5. COLLOQUIAL LEBANESE ARABIC

1. ɛžit sælma min is suˀ
   Salma came from the market.
2. šɛrbit sælma ˀæhwey
   Salma drank coffee.
3. ḥakit sælma maˀ el xæ·dæm
   Salma talked with the servant.
4. ɛžɛ sami·r min is suˀ
   Samiir came from the market.
5. šɛrɛb sami·r ˀæhwey
   Samiir drank coffee.
6. ḥakɛ sami·r maˀ el xæ·dæm
   Samiir talked with the servant.
7. ɛžit sælma min is suˀ wæ šɛrɛb sami·r ˀæhwey
   Salma came from the market and Samiir drank coffee.
8. šɛrbit sælma ˀæhwey wæ ḥakɛ sami·r maˀ el xæ·dæm
   Salma drank coffee and Samiir talked with the servant.

9. εžε sami·r min is suˀ wæ ḥakit sælma mả el xæ·dæm
   Samiir came from the market and Salma talked with the servant.
10. εžε sami·r min is suˀ wæ ḥakε mả el xæ·dæm
   Samiir came from the market and talked with the servant.
11. ḥakit sælma mả el xæ·dæm wæ šεrbit ˀæhwey
   Salma talked with the servant and drank coffee.
12. šεrbit sælma ˀæhwey wæ ḥakit mả el xæ·dæm
   Salma drank coffee and talked with the servant.

But not:
*εžit sami·r min is suˀ
*εžε sælma min is suˀ
*εžε sami·r min is suˀ wæ ḥakit mả el xæ·dæm
*šεrbit sælma ˀæhwey wæ hakε mả el xæ·dæm

6. KAIWA-GUARANI, a language of Brazil

1. oho ǰari okoɨpɨ — *Grandmother went to her garden.*
2. oho ǰari padabipɨ — *Grandmother went to Panambi.*
3. avati oǰotɨ̃ ǰari — *Grandmother planted corn.*
4. kubada oǰotɨ̃ ǰari — *Grandmother planted beans.*
5. avati oqeru ǰari — *Grandmother brought corn.*
6. kubada oqeru ǰari — *Grandmother brought beans.*
7. avati hoˀu ǰari — *Grandmother ate corn.*
8. kubada hoˀu ǰari — *Grandmother ate beans.*
9. oho ǰari okoɨpɨ oǰotɨ̃ haqã avati
   Grandmother went to her garden to plant corn.
10. oho ǰari padabipɨ oqeru haqã avati
   Grandmother went to Panambi to bring corn.
11. oho ǰari okoɨpɨ oǰotɨ̃ haqã kubada
   Grandmother went to her garden to plant beans.
12. oǰotɨ̃ haqã avati oho okoɨpɨ ǰari
   Grandmother went to her garden to plant corn.
13. oǰotɨ̃ haqã kubada oho padabipɨ ǰari
   Grandmother went to Panambi to plant beans.
14. oqeru haqã avati oho padabipɨ ǰari
   Grandmother went to Panambi to bring corn.
15. oqeru haqã kubada oho okoɨpɨ ǰari
   Grandmother went to her garden to bring beans.

16. oho rabõ okoɨpɨ oǰotɨ̃ ǰari avati
If she goes to her field, grandmother will plant corn.
17. oho rabõ padabipɨ oqeru ǰari kubada
If she goes to Panambi, grandmother will bring beans.

But not:

*haqã oqeru avati oho padabipɨ̃ ǰari
*oho ǰari padabipɨ oqeru avati haqã
*rabõ oho okoɨpɨ oǰotɨ̃ ǰari avati
*oho okoɨpɨ rabõ oǰotɨ̃ ǰari avati
*oho ǰari padabipɨ oqeru avati rabõ
*oho ǰari padabipɨ rabõ oqeru avati

7. MODERN GREEK

1. pjos kaθaˈrizi to ˈspiti
Who is cleaning the house?
2. afˈtos kaθaˈrizi to ˈspiti
He is cleaning the house.
3. eγˈo kaθaˈrizo to ˈspiti
I am cleaning the house.
4. pjos ðjorˈθoni to ˈspiti
Who is fixing the house?
5. afˈtos ðjorˈθoni to ˈspiti
He is fixing the house.
6. eγˈo ðjorˈθono to ˈspiti
I am fixing the house.
7. pjos ðjorˈθoni ke kaθaˈrizi to ˈspiti
Who is fixing and cleaning the house?
8. eγˈo ðjorˈθono ke kaθaˈrizo to ˈspiti
I am fixing and cleaning the house.
9. afˈtos kaθaˈrizi ke ðjorˈθoni to ˈspiti
He is cleaning and fixing the house.
10. ti kaθaˈrizi
What is he cleaning?
11. ti ðjorˈθono
What am I fixing?
12. ti kaθaˈrizi ke ðjorˈθoni
What is he cleaning and fixing?

13. ti ðjorθóno ke kaθarízo
    What am I fixing and cleaning?
14. ti kaθarízo ke ðjorθóno
    What am I cleaning and fixing?
15. pjos kaθárise to spíti
    Who cleaned the house?
16. aftós kaθárise to spíti
    He cleaned the house.
17. eγó kaθárisa to spíti
    I cleaned the house.
18. pjos ðjórθose to spíti
    Who fixed the house?
19. eγó ðjórθosa to spíti
    I fixed the house.
20. pjos ðjórθose ke kaθárise to spíti
    Who fixed and cleaned the house?
21. aftós ðjórθose ke kaθárise to spíti
    He fixed and cleaned the house.
22. eγó kaθárisa ke ðjórθosa to spíti
    I cleaned and fixed the house.
23. ti ðjórθosa
    What did I fix?
24. ti kaθárise
    What did he clean?
25. ti kaθárisa ke ðjórθosa
    What did I fix and clean?
26. ti kaθárise ke ðjórθise
    What did he clean and fix?
27. ti ðjórθise ke kaθárise
    What did he fix and clean?

But not:

*aftós kaθarízo to spíti
*eγó kaθárise to spíti
*pjos kaθarízo to spíti
*pjos kaθárisa to spíti
*pjos kaθarízi ke ðjórθose to spíti
*ti kaθárisa to spíti
*pjos aftós kaθárise to spíti
*ti kaθárisa ke kaθárise to spíti

8. MANDARIN CHINESE[6]

1. wǒ mǎi shū	*I buy books.*
2. wǒ bù mǎi shū	*I don't buy books.*
3. wǒ mǎile shū	*I have bought books.*
4. wǒ méiyou mǎi shū	*I have not bought books.*
5. wǒ gǎn lái	*I dare to come.*
6. wǒ bù gǎn lái	*I don't dare to come.*
7. wǒ gǎn lái bù gǎn	*Do I dare to come?*
8. wǒ gǎn bù gǎn lái	*Do I dare to come?*
9. wǒ gǎn mǎi shū	*I dare to buy books.*
10. wǒ gǎn mǎi shū bù gǎn	*Do I dare to buy books?*
11. wǒ gǎn bù gǎn mǎi shū	*Do I dare to buy books?*
12. wǒ mài shū	*I sell books.*
13. wǒ màile shū	*I have sold books.*
14. wǒ bù mài shū	*I don't sell books.*
15. wǒ méiyou mài shū	*I have not sold books.*
16. wǒ màile shū méiyou	*Have I sold books?*
17. wǒ yǒu méiyou mài shū	*Have I sold books?*
18. wǒ mài shū bù mài	*Do I sell books?*
19. wǒ mài bù mài shū	*Do I sell books?*

But not:

*wǒ yǒu mǎi shū
*wǒ mǎile shū méi
*wǒ mǎi shū bú

9. GERMAN

1. ix bin arm
   I am poor.
2. er ist arm
   He is poor.
3. ix bin arm unt er ist arm
   I am poor and he is poor.
4. ix bin alt
   I am old.

[6] This exercise is by courtesy of William S-Y. Wang.

5. ix bin alt unt ix bin arm
   I am old and I am poor.
6. er ist arm unt ix bin alt
   He is poor and I am old.
7. er ist arm ɔbglaix ix alt bin
   He is poor, although I am old.
8. ix bin alt ɔbglaix er arm ist
   I am old, although he is poor.
9. ɔbglaix ix alt bin bin ix arm
   Although I am old, I am poor.
10. ɔbglaix er arm ist bin ix alt
    Although he is poor, I am old.
11. ix var arm
    I was poor.
12. er var alt
    He was old.
13. ix var arm unt er var alt
    I was poor and he was old.
14. er var alt unt er var arm
    He was old and he was poor.
15. ɔbglaix er alt var var er arm
    Although he was old, he was poor.
16. er var alt ɔbglaix ix arm var
    He was old, although I was poor.
17. ix verdə alt zain
    I will be old.
18. er virt arm zain
    He will be poor.
19. ix verdə alt zain unt er virt arm zain
    I will be old and he will be poor.
20. ix verdə alt zain ɔbglaix er arm zain virt
    I will be old, although he will be poor.
21. er virt alt zain ɔbglaix ix arm zain verdə
    He will be old, although I will be poor.
22. ɔbglaix er arm zain virt verdə ix alt zain
    Although he will be poor, I will be old.
23. ɔbglaix ix arm zain verdə virt er alt zain
    Although I will be poor, he will be old.
24. ɔbglaix er alt zain virt virt er arm zain
    Although he will be old, he will be poor.

But not:

*bin ix arm
*ix arm bin
*er bin arm
*ix bin arm ɔbglaix er ist alt
*ix bin arm unt er alt ist
*ɔbglaix ix bin arm er ist alt
*ix verdə zain arm
*verdə ix arm zain ɔbglaix er alt zain virt

10. ENGLISH

1. Bob is coming
2. John is coming
3. is John or Bob coming
4. is John or is Bob coming
5. is John coming or is Bob coming
6. either John or Bob is coming
7. either John is coming or Bob is
8. who is coming
9. Tom is going
10. John is going
11. is Tom or John going
12. is Tom or is John going
13. is Tom going or is John
14. who is going
15. either Tom or John is going
16. either Tom is going or John is
17. is Tom coming or going
18. is John coming or going
19. is Tom or John coming or going
20. is Tom coming or going or is John coming or going
21. is Tom coming or going or is John
22. who is coming or going
23. who is going or coming
24. either Tom or John is either coming or going
25. either Tom or John is either going or coming
26. either Tom or John is going
27. either John or Tom is going

28. either John or Tom is coming
29. either John or Tom or Bob is either coming or going
30. is John or Bob or Tom coming or going
31. is John or Bob either coming or going
32. who is either coming or going
33. who is either going or coming
34. is Tom or Bob going or is John

But not:

*is coming Bob
*John is coming or is Bob coming
*either John or Tom is
*Tom or John is going
*either is Tom coming or going
*is who going
*who Bob is going
*is Tom or who going
*either Tom or who is going

chapter eight

EMBEDDING

INTRODUCTION

In Chapter 7 we saw how to specify sentences derived by conjoining one sentence to another. The purpose of this chapter is to illustrate the specification of sentences derived by embedding one sentence into another, i.e. to illustrate how complex sentences are derived.

In traditional terminology the embedded sentence of a complex sentence is referred to as the **dependent** or **subordinate clause,** while the other part of the complex sentence is referred to as the **independent clause.** The essential differences between these two types of clauses are that (1) while an independent clause can stand alone as a sentence, a subordinate clause cannot (i.e. it requires the occurrence of an independent clause) and (2) while an independent clause cannot function (i.e. be used) as a noun, adjective, adverb, etc., a subordinate clause can.

The following problems illustrate some of the more

common functions that subordinate clauses are said to have: the subordinate clauses in Problems 57 and 58 function as time adverbs; in Problems 59, 60, 61, and 67 they function as noun complements; in Problems 62 and 63 they function as adjective intensifiers; and in the remaining problems (64 to 66, 68) they function as noun modifiers.

8.1 DATA

PROBLEM 57: KRIO

1. ustɛm a slip	*When did I sleep?*
2. a slip yɛstade	*I slept yesterday.*
3. mi brɔda wok	*My brother worked.*
4. a slip we mi brɔda wok	*I slept when my brother worked.*
5. mi sista wok	*My sister worked.*
6. a slip we mi sista wok	*I slept when my sister worked.*
7. ustɛm mi sista it	*When did my sister eat?*
8. mi sista it yɛstade	*My sister ate yesterday.*
9. mi sista it we mi brɔda wok	*My sister ate when my brother worked.*
10. a wok	*I work.*
11. mi sista it we a wok	*My sister ate when I worked.*
12. mi brɔda slip	*My brother slept.*
13. mi sista it we mi brɔda slip	*My sister ate when my brother slept.*
14. a it	*I ate.*
15. a slip we a it	*I slept when I ate.*
16. mi sista it we a it	*My sister ate when I ate.*
17. ustɛm mi brɔda wok	*When did my brother work?*
18. mi brɔda wok yɛstade	*My brother worked yesterday.*
19. mi brɔda wok tide	*My brother worked today.*
20. mi brɔda wok we a wok	*My brother worked when I worked.*
21. mi brɔda wok we a slip	*My brother worked when I slept.*
22. mi brɔda wok we a it	*My brother worked when I ate.*
23. mi brɔda wok we mi sista wok	*My brother worked when my sister worked.*
24. mi brɔda wok we mi sista it	*My brother worked when my sister ate.*

25. mi sista slip — *My sister slept.*
26. mi brɔda wok we mi sista slip — *My brother worked when my sister slept.*

But not:

*a slip yɛstade we mi sista wok
*a slip we a slip
*a slip we mi sista it yɛstade
*mi sista it we mi sista it
*ustɛm a slip we mi sista wok

The above sentences are either simple or complex. The simple sentences are all intransitive and are either declarative or interrogative. Simple declarative sentences consist of a pronoun or of a determiner and a noun as the subject, followed by a predicate consisting either of a verb or of a verb followed by an adverb of time. Simple interrogative sentences differ from simple declarative sentences in that they contain the adverbial question-word *ustɛm* 'when,' which (1) is mutually exclusive with the adverbs of time and (2) always occurs at the beginning of a sentence.

The complex sentences are declarative and differ from the corresponding simple sentences in that they consist of two simple declarative sentences, neither of which contains an adverb of time, and one of which is subordinated to the other (i.e. linked to it) by the particle *we* 'when.' Notice that the subordinate sentence occupies the same position as the time adverbs of simple sentences. (Put differently, subordinate sentences and time adverbs are mutually exclusive.) Notice, finally, that complex sentences cannot consist of two lexically identical simple sentences.

PROBLEM 58: ROGLAI

1. ama naw
   Father went.
2. ama naw tubrəy
   Father went yesterday.
3. adəy ˀbək bu
   The child ate rice.
4. ama naw judəy adəy ˀbək bu
   Father went after the child ate rice.

5. adəy ʔbək bu tubrəy
   The child ate rice yesterday.
6. adəy ʔbək bu judəy ama naw
   The child ate rice after the father went.
7. tubrəy ama naw
   Yesterday father went.
8. judəy adəy ʔbək bu ama naw
   After the child ate rice, the father went.
9. tubrəy adəy ʔbək bu
   Yesterday the child ate rice.
10. judəy ama naw adəy ʔbək bu
    After father went, the child ate rice.
11. adəy naw musu·p
    The child went early in the morning.
12. ama ʔbək ika·t
    Father ate fish.
13. adəy naw judəy ama ʔbək ika·t
    The child went after the father ate fish.
14. adəy naw juma ama ʔbək ika·t
    The child went before father ate fish.
15. musu·p adəy naw
    Early in the morning the child went.
16. judəy ama ʔbək ika·t adəy naw
    After the father ate fish, the child went.
17. juma ama ʔbək ika·t adəy naw
    Before the father ate fish, the child went.
18. ama naw juma adəy ʔbək bu
    Father went before the child ate rice.
19. juma adəy ʔbək bu ama naw
    Before the child ate rice, the father went.
20. adəy ʔbək ika·t tubrəy
    The child ate fish yesterday.
21. tubrəy adəy ʔbək ika·t
    Yesterday the child ate fish.
22. judəy ama naw adəy ʔbək ika·t
    After father went, the child ate fish.
23. juma ama naw adəy ʔbək ika·t
    Before father went, the child ate fish.

But not:

*bu ʔbək ama
*ama naw juma ama ʔbək bu

*ama naw musu·p juma adəy ˀbək bu
*musu·p ama naw juma adəy ˀbək bu
*ama naw juma adəy ˀbək bu musu·p

In the above data the simple sentences are either transitive or intransitive. The subject of both these types of sentences is a human noun. The predicate of an intransitive sentence is an intransitive verb, while the predicate of a transitive sentence is a transitive verb followed by a non-human noun. An adverb of time may occur in both these types of sentences; when it does, it is either at the very beginning or the very end of a sentence.

The complex sentences are also transitive or intransitive and differ from the corresponding simple sentences in that they consist of two simple sentences, neither of which contains an adverb of time, and one of which is subordinated to the other by one of the particles, *judəy* 'after' or *juma* 'before.' Notice that the position of time adverbs in simple sentences and the position of the subordinate sentences in complex sentences are the same; i.e. subordinate sentences and time adverbs are mutually exclusive, and both occur either at the beginning or at the end of a sentence.

PROBLEM 59: JAPANESE

1. nara wa hanasi o kiita
   Nara heard the story.
2. anata wa nara o kiita
   You heard Nara.
3. ǰon wa hanasi o šinzita
   John believed the story.
4. nara wa ǰon o šinzita
   Nara believed John.
5. anata wa nara ga hanasi o kiita to šinzita
   You believed that Nara heard the story.
6. nara wa ǰon ga hanasi o šinzita to kiita
   Nara heard that John believed the story.
7. ǰon wa šiawase da
   John was happy.
8. anata wa ǰon ga šiawase da to kiita
   You heard that John was happy.
9. nara wa daigakusei da
   Nara was a student.

10. ǰon wa nara ga daigakusei da to šinzita
    John believed that Nara was a student.
11. nara wa anata ga daigakusei da to kiita
    Nara heard that you were a student.
12. daigakusei wa nara ga šiawase da to šinzita
    The student believed that Nara was happy.
13. ǰon wa anata ga šiawase da to kiita
    John heard that you were happy.

But not:

*hanasi wa nara o kiita
*hanasi wa šiawase da
*ǰon wa hanasi da
*anata wa ǰon ga kiita to šiawase da
*ǰon wa nara ga kiita to daigakusei da

The above simple sentences are either transitive or copulative. The subject of both these types of sentences is either a name, pronoun, or animate noun, followed by the subject marker *wa*. The predicate follows the subject and, in transitive sentences, consists of either a name or an inanimate noun followed by the object marker *o* and a transitive verb, while in copulative sentences it is either an animate noun or an adjective, followed by a copulative verb.

The complex sentences are transitive and differ from the corresponding simple sentences in that they consist of two simple sentences, one of which is subordinated to the other and is followed by *to* 'that.' In traditional terminology, the subordinate sentence is a "complement that-clause"; i.e. the subordinate sentence occurs in the same position as the complement of simple transitive sentences (i.e. the object) and thus is mutually exclusive with this complement. Notice that although a subordinate sentence does not occur as a complement of a copulative verb, it may be either transitive or copulative and its subject marker is always *ga*.

PROBLEM 60: KRIO

1. di klak mɛmba di uman
   The clerk remembers the woman.
2. di klak mɛmba di stori
   The clerk remembers the story.

3. di klak rid di stori
   The clerk read the story.
4. di uman rid di njuz
   The woman read the news.
5. di klak mɛmba se di uman rid di stori
   The clerk remembers that the woman read the story.
6. di uman mɛmba se di klak rid di njuz
   The woman remembers that the clerk read the news.
7. di tiča no di stori
   The teacher knows the story.
8. di tiča no se di uman rid di njuz
   The teacher knows that the woman read the news.
9. di tiča mɛmba se di klak no di stori
   The teacher remembers that the clerk knows the story.
10. di fama gɛt di lɛta
    The farmer has the letter.
11. di klak no se di fama gɛt di lɛta
    The clerk knows that the farmer has the letter.
12. di uman mɛmba se di tiča gɛt di lɛta
    The woman remembers that the teacher has the letter.
13. di uman mit di tiča
    The woman met the teacher.
14. di klak no se di uman mit di tiča
    The clerk knows that the woman met the teacher.
15. di uman mɛmba se di tiča mit di fama
    The woman remembers that the teacher met the farmer.
16. di fama ɛp di uman
    The farmer helped the woman.
17. di tiča no se di fama ɛp di uman
    The teacher knows that the farmer helped the woman.
18. di fama no se di tiča mɛmba di njuz
    The farmer knows that the teacher remembers the news.
19. di klak sabi di tiča
    The clerk knows the teacher.
20. di uman no se di klak sabi di tiča
    The woman knows that the clerk knows the teacher.
21. di fama mɛmba se di uman sabi di klak
    The farmer remembers that the woman knows the clerk.
22. di tiča no se di fama no se di uman sabi di klak
    The teacher knows that the farmer knows that the woman knows the clerk.

23. di uman no se di klak mɛmba se di tiča ɛp di fama
    The woman knows that the clerk remembers that the teacher helped the farmer.
24. di klak mɛmba se di uman no se di fama mɛmba di stori
    The clerk remembers that the woman knows that the farmer remembers the story.

But not:

*di klak rid di tiča
*di fama gɛt di klak
*di tiča mit di stori
*di klak no di tiča
*di uman sabi di njuz
*di uman sabi se ...
*di klak gɛt se ...
*di uman mit se ...
*di fama ɛp se ...
*di tiča rid se ...

The simple sentences above are transitive and consist of a subject, which is a determiner and a noun, followed by a predicate; the predicate is a verb followed by an object, which is a determiner and a noun. All subject nouns are animate, while object nouns are (1) animate after the verbs *sabi* 'know,' *ɛp* 'help,' and *mit* 'meet,' (2) inanimate after the verbs *no* 'know,' *rid* 'read,' and *gɛt* 'have,' and (3) either animate or inanimate after the verb *mɛmba* 'remember.'

The complex sentences are transitive and differ from the simple sentences in that they consist of two or more simple sentences, one of which is independent while the others are subordinated by the particle *se* 'that.' If there is only one subordinate sentence, it is subordinated to the independent sentence, and if there are two subordinate sentences, one is subordinated to the independent sentence while the other is subordinated to the subordinate sentence. The subordinate sentences are complement that-clauses of independent (or subordinate) sentences, but of only two verbs, *mɛmba* and *no;* that is, subordinate sentences can be complements of only these two verbs.

PROBLEM 61: ENGLISH

1. Jim heard the man
2. Jim heard the truth
3. the man came

4. Jim heard that the man came
5. Bill heard the truth
6. Jim and Bill heard the truth
7. Bill and Jim heard that the man came
8. the man heard the truth
9. Jim came
10. the man heard that Jim came
11. Bill came
12. Bill and Jim came
13. Jim and the man came
14. the man heard that Jim and Bill came
15. the truth was heard by Jim
16. that the man came was heard by Jim
17. the truth was heard by Bill
18. the truth was heard by Jim and Bill
19. the truth was heard by Jim and the man
20. that the man came was heard by Jim and Bill
21. the truth was heard by the man
22. Jim was heard by Bill
23. that Jim came was heard by the man
24. that Bill and Jim came was heard by the man

But not:

*the truth heard Jim
*the truth came
*Bill came that the man heard the truth
*the man came that Jim heard the truth
*the truth was came by Jim

The above sentences are simple, compound, or complex. The simple sentences are either transitive or intransitive. The subject of the intransitive sentences is a name or a determiner and an animate noun, and the predicate is an intransitive verb. The transitive sentences are either active or passive. Simple active sentences have a name or a determiner followed by an animate noun as the subject and, as the predicate, have a transitive verb followed by an object, which is a determiner followed by either an animate or abstract noun. Simple passive sentences differ from simple active sentences in that the subject of the passive sentences is identical to the object of corresponding active sentences and the predicate of passive sentences is a verb preceded by *was* and followed by a prepositional phrase which consists of the preposition *by* and an object which is identical to the subject of corresponding active sentences.

Compound sentences differ from simple sentences in that in intransitive and active transitive sentences the subject is compound, while in passive sentences the prepositional object is compound. The compound subjects and prepositional objects are joined by the conjunction *and.*

The complex sentences are active or passive transitive sentences and differ from the corresponding simple and compound sentences in that they consist of one simple and one compound sentence or of two simple sentences, one of which is subordinated to the other by the particle *that.* The subordinate sentence is always an intransitive that-clause, while the independent sentence is always transitive. In complex active sentences the subordinate sentence is a complement, while in complex passive sentences, it is the subject. Notice, finally, the compounding within complex sentences: (1) in active sentences the subject of either the independent or the subordinate sentence is compound; and (2) in passive sentences either the subject of the subordinate sentence or the prepositional object of the independent sentence is compound.

PROBLEM 62: BULGARIAN (Eastern variety)

1. boris e pročut	*Boris is famous.*
2. ivan e pročut	*Ivan is famous.*
3. boris e mnogo pročut	*Boris is very famous.*
4. boris e po pročut ot ivan	*Boris is more famous than Ivan.*
5. ivan e dosta pročut	*Ivan is rather famous.*
6. ivan e po pročut ot boris	*Ivan is more famous than Boris.*
7. aleksandər e star	*Alexander is old.*
8. boris e dosta star	*Boris is rather old.*
9. boris e po star ot aleksandər	*Boris is older than Alexander.*
10. gradət e star	*The city is old.*
11. boris e po star ot ivan	*Boris is older than Ivan.*
12. vinoto e mnogo star	*The wine is very old.*
13. vinoto e po star ot ivan	*The wine is older than Ivan.*
14. gradət e dosta pročut	*The city is rather famous.*
15. gradət e po pročut ot vinoto	*The city is more famous than the wine.*
16. gradət e po pročut ot boris	*The city is more famous than Boris.*
17. aleksandər e po star ot ivan	*Alexander is older than Ivan.*

But not:

*ivan e po dosta star ot boris
*vinoto e mnogo star ot gradət

*ivan e star ot boris
*ivan e po star boris

The above sentences are copulative and differ from each other primarily in that some contain predicate adjectives in the "positive degree" (e.g. sentences 1, 3, and 5), while others contain predicate adjectives in the "comparative degree" (e.g. sentences 4, 6, and 13).

Sentences with adjectives in the positive degree consist of a name or noun as the subject, followed by a copulative verb, which is, in turn, followed by an adjective, as the predicate. The adjective may be preceded by one of the adjective intensifiers *mnogo* 'very' or *dosta* 'rather.'

Sentences with adjectives in the comparative degree differ from those with adjectives in the positive degree in that (1) the adjective has a complement, which is either a noun or a name, and (2) the adjective is flanked by the (comparative) particles *po* ... *ot.* The predicate of these sentences, then, always consists of a verb, *po,* an adjective, *ot,* and either a name or a noun.

Finally, notice that the comparative particles and the adjective complement are mutually exclusive with the adjective intensifiers.

PROBLEM 63: GERMAN

1.	karl ist klain	*Carl is short.*
2.	klaus ist klain	*Claus is short.*
3.	klaus ist ze·r klain	*Claus is very short.*
4.	klaus ist klainər als karl	*Claus is shorter than Carl.*
5.	klaus ist zo· klain vi· karl	*Claus is as short as Carl.*
6.	jo·han ist ze·r dik	*John is very fat.*
7.	jo·han ist dikər als klaus	*John is fatter than Claus.*
8.	jo·han ist zo· dik vi· klaus	*John is as fat as Claus.*
9.	klaus ist dik	*Claus is fat.*
10.	karl ist tsimliç dik	*Carl is rather fat.*
11.	karl ist dikər als klaus	*Carl is fatter than Claus.*
12.	karl ist zo· dik vi· jo·han	*Carl is as fat as John.*
13.	jo·han ist tsimliç klain	*John is rather short.*
14.	jo·han ist klainər als klaus	*John is shorter than Claus.*
15.	jo·han ist zo· klain vi· karl	*John is as short as Carl.*
16.	karl ist zo· klain vi· klaus	*Carl is as short as Claus.*
17.	karl ist klainər als jo·han	*Carl is shorter than John.*
18.	klaus ist dikər als jo·han	*Claus is fatter than John.*
19.	klaus ist zo· dik vi· karl	*Claus is as fat as Carl.*

20. karl ist auf dem berg — *Carl is on the mountain.*
21. klaus ist auf dem plats — *Claus is on the square.*
22. jo·han ist auf dem berg — *John is on the mountain.*

But not:

*karl ist zo· ze·r klain vi· klaus
*karl ist ze·r klainər als klaus
*karl ist klain auf dem berg
*karl ist klainər als auf dem berg
*karl ist zo· klain vi· auf dem berg
*karl ist klainər als karl
*karl ist zo· klain vi· karl
*karl ist klain als klaus
*karl ist klainər klaus

The above sentences are either intransitive or copulative. Both types consist of a subject, which is always a name, followed by a predicate. The predicate of intransitive sentences is an intransitive verb followed by a locative phrase, which is a preposition followed by a determiner and a noun. The predicate of copulative sentences is a copulative verb followed by an adjective, which is in either the positive or the comparative degree.

Predicates of copulative sentences which have an adjective in the positive degree consist of that adjective, or that adjective preceded by one of the intensifiers *ze·r* 'very' or *tsimliç* 'rather.' Predicates of copulative sentences which have an adjective in the comparative degree differ from those with an adjective in the positive degree in that (1) the adjective is flanked by the particles *zo·* ... *vi·*, or is followed by the particles *ər* and *als,* and (2) the predicates contain an adjective complement, which is always a name and which is preceded by the last comparative particle.

Notice, finally, that the comparative particles and adjective complement are mutually exclusive with the adjective intensifiers and that although the adjective complement and the subject must differ lexically, they both must be names.

PROBLEM 64: MODERN GREEK

1. o andras γirevi ton maθiti
   The man is looking for the student.
2. o andras irθe
   The man came.

3. o andras pu irθe γirevi ton maθiti
   The man who came is looking for the student.
4. o andras pu γirevi ton maθiti irθe
   The man who is looking for the student came.
5. o maθitis γirevi ton andra
   The student is looking for the man.
6. o maθitis irθe
   The student came.
7. o maθitis pu irθe γirevi ton andra
   The student who came is looking for the man.
8. o maθitis pu γirevi ton andra irθe
   The student who is looking for the man came.
9. irθe o andras
   Did the man come?
10. irθe o andras pu γirevi ton maθiti
    Did the man who is looking for the student come?
11. γirevi ton maθiti o andras
    Is the man looking for the student?
12. γirevi ton maθiti o andras pu irθe
    Is the man who came looking for the student?

But not:

*o andras pu o andras irθe γirevi ton maθiti
*irθe o andras pu andras γirevi ton maθiti
*irθe pu o andras γirevi ton maθiti

The simple sentences above are either declarative or interrogative. Simple declarative sentences are either transitive or intransitive and consist of a determiner and a noun as the subject, which is followed by an intransitive verb or by a transitive verb and a determiner followed by a noun as the predicate. (Notice that the determiner agrees in case with the following noun.) Simple interrogative sentences differ from the declarative sentences only in that the predicate precedes the subject; i.e. the order of the subject and predicate in simple interrogative sentences is predicate – subject.

The complex sentences are declarative or interrogative and differ from the corresponding simple sentences in that they consist of two simple sentences (one transitive and the other intransitive), one of which is subordinated to the other as a relative clause (i.e. a clause which modifies a noun phrase).

Notice that the relative clause is subordinated only to the subject of an independent sentence, always immediately follows this subject, and that *pu* 'who' is the subject of the relative clause. Notice, also, that the order of the subject and predicate in complex sentences is the same as that of simple declarative and interrogative sentences, respectively: in complex declarative sentences, the subject precedes the predicate, and in complex interrogative sentences, the subject follows the predicate.

PROBLEM 65: KOREAN

1. aika chinkuta	*The boy is a friend.*
2. chinkuka aita	*The friend is a boy.*
3. jøki aika kanta	*The boy goes there.*
4. jøki kanʉn aika chinkuta	*The boy who goes there is a friend.*
5. jøki chinkuin aika kanta	*The boy who is a friend goes there.*
6. salami chinkuta	*The man is a friend.*
7. salami onta	*The man comes (is coming).*
8. onʉn salami chinkuta	*The man who is coming is a friend.*
9. chinkuin salami onta	*The man who is a friend is coming.*
10. aika onta	*The boy comes (is coming).*
11. onʉn aika chinkuta	*The boy who is coming is a friend.*
12. chinkuin salami onta	*The man who is a friend is coming.*
13. jatoŋchaka alʉmtapta	*The car is pretty.*
14. jøki jatoŋchaka onta	*The car comes (is coming) there.*
15. jøki onʉn jatoŋchaka alʉmtapta	*The car that is coming there is pretty.*
16. jøki alumtaʉn jatoŋchaka onta	*The car that is pretty is coming there.*
17. salami alʉmtapta	*The man is handsome.*
18. mataŋe salami kanta	*The man is going into the garden.*
19. mataŋe kanʉn salami alʉmtapta	*The man who is going into the garden is handsome.*

20. mataŋe alumtaʉn salami kanta — *The man who is handsome is going into the garden.*

21. mataŋe onʉn aika chinkuta — *The boy who is coming into the garden is a friend.*

22. mataŋe kanʉn jatoŋchaka alʉmtapta — *The car that is going into the garden is pretty.*

But not:

*jøki aika kanʉn aika chinkuta
*mataŋe kanuin salami alʉmtapta
*chinkuʉn salami onta
*aika jatoŋchata

Additional information:

(1) Every sentence ends in *ta,* which signals the end of a statement.
(2) The *n* in the verb stems *kan* 'go' and *on* 'come' signals the present tense.

The above sentences are either simple or complex. The simple sentences are either copulative or intransitive, with a subject consisting of a noun followed by a subject marker, which is *ka* when the preceding word ends in a vowel and *i* otherwise. In simple intransitive sentences the subject is followed by an intransitive verb. A location adverb sometimes occurs in these sentences, and when it does, it is always at the beginning of a sentence. In simple copulative sentences the subject is followed by either an adjective or an animate noun.

The complex sentences are copulative or intransitive and differ from the corresponding simple sentences in that they consist of two simple sentences (one intransitive and the other copulative), one of which is subordinated to the other as a relative clause. Notice that relative clauses (1) are subordinated only to subject nouns and always immediately precede these nouns, (2) do not contain an overt subject, and (3) always end with a particle, which is *in* if the preceding word is a noun, but *ʉn* otherwise (notice that the consonant *p* in *alʉmtap* 'pretty' does not occur before *ʉn*). Notice, further, that regardless of whether a sentence is simple or complex, there never is more than one adverb or sentence-final particle. Notice, finally, that the predicates of the independent sentence and the subordinate sentence cannot be lexically identical.

PROBLEM 66: THAI[1]

1. mǎ· kin rew
The dog eats fast.
2. mǎ· tua ní· kin rew
This dog eats fast.
3. mǎ· tua nán kin rew
That dog eats fast.
4. mǎ· wîŋ chá·chá·
The dog runs slowly.
5. mǎ· tua ní· wîŋ chá·chá·
This dog runs slowly.
6. mǎ· tua nán wîŋ chá·chá·
That dog runs slowly.
7. mǎ· tua thî· kin rew (nán) wîŋ chá·chá·
The dog that eats fast runs slowly.
8. mǎ· tua thî· wîŋ chá·chá· (nán) kin rew
The dog that runs slowly eats fast.
9. mɛ·w wîŋ rew
The cat runs fast.
10. mɛ·w tua ní· wîŋ rew
This cat runs fast.
11. mɛ·w kin thî· bâ·n
The cat eats at the house.
12. mɛ·w tua nán kin thî· bâ·n
That cat eats at the house.
13. mɛ·w tua thî· wîŋ rew (nán) kin thî· bâ·n
The cat that runs fast eats at the house.
14. mɛ·w tua thî· kin thî· bâ·n (nán) wîŋ rew
The cat that eats at the house runs fast.
15. nákrian kin chá·chá·
The student eats slowly.
16. nákrian khon ní· kin chá·chá·
This student eats slowly.
17. nákrian khon nán kin chá·chá·
That student eats slowly.
18. nákrian rian thî· ro·ŋrian
The student studies at the school.
19. nákrian khon thî· kin chá·chá· (nán) rian thî· ro·ŋrian
The student who eats slowly studies at the school.

[1] The parentheses around *nán* 'that' mean that the occurrence of this particle is optional in the sentence in question.

20. nákrian khon thî· rian thî· ro·ŋrian (nán) kin chá·chá·
    The student who studies at the school eats slowly.
21. khru· khon ní· rian rew
    This teacher learns fast.
22. khru· khon thî· rian rew (nán) wîŋ chá·chá·
    The teacher who learns fast runs slowly.
23. mǎ· tua thî· rian chá·chá· (nán) kin chá·chá·
    The dog that learns slowly eats slowly.
24. khru· khon thî· kin thî· ro·ŋrian (nán) rian thî· ro·ŋrian
    The teacher who eats at the school studies at the school.
25. mɛ·w nyàj
    The cat is tired.
26. mǎ· di·
    The dog is good.
27. mǎ· tua ní· di·
    This dog is good.
28. mǎ· wîŋ rew
    The dog runs fast.
29. mǎ· tua di· wîŋ rew
    The good dog runs fast.
30. mǎ· tua thî· wîŋ rew (nán) di·
    The dog that runs fast is good.
31. khru· khon nán nyàj
    That teacher is tired.
32. khru· khon nyàj kin thî· bâ·n
    The tired teacher eats at the house.
33. khru· khon thî· kin thî· bâ·n (nán) nyàj
    The teacher who eats at the house is tired.
34. nákrian khon di· nyàj
    The good student is tired.
35. mɛ·w tua nyàj di·
    The tired cat is good.
36. mɛ·w tua di· rian rew
    The good cat learns fast.

But not:

*mɛ·w khon ní· kin rew
*khru· tua nán kin thî· bâ·n
*mɛ·w tua thî· di· nán wîŋ rew
*khru· khon kin rew di·
*mɛ·w kin thî· chá·chá·

The simple sentences above are either intransitive or copulative. In both these types of sentences the subject is a noun which may be followed by a classifier and either a determiner or an adjective. Notice that (1) the classifier and determiner are mutually dependent; (2) determiners are mutually exclusive with the adjectives and have regular tone (it is always high); and (3) the classifier *khon* occurs with human nouns while the classifier *tua* occurs with all other nouns. The predicate of simple intransitive sentences follows the subject and consists of an intransitive verb and either an adverb or an adverbial phrase consisting of the preposition *thî·* 'at' followed by an inanimate noun. The predicate of simple copulative sentences follows the subject and consists only of a (verbal) adjective.

The complex sentences are intransitive and copulative and differ from the corresponding simple sentences in that they consist of two simple sentences, one of which is subordinated to the other as a relative clause. This subordination is subject to the restriction that relative clauses can be subordinated only to subject nouns.

Finally, notice that (1) the subject of a relative clause is *thî·* 'who' or 'that' and (2) relative clauses occur only after a classifier and before either the determiner *nán* or the predicate of the independent sentences.

PROBLEM 67: FRENCH

Declaratives

1. s e la fam	*It is the woman.*
2. s e la bul	*It is the ball.*
3. la fam frap la bul	*The woman is hitting the ball.*
4. la bul frap la fam	*The ball is hitting the woman.*
5. s e kø la fam frap la bul	*It's that (because) the woman is hitting the ball.*
6. s e kø la bul frap la fam	*It's that (because) the ball is hitting the woman.*
7. s e la fam ki frap la bul	*It is the woman who is hitting the ball.*
8. s e la bul ki frap la fam	*It is the ball that is hitting the woman.*
9. s e la bul kø la fam frap	*It is the ball that the woman is hitting.*
10. s e la fam kø la bul frap	*It is the woman that the ball is hitting.*

Yes-No Questions

1a. ɛ s la fam	*Is it the woman?*
2a. ɛ s la bul	*Is it the ball?*
3a. ɛ s kø la fam frap la bul	*Is the woman hitting the ball?*
4a. ɛ s kø la bul frap la fam	*Is the ball hitting the woman?*
5a. ɛ s kø la fam frap la bul	*Is the woman hitting the ball?*
6a. ɛ s kø la bul frap la fam	*Is the ball hitting the woman?*
7a. ɛ s la fam ki frap la bul	*Is it the woman who is hitting the ball?*
8a. ɛ s la bul ki frap la fam	*Is it the ball that is hitting the woman?*
9a. ɛ s la bul kø la fam frap	*Is it the ball that the woman is hitting?*
10a. ɛ s la fam kø la bul frap	*Is it the woman that the ball hits?*

Wh-Questions

1b. ki ɛ s	*Who is it?*
2b. k ɛ s	*What is it?*
3b. ki frap la bul	*Who is hitting the ball?*
kø frap la fam	*What is the woman hitting?*
4b. Same as 8b and 10b.	
5b. none	
6b. none	
7b. ki ɛ s ki frap la bul	*Who (is it that) is hitting the ball?*
8b. k ɛ s ki frap la fam	*What (is it that) is hitting the woman?*
9b. k ɛ s kø la fam frap	*What is (it that) the woman (is) hitting?*
10b. ki ɛ s kø la bul frap	*Who is (it that) the ball (is) hitting?*

But not:

*kø frap la fam (if *kø* is the subject)
*ki frap la bul (if *ki* is the object)
*s e la fam kø frap la bul
*s e la bul ki la fam frap
*ɛ s la fam kø frap la bul
*ɛ s la bul ki la fam frap
*ki ɛ s kø frap la bul
*k ɛ s ki la fam frap

The first four sentences (except 4b) in each of the above sets are simple sentences, and the last six sentences (and 4b) are complex sentences. The first two simple sentences are always copulative sentences, and the last two are always transitive sentences. The complex sentences are all copulative sentences. The last four of these are what are called "cleft sentences"; i.e. they are sentences in which one of the constituents of the subordinate clause is also a constituent of the (copulative) independent clause; the subordinate clause is thus split or cleft by the subordinating morpheme and is only partially embedded in the independent clause.

Simple declarative copulative sentences have a pronoun as the subject and a copulative verb followed by a determiner and a noun as the predicate. Simple declarative transitive sentences have a determiner and a noun as the subject and a transitive verb followed by a determiner and a noun as the predicate.

Complex declarative sentences differ from simple declarative sentences in that they consist of two simple sentences, one of which is subordinated to the other as a complement. The independent clause is copulative and the subordinate clause is transitive. More specifically, the complex declarative sentences consist of *s e* 'it is' followed by either a complete sentence which is introduced by the subordinating particle *kø* 'that' or by a noun phrase followed by a clause introduced by one of the subordinating particles *ki* or *kø* (*ki* may be considered the subject of such clauses and *kø* the object).

Simple transitive yes-no questions (3a and 4a) differ from the corresponding declarative sentences only in that ε *s kø* occurs at the beginning of the sentence. The complex and simple copulative yes-no sentences differ from the corresponding declarative sentences only in that the order of the pronoun and the copulative verb is the reverse of that in the declarative sentences. (Notice that the pairs of sentences 3a and 5a and 4a and 6a are identical.)

Simple copulative wh-questions begin with *ki* (or *k*), which is followed by a verb and a pronoun, while the simple transitive wh-questions begin with *ki,* which is followed by the verb and an object noun phrase, or with *kø,* which is followed by the verb and a subject noun phrase.

Complex wh-questions begin with either *ki* or *kø* (or *k*), which is followed by a verb, a pronoun, and a clause introduced by *ki* or *kø.*

Notice that (1) complex declarative sentences containing that-clauses have yes-no equivalents but do not have wh-equivalents; and (2) simple transitive sentences have ε *s kø* in the corresponding yes-no questions, and, except sentence 4, either *ki* (which is mutually exclusive with an animate noun phrase) or *kø* (which is mutually exclusive with an inanimate noun phrase) in the corresponding wh-questions.

Finally, notice the following morphophonemic changes: (1) the copulative verb is ε before a pronoun, and *e* otherwise; and (2) the *ø* of *kø* drops before a vowel.

PROBLEM 68: ENGLISH

Set I

1. the girl likes Bill
2. Bill likes the girl
3. the girl is from Athens
4. Bill likes the girl who is from Athens
5. Bill likes the girl that is from Athens
6. Bill likes the girl from Athens
7. the girl who Bill likes is from Athens
8. the girl that Bill likes is from Athens
9. the girl Bill likes is from Athens
10. Jim likes the plant
11. the plant is from Athens
12. Jim likes the plant which is from Athens
13. Jim likes the plant that is from Athens
14. Jim likes the plant from Athens
15. the plant which Jim likes is from Athens
16. the plant that Jim likes is from Athens
17. the plant Jim likes is from Athens

Set II

18. Peter is nice
19. Peter likes the boy
20. the boy is nice
21. Peter likes the boy who is nice
22. Peter likes the boy that is nice
23. Peter likes the nice boy
24. the boy who Peter likes is nice
25. the boy that Peter likes is nice
26. the boy Peter likes is nice
27. Bill likes a car
28. a car is cheap
29. Bill likes a car which is cheap
30. Bill likes a car that is cheap
31. Bill likes a cheap car
32. a car which Bill likes is cheap
33. a car that Bill likes is cheap
34. a car Bill likes is cheap

Set III

35. Jim has a car
36. the car is Jim's

37. Jim has a car which is cheap
38. Jim has a car that is cheap
39. Jim has a cheap car
40. Bill likes the car which is Jim's
41. Bill likes the car that is Jim's
42. Bill likes Jim's car
43. the car which Bill likes is Jim's
44. the car that Bill likes is Jim's
45. the car Bill likes is Jim's
46. the car which is Jim's is cheap
47. the car that is Jim's is cheap
48. Jim's car is cheap
49. Bill has a boy
50. the boy is Bill's
51. Bill has a boy who is nice
52. Bill has a boy that is nice
53. Bill has a nice boy
54. Peter likes the boy who is Bill's
55. Peter likes the boy that is Bill's
56. Peter likes Bill's boy
57. the boy who Peter likes is Bill's
58. the boy that Peter likes is Bill's
59. the boy Peter likes is Bill's
60. the boy who is Bill's is nice
61. the boy that is Bill's is nice
62. Bill's boy is nice

But not:

*Bill is from the girl
*Athens is from Athens
*the girl is from Jim
*Bill likes the girl likes a car
*Bill likes the girl which is from Athens
*the girl which Bill likes is from Athens
*Bill likes the plant who is from Athens
*the plant who Bill likes is from Athens
*Peter likes the boy which is nice
*the boy which Peter likes is nice
*Bill likes a car who is cheap
*the car who Bill likes is cheap
*a car is Jim's
*a boy is Jim's

*Jim is the car's
*the girl is the car's
*Jim is the girl's
*Any sentence in which the verb is either *likes* or *has* and the subject is an inanimate noun phrase, e.g. **the car likes Bill*, **the car likes the girl*, **the plant has Bill*, or **the plant has the girl*.
*Any sentence in which the possessed word is a name, e.g. **Bill likes the girl's Jim* or **the car's Jim is nice*.
*Any sentence in which the possessor is an inanimate noun, e.g. **Bill likes the car's girl*, **the plant's boy is nice*, **Bill likes the plant's car*, or **the plant's car is cheap*.

Set I. The simple sentences of this set are either transitive or intransitive. The subject of both these types of sentences is either a proper name or a determiner followed by an animate noun. The predicate of intransitive sentences is an intransitive verb followed by a locative phrase (a preposition followed by a place name), while the predicate of transitive sentences is a transitive verb followed by a determiner and a noun, which is sometimes followed by the same prepositional phrase as that in intransitive sentences. (Notice, however, the similarity between sentences 4, 5, and 6, and sentences 12, 13, and 14.)

The complex sentences of Set I are transitive or intransitive and differ from the corresponding simple sentences in that they consist of two simple sentences (one transitive and the other intransitive), one of which is subordinated to the other as a relative clause. Notice that relative clauses (1) are subordinated to subject or object noun phrases and always immediately follow them and (2) sometimes have *who* (or *that*) or *which* (or *that*) as their subject or as their object. Whenever *who, which,* or *that* occurs in a relative clause, it always begins the clause. The order of elements in relative clauses is either *who, which* (or *that*) – verb – object or *who, which* (or *that*) – subject – verb.

Set II. The simple sentences of this set are transitive or copulative. The transitive sentences differ from those of Set I in that an adjective may occur in the object noun phrase (between the determiner and the noun). The subject of simple copulative sentences is a proper name or a determiner followed by a noun, and the predicate is a copulative verb followed by an adjective.

The complex sentences of this set are transitive or copulative. The transitive complex sentences differ from those in Set I only in that their relative clauses include simple sentences of Set II.

Set III. The simple sentences of this set differ from those of Sets I and II in that in Set III (1) the transitive sentences have a predicate which consists of either the verb *has* followed by a determiner and a noun (with or without the adjective between them), or a transitive verb followed by a possessive phrase; and (2) the copulative sentences may contain possessive phrases as the subject (e.g. sentence 48) or a possessor as a complement (e.g. sentence 36). A possessive phrase consists of a name followed by the possessive suffix *'s* (the possessor), which, in turn, is followed by a noun (the possessed). Notice that if the complement is a possessor, the determiner preceding the (possessed) subject noun must be *the* and that when the possessor is followed by a (possessed) noun, it is the determiner of that noun.

The complex sentences of Set III differ from those of Sets I and II only in that some of their relative clauses are simple sentences of Set III.

The subject or object of the relative clauses is *who* (or *that*) if the preceding noun is animate, and *which* (or *that*) if the preceding noun is inanimate. Notice that *who, which,* and *that* can be omitted from a relative clause only if they are the object of the clause, e.g. *the boy (who) Peter likes is here, Peter likes the boy who is Bill's,* but not **Peter likes the boy is Bill's* or **Bill likes the girl likes a car.*

8.2 SOLUTIONS

SOLUTION 57: KRIO

1. $S \rightarrow NP + V(Tm)$
2. $Tm \rightarrow Ta, Tms$
3. $Tms \rightarrow Td$
4. $NP \rightarrow \begin{Bmatrix} Pron \\ Det + N \end{Bmatrix}$
5. $Det \rightarrow mi$
6. $N \rightarrow$ *brɔda, sista*
7. $Pron \rightarrow a$
8. $V \rightarrow$ *slip, wok, it*
9. $Ta \rightarrow$ *yɛstade, tide, ustɛm*
10. Temb

$$\left.\begin{matrix} NP + V - Td \\ NP' + V' \end{matrix}\right\} \Rightarrow NP + V - we + NP' + V'$$

where $NP \neq NP'$ or $V \neq V'$

or, alternatively

10′. Temb

$$NP + \left.\begin{matrix} V - Td \\ S \end{matrix}\right\} \Rightarrow NP + V - we + S$$

where $S = NP' + V'$ and $NP \neq NP'$ or $V \neq V'$

11. Tob question

$X + Tm \Rightarrow Tm + X$

where $Tm = ust\varepsilon m$

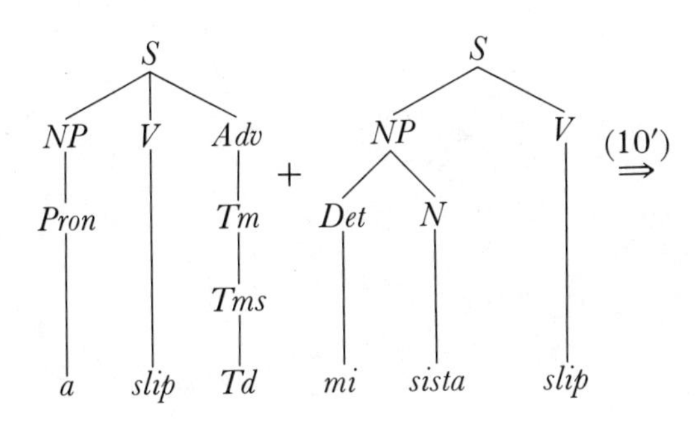

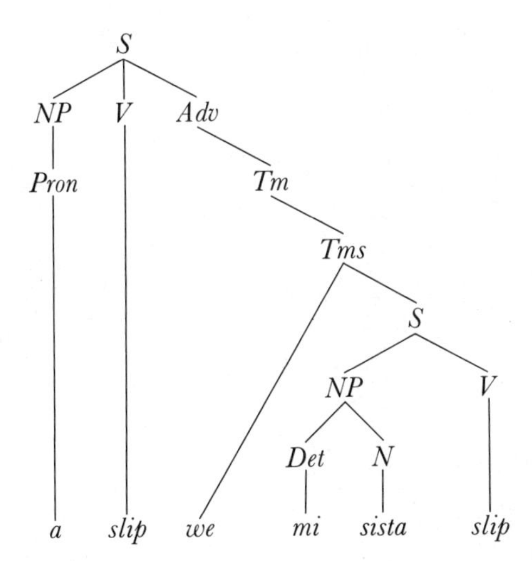

SOLUTION 58: ROGLAI

1. $S \rightarrow N + Vb(Tm)$
2. $Tm \rightarrow Ta, Tms$
3. $Tms \rightarrow Td$

4. $Vb \rightarrow \begin{Bmatrix} Vtr + N \\ Vin \end{Bmatrix}$

5. $N \rightarrow \begin{Bmatrix} Nh \ / \ \#\text{—} \\ Nnh \end{Bmatrix}$

6. *Nh* → *ama, adəy*
7. *Nnh* → *bu, ika·t*
8. *Vtr* → *ˀbək*
9. *Vin* → *naw*
10. *Ta* → *musu·p, tubrəy*
11. Temb

$$\begin{Bmatrix} X - Td \\ S \end{Bmatrix} \Rightarrow X - \begin{Bmatrix} judəy \\ juma \end{Bmatrix} S$$

where $S \neq Y + Tm$

12. Topt

$$X + Tm \Rightarrow Tm + X$$

SOLUTION 59: JAPANESE

1. $S \rightarrow NP + VP$

2. $VP \rightarrow \begin{Bmatrix} Pred + Vcop \\ \begin{Bmatrix} NP \\ Comp \end{Bmatrix} Vtr \end{Bmatrix}$

3. *Pred* → *NP, Adj*
4. *Vtr* → *OM* + *Vt*
5. *Comp* → *Cd*

6. $NP \rightarrow \begin{Bmatrix} N + SM \ / \ \#\text{—} \\ N \end{Bmatrix}$

7. $N \rightarrow \begin{Bmatrix} Nan \ / \begin{Bmatrix} \text{—}SM \\ SM\text{—}Vcop \end{Bmatrix} \\ Nan \\ Nin \end{Bmatrix}$

8. *SM* → *wa*
9. *Nan* → *nara, ǰon, anata, daigakusei*
10. *Nin* → *hanasi*
11. *Adj* → *šiawase*
12. *Vcop* → *da*
13. *Vt* → *kiita, šinzita*

14. Temb

$$\left.\begin{matrix} NP - Cd - Vtr \\ S \end{matrix}\right\} \Rightarrow NP - S - Vtr$$

where $S \neq X + Cd + Y$

15. Tob

$$OM \Rightarrow \left\{\begin{matrix} to \; / \; Comp\_\_ \\ o \end{matrix}\right\}$$

16. Tob

$$X + wa + Y + wa + Z \Rightarrow X + wa + Y + ga + Z$$

SOLUTION 60: KRIO

1. $S \rightarrow NP + VP$
2. $VP \rightarrow Vtr \left\{\begin{matrix} NP \\ Comp \end{matrix}\right\}$
3. $Vtr \rightarrow \left\{\begin{matrix} Vts \; / \; \_\_Comp \\ Vt \\ Vts \end{matrix}\right\}$
4. $Comp \rightarrow Cd$
5. $Vts \rightarrow Vts_1, Vts_2$
6. $Vt \rightarrow Vt_1, Vt_2$
7. $NP \rightarrow Det + N$
8. $N \rightarrow \left\{\begin{matrix} \left\{\begin{matrix} Nan \\ Nin \end{matrix}\right\} / \; Vts_1 + Det\_\_ \\ Nin \; / \left\{\begin{matrix} Vts_2 \\ Vt_1 \end{matrix}\right\} Det\_\_ \\ Nan \end{matrix}\right\}$
9. $Det \rightarrow$ *di*
10. $Nan \rightarrow$ *klak, uman, tiča, fama*
11. $Nin \rightarrow$ *stori, njuz, lɛta*
12. $Vts_1 \rightarrow$ *mɛmba*
13. $Vts_2 \rightarrow$ *no*
14. $Vt_1 \rightarrow$ *rid, gɛt*
15. $Vt_2 \rightarrow$ *ɛp, mit, sabi*
16. Temb

$$\left.\begin{matrix} X - Cd \\ S \end{matrix}\right\} \Rightarrow X - se + S$$

where $S \neq Y + Cd$

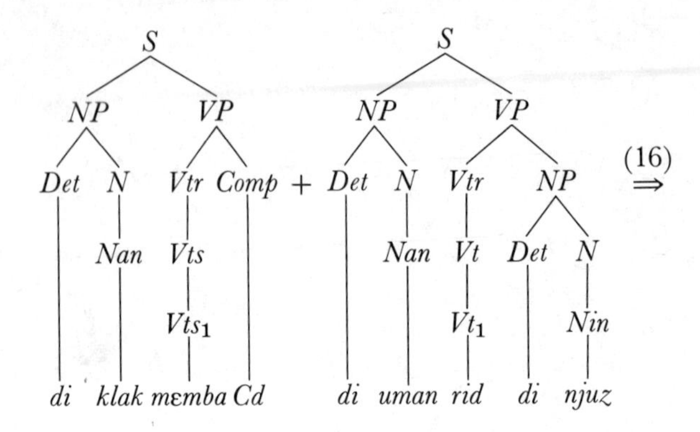
S
NP
VP
Det
N
Vtr
Comp
+
Det
N
Vtr
NP
(16)
⇒
Nan
Vts
Nan
Vt
Det
N
Vts1
Vt1
Nin
di
klak
mɛmba
Cd
di
uman
rid
di
njuz

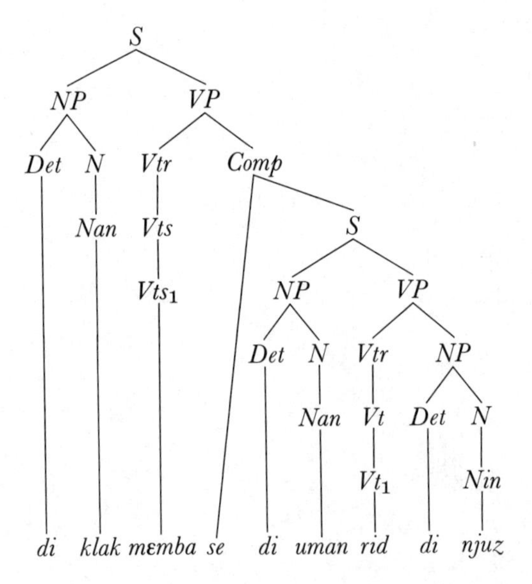
S
NP
VP
Det
N
Vtr
Comp
Nan
Vts
S
Vts1
NP
VP
Det
N
Vtr
NP
Nan
Vt
Det
N
Vt1
Nin
di
klak
mɛmba
se
di
uman
rid
di
njuz

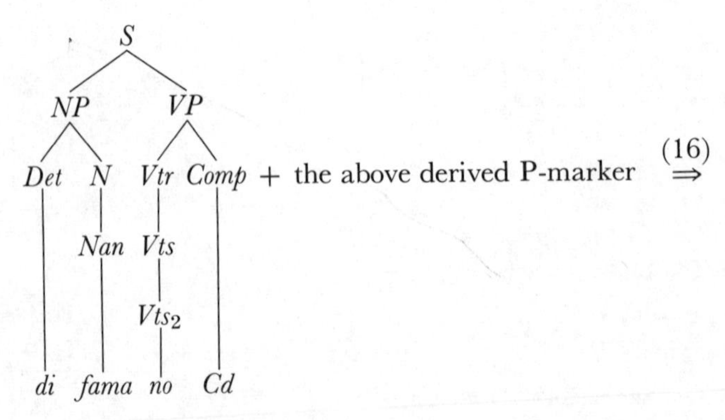
S
NP
VP
Det
N
Vtr
Comp
+ the above derived P-marker
(16)
⇒
Nan
Vts
Vts2
di
fama
no
Cd

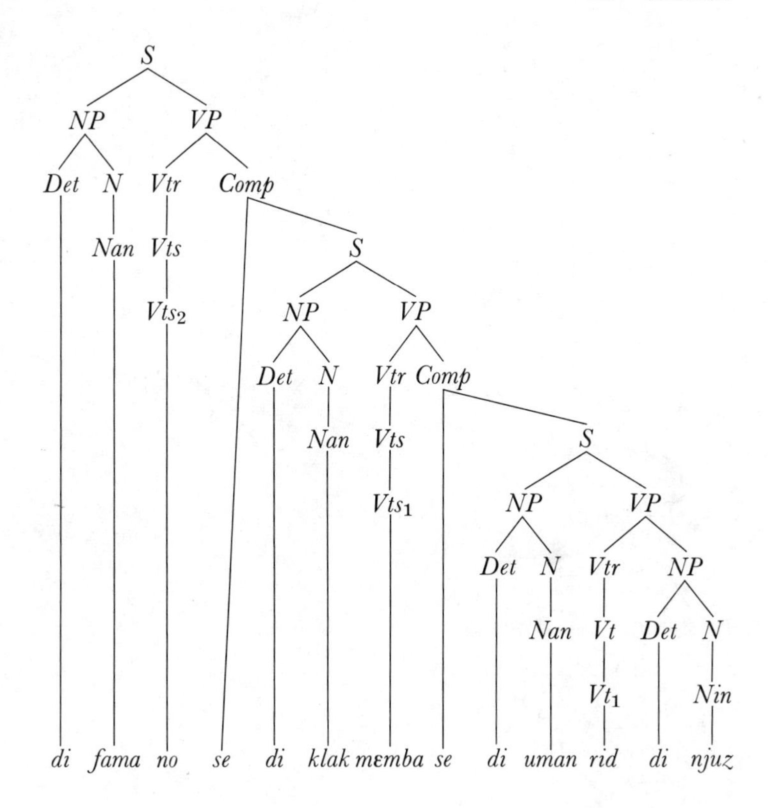

SOLUTION 61: ENGLISH

1. $S \rightarrow NP + VP$
2. $VP \rightarrow \begin{Bmatrix} Vtr + Pred \\ Vin \end{Bmatrix}$
3. $Pred \rightarrow NP, Comp$
4. $Comp \rightarrow Cd$
5. $NP \rightarrow \begin{Bmatrix} Name \\ Det + N \end{Bmatrix}$
6. $N \rightarrow \begin{Bmatrix} Nan \ / \ \#Det\_\_ \\ Nan \\ Nab \end{Bmatrix}$
7. $Name \rightarrow Jim, Bill$
8. $Det \rightarrow the$

9. $Nan \rightarrow man$
10. $Nab \rightarrow truth$
11. $Vtr \rightarrow heard$
12. $Vin \rightarrow came$
13. Temb

$$\left.\begin{matrix} X - Cd \\ S \end{matrix}\right\} \Rightarrow X - that + S$$

where $S = NP + Vin$

14. Tconj

$$\left.\begin{matrix} X - NP - VP \\ X - NP' - VP' \end{matrix}\right\} \Rightarrow X - NP + and + NP' - VP$$

where $VP = VP'$

15. Topt passive

$$NP - Vtr - Pred \Rightarrow Pred - was + Vtr - by + NP$$

SOLUTION 62: BULGARIAN

1. $S \rightarrow NP + VP$
2. $VP \rightarrow Vcop + Adj$
3. $Adj \rightarrow (Int)A$
4. $Int \rightarrow Ia, Ins$
5. $Ins \rightarrow Id$
6. $NP \rightarrow Name, N$
7. *Name* → *boris, ivan, aleksandər*
8. *N* → *gradət, vinoto*
9. *Ia* → *mnogo, dosta*
10. *A* → *pročut, star*
11. *Vcop* → *e*
12. Temb

$$\left.\begin{matrix} X - Id - A \\ S \end{matrix}\right\} \Rightarrow X - po + ot + S - A$$

where $S = NP' + Vcop' + A'; A = A'$

13. Tob

$$X + Ins + A \Rightarrow X + A + Ins$$

14. Tob

$$X + A + Y + NP + VP \Rightarrow X + A + Y + NP$$

15. Tob

$$X + A + po + Y \Rightarrow X + po + A + Y$$

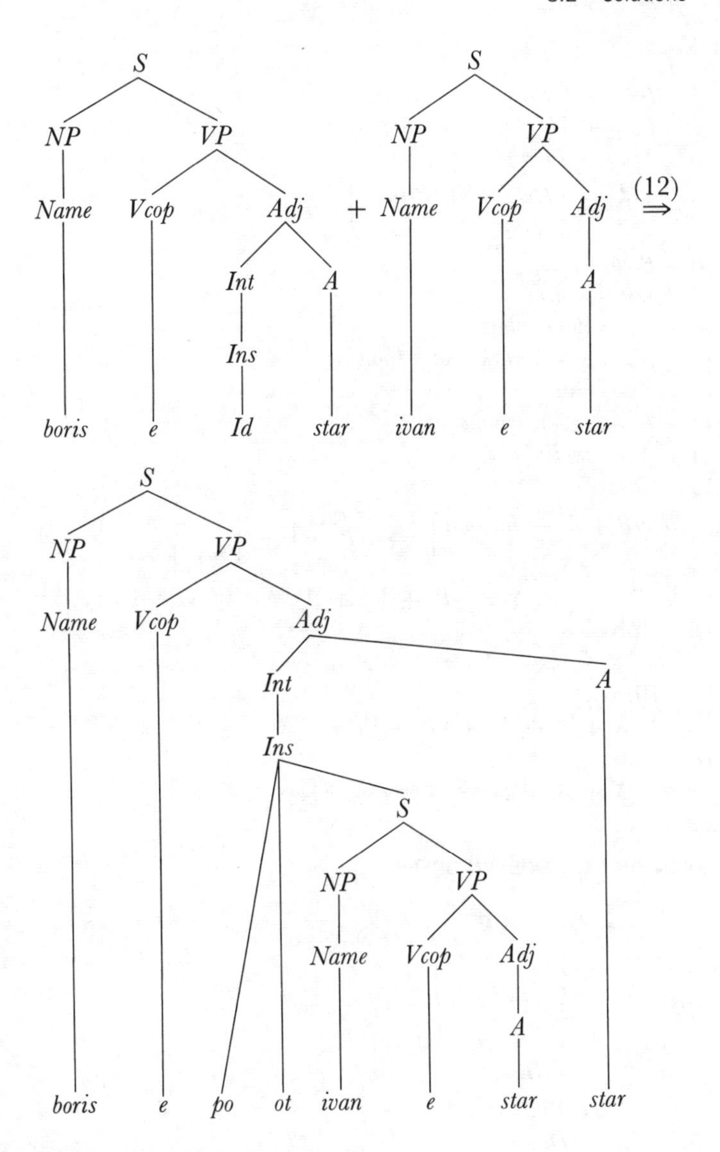

SOLUTION 63: GERMAN

1. $S \rightarrow NP + VP$
2. $VP \rightarrow V\begin{Bmatrix} Adj \\ Loc \end{Bmatrix}$
3. $Adj \rightarrow (Int)A$

4. $Int \rightarrow Ia, Ins$
5. $Ins \rightarrow Id$
6. $Loc \rightarrow Prep + NP$
7. $NP \rightarrow \begin{Bmatrix} Det + N \,/\, Prep\_\_ \\ Name \end{Bmatrix}$
8. $Prep \rightarrow auf$
9. $Det \rightarrow dem$
10. $N \rightarrow berg, plats$
11. $Name \rightarrow karl, klaus, jo \cdot han$
12. $V \rightarrow ist$
13. $Ia \rightarrow ze \cdot r, tsimliç$
14. $A \rightarrow klain, dik$
15. Temb

$$\left.\begin{matrix} NP + V - Id - A \\ S \end{matrix}\right\} \Rightarrow NP + V - \begin{Bmatrix} ər + als \\ zo\cdot + vi\cdot \end{Bmatrix} S - A$$

where $S = NP' + V' + A'$; $NP \neq NP'$; $A = A'$

16. Tob

$$X + Ins + A \Rightarrow X + A + Ins$$

17. Tob

$$X + A + Y + NP + VP \Rightarrow X + A + Y + NP$$

18. Tob

$$X + A + zo\cdot + Y \Rightarrow X + zo\cdot + A + Y$$

SOLUTION 64: MODERN GREEK

1. $S \rightarrow NP + VP$
2. $VP \rightarrow \begin{Bmatrix} Vtr + NP \\ Vin \end{Bmatrix}$
3. $NP \rightarrow \begin{Bmatrix} Nn(Rel) \,/\, \#\_\_ \\ Nn \end{Bmatrix}$
4. $Rel \rightarrow Rld$
5. $Nn \rightarrow Det + N$
6. $Det \rightarrow D$
7. $N \rightarrow Ns + Ca$
8. $Ca \rightarrow \begin{Bmatrix} Acc \,/\, \_\_\# \\ Nom \end{Bmatrix}$
9. $Ns \rightarrow andra, ma\theta iti$
10. $Vtr \rightarrow \gamma irevi$
11. $Vin \rightarrow ir\theta e$

12. Temb

$$\left.\begin{matrix} X - Rld - VP \\ X + VP' \end{matrix}\right\} \Rightarrow X - pu + VP' - VP$$

13. Tob agreement

$$D - Ns + Ca \Rightarrow D + Ca - Ns + Ca$$

14. Topt question

$$NP + VP \Rightarrow VP + NP$$

15. Tob

$$D \begin{bmatrix} Nom \\ Acc \end{bmatrix} \Rightarrow \begin{bmatrix} o \\ ton \end{bmatrix}$$

16. Tob

$$\begin{bmatrix} Nom \\ Acc \end{bmatrix} \Rightarrow \begin{bmatrix} s \\ \emptyset \end{bmatrix}$$

SOLUTION 65: KOREAN

1. $S \rightarrow NP + VP + SFM$
2. $VP \rightarrow \begin{Bmatrix} V(Loc) \\ Pred \end{Bmatrix}$
3. $V \rightarrow Vs + Pres$
4. $Pred \rightarrow NP, Adj$
5. $NP \rightarrow \begin{Bmatrix} (Rel)Nn \;/\; \#\text{—} \\ N \end{Bmatrix}$
6. $Rel \rightarrow Rld$
7. $Nn \rightarrow N + SM$
8. $N \rightarrow \begin{Bmatrix} Nan \;/\; \text{—}SFM \\ Nan \\ Nin \end{Bmatrix}$
9. $Pres \rightarrow n$
10. $Nin \rightarrow$ *jatoŋcha*
11. $Nan \rightarrow$ *ai, salam, chinku*
12. $Adj \rightarrow$ *alɨmtap*
13. $Vs \rightarrow$ *ka, o*
14. $Loc \rightarrow$ *jøki, mataŋe*
15. $SFM \rightarrow$ *ta*
16. Temb

$$\left.\begin{matrix} Rld - Nn - VP + SFM \\ Nn' + VP' + SFM' \end{matrix}\right\} \Rightarrow VP' + R - Nn - VP + SFM$$

where $Nn = Nn'$; $VP \neq VP'$

or, preferably,

$$\left.\begin{matrix} Rld - X - VP + Y \\ X + VP' + Y \end{matrix}\right\} \Rightarrow VP' + R - X - VP + Y$$

where $VP \neq VP'$

17. Tob

$$X + Loc + Y + Loc \Rightarrow X + Y + Loc$$

18. Tob

$$X + Loc \Rightarrow Loc + X$$

19. Tob

$$R \Rightarrow \left\{\begin{matrix} in\ /\ N\_\_ \\ \text{ʉ}n \end{matrix}\right\}$$

20. Tob

$$p + \text{ʉ}n \Rightarrow \text{ʉ}n$$

21. Tob

$$SM \Rightarrow \left\{\begin{matrix} i\ /\ C\_\_ \\ ka \end{matrix}\right\}$$

SOLUTION 66: THAI

1. $S \rightarrow NP + VP$
2. $VP \rightarrow \left\{\begin{matrix} V + Adv \\ Adj \end{matrix}\right\}$
3. $Adv \rightarrow Man, Loc$
4. $Loc \rightarrow Prep + N$
5. $NP \rightarrow N(Det)$
6. $Det \rightarrow Cl(Rel)D$
7. $Rel \rightarrow Rld$
8. $N \rightarrow \left\{\begin{matrix} Nin\ /\ Prep\_\_ \\ Nan \end{matrix}\right\}$
9. $Nan \rightarrow N_1, N_2$
10. $Cl \rightarrow \left\{\begin{matrix} khon\ /\ N_1\_\_ \\ tua \end{matrix}\right\}$
11. $N_1 \rightarrow$ *nákrian, khru·*
12. $N_2 \rightarrow$ *mɛ·w, mǎ·*
13. $Nin \rightarrow$ *bâ·n, ro·ŋrian*
14. $D \rightarrow \left\{\begin{matrix} nan\ /\ Rld\_\_ \\ ni\cdot \\ nan \end{matrix}\right\}$
15. $Adj \rightarrow$ *di·, nyàj*

16. $V \rightarrow kin, w\hat{i}\eta, rian$
17. $Man \rightarrow rew, ch\acute{a}\cdot ch\acute{a}\cdot$
18. $Prep \rightarrow th\hat{i}\cdot$
19. Temb

$$\left.\begin{array}{c} X - Rld - D + VP \\ X + D' + VP' \end{array}\right\} \Rightarrow X - R + VP' - D + VP$$

20. T

$$X + Rel + D + Y \Rightarrow X + Rel + Y$$

obligatory if *Rel* dominates *VP* and $VP = Adj$;
optional otherwise (i.e. if *Rel* dominates *VP* and $VP \neq Adj$)

21. Tob

$$R \Rightarrow \left\{\begin{array}{l} \emptyset / \_\_Adj \\ th\hat{i}\cdot \end{array}\right\}$$

22. Tob

$$Vw]_D \Rightarrow \acute{V}w]_D$$

SOLUTION 67: FRENCH

1. $S \rightarrow NP + VP$
2. $VP \rightarrow Vb \left\{\begin{array}{c} NP \\ Comp \end{array}\right\}$
3. $Vb \rightarrow \left\{\begin{array}{l} Vcop / \_\_Comp \\ Vcop \\ Vtr \end{array}\right\}$
4. $Comp \rightarrow Cd$
5. $NP \rightarrow \left\{\begin{array}{l} Pron / \_\_Vcop \\ Det + N \end{array}\right\}$
6. $N \rightarrow Nan, Nin$
7. $Det \rightarrow la$
8. $Nan \rightarrow fam$
9. $Nin \rightarrow bul$
10. $Pron \rightarrow s$
11. $Vcop \rightarrow e$
12. $Vtr \rightarrow frap$
13. Topt

$$X + Det + N + Y \Rightarrow WH + Det + N + X + Y$$

This rule may be reapplied to any matrix sentence (i.e. any sentence not dominated by *Comp*) not containing *WH* (i.e. *X* and $Y \neq W + WH + Z$).

14. Temb

$$\left.\begin{array}{c} X - Cd \\ WH + Det + N_1 + Y \end{array}\right\} \Rightarrow$$

$$X + Det + N_1 - WH + Det + N_1 + Y$$

$$Y \neq W + Vcop + Z$$

This rule is obligatory for constituent strings having the form:

(a) $WH + Det + Nin + V + W$

(b) $WH + Det + Nan + Det + W$

15. Temb

$$\left.\begin{array}{c} X - Cd \\ S \end{array}\right\} \Rightarrow X - WH + S$$

where $S \neq WH + Z$ and $S \neq Y + Vcop + W$

16. T

$$X + NP + Vb + Y \Rightarrow X + Vb + NP + Y$$

where $X + NP + Vb + Y$ is not a constituent sentence (i.e. is form not dominated by *Comp*)

obligatory if $X = WH + Det + N$

optional if $X = null$ and $NP = Pron$

17. Tob

$$\# WH + Det \begin{bmatrix} Nan \\ Nin \end{bmatrix} \Rightarrow \# \begin{bmatrix} ki \\ kø \end{bmatrix}$$

18. Tob

$$WH + S \Rightarrow kø + S$$

19. Tob

$$WH + Det + N \Rightarrow \begin{Bmatrix} ki \,/\, \_Vb \\ kø \end{Bmatrix}$$

20. Tob

$$kø + Vw \Rightarrow k + Vw$$

21. Tob

$$e + s \Rightarrow \varepsilon + s$$

SOLUTION 68: ENGLISH

1. $S \rightarrow NP + VP$

2. $VP \rightarrow \begin{Bmatrix} BE \begin{Bmatrix} Adj \\ Loc \end{Bmatrix} \\ V + NP \end{Bmatrix}$

3. $Loc \rightarrow Prep + NP$

4. $V \rightarrow V_1, V_2$

5. $NP \rightarrow \begin{Bmatrix} Det + N(Rel) \;/\; V_2\_\_ \\ Name \;/\; Prep\_\_ \\ Name \\ Det + N(Rel) \end{Bmatrix}$

6. $Name \rightarrow \begin{Bmatrix} Name_1 \;/\; Prep\_\_ \\ Name_2 \end{Bmatrix}$

7. $N \rightarrow \begin{Bmatrix} Nan \;/\; \_\_(Rel)\begin{Bmatrix} V_1 \\ V_2 \end{Bmatrix} \\ Nan \\ Nin \end{Bmatrix}$

8. $Det \rightarrow D$
9. $Rel \rightarrow Rld$
10. $Prep \rightarrow$ *from*
11. $D \rightarrow$ *the, a*
12. $Adj \rightarrow$ *nice, cheap*
13. $Nan \rightarrow$ *girl, boy*
14. $Nin \rightarrow$ *plant, car*
15. $Name_1 \rightarrow$ *Athens*
16. $Name_2 \rightarrow$ *Bill, Jim, Peter*
17. $BE \rightarrow$ *is*
18. $V_1 \rightarrow$ *likes*
19. $V_2 \rightarrow$ *has*
20. Topt possessive

$$NP + V_2 + D + N(Rel) \Rightarrow the + N(Rel) is + NP + \text{'s}$$
$$NP \neq X + Rel + Y$$

21. Temb

$$\left.\begin{matrix} X - Det + N - Rld - Y \\ W + Det' + N' + Z \end{matrix}\right\} \Rightarrow$$
$$X - Det + N - WH + Det' + N' + W + Z - Y$$

where $Det + N = Det' + N'$; $Z \neq \begin{Bmatrix} Rel \\ is \end{Bmatrix} U$

22. Topt

$$X + WH + Det + N\begin{bmatrix} is + Z \\ Y \end{bmatrix} \Rightarrow X\begin{bmatrix} Z \\ Y \end{bmatrix}$$
$$Y \neq V + W$$

23. Tob

$$X + D + N\begin{bmatrix} Adj \\ NP + \text{'s} \end{bmatrix} Y \Rightarrow X\begin{bmatrix} D + Adj \\ NP + \text{'s} \end{bmatrix} N + Y$$

24. Tob

$$WH + Det \begin{bmatrix} Nan \\ Nin \end{bmatrix} \Rightarrow \begin{bmatrix} who \\ which \end{bmatrix}$$

25. Topt

$$\begin{Bmatrix} who \\ which \end{Bmatrix} \Rightarrow that$$

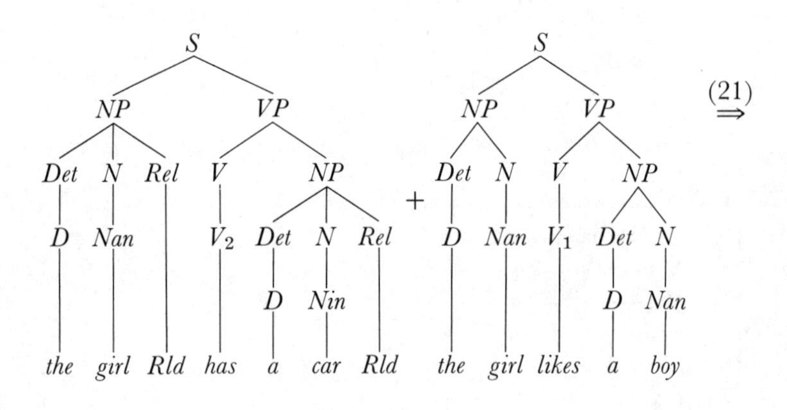

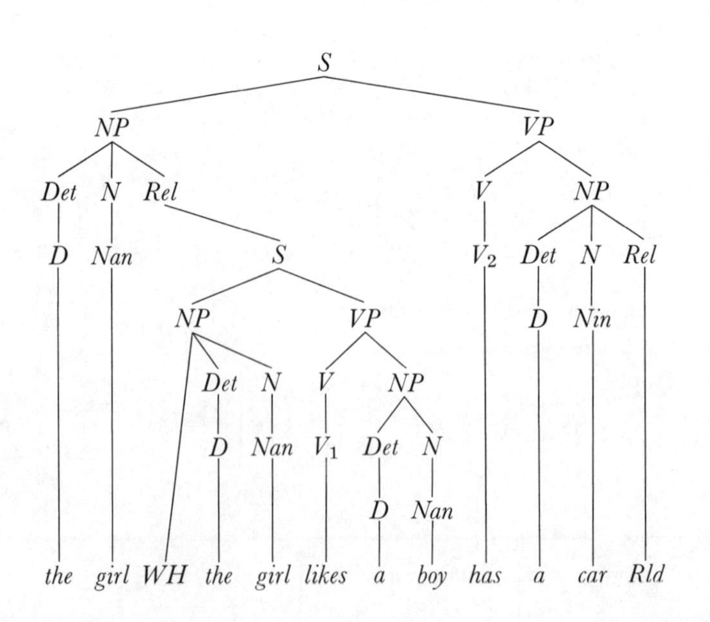

the preceding P-marker + [$_S$ [$_{NP}$ [$_{Det}$ [$_D$ *a*]] [$_N$ [$_{Nin}$ *car*]]] [$_{VP}$ [$_{BE}$ *is*] [$_{Adj}$ *nice*]]] $\overset{(21)}{\Rightarrow}$

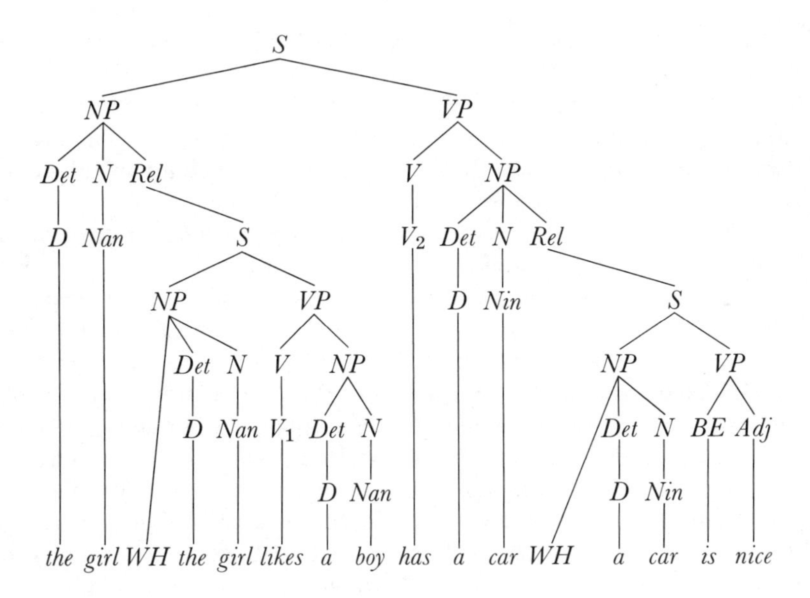

8.3 DISCUSSION OF SOLUTIONS

8.3.1 The derivation of complex sentences

In the preceding solutions complex sentences are derived from two (initially, simple) sentences by an embedding rule that works in the following manner. One of the source sentences is designated as the **matrix sentence** (which is defined in the top line of the structural description) and the other as the **constituent sentence** (which is defined in the second line of the structural description).[2] The constituent sentence is then embedded into the matrix sentence, usually along with a "subordinating" morpheme, through the operation of replacement, generating a complex sentence of the same sentence type as the matrix sentence; e.g. if the matrix sentence is copulative, the complex sentence generated by the embedding rule is copulative also. More specifically, a P-marker representing a constituent sentence replaces one of the terminal symbols in a P-marker representing a matrix sentence, producing a derived P-marker representing a complex sentence which is always the same sentence type as the matrix sentence.[3] For example, in Solution 59 (Japanese) the complex transitive sentence *anata wa ǰon ga šiawase da to kiita* 'you heard that John was happy' is generated through the application of rules (14) to (16) as follows: by rule (14) *Cd* in the (transitive) matrix P-marker terminating in *anata wa Cd OM kiita* is replaced by the (copulative) constituent P-marker terminating in *ǰon wa šiawase da* 'John was happy,' producing the (transitive) derived P-marker terminating in *anata wa ǰon wa šiawase da OM kiita,* which the application of rules (15) and (16) changes to *anata wa ǰon ga šiawase da to kiita.*

The symbol which is replaced in a matrix P-marker by a constituent P-marker is called a **dummy symbol;** i.e. it is a terminal symbol which must be obligatorily replaced through the application of an embedding rule. (In the preceding solutions all the dummy symbols end in the letter *d.*) In rule (14) of Solution 59 (Japanese), for example, the symbol *Cd* which is replaced by a constituent P-marker is a dummy symbol; similarly, in rule (15) of Solution 63 the symbol *Id* is a dummy symbol.

The motivation for introducing dummy symbols into a grammar is, in brief, that their use considerably simplifies a grammar; specifically: (1) we thus obtain an easily specifiable derived constituent structure; the replacing elements take on the structure of the dummy element (i.e. they are attached to the same node to which the dummy symbol was attached); (2) since only the dummy symbol is replaced through the embedding rule, we have a constituent structure label for embedded sentences to which we can refer in later T-rules, thus simplifying the statement of these rules (i.e. we can thus distinguish between the matrix

[2] Following the terminology established by R. B. Lees, *The Grammar of English Nominalizations,* Indiana University Research Center in Anthropology, Folklore, and Linguistics, Publication 12 (*International Journal of American Linguistics,* vol. 26, no. 3, pt. 2, 1960). See especially the introduction to chap. 3.

[3] In almost all the published literature, embedding rules operate in the same manner. However, see Charles J. Fillmore, "The Position of Embedding Transformations in a Grammar," *Word,* vol, 19, no. 2, pp. 208–231, 1963, in which complex sentences are derived through "transformational expansion rules."

P-marker and the constituent P-marker within the derived P-marker produced by an embedding rule); e.g. see rules (13) and (16) of Solution 67 (French); and (3) since every matrix P-marker is characterized by at least one dummy symbol, we thus have a simple formal specification of the set "matrix P-markers."

By applying an embedding rule once, a complex sentence containing one embedded sentence is generated. The specification of (the structure of) complex sentences containing more than one embedded sentence is such that they are derived only by embedding a complex sentence into a simple sentence and never vice versa. That is, the domain of an embedding rule is stated in such a way that the product of the rule can be used only as a constituent P-marker and never as a matrix P-marker. For example, rule (16) of Solution 60 (Krio) is written in such a way that the product of that rule can serve only as a constituent P-marker. To derive a complex sentence such as *di uman no se di klak mɛmba se di tiča ɛp di fama* 'the woman knows that the clerk remembers that the teacher helped the farmer,' therefore, we apply rule (16) once; i.e. we embed a constituent P-marker terminating in *di tiča ɛp di fama* 'the teacher helped the farmer' into a matrix P-marker terminating in *di klak mɛmba Cd,* thus producing a derived P-marker terminating in *di klak mɛmba se di tiča ɛp di fama* 'the clerk remembers that the teacher helped the farmer'; and then, by reapplying rule (16), we embed the latter into a matrix P-marker terminating in *di uman no Cd,* producing a derived P-marker terminating in *di uman no se di klak mɛmba se di tiča ɛp di fama.*

In other words, the embedding rules are restricted such that only underlying P-markers containing a dummy symbol can serve as the matrix P-marker of an embedding rule (i.e. only simple sentences can serve as matrix sentences), while either an underlying P-marker not containing a dummy symbol or a P-marker derived through the application of the embedding rule (and any preceding single-base transformations) can serve as a constituent P-marker (i.e. both simple and complex sentences can serve as constituent sentences). The only time the product of an embedding rule can serve as a matrix P-marker is when the matrix P-marker originally contained more than one dummy symbol, as, for example, does the matrix P-marker given for Solution 68 (English). By convention, in all such cases, the left-most occurrence of a dummy symbol is replaced first, and the product of the application of the rule is used again as the matrix P-marker (since it still contains a dummy symbol, clearly it cannot serve as a constituent P-marker); each successively left-most occurrence of a dummy is replaced in this way until no dummy symbols are left in the matrix P-marker.

Now, the reason we do not permit derived P-markers representing complex sentences (or P-markers representing sentences with any kind of compounding) to serve as matrix P-markers is that the embedding rules themselves, as well as the statement of later transformations, are, as a result, simplified. Specifically, since complex sentences are specified as simple sentences within simple sentences within simple sentences (*ad infinitum*), later T-rules can be specified as operating either on the entire derived P-marker assigned by an embedding rule or on the easily distinguishable matrix and constituent P-markers within it. (Notice that this implies that the embedding rules must come very early in the transformational part of a grammar.) If, however, we were to permit P-markers derived through an embedding rule to serve as matrix P-markers, (a) the embedding rules themselves would be much more complicated in order to allow for embedding into complex sentences, e.g. to allow embedding not only into simple intransitive or active sentences but also into complex intransitive or active sentences and embedded active or copulative sentences, etc. (i.e. we no longer would have an easily specifiable set of matrix P-markers), and (b) clearly, as a result, later T-rules would also be more complicated. Similar, and even greater, complications would arise if we allowed derived P-markers with conjoined constituents to serve as either matrix or constituent P-markers.

Finally, since matrix P-markers contain dummy symbols, the application of embedding rules is obligatory for matrix P-markers. It is not obligatory for constituent P-markers, however, unless expressly stated as such, as, for example, in rule (14) of Solution 67 (French), which specifies that any P-markers of the form *WH* + *Det* + *Nin* + *V* + *W* and *WH* + *Det* + *Nan* + *Det* + *W* must serve as constituent P-markers of that rule. This restriction on rule (14) prevents the generation of sentences such as **kø frap la fam* (if *kø* is the subject) and **ki frap la bul* (if *ki* is the object).

8.3.2 Introducing constituent-types that have dummy constituents

The first consideration in specifying complex sentences is the introduction of constituent-types which have dummy constituents, or, in other words, the introduction of symbols that terminate in dummy symbols. In general, this is determined by the same considerations as those for introducing any constituent-type in the phrase structure grammar (discussed in Chapter 4). Specifically, we (1) regard subordinate sentences as constituents of simple sentences, (2) observe the co-occurrence relations the subordinate sentences exhibit with the other constituents in simple sentences, and (3) using a class symbol, such as *Comp*, *Rel*, or *Tms*, to represent the subordinate sentences, specify these relations in precisely the same manner that co-occurrence relations between classes in simple sentences are specified. These symbols are then expanded into the appropriate dummy symbols.

The co-occurrence relations that subordinate sentences exhibit have been pointed out in the discussions of the data of the preceding problems. Specifically, some subordinate sentences are mutually exclusive with a particular class, while others have a simple dependency relation with another class.

Whenever embedded sentences are mutually exclusive with various constituents of the same type, the symbol that is expanded into a dummy element is postulated to be a constituent of that type. For example, in Solution 58 (Roglai) *Tms* is postulated by rule (2) to be a constituent of the type *Tm* since embedded sentences subordinated by either *juma* or *judəy* are mutually exclusive with the time adverbs *tubrəy* 'yesterday' and *musu·p* 'early in the morning.' The symbol that terminates in a dummy symbol is introduced in this same manner in Solutions 57 to 63. (It should be noted that since no use is made of *Tms* in Solutions 57 [Krio] and 58 [Roglai], its postulation is not justified; the dummy element *Td* could have been postulated in both solutions to be a constituent of the type *Tm*. The postulation of *Tms,* therefore, is based on the anticipation that a more comprehensive grammar of these languages will justify it.)

In Solutions 64 to 66 and 68 the symbol that terminates in a dummy is postulated to be an optional constituent of a constituent-type, i.e. that constituent-type which relative clauses are said to modify. For example, in Solution 66 (Thai) *Rel* is postulated to be a constituent of *Det,* and its selection is dependent on the selection of both *Cl* and *D*. Similarly, in Solution 64 (Modern Greek) *Rel* is postulated by rule (3) to be an optional constituent of subject noun phrases, and its selection is dependent on the selection of a sentence-initial *Nn.*

Some of the subordinate clauses in Problem 67 (French) could be interpreted to be optional constituents of noun phrases, i.e. to be relative clauses. That is to say, it would seem that, in place of rules (2) to (4) of Solution 67, it would be possible to have the following four rules:

$$2.\quad VP \rightarrow Vb\begin{Bmatrix} NP(Rel) \\ Comp \end{Bmatrix}$$

$$3.\quad Vb \rightarrow \begin{Bmatrix} Vcop\ /\ \_\begin{Bmatrix} NP + Rel \\ Comp \end{Bmatrix} \\ Vcop \\ Vtr \end{Bmatrix}$$

$$4.\quad Rel \rightarrow Rld$$

$$5.\quad Comp \rightarrow Cd$$

The above underlying structure is not postulated for complex sentences, however, first because it is known, on the basis of other data, that they are not relative clauses, but aside from this, because the grammar for these data is considerably simplified by postulating that there is only one constituent-type that has a dummy constituent, i.e. *Cd*, rather than postulating that there are two constituent-types that have dummy constituents.

Specifically, the grammar is simplified first in that the number of restrictions that must be imposed on some of the T-rules of the grammar are minimized. For example, had these clauses been introduced with *NP* as *NP(Rel)*, we would have had to impose another restriction on rule (13), i.e. that $Y \neq Rel + W$, to ensure that when rule (14) is applied, it will not generate ungrammatical sentences. Second, had we postulated two constituent-types having dummy constituents, we would not be making the generalization that not only do the two types of subordinate sentences involve the same noun phrases of independent sentences, but in addition that the type of sentence that can serve as a matrix sentence is the same in both types of embedding; i.e. they are copulative sentences.

If the reader should choose to specify cleft sentences in the manner illustrated in Solution 67 (see also note 6 of 8.4), he should bear in mind that since there are no noun phrase complements in the underlying structure of the matrix sentences, this noun phrase must be provided by the embedding rule itself. That is to say, as we can see in Solution 67, since the general structure of the matrix P-markers to which rule (14) applies is $X - Cd$ (i.e. $Pron - Vcop - Cd$), the structural change must provide the proper noun phrase complement. This is done by specifying that the subject noun phrase of the constituent sentence must be reduplicated and added to the matrix sentence.

8.3.3 Format of embedding rules

The notational conventions adopted for stating embedding rules are essentially the same as those adopted for stating conjoining rules, as we can see from rule (10) of Solution 57 (Krio):

10. Temb

$$\left.\begin{array}{c} NP + V - Td \\ NP' + V' \end{array}\right\} \Rightarrow NP + V - we + NP' + V'$$

where $NP \neq NP'$ or $V \neq V'$

Temb indicates that the rule is an embedding rule.

The two lines of the structural description, together with the set of conditions imposed on the P-markers defined in the structural description, define the domain of the rule. Again the two lines are enclosed on the right by a right-hand brace, indicating that the rule operates simultaneously on both P-markers. The top line represents the general structure of the matrix P-markers to which the rule applies, and the lower line defines the general structure of the constituent P-markers. Prime marks are used in defining constituent P-markers whenever there may be any ambiguity regarding the derived constituent structure assigned by the rule. The same notational devices, i.e. the equality and inequality signs, are used to impose restrictions on the P-markers defined in the structural description. In rule (10) above, $NP \neq NP'$ or $V \neq V'$ means that the strings dominated by *NP* or *V* of the matrix P-marker must differ by at least one string from the strings dominated by either *NP* or *V* in the constituent P-marker.

The arrow and structural change follow the structural description; and hyphens and pluses are used to indicate the grouping of symbols for proper attachment in the derived P-marker.

8.3.4 Considerations for writing embedding rules

There are two main considerations for writing embedding rules, namely, (1) the domain of the rule and (2) the derived constituent structure assigned.

(1) **Domain of the rule.** Although the domain of embedding rules is, like that of conjoining rules, defined in two parts, the considerations involved in specifying the domain of these two types of rules are somewhat different, since the two source P-markers defined in the structural description of an embedding rule, unlike those of a conjoining rule, must not be identical. The specification of the domain of embedding rules is discussed in two parts: the specification of the matrix and of the constituent P-markers, respectively.

(a) By definition, a matrix P-marker is a P-marker which has (at least) one dummy symbol as one of its terminal nodes. The sets of P-markers which can serve as matrix P-markers are, therefore, determined by the way we have written the P-rules of a grammar (discussed in 8.3.2). For example, in Solution 61 (English) any underlying P-markers containing *Cd* are matrix P-markers. Similarly, in Solution 62 (Bulgarian) any underlying P-markers containing *Id* are matrix P-markers. Clearly, then, one of the symbols in the structural description of the matrix P-markers must be the dummy symbol.

The specification of the remaining structure of matrix P-markers should be as general as possible; i.e. either cover symbols or high order class symbols (or both) should be used to define the matrix P-markers. How general the definition of matrix P-markers can be depends largely on the various restrictions that must be imposed on them. For example, the general structure of matrix P-markers in Solution 63 (German) is defined by rule (15) as $NP - V - Id - A$. NP is the only high order symbol in the structural description because we must impose certain restrictions on A of the matrix and the constituent P-markers. As another example, in the structural description of rule (12) of Solution 64 (Modern Greek), the matrix P-markers are defined as $X - Rld - VP$. The symbol X (rather than Nn or NP) is used to obviate the necessity of adding "where $Nn = Nn'$"; i.e. we have taken advantage of the fact that identical cover symbols in a rule indicate identical strings and thereby make it unnecessary to add the restriction that the strings dominated by Nn in the matrix P-marker and the constituent P-marker must be identical. Since VP is the only constituent that can follow Rld, and since there are no restrictions on it, it is used in the structural description rather than another cover symbol. As a last example, in rule (21) of Solution 68 (English) the matrix P-markers are defined as $X - Det + N - Rld - Y$ in the structural description. The cover symbols X and Y are used because either a subject or an object noun phrase (or both) can be modified by a relative clause, and $Det + N$ is used because not only is it the only type of noun phrase in the data that can be modified in this way, but because we must impose certain restrictions on the $Det + N$ of matrix and of constituent P-markers. Notice that since we have used X and Y and have not restricted them, P-markers representing the underlying structure of both transitive and intransitive sentences are specified as matrix P-markers.

(b) By definition, underlying P-markers not containing a dummy symbol and derived P-markers can potentially serve as constituent P-markers. Which particular sets of underlying and derived P-markers are specified as constituent P-markers depends, of course, on which types of sentences are to be embedded.

The most important points to remember with regard to the specification of constituent P-markers in the structural description of an embedding rule are that (a) a dummy symbol must not appear in it and (b) these P-markers should be defined as generally as possible. We can then impose any necessary restrictions upon constituent and matrix P-markers below the structural description of the embedding rule. For example, in rule (14) of Solution 59 (Japanese) the constituent P-marker is defined as S in the structural description; and in rule (13) of Solution 61

(English) the constituent P-marker is defined as *S* in the structural description and then is defined below it as *NP* + *Vin*.

It should be noticed that the conditions below the structural description specify whether the product of the embedding rule can be used as a constituent P-marker. The condition below rule (14) of Solution 59 (Japanese) and that below rule (16) of Solution 60 (Krio), for example, are such that the product of these rules can be used as a constituent P-marker. In contrast, the restrictions of rule (10) in Solution 57 (Krio) are such that the product of the rule cannot be used as a constituent P-marker. The same is true of the restrictions on the embedding rules of Solutions 58 and 62 to 66.

We sometimes must define the constituent P-marker other than as *S* in the structural description. This may be because of (1) the structural change that must be specified, (2) the restrictions that must be imposed on the various constituents of the matrix and constituent P-markers, or (3) both (1) and (2). For example, in rule (14) of Solution 67 (French) we have no choice but to define the constituent P-markers other than as *S* because of the structural change that must be specified. That is to say, if the constituent P-markers were defined as *S*, we would have no way of showing that the derived constituent structure must be such that the subject *Det* + *N* of the constituent P-marker is reduplicated and attached to the matrix P-marker and that *WH* must be attached to the noun phrase of the constituent P-marker. Notice, however, that by following the required *WH* + *Det* + *N* by the cover symbol *X*, which is restricted to be "any string not containing *Vcop*" (and which, therefore, can be either *NP* + *Vtr* or *Vtr* + *NP*), we are still defining the constituent P-markers of rule (14) in a general manner. Similarly, in the structural description of rule (21) of Solution 68 (English), the constituent P-markers are defined as *W* + *Det′* + *N′* + *Z* since, if we had defined them as *S* (and then restricted *S* below the structural description), there would be no way to show the proper attachment of the *WH* morpheme after embedding. Despite this, by using cover symbols in the structural description to represent the remaining structure of constituent P-markers and restricting the cover symbols below the structural description, rule (21) is a very general rule, since any P-marker with the general structure *NP* + *VP* but not containing *Rel* can serve as a constituent P-marker.

It should be noticed that, as in conjoining rules, when any symbol that appears in the structural description of an embedding rule is not specifically restricted below this rule, this means that there are no restrictions on the constituent-type(s) it represents. For example, since in rule (16) of Solution 60 (Krio) no restrictions are added to either the matrix or the constituent P-markers (other than the restriction that the latter P-markers cannot contain *Cd*), the strings dominated by *NP* and *Vts* in the matrix P-marker may be either the same as or different from those dominated by *NP* and *Vts* in constituent P-markers.

It should also be noted that aside from the desire to generalize, another motivation for defining constituent P-markers as *S* whenever possible is that subordinating morphemes are thus attached to the same node as *S*. While there is no particular reason why this is desirable in the preceding solutions, such an attachment of the subordinating morphemes may result in a simplification of other T-rules in the grammar (see, for example, the solution in note 6 of 8.4).

(2) **Derived constituent structure.** There are two points to remember with regard to the constituent structure assigned by embedding rules: (a) the constituent P-marker within the P-marker derived through embedding should represent an entire sentence; and (b) the constituent structure of the embedded P-marker is the same as that of the symbol it has replaced.

(a) The derived constituent structure assigned by embedding rules should be such that P-markers representing *entire* sentences replace the dummy symbol. Then later T-rules can optionally or obligatorily perform various operations on the constituent or matrix P-marker within the derived P-marker or on the entire derived P-marker. Although this was not done in Solutions 64, 65, and 66 (Modern Greek, Korean, and Thai, respectively), it is nevertheless very desirable because in the long run the practice of embedding entire sentences will simplify a grammar.

For example, in rule (21) of Solution 68 (English) we cannot embed (the constituent P-marker) $W + Det' + N' + Z$ and simultaneously delete $Det' + N'$, for two reasons. First, because the deletion of $Det' + N'$ is contingent upon its position relative to the other constituents in the constituent P-markers (e.g. $Det' + N'$ cannot be deleted if V immediately follows it); and second, because different morphophonemic changes are effected depending on whether N' is animate or inanimate. Clearly, if we had managed to combine both the embedding and deletion within one rule, the resulting grammar would be much more complicated than Solution 68.

As we just saw, however, by not embedding P-markers representing entire sentences, a constituent-type that must be referred to in later T-rules might be deleted. This may complicate the ordering of rules as well as the rules themselves. For example, if Problem 64 (Modern Greek) were extended to include complex sentences having copulative subordinate clauses, an additional rule would be necessary in the solution to specify agreement between a subject noun and a predicate adjective.

Given this situation, combining the operations of embedding and deletion in one rule, as does rule (12) of Solution 64, would require either that the specification of agreement precede embedding, and this is undesirable for a number of reasons (discussed in 8.3.5), or that the specification of agreement following embedding be more complicated than necessary, since agreement would now have to be specified between the subject of the matrix P-marker and the predicate adjective of the constituent P-marker. For reasons such as these, then, Solutions 64, 65, and 66 must be considered objectionable, despite the fact that they work.

(b) Since embedding rules are substitution transformations, the derived constituent structure assigned by them is clear: the embedded P-markers take on the structure of the symbol they have replaced in the matrix P-marker, while the remaining structure of the matrix P-marker remains the same. For example, as we can see from the P-markers given for Solution 57 (Krio), since the constituent P-marker replaces *Td* of the matrix P-marker, it is attached to *Tms* in the derived P-marker, while the rest of the matrix P-marker remains unchanged. Similarly, from the P-markers below Solution 62 (Bulgarian) we can see that, since the constituent P-marker replaces *Id* of the matrix P-marker, it is attached to *Ins* in the derived P-marker, while the rest of the matrix P-marker remains unchanged.

8.3.5 Ordering transformations

Although only a few of the preceding solutions contain more than one syntactic transformation, clearly, given the manner we have chosen to specify the derivation of complex sentences, a grammar will be simplified if the embedding rules are either the first set of rules or among the first rules of the transformational part of it, since all other complex sentence types can then be derived from the P-markers produced by the embedding rules; i.e. the optional singulary transformations will apply to complex as well as to simple sentences.

Solution 64 (Modern Greek) is the only solution in which we have an agreement rule; it follows the embedding rule for essentially the same reason that agreement rules followed the conjoining rule in Solution 55 of Chapter 7 (see 7.3.4). In Solution 61 (English) the embedding rule precedes the conjoining rule because this order simplifies the solution. That is, since only P-markers underlying kernel sentences can serve as matrix P-markers and only underlying P-markers not containing a dummy symbol or P-markers derived through the application of the embedding rule (or certain previous singulary transformations) can serve as constituent P-markers, if the conjoining rule preceded the embedding rule, we would have to restrict both the conjoining rule and the embedding rule. Specifically, we would have to restrict the conjoining rule not to apply to underlying P-markers containing a dummy symbol and then to restrict the constituent P-markers of the embedding rule such that they could not contain conjoined constituents. In addition, we would have to allow looping back to reapply the conjoining rule in order to generate complex sentences that have compounded constituents.

The order of embedding rules relative to each other, however, seems to be arbitrary. For example, in Solution 67 (French) rule (15) could precede rule (14) without affecting any part of the transformational part of the grammar.

Up until this chapter, the rules of a grammar were always strictly ordered; i.e. they were ordered in such a way that in deriving any sentence, once we had applied a rule, it was not permissible to go back and reapply it after applying one or more later rules. This restriction has been lifted on T-rules in Solution 67, however, to illustrate another way in which rules can be ordered. In this solution we derive complex wh-questions by applying rules (13) and (14) and then looping back and reapplying rule (13). For example, we derive the sentence *ki ɛ s ki frap la bul* 'who is it that is hitting the ball?' as follows:

$$\textit{la fam frap la bul} \overset{(13)}{\Rightarrow} \textit{WH la fam frap la bul}$$

$$\left.\begin{array}{c} \textit{s e Cd} \\ \textit{WH la fam frap la bul} \end{array}\right\} \overset{(14)}{\Rightarrow} \textit{s e la fam WH la fam frap la bul}$$

$$\overset{(13)}{\Rightarrow} \textit{WH la fam s e WH la fam frap la bul} \overset{(16)}{\Rightarrow} \textit{WH la fam e s}$$

$$\textit{WH la fam frap la bul} \overset{(17)}{\Rightarrow} \textit{ki e s WH la fam frap la bul} \overset{(19)}{\Rightarrow}$$

$$\textit{ki e s ki frap la bul} \overset{(21)}{\Rightarrow} \textit{ki } \varepsilon \textit{ s ki frap la bul}$$

The main consideration when allowing one or more T-rules to be reapplied after later T-rules have been applied is that they be properly restricted. For example, rule (13) of Solution 67 is restricted so that it can be reapplied only to "any matrix P-marker not containing *WH*."

Since it is not clear that the advantages of allowing looping of rules outweigh the advantages of having strict ordering of rules within a grammar, it is suggested that the reader stick to strictly ordered rules and give that ordering which results in the simplest grammar.[4]

[4] For a discussion of some advantages of allowing looping in a grammar, see Charles J. Fillmore, "The Position of Embedding Transformations in a Grammar," *Word*, vol. 19, no. 2, pp. 208–231, 1963.

8.3.6 The specification of noun modifiers

In Problems 66 (Thai) and 68 (English) we have both predicate adjectives and adjective modifiers, i.e. adjectives that are the complement of a copulative verb, or, as is the case in Thai, verbal adjectives, and adjectives that modify nouns, respectively. In the solutions for both these problems, sentences containing adjective modifiers are derived through a relative embedding rule. In other words, adjective modifiers are omitted from the phrase structure grammar and are introduced via a relative embedding rule. We thus considerably simplify our grammar (at the very least) in that (1) the rules are fewer in number and less complicated and (2) we make at least one generalization, namely, that embedded copulative sentences having predicate adjectives and adjective modifiers have the same relationship to nouns; i.e. they both modify them.[5]

In the English solution *Adj* is introduced in the phrase structure grammar as a predicate adjective (see rule [2]). Rule (21) then embeds a copulative sentence such as *the boy is nice* into *Bill likes the boy,* producing *Bill likes the boy WH the boy is nice,* which rule (22) changes into *Bill likes the boy nice,* which rule (23) changes to *Bill likes the nice boy.* Now, if we had introduced the adjective both as a complement of copulative sentences and as a modifier of nouns (i.e. as a constituent of a noun phrase) in the phrase structure grammar, we would be unnecessarily complicating not only the P-rules but, more important, the T-rules of this grammar, since we would have to restrict rule (22) not to apply to copulative verbs followed by a predicate adjective. If the latter were done, not only would we have an additional restriction on rule (22), but as a result, we could not reveal that embedded copulative sentences and adjective modifiers have the same relation to nouns. Clearly, then, even for data as restricted as Problem 68, the specification of sentences containing adjective modifiers as embeddings of copulative sentences considerably simplifies the grammar.

What we have just said about adjective modifiers in Solution 68 also applies to adjective modifiers in Solution 66. The adjectives in Solution 66 are introduced in the phrase structure grammar as verbal adjectives (see rule [2]); thus application of the P-rules produces

[5] One complication that is immediately avoided is that illustrated in Solution 39 (Spanish) of Chapter 5, namely, that in order to avoid writing a complicated agreement rule (because of the position of an adjective in a noun phrase) the constituent-type having the grammatical categories gender, number, and person as constituents had to be postulated twice: once as a constituent of pronouns and again as a constituent of nouns. By introducing adjective modifiers via a relative embedding rule, this complication does not arise.

copulative sentences such as *mǎ· di·* 'the dog is good.' Rule (19), the relative embedding rule, then specifies that a sentence such as *mǎ· di·* is embedded into a sentence such as *mǎ· tua nán wîŋ rew* 'that dog runs fast,' producing *mǎ· tua di· nán wîŋ rew,* which rule (23) changes (by obligatorily deleting *nán*) into *mǎ· tua di· wîŋ rew* 'the good dog runs fast.'

In Problem 68 we also have an example of what is traditionally called a "post-nominal modifier," i.e. the prepositional phrases in the transitive sentences of Set I. These modifiers are handled in Solution 68 in precisely the same manner as adjective modifiers and for precisely the same reason. That is, sentences such as *Bill likes the girl from Athens* are derived through the application of a relative embedding rule and a deletion rule (in fact, two of the three rules that specify sentences containing adjective modifiers) as follows: rule (21) embeds *WH the girl is from Athens,* for example, into *Bill likes the girl Rld,* producing *Bill likes the girl WH the girl is from Athens,* which rule (22) changes to *Bill likes the girl from Athens.*

8.3.7 Possessives

Problem 68 (English) is the only problem in which there are sentences having possessives (either as part of the subject or as a complement). In the solution for this problem these sentences are derived from kernel sentences containing the verb *to have.* The reason for this is that the difference between these kernel sentences and sentences containing possessives can be accounted for by postulating that the latter sentences have undergone an optional singulary transformation that the former have not. We can therefore omit the introduction of possessives from the phrase structure grammar and derive them from kernel sentences containing the verb *to have,* thus simplifying both the phrase structure and the transformational part of the grammar.

This is possible because the possessive morpheme *'s* and the verb *to have* behave alike in a number of situations. Specifically, the grammatical constraints on the subject and object of kernel sentences containing the verb *to have* are, in general, the same as those on possessor and possessed, respectively, as we can see in the examples below. Notice, in particular, that if it is grammatical to say that "X *has* a Y," the phrase "X*'s* Y" or "the X*'s* Y" is grammatical also, and if it is ungrammatical to say that "X *has* a Y," the phrase "X*'s* Y" or "the X*'s* Y" is ungrammatical also:

Jim has a car.	Jim's car (is nice).
A girl has a car.	A girl's car (is blue).

The girl has a plant.	The girl's plant (died).
*The plant has a girl.	*The plant's girl (is nice).
*A car has Jim.	*The car's Jim (is blue).

In brief, if a sentence containing *has* is grammatical, it will be grammatical also if we substitute *'s* for *has* (and the determiner) and add a predicate. Similarly, if a sentence containing *has* is ungrammatical, it will be ungrammatical also if we substitute *'s* for *has* (and the determiner) and add a predicate.

To generate English sentences containing possessives, we apply the rules of Solution 68 as follows:

(1) First we take a P-marker underlying a kernel sentence such as *Jim has a car* and, by applying rule (20), we derive from it the copulative sentence *the car is Jim's.*[6] Notice that one of the changes specified is that the determiner preceding the possessed noun must be *the.* Rule (20) thus is an optional single-base transformation through which we derive copulative sentences containing possessors as complements (e.g. *is Jim's*) from transitive sentences whose verb is *to have.*

(2) The product of rule (20), i.e. *the car is Jim's,* is then embedded by the relative embedding rule, rule (21), into a matrix P-marker representing a sentence such as *Bill likes a car,* producing *Bill likes a car which is Jim's.* That is, the P-marker resulting from the application of rule (20) can be used as a constituent P-marker in the relative embedding rule to derive complex sentences having relative clauses containing possessor complements.

(3) Rule (22) may then be applied to the product of the embedding rule, e.g. to *Bill likes a car which is Jim's,* producing *Bill likes a car Jim's.* We then must apply rule (23), which shifts the possessive complement to precede the object noun and at the same time deletes the determiner preceding that noun, in order to get *Bill likes Jim's car.*

By the above procedure, then, we are able to derive both possessor complements (e.g. *is Jim's*) and possessor-possessed noun phrases (e.g. *Jim's car*).

To summarize, sentences containing possessives are derived through four rules of the grammar, i.e. rules (20) to (23). The application of rule (20) alone generates sentences such as *the car is Jim's* and *the car is the girl's.* The application of both rules (20) and (21) generates sentences such as *the car which is Jim's is nice* and *the car which is the girl's is*

[6] This is only one of several ways possible to specify English sentences containing possessive complements.

nice. The application of rules (20) to (23) inclusive generates sentences such as *Jim's car is nice* and *the girl's car is nice.* It should be noted, however, that since rules (21), (22), and (23) are used to derive other sentences besides those containing possessives (i.e. sentences containing relative clauses that do not have possessives and sentences containing the noun modifiers discussed in 8.3.6), rule (20) is the only additional rule introduced in the grammar to derive sentences containing possessives.

8.3.8 Kernel and derived sentences

As we saw in 1.7, the distinction of obligatory and optional transformations provides the formal characterization of kernel and derived sentences: those sentences whose structural descriptions include only obligatory transformations are kernel sentences, while those sentences whose structural descriptions include at least one optional transformation are derived sentences. The way we have derived complex sentences, however, i.e. through embedding rules that are obligatory for all matrix and some constituent P-markers, conflicts with this characterization. That is, we now have sentences which we want considered not kernel but derived sentences generated by T-rules that are obligatory (in a specific sense). Clearly, since the distinction of optional-obligatory transformations is inadequate for characterizing kernel and derived sentences, we must modify the theory presented in this book at least in the specific area of conflict. This will require not only questioning the need for the notion of kernel and derived sentences and, if we think it necessary, deciding upon another formal characterization of them, but also questioning the need for and significance of optional and obligatory T-rules.

8.4 NOTES

1. Because of the way we have chosen to derive complex sentences, it is redundant to specify for each embedding rule the condition that a constituent P-marker cannot contain a dummy symbol. (It is for pedagogical reasons only that this practice was followed in the preceding solutions.) All that is necessary is to state at the outset that this condition is imposed by convention on the grammar.

In fact, all conventions are adopted for this purpose, i.e. to simplify a grammar; whenever a convention adopted for one grammar also holds for other grammars, the convention is considered part of the general theory on which grammars are based.

2. A number of the preceding solutions can be simplified by at least one of the following ways.

First, they can be simplified by lifting the restriction that the independent and subordinate clauses be lexically different (which was imposed on Problems 57, 63, and 65 simply to be able to illustrate the use of the inequality sign to impose lexical constraints) and then using cover symbols in the structural description and structural change of the embedding rule.

Second, whenever there is more than one subordinating morpheme, these morphemes can be introduced in the phrase structure grammar. For example, we can simplify Solution 58 (Roglai) by rewriting rule (2) as follows:

$$Tm \rightarrow Ta,\ Tc + Tms$$

adding the following rule:

$$Tc \rightarrow \textit{judəy, juma}$$

and rewriting rule (11) as follows:

$$\left.\begin{matrix} X + Td \\ S \end{matrix}\right\} \Rightarrow X + S$$

where $S \neq Y + Tm$

3. In Solution 59 (Japanese) the particle *to* is handled as an object marker (*OM*). Specifically, *OM* is specified as a single morpheme which, by rule (15), has the pronunciation *to* in the context *Comp* and *o* otherwise. The following are two of several alternative ways of handling *to*.

to could be split into two morphemes, *t* and *o*; i.e. we could claim that *o* is the object marker and *t* is a subordinating morpheme. If this alternative were adopted, the only changes that would be necessary in Solution 59 would be to (1) introduce *t* after *S* in the structural change of rule (14) and (2) omit rule (15).

A third way of handling the particle *to* is to postulate it as a subordinating morpheme, i.e. a morpheme introduced via the embedding rule, rule (14). The essential changes this alternative would require are to (1) postulate that *OM* is a constituent of an object noun instead of a verb, (2) introduce *to* by the embedding rule, and (3) omit rule (15).

Which of the various alternatives is the best cannot be decided on the basis of the data given, nor on the basis of any effect on the simplicity of the grammar.

4. In Problem 61 (English) we have our only example of passive sentences. Notice that in the solution for this problem, the rule that

specifies passive sentences follows the embedding and conjoining rules and that this one rule forms the passive of either simple, compound, or complex sentences. Because of the way the data were restricted, however, the passive rule, although it works, is unsatisfactory. A more comprehensive grammar of English would have a passive rule such as that in C. J. Fillmore.[7]

5. The solutions for Problems 62 (Bulgarian) and 63 (German) specify that sentences with adjectives in the comparative degree are derived through embedding. The comparatives illustrated in these problems are similar to two of the three types of comparative constructions exhibited in English. That is, in English we have comparatives such as (1) *John is taller than Jim,* (2) *John is as tall as Jim,* and (3) *John is as smart as Jim is stupid* and *he is as tall as I am fat.* The comparatives in Problem 62 are similar to (1), and those in Problem 63 are similar to (1) and (2). All three types of comparative constructions are derived by embedding rules by R. B. Lees[8] but by adjunction transformations by C. S. Smith.[9]

6. Solution 67 (French) was written to illustrate looping and to illustrate that embedding rules may sometimes be obligatory for certain constituent P-markers. A simpler (and more reasonable) solution for Problem 67 is the following, in which the rules are strictly ordered:[10]

1–3. Same as in Solution 67

4. $Comp \rightarrow WH + Cd$

5–12. Same as in Solution 67

13. Temb

$$\left.\begin{matrix} X + Cd \\ S \end{matrix}\right\} \Rightarrow X + S$$

where $S \neq Y + Vcop + Z$

14. Topt

$$X + WH + Y + NP + Z \Rightarrow X + NP - WH + NP - Y + Z$$

15. Topt wh-question

$$X + Det + N + Y \Rightarrow WH + Det + N + X + Y$$

where (1) $X = Pron + Vcop$; or
(2) $X = null$ and $N = Nan$; or
(3) $X = NP + Vb$ and $N = Nin$

[7] "The Position of Embedding Transformations in a Grammar," *op. cit.*, p. 228.

[8] "Grammatical Analysis of the English Comparative Construction," *Word,* vol. 17, no. 2, pp. 171–185, 1961.

[9] "A Class of Complex Modifiers in English," *Language,* vol. 37, no. 3, pt. 1, pp. 342–365, 1961.

[10] This solution was suggested by Ronald Langacker.

16. T yes-no question
    $X + NP + Vb + Y \Rightarrow X + Vb + NP + Y$
    obligatory if $X = WH + NP$
    optional if $X = null$ and $NP = Pron$

17–21. Same as in Solution 67

The above solution is a better solution than that given in 8.2 not only because it is simpler but (a) it formally characterizes wh-questions and yes-no questions and (b) it specifies that sentences whose complements are cleft and those whose complements are not cleft are related.

8.5 COLLATERAL READINGS

Fillmore, Charles J.: "The Position of Embedding Transformations in a Grammar," *Word,* vol. 19, no. 2, pp. 208–231, 1963.
Katy, J. J. and P. M. Postal: *An Integrated Theory of Language Descriptions,* The M.I.T. Press, Cambridge, Mass., 1964, pp. 122–144.
Lees, Robert B.: "Grammatical Analysis of the English Comparative Construction," *Word,* vol. 17, no. 2, pp. 171–185, 1961.
———: "A Multiply Ambiguous Adjectival Construction in English," *Language,* vol. 36, no. 2, pt. 1, pp. 207–221, 1960.
Smith, Carlota S.: "A Class of Complex Modifiers in English," *Language,* vol. 37, no. 3, pt. 1, pp. 342–365, 1961.
———: "Determiners and Relative Clauses in a Generative Grammar of English," *Language,* vol. 40, no. 1, pp. 37–52, 1964.

8.6 EXERCISES

1. SAMOAN

1. o ia o se taŋata	*He is a man.*
2. na sau ia	*He came.*
3. o ia o le taŋata na sau	*He is the man who came.*
4. o ioane o se taŋata	*John is a man.*
5. na savali ioane	*John walked.*
6. o ioane ia o le taŋata na savali	*John is the man who walked.*
7. o ioane o le taŋata na savali	*John is the man who walked.*

8.	o le taŋata na savali o ioane ia	*The man who walked is John.*
9.	o le taŋata na savali o ioane	*The man who walked is John.*
10.	o aˀu o se taŋata	*I am a man.*
11.	na tamoˀe aˀu	*I ran.*
12.	o aˀu o le taŋata na tamoˀe	*I am the man who ran.*
13.	o le taŋata na tamoˀe o aˀu ia	*The man who ran is I.*
14.	o le taŋata na tamoˀe o aˀu	*The man who ran is I.*
15.	o le taŋata na sau o le taŋata ia	*The man who came is he.*
16.	na sau le taŋata	*The man came.*
17.	na tamoˀe le taŋata	*The man ran.*

But not:

*o le taŋata na sau o ia
*o le taŋata na sau o ia ia
*na sau o ia
*aˀu o se taŋata
*o aˀu se taŋata

2. PERSIAN

1.	man mahmud ra didam	*I saw Mahmud.*
2.	man mahmud ra sɔate dæh didam	*I saw Mahmud at ten o'clock.*
3.	mahmud amad	*Mahmud came.*
4.	man mahmud ra didam vaqtikeh amad	*I saw Mahmud when he came.*
5.	mahmud man ra did	*Mahmud saw me.*
6.	mahmud man ra sɔate dɨ did	*Mahmud saw me at two o'clock.*
7.	man amedam	*I came.*
8.	mahmud man ra did vaqtikeh amedam	*Mahmud saw me when I came.*
9.	man u ra didam	*I saw him.*
10.	man u ra sɔate dɨ didam	*I saw him at two o'clock.*
11.	u ræft	*He went.*
12.	man u ra didam vaqtikeh ræft	*I saw him when he went.*

13. u man ra šænid — *He heard me.*
14. u man ra sɔate dæh šænid — *He heard me at ten o'clock.*
15. man ræftam — *I went.*
16. u man ra šænid vaqtikeh ræftam — *He heard me when I went.*

But not:

*man mahmud ra did
*mahmud amedam
*man mahmud ra vaqtikeh amad didam
*man u ra sɔate dɨ didam vaqtikeh ræft

3. ROGLAI

1. haphe bent — *Haphe is little.*
2. haphe bent ˀwan — *Haphe is very little.*
3. pitonk bent — *Pitonk is little.*
4. pitonk bent luh — *Pitonk is quite small.*
5. dwək bent — *Duok is small.*
6. haphe si pitonk bent — *Haphe and Pitonk are small.*
7. pitonk si dwək bent luh — *Pitonk and Duok are quite small.*
8. haphe si pitonk si dwək bent — *Haphe, Pitonk, and Duok are small.*
9. haphe bent ralaw di pitonk — *Haphe is smaller than Pitonk.*
10. pitonk bent ralaw di dwək — *Pitonk is smaller than Duok.*
11. haphe bent ralaw di dwək — *Haphe is smaller than Duok.*
12. haphe si pitonk bent ralaw di dwək — *Haphe and Pitonk are smaller than Duok.*
13. haphe bent ralaw di pitonk si dwək — *Haphe is smaller than Pitonk and Duok.*
14. haphe bent ralaw di avih — *Haphe is the smallest.*
15. dwək jway — *Duok is clever.*
16. dwək jway ˀwan — *Duok is very clever.*
17. pitonk jway — *Pitonk is clever.*

18.	pitonk jway luh	*Pitonk is quite clever.*
19.	haphe jway	*Haphe is clever.*
20.	dwək si pitonk jway	*Duok and Pitonk are clever.*
21.	pitonk si haphe jway ʔwan	*Pitonk and Haphe are very clever.*
22.	haphe si dwək si pitonk jway	*Haphe, Duok, and Pitonk are clever.*
23.	dwək jway ralaw di pitonk	*Duok is more clever than Pitonk.*
24.	pitonk jway ralaw di haphe	*Pitonk is more clever than Haphe.*
25.	dwək jway ralaw di haphe	*Duok is more clever than Haphe.*
26.	dwək si pitonk jway ralaw di haphe	*Duok and Pitonk are more clever than Haphe.*
27.	dwək jway ralaw di pitonk si haphe	*Duok is more clever than Pitonk and Haphe.*
28.	dwək jway ralaw di avih	*Duok is the most clever.*
29.	lamo ghəng ralaw di un	*The cow is bigger than the pig.*
30.	un ghəng ralaw di asəw	*The pig is bigger than the dog.*
31.	lamo ghəng ralaw di avih	*The cow is the biggest.*
32.	pitonk jway luʔ	*Is Pitonk clever?*
33.	pitonk jway luh luʔ	*Is Pitonk quite clever?*
34.	un ghəng ralaw di lamo luʔ	*Is the pig bigger than the cow?*
35.	haphe bent si jway	*Haphe is small and clever.*
36.	haphe bent ma jway	*Haphe is small but clever.*
37.	haphe bent ma pitonk jway	*Haphe is little but Pitonk is clever.*
38.	haphe bent ralaw di pitonk ma pitonk jway ralaw di haphe	*Haphe is smaller than Pitonk but Pitonk is more clever than Haphe.*
39.	pitonk bent ralaw di dwək si jway ralaw di haphe	*Pitonk is smaller than Duok but more clever than Haphe.*

40. pitonk bent ralaw di dwək ma jway ralaw di haphe	*Pitonk is smaller than Duok but more clever than Haphe.*
41. haphe bent ralaw di avih ma dwək jway ralaw di avih	*Haphe is the smallest but Duok is the most clever.*

But not:

*haphe bent luh ralaw di pitonk
*haphe bent ralaw di avih pitonk
*haphe bent ʔwan di avih
*haphe ma pitonk bent

4. SPANISH

1. pepe es muy timido	*Pepe is very shy.*
2. ana es timida	*Ann is shy.*
3. pepe es mas timido ke ana	*Pepe is more shy than Ann.*
4. ana es muy timida	*Ann is very shy.*
5. ana es menos timida ke pepe	*Ann is less shy than Pepe.*
6. el ixo es alto	*The son is tall.*
7. la ixa es bien alta	*The daughter is quite tall.*
8. la ixa es mas alta ke el ixo	*The daughter is taller than the son.*
9. la ixa es menos alta ke pepe	*The daughter is less tall than Pepe.*
10. pepe es mas alto ke ana	*Pepe is taller than Ann.*
11. el gato es fiel	*The cat* (masc.) *is faithful.*
12. la gata es algo fiel	*The cat* (fem.) *is somewhat faithful.*
13. la gata es (algo) mas fiel ke el ixo[11]	*The cat* (fem.) *is (somewhat) more faithful than the son.*

[11] Parentheses around a Spanish word mean that the word is optional in that sentence.

14. pepe es (algo) menos fiel ke la ixa	*Pepe is (somewhat) less faithful than the daughter.*
15. ana es (algo) menos timida ke el ixo	*Ann is (somewhat) less shy than the son.*
16. pepe es bastante fiel	*Pepe is rather faithful.*
17. pepe es (bastante) menos fiel ke la gata	*Pepe is (rather) less faithful than the cat* (fem.)
18. el ixo es (algo) mas alto ke pepe	*The son is (somewhat) taller than Pepe.*
19. la ixa es (bastante) mas timida ke ana	*The daughter is (rather) more shy than Ann.*
20. el gata es (bastante) menos alto ke el ixo	*The cat* (masc.) *is (rather) less tall than the son.*
21. pepe xuega mučo	*Pepe plays a lot.*
22. pepe kien es mas timido ke ana xuega mučo	*Pepe, who is more shy than Ann, plays a lot.*
23. pepe kien xuega mučo es mas timido ke ana	*Pepe, who plays a lot, is more shy than Ann.*
24. ana kien es menos alta ke la ixa xuega mučo	*Ann, who is less tall than the daughter, plays a lot.*
25. ana kien xuega mučo es menos alta ke la ixa	*Ann, who plays a lot, is less tall than the daughter.*
26. el gato ke es (algo) mas fiel ke pepe xuega mučo	*The cat* (masc.), *which is (somewhat) more faithful than Pepe, plays a lot.*
27. el gato ke xuega mučo es (algo) mas fiel ke pepe	*The cat* (masc.), *which plays a lot, is (somewhat) more faithful than Pepe.*
28. la gata ke es (bastante) menos alta ke el ixo xuega mučo	*The cat* (fem.), *which is less tall than the son, plays a lot.*
29. la ixa deskansa mučo	*The daughter rests a lot.*
30. la ixa kien es (algo) mas alta ke pepe deskansa mučo	*The daughter, who is (somewhat) taller than Pepe, rests a lot.*

31. el ixo kien deskansa mučo es (bastante) menos fiel ke ana — *The son, who rests a lot, is (rather) less faithful than Ann.*
32. la gata ke es mas timida ke el gato deskansa mučo — *The cat* (fem.), *which is more shy than the cat* (masc.), *rests a lot.*
33. pepe kien deskansa mučo es menos fiel ke el ixo — *Pepe* (masc.), *who rests a lot, is less faithful than the son.*
34. el ixo kien xuega mučo es mas alto ke ana — *The son, who plays a lot, is taller than Ann.*

But not:

*pepe es mas timida
*ana es timido
*pepe es muy mas timido ke ana
*ana es muy menos timida ke pepe
*la ixa es bien mas (*or* menos) alta ke el ixo
*pepe es mas timido ke pepe
*la ixa es menos alta ke la ixa
*pepe ke es mas timido ke ana xuega mučo
*la gata (*or* el gato) kien es mas fiel ke pepe xuega mučo

5. VIETNAMESE

1. ba nay muə mot ka·y ba·n — *This woman buys a table.*
2. ba nay muə mot diəw — *This woman buys a thing.*
3. oŋ nay muən mot ka·y ba·n — *This man wants a table.*
4. oŋ nay muən mot diəw — *This man wants a thing.*
5. oŋ nay muən zi — *What does this man want?*
6. oŋ nay muən ba nay muə mot ka·y ba·n — *This man wants this woman to buy a table.*
7. oŋ nay muə mot ka·y ge — *This man buys a chair.*
8. oŋ nay muən muə mot ka·y ge — *This man wants to buy a chair.*
9. toy thəy mot kɔn ga — *I see a chicken.*
10. toy thəy ba nay — *I see this woman.*
11. toy thəy a·y — *Who do I see?*
12. ba nay muə mot kɔn ga — *This woman buys a chicken.*
13. toy thəy zi — *What do I see?*

14. toy thəy ba nay muə mot kɔn ga	*I see this woman buy a chicken.*
15. oŋ nay muə mot kɔn hew	*This man buys a pig.*
16. oŋ nay biət toy	*This man knows me.*
17. toy biət oŋ nay	*I know this man.*
18. toy biət a·y	*Who do I know?*
19. toy biət diəw nay	*I know this thing.*
20. toy biət zi	*What do I know?*
21. toy biət oŋ nay muə mot kɔn hew	*I know that this man buys a pig.*
22. toy muə kɔn hew nay	*I buy this pig.*
23. toy biət muə kɔn hew nay	*I know how to buy this pig.*
24. toy biət toy muə kɔn hew nay	*I know that I buy this pig.*
25. oŋ nay muən ba nay muə zi	*What does this man want this woman to buy?*
26. oŋ nay muən muə zi	*What does this man want to buy?*
27. a·y muə mot ka·y ba·n	*Who buys a table?*
28. oŋ nay muən a·y muə mot ka·y ba·n	*Who does this man want to buy a table for?*
29. oŋ nay muən toy muə mot ka·y ba·n	*This man wants to see me buy a table.*
30. oŋ nay muən toy thəy ba nay muə mot kɔn ga	*This man wants me to see this woman buy a chicken.*
31. toy thəy ba nay biət oŋ nay muən muə mot ka·y ba·n	*I see that this woman knows that this man wants to buy a table.*
32. toy thəy oŋ nay biət muə mot ka·y ba·n	*I see that this man knows how to buy a table.*
33. ba nay kɔ mot kɔn hew	*This woman has a pig.*
34. oŋ nay muə kɔn hew ba nay kɔ	*This man buys the pig this woman has.*
35. oŋ nay muə kɔn hew kuə ba nay	*This man buys this woman's pig.*
36. oŋ nay muə kɔn hew ba nay	*This man buys this woman's pig.*
37. toy kɔ mot ka·y ba·n	*I have a table.*
38. ba nay muən mot ka·y ba·n toy kɔ	*This woman wants a table I have.*
39. oŋ nay muən ba nay muə ka·y ba·n toy kɔ	*This man wants this woman to buy the table I have.*

40. oŋ nay muən muə ka·y ba·n toy	*This man wants to buy my table.*
41. oŋ nay muən ba nay muə ka·y ba·n kuə toy	*This man wants this woman to buy my table.*
42. oŋ nay muən ba nay muə ka·y ba·n nay kuə toy	*This man wants this woman to buy this table of mine.*
43. ka·y ba·n nay kuə toy	*This table is mine.*
44. ka·y ge nay kuə ba nay	*This chair is this woman's.*
45. ka·y ge nay kuə a·y	*Whose chair is this?*
46. toy kɔ zi	*What do I have?*
47. toy kɔ kɔn hew ba nay thəy	*I have the pig this woman sees.*
48. toy kɔ kɔn hew ba nay muə	*I have the pig this woman buys.*
49. toy muə kɔn hew ba nay muən	*I buy the pig this woman wants.*
50. toy muə kɔn hew ba nay biət	*I buy the pig this woman knows.*

But not:

*toy muən toy muə mot ka·y ba·n
*ba nay thəy muə mot kɔn ga
*toy muə thəy ba nay
*toy nay muə mot kɔn hew
*toy biət mot ka·y diəw
*toy biət mot ka·y ba
*toy biət mot kɔn ba
*ka·y ba·n muə mot kɔn hew
*toy biət mot ba
*diəw nay biət toy
*zi biət toy
*toy thəy mot ka·y ga
*oŋ nay muən ba nay muə ka·y ba·n nay toy
*ka·y ba·n nay toy

6. OKINAWAN

1. wan ne ʔya n·čan	*I saw you.*
2. wan ne taro n·čan	*I saw Taro.*
3. wan ne rajio n·čan	*I saw the radio.*

4. ˀya ya wan n·čan — *You saw me.*
5. ˀya ya nugana n·čan — *You saw something*
6. taro ya nugana n·čan — *Taro saw something.*
7. wan ne nugana čičan — *I heard something.*
8. ˀya ya rajio čičan — *You heard the radio.*
9. ˀya ya uta čičan — *You heard a song.*
10. taro ya uta čičan — *Taro heard a song.*
11. ˀya ya utatan — *You sang.*
12. taro ya waratan — *Taro laughed.*
13. taro ya katatan — *Taro talked.*
14. wan ne načan — *I cried.*
15. wan ne ˀya n·čun — *I (will) see you.*
16. wan ne nugana čičun — *I (will) hear something.*
17. ˀya ya utain — *You (will) sing.*
18. taro ya warain — *Taro (will) laugh.*
19. taro ya katain — *Taro (will) talk.*
20. wan ne načun — *I (will) cry.*
21. wan ne ˀya n·čo·n — *I'm seeing you.*
22. wan ne nugana čičo·n — *I'm hearing something.*
23. ˀya ya utato·n — *You are singing.*
24. taro ya warato·n — *Taro is laughing.*
25. taro ya katato·n — *Taro is talking.*
26. wan ne načo·n — *I'm crying.*
27. wan ne ˀya ga utaiši n·čan — *I saw you sing.*
28. wan ne taro ga waraiši n·čan — *I saw Taro laugh.*
29. wan ne taro ga kataiši čičan — *I heard Taro talk.*
30. ˀya ya wan ga načo·ši n·čan — *You saw me crying.*
31. wan ne ˀya ga utato·ši n·čan — *I saw you singing.*
32. wan ne taro ga warato·ši n·čan — *I saw Taro laughing.*
33. wan ne taro ga katato·ši čičan — *I heard Taro talking.*
34. ˀya ya wan ga načo·ši čičan — *You heard me crying.*
35. wan ne ˀya ga utaiši n·čun — *I (will) see you sing.*
36. wan ne ˀya ga utato·ši n·čun — *I (will) see you singing.*
37. ˀya ya wan ga načuši čičo·n — *You're hearing me cry.*
38. ˀya ya wan ga načo·ši čičo·n — *You're hearing me crying.*
39. wan ne ˀya tu taro n·čan — *I saw Taro and you.*
40. taro tu wan ne ˀya n·čan — *Taro and I saw you.*
41. wan tu taro ya ˀya n·čan — *I and Taro saw you.*
42. ˀya tu taro ya wan n·čan — *You and Taro saw me.*
43. taro tu wan ne utain — *Taro and I (will) sing.*

44. wan tu ˀya ya utain	*I and you will sing.*
45. wan ne ˀya tu taro ga utato·ši n·čan	*I saw you and Taro singing.*
46. wan tu ˀya ya taro ga utato·ši n·čan	*I and you saw Taro singing.*
47. wan ne rajio tu taro n·čan	*I saw the radio and Taro.*

But not:

*wan ne taro čičan
*ˀya ya wan čičan
*rajio ya wan n·čan
*nugana ya ˀya čičan
*ˀya ya wan ga n·čuši čičan
*wan ne ˀya ga čičuši n·čan
*Any complex sentence in which the verb of the dependent clause is in the past or present-future tense, e.g. **wan ne ˀya ga utain n·čan.*

7. KOREAN

1. yøki jipi issʉmnita	*Here is a house.*
2. kʉ salami jipesø samnita	*That man lives in this house.*
3. yøki kʉ salami sanʉn jipi issʉmnita	*Here is the house that man lives in.*
4. kʉ salami i jipesø salassʉmnita	*That man lived in this house.*
5. yøki kʉ salami san jipi issʉmnita	*Here is the house that man lived in.*
6. kʉ salami i jipesø salkessʉmnita	*That man will live in this house.*
7. yøki kʉ salami sal jipi issʉmnita	*Here is the house that man will live in.*
8. yøki mataŋi issʉmnita	*Here is a garden.*
9. kʉ aituli i mataŋesø nomnita	*Those children are playing in this garden.*
10. yøki kʉ aituli nonʉn mataŋi issʉmnita	*Here is the garden those children are playing in.*
11. kʉ aituli i mataŋesø nolassʉmnita	*Those children played in this garden.*

12. yøki kʉ aituli non mataŋji issʉmnita — *Here is the garden those children played in.*
13. kʉ aituli i mataŋesø nolkessʉmnita — *Those children will play in this garden.*
14. yøki kʉ aituli nol mataŋji issʉmnita — *Here is the garden those children will play in.*
15. jøki tosøkwani issʉmnita — *There is a library.*
16. i haksäŋji jø tosøkwanesø koŋpu hamnita — *This student studies in that library.*
17. jøki i haksäŋji koŋpu hanʉn tosøkwani issʉmnita — *There is the library this student studies in.*
18. i haksäŋji jø tosøkwanesø koŋpu hassʉmnita — *This student studied in that library.*
19. jøki i haksäŋji koŋpu han tosøkwani issʉmnita — *There is the library this student studied in.*
20. i haksäŋji jø tosøkwanesø koŋpu hakessʉmnita — *This student will study in that library.*
21. jøki i haksäŋji koŋpu hal tosøkwani issʉmnita — *There is the library this student will study in.*
22. køki samusili issʉmnita — *There is an office.*
23. sønsa nimi kʉ samusilesø il hamnita — *A teacher works in that office.*
24. køki sønsäŋnimi il hanʉn samusili issʉmnita — *There is the office a teacher works in.*
25. kʉ salami haksäŋʉl jhassʉmnita — *That man is looking for the student.*
26. haksäŋji kʉ salamʉl jhassʉmnita — *The student is looking for that man.*
27. kʉ salami jø tosøkwanesø koŋpu hanʉn haksäŋʉl jhassʉmnita — *That man is looking for the student who studies in this library.*
28. kʉ tosøkwanesø ko pu hanʉn haksa i kʉ salamʉl jhassʉmnita — *The student who studies in that library is looking for that man.*
29. kʉ tosøkwanesø ko pu hanʉn haksa i i jipesø sanʉn salamʉl jhassʉmnita — *The student who studies in that library is looking for the man who lives in this house.*

But not:

*yøki jipʉl issʉmnita
*kʉ salami i jipi samnita

*kʉ salamesø i jipesø samnita
*kʉ salami jipe sanʉn
*yøki kʉ salami samnita jipi issʉmnita

Additional information:
kʉ, køki refer to things in sight.
jø, jøki refer to things out of sight.

8. FRENCH

Declaratives

1. s e la fam	*It is the woman.*
2. s e la bul	*It is the ball.*
3. la fam frap la bul	*The woman is hitting the ball.*
4. la bul frap la fam	*The ball is hitting the woman.*
5. ɛl frap la bul	*She (it) is hitting the ball.*
6. ɛl frap la fam	*She (it) is hitting the woman.*
7. la fam tõb	*The woman is falling.*
8. la bul tõb	*The ball is falling.*
9. ɛl tõb	*She (it) is falling.*
10. s e kø la fam frap la bul	*It's that the woman is hitting the ball.*
11. s e kø la bul frap la fam	*It's that the ball is hitting the woman.*
12. s e k ɛl frap la bul	*It's that she (it) is hitting the ball.*
13. s e k ɛl frap la fam	*It's that she (it) is hitting the woman.*
14. s e kø la fam tõb	*It's that the woman is falling.*
15. s e kø la bul tõb	*It's that the ball is falling.*
16. s e k ɛl tõb	*It's that she (it) is falling.*
17. s e la fam ki frap la bul	*It is the woman who is hitting the ball.*
18. s e la bul ki frap la fam	*It is the ball that is hitting the woman.*
19. s e la bul kø la fam frap	*It is the ball that the woman is hitting.*
20. s e la fam kø la bul frap	*It is the woman that the ball is hitting.*
21. s e la fam k ɛl frap	*It is the woman that she (it) is hitting.*
22. s e la bul k ɛl frap	*It is the ball that she (it) is hitting.*
23. s e la fam ki tõb	*It is the woman who is falling.*
24. s e la bul ki tõb	*It is the ball that is falling.*

Yes-No Questions

1a.	ɛ s la fam ɛ s kø s e la fam	*Is it the woman?*
2a.	ɛ s la bul ɛ s kø s e la bul	*Is it the ball?*
3a.	ɛ s kø la fam frap la bul la fam frapt ɛl la bul	*Is the woman hitting the ball?*
4a.	ɛ s kø la bul frap la fam la bul frapt ɛl la fam	*Is the ball hitting the woman?*
5a.	ɛ s k ɛl frap la bul frapt ɛl la bul	*Is she (it) hitting the ball?*
6a.	ɛ s k ɛl frap la fam frapt ɛl la fam	*Is she (it) hitting the woman?*
7a.	ɛ s kø la fam tõb la fam tõbt ɛl	*Is the woman falling?*
8a.	ɛ s kø la bul tõb la bul tõbt ɛl	*Is the ball falling?*
9a.	ɛ s k ɛl tõb tõbt ɛl	*Is she (it) falling?*
10a.	ɛ s kø la fam frap la bul	*Is the woman hitting the ball?*
11a.	ɛ s kø la bul frap la fam	*Is the ball hitting the woman?*
12a.	ɛ s k ɛl frap la bul	*Is she (it) hitting the ball?*
13a.	ɛ s k ɛl frap la fam	*Is she (it) hitting the woman?*
14a.	ɛ s kø la fam tõb	*Is the woman falling?*
15a.	ɛ s kø la bul tõb	*Is the ball falling?*
16a.	ɛ s k ɛl tõb	*Is she (it) falling?*
17a.	ɛ s la fam ki frap la bul ɛ s kø s e la fam ki frap la bul	*Is it the woman who is hitting the ball?*
18a.	ɛ s la bul ki frap la fam ɛ s kø s e la bul ki frap la fam	*Is it the ball that is hitting the woman?*
19a.	ɛ s la bul kø la fam frap ɛ s kø s e la bul kø la fam frap	*Is it the ball that the woman is hitting?*
20a.	ɛ s la fam kø la bul frap ɛ s kø s e la fam kø la bul frap	*Is it the woman that the ball is hitting?*

21a. ɛ s la fam k ɛl frap ɛ s kø s e la fam k ɛl frap	*Is it the woman that she (it) is hitting?*
22a. ɛ s la bul k ɛl frap ɛ s kø s e la bul k ɛl frap	*Is it the ball that she (it) is hitting?*
23a. ɛ s la fam ki tõb ɛ s kø s e la fam ki tõb	*Is it the woman who is falling?*
24a. ɛ s la bul ki tõb ɛ s kø s e la bul ki tõb	*Is it the ball that is falling?*

Wh-Questions

1b. ki ɛ s ki ɛ s kø s e	*Who is it?*
2b. k ɛ s k ɛ s kø s e	*What is it?*
3b. ki frap la bul	*Who is hitting the ball?*
kø frap la fam	*What is the woman hitting?*
k ɛ s kø la fam frap	*What is the woman hitting?*
4b. ki la bul frapt ɛl	*Who is the ball hitting?*
Same as 18b and 20b	
5b. ki frap la bul	*Who is hitting the ball?*
kø frapt ɛl	*What is she (it) hitting?*
6b. ki frap la fam	*Who is hitting the woman?*
ki frapt ɛl	*Who is she (it) hitting?*
7b. ki tõb	*Who is falling?*
8b. k ɛ s ki tõb	*What is falling?*
9b. ki tõb	*Who is falling?*
10b–16b. none	
17b. ki ɛ s ki frap la bul ki ɛ s kø s e ki frap la bul	*Who (is it that) is hitting the ball?*
18b. k ɛ s ki frap la fam k ɛ s kø s e ki frap la fam	*What is hitting the woman?*
19b. k ɛ s kø la fam frap k ɛ s kø s e kø la fam frap	*What is (it that) the woman (is) hitting?*
20b. ki ɛ s kø la bul frap ki ɛ s kø s e kø la bul frap	*Who is (it that) the ball (is) hitting?*
21b. ki ɛ s k ɛl frap ki ɛ s kø s e k ɛl frap	*Who is (it that) she (it) (is) hitting?*
22b. k ɛ s k ɛl frap k ɛ s kø s e k ɛl frap	*What is (it that) she (it) (is) hitting?*

23b. ki ɛ s ki tõb
ki ɛ s kø s e ki tõb } *Who (is it that) is falling?*

24b. k ɛ s ki tõb
k ɛ s kø s e ki tõb } *What (is it that) is falling?*

But not:

*s e ɛl
*la fam frap ɛl
*kø frap la fam (if *kø* is the subject)
*ki frap la bul (if *ki* is the object)
*kø tõb
*s e ɛl ki frap la bul
*s e ɛl ki la bul frap
*s e ɛl ki tõb
*s e la fam kø frap la bul
*s e la bul ki la fam frap
*s e la fam kø tõb
*frap la fam la bul
*ɛ s kø la fam frapt ɛl la bul
*tõb la bul
*kø tõbt ɛl
*ki tõbt ɛl
*kø la fam frapt ɛl
*ɛ s la fam kø frap la bul
*ɛ s la bul ki la fam frap
*ki ɛ s kø frap la bul
*ki ɛ s la bul ki frap
*k ɛ s ki la fam frap

9. ENGLISH

Statements

1. Tom saw the man
2. Mary saw the dog
3. the dog saw Tom
4. the man saw Mary
5. the man came
6. the dog came
7. Tom came
8. Mary came

9. Tom saw the man come
10. Mary saw the dog come
11. the dog saw Tom come
12. the man saw Mary come
13. Tom saw the man who came
14. Mary saw the dog which came
15. the dog saw the Tom who came
16. the man saw the Mary who came
17. Tom saw the man that came
18. Mary saw the dog that came
19. the dog saw the Tom that came
20. the man saw the Mary that came
21. the Tom who came saw the man
22. the Mary who came saw the dog
23. the dog which came saw Tom
24. the man who came saw Mary
25. the Tom that came saw the man
26. the Tom that came saw the man come
27. the man who came saw Mary come
28. the dog that came saw the Tom that came
29. the man who came saw the Mary who came
30. the dog which came saw the Mary that came

Questions

1a. who saw the man
who did Tom see

2a. who saw the dog
what did Mary see

3a. what saw Tom
who did the dog see

4a. who saw Mary
who did Mary see

5a. who came

6a. what came

7a. who came

8a. who came

9a. who saw the man come
who did Tom see come

10a. who saw the dog come
what did Mary see come

11a. what saw Tom come
who did the dog see come

12a. who saw Mary come
who did the man see come
13a. who saw the man who came
which man did Tom see
14a. who saw the dog which came
which dog did Mary see
15a. what saw the Tom who came
which Tom did the dog see
16a. who saw the Mary who came
which Mary did the man see
17a. who saw the man that came
which man did Tom see
18a. who saw the dog that came
which dog did Mary see
19a. what saw the Tom that came
which Tom did the dog see
20a. who saw the Mary that came
which Mary did the man see
21a. which Tom saw the man
who did the Tom who came see
22a. which Mary saw the dog
what did the Mary who came see
23a. which dog saw Tom
who did the dog which came see
24a. which man saw Mary
who did the man who came see
25a. which Tom saw the man
who did the Tom that came see
26a. which Tom saw the man come
who did the Tom that came see come
27a. which man saw Mary come
who did the man who came see come
28a. which dog saw the Tom that came
which Tom did the dog that came see
29a. which man saw the Mary who came
which Mary did the man who came see
30a. which dog saw the Mary that came
which Mary did the dog which came see

But not:

*the Tom saw the man
*the man saw the Mary

*man came
*Tom came the man
*Mary saw
*Tom saw the man came
*the man come
*Tom saw the man which came
*Mary saw the dog who came
*the man saw Mary who came
*dog which come saw Tom
*Tom who came saw the dog
*the Tom that came saw the man came
*who did Tom saw
*who saw the man came
*who saw who came
*who man did Tom see
*who Tom did the dog see
*who did Tom who came see

10. KRIO

Questions	*Statements*
	Part I
1. udat de slip *Who is sleeping?*	1a. pikin de slip *A child is sleeping.* di pikin de slip *The child is sleeping.*
2. udat it *Who ate?*	2a. pikin it *A child ate.* di pikin it *The child ate.*
3. us pikin de slip *Which child is sleeping?*	3a. pikin we it de slip *A child who ate is sleeping.* di pikin we it de slip *The child who ate is sleeping.*
4. us pikin it *Which child ate?*	4a. pikin we de slip it *A child who is sleeping ate.* di pikin we de slip it *The child who is sleeping ate.*

5. wetin go it
What will eat?

5a. pus go it
A cat will eat.
di pus go it
The cat will eat.

6. wetin de rɔn
What is running?

6a. pus de rɔn
A cat is running.
di pus de rɔn
The cat is running.

7. us pus go it
Which cat will eat?

7a. pus we de rɔn go it
A cat that is running will eat.
di pus we de rɔn go it
The cat that is running will eat.

8. us pus de rɔn
Which cat is running?

8a. di pus we go it de rɔn
The cat that will eat is running.

9. wetin taya
What is tired?

9a. di pus taya
The cat is tired.

10. udat taya
Who is tired?

10a. di tiča taya
The teacher is tired.

11. udat go bizi
Who will be busy?

11a. di tiča go bizi
The teacher will be busy.

12. udat de bizi
Who is becoming busy?

12a. tiča de bizi
A teacher is becoming busy.

13. us tiča taya
Which teacher is tired?

13a. di tiča we go bizi taya
The teacher who will be busy is tired.
di bizi tiča taya
The busy teacher is tired.

14. us tiča go bizi
Which teacher will be busy?

14a. tiča we taya go bizi
A teacher who is tired will be busy.
taya tiča go bizi
A tired teacher will be busy.

15. wetin bɛt di dɔg
What bit the dog?

15a. di pus bɛt di dɔg
The cat bit the dog.

16. wetin di pus bɛt
What did the cat bite?

16a. di pus bɛt di dɔg
The cat bit the dog.

17. us pus bɛt dɔg
Which cat bit a dog?

17a. di pus we go rɔn bɛt dɔg
The cat that will run bit a dog.
di taya pus bɛt dɔg
The tired cat bit a dog.

18. us dɔg di pus bɛt
    Which dog did the cat bite?

18a. di pus bɛt di dɔg we de it
    The cat bit the dog that is eating.
    di pus bɛt di bizi dɔg
    The cat bit the busy dog.

19. udat gɛt di dɔg
    Who has the dog?

19a. di tiča gɛt di dɔg
    The teacher has the dog.

20. wetin di tiča gɛt
    What does the teacher have?

20a. di tiča gɛt dɔg
    The teacher has a dog.

21. us tiča slip
    Which teacher slept?

21a. di tiča we gɛt dɔg slip
    The teacher who has a dog slept.

22. us tiča gɛt dɔg
    Which teacher has a dog?

22a. di tiča we bizi gɛt dɔg
    The teacher who is busy has a dog.
    di bizi tiča gɛt dɔg
    The busy teacher has a dog.

23. us dɔg de it
    Which dog is eating?

23a. di dɔg we di tiča gɛt de it
    The dog that the teacher has is eating.
    di tiča in dɔg de it
    The teacher's dog is eating.

24. us dɔg bɛt us pus
    Which dog bit which cat?

24a. di dɔg we di pikin gɛt bɛt di pus we di tiča gɛt
    The dog that the child has bit the cat that the teacher has.
    di pikin in dɔg bɛt di tiča im pus
    The child's dog bit the teacher's cat.

But not:

*udat di pikin bizi
*udat us go it
*us taya pus rɔn
*us de it
*di pus taya bɛt di dɔg
*di we it pikin de rɔn
*di dɔg bizi we di tiča
*wetin di tiča
*udat di pikin
*di pikin pus slip

Part II

25. wetin di pikin gɛt
    What does the child have?

25a. di pikin gɛt pus
    The child has a cat.

26. wetin di tiča lɛk
    What does the teacher like?

26a. di tiča lɛk di pus
    The teacher likes the cat.

27. udat di tiča lɛk
    Who does the teacher like?

27a. di tiča lɛk di pikin we gɛt pus
    The teacher likes the child who has a cat.

28. udat im pus di tiča lɛk
    Whose cat does the teacher like?

28a. di tiča lɛk di pikin im pus
    The teacher likes the child's cat.

29. wetin di tiča gɛt
    What does the teacher have?

29a. di tiča gɛt os
    The teacher has a house.

30. wetin di pikin si
    What did the child see?

30a. di pikin si di os
    The child saw the house.

31. udat di pikin si
    Who did the child see?

31a. di pikin si di tiča we gɛt os
    The child saw the teacher who has a house.

32. udat ĩ os di pikin si
    Whose house did the child see?

32a. di pikin si di tiča ĩ os
    The child saw the teacher's house.

33. wetin yu gɛt
    What do you have?

33a. a gɛt sista
    I have a sister.

34. wetin yu sista lɛk
    What does your sister like?

34a. mi sista lɛk di dɔg
    My sister likes the dog.

35. udat in dɔg yu sista lɛk
    Whose dog does your sister like?

35a. mi sista lɛk di pikin in dɔg
    My sister likes the child's dog.

36. udat im pikin in dɔg yu sista lɛk
    What child's dog does your sister like?

36a. mi sista lɛk di tiča im pikin in dɔg
    My sister likes the teacher's child's dog.

37. wetin i gɛt
    What does he have?

37a. i gɛt ɔs
    He has a horse.

38. wetin ĩ ɔs si
    What did his horse see?

38a. ĩ ɔs si yu pus
    His horse saw your cat.

39. wetin in sista lɛk
    What does his sister like?

39a. in sista lɛk ĩ ɔs
    His sister likes his horse.

40. wetin a gɛt
    What do I have?

40a. yu gɛt brɔda
    You have a brother.

41. udat im brɔda lɛk yu ɔs
Whose brother likes your horse?

41a. yu brɔda lɛk mi ɔs
Your brother likes my horse.

42. udat gɛt got
Who has a goat?

42a. di tiča im brɔda gɛt got
The teacher's brother has a goat.

43. udat si iŋ got
Who saw his goat?

43a. i si iŋ got
He saw his goat.

44. udat iŋ got yu si
Whose goat did you see?

44a. a si mi brɔda im pikin iŋ got
I saw my brother's child's goat.

45. wetin di pikin in sista im pus si
What did the child's sister's cat see?

45a. di pus si yu pikin iŋ got
The cat saw your child's goat.

But not:

*yu gɛt yu brɔda
*udat pikin yu sista si
*us tiča us pikin lɛk
*wetin im pus di tiča lɛk
*di tiča lɛk di pikin dɔg
*wetin iŋ gɛt
*i gɛt di sista
*yu gɛt di got
*wetin pikin di tiča lɛk
*im pus di pikin lɛk
*di pikin gɛt wetin
*udat di pikin si im pus
*udat i pus yu lɛk
*udat lɛk yu yu os
*a si di pikin we i gɛt pus
*a si di pus di pikin gɛt

Part III

46. ustɛm wi go it
When will we eat?

46a. wi go it sɔmtɛm
We will eat sometime.
wi go it naw
We will eat now.
wi go it we mi brɔda grap
We will eat when my brother gets up.

47. ustɛm yu brɔda go grap
When will your brother get up?

47a. mi brɔda go grap sɔmtɛm
My brother will get up sometime.
mi brɔda go grap naw
My brother will get up now.
mi brɔda go grap we wi it
My brother will get up when we eat.
we wi it mi brɔda go grap
When we eat, my brother will get up.
mi brɔda go grap sɔmtɛm we wi it
My brother will get up sometime, when we eat.
naw we wi it mi brɔda go grap
Now, when we eat, my brother will get up.

48. ustɛm i slip
When did he sleep?

48a. i slip sɔmtɛm
He slept sometime.
i slip yɛstade
He slept yesterday.
i slip we in sista wok
He slept when his sister worked.

49. ustɛm in sista wok
When did his sister work?

49a. in sista wok yɛstade
His sister worked yesterday.
in sista wok yɛstade we i slip
His sister worked yesterday when he slept.
in sista wok we i slip
His sister worked when he slept.
yɛstade we i slip in sista wok
Yesterday, when he slept, his sister worked.

50. ustɛm im brɔda slip
When did his brother sleep?

50a. im brɔda slip we i wok yɛstade
His brother slept when he worked yesterday.

51. ustɛm yu de wok
When are you working?

51a. a de wok we mi brɔda it
I'm working when my brother is eating.

52. ustɛm mi sista de it
When is my sister eating?

52a. naw we wi wok yu sista de it
Now, when we're working, your sister is eating.

53. ustɛm di pus go lɛk di dɔg
When will the cat like the dog?

53a. di pus go lɛk di dɔg we i slip
The cat will like the dog when he sleeps.

54. ustɛm di tiča go taya
When will the teacher be tired?

54a. we i bizi i go taya
When he's busy he will be tired.

55. ustɛm di pikin taya
When is the child tired?

55a. di pikin taya we di tiča taya
The child is tired when the teacher is tired.

56. ustɛm yu go gɛt ɔs
When will you have a horse?

56a. we a gɛt os a go gɛt ɔs
When I have a house, I'll have a horse.

But not:

*im brɔda wok ustɛm
*im brɔda it go naw
*in de wok naw
*a it we yɛstade
*we i go taya i go bizi
*di pikin de slip we di pus de rɔn
*mi sista wok we it

APPENDIX

A. Vocabulary Symbols

The following are the vocabulary symbols, other than lexical morphemes, used in this book.

A, *Adj* = adjective
Acc = accusative (case)
Ad, *Adv* = adverb
Afa = adjective affix
Afn = noun affix
Afp = pronoun affix
Afv = verb affix
As = adjective stem
Aspe = aspect
Aux = auxiliary verb or phrase

BE = the verb "be"

C = cover symbol for any consonant
Ca = case
Cd = complement dummy
Cl = classifier
Co = concreteness
Comp = complement

D, *Det* = determiner
Dat = dative (case)
Def = definite
Dim = diminutive

F = feminine
Fir = first (person)

G = gender
Gen = genitive (case)

Ia, *Ins*, *Int* = intensifier
Id = intensifier dummy
Impe = imperative
Indef = indefinite
Instr = instrumental (case)
IO = indirect object

Loc = locative adverb or phrase

M = masculine (modal in Solution 48)
Man = manner adverb

N = noun
Nab = abstract noun
Name = proper name
Nan = animate noun
Neg, *Ng* = negative
Neu = neuter
Nfan = noun (stem) feminine animate
Nfin = noun (stem) feminine inanimate
Nh = human noun
Nin = inanimate noun
Nman = noun (stem) masculine animate
Nmin = noun (stem) masculine inanimate
Nn, *NP* = noun phrase
Nnh = non-human noun
Nom = nominative (case)
Non-Fir = non-first (person)
Ns = noun stem
Nsf = feminine noun stem
Nsm = masculine noun stem
Nsn = neuter noun stem
Nu = number
Nuc = nucleus

OM = object marker

Pas = past (tense)
Per = person

Pl = plural
PM = person marker
PP = prepositional phrase
Pr, *Pron* = pronoun
Pred = predicate
Prep = preposition
Pres = present (tense)
Prt = particle

QM = question marker

Rel = relative
Rld = relative dummy

S = sentence
Sec = second (person)
SFM = sentence-final marker
Sg = singular
SM = subject marker

T = tense
Ta, *Tm*, *Tms* = time adverb
Tc = temporal conjunction
Td = time dummy
Thi = third (person)

U = cover symbol

V = verb
Vb = verb or verb phrase
Vcop = copulative verb
Vin = intransitive verb
VP = verb phrase
Vs = verb stem
Vsc = copulative verb stem
Vst = transitive verb stem
Vt, *Vtr* = transitive verb
Vtc = complex transitive verb
Vts = transitive verb taking a sentence complement
Vw = cover symbol for any vowel

W = word (in Chapter 3), cover symbol (elsewhere)

X, *Y*, *Z* = cover symbols

B. Special Symbols

Symbol	*Page defined on*
+	8
#	8–9
=	7–8, 246–247
≠	7–8, 246–247
→	9
⇒	9
( )	9–10
{ }	11–12
[ ]	13
]	119–120
}	246
–	30

SELECTED BIBLIOGRAPHY

Bach, Emmon: *An Introduction to Transformational Grammars,* Holt, Rinehart and Winston, Inc., New York, 1964.

———: "The Order of Elements in a Transformational Grammar of German," *Language,* vol. 38, no. 3, pt. 1, pp. 263–269, 1962.

Boyd, Julian C., and Harold V. King: "Annotated Bibliography of Generative Grammar," *Language Learning,* vol. 12, no. 4, pp. 307–312, 1962.

Chomsky, Noam: "Some Methodological Remarks on Generative Grammar," *Word,* vol. 17, no. 2, pp. 219–239, 1961.

———: *Syntactic Structures,* Mouton and Co., The Hague, 1957 (2d printing with additional bibliography, 1962).

———: "A Transformational Approach to Syntax," *Third Texas Conference on Problems of Linguistic Analysis in English,* University of Texas, Austin, Texas, 1962, pp. 124–158 (discussion, pp. 158–186).

———: "Explanatory Models in Linguistics," in E. Nagel, P. Suppes, and A. Tarski (eds.), *Logic, Methodology, and Philosophy of Science: Proceedings of the 1960 International Congress,* Stanford University Press, Stanford, Calif., 1962, pp. 528–550.

———: *Aspects of the Theory of Syntax,* The M.I.T. Press, Cambridge, Mass., 1965.

———, Morris Halle, and Fred Lukoff: "On Accent and Juncture in English," in *For Roman Jakobson,* Mouton and Co., The Hague, 1956, pp. 65–80.

Fillmore, Charles J.: *Indirect Object Constructions in English and the Ordering of Transformations,* Ohio State Research Foundation, Project of Syntactic Analysis, Report 1, Columbus, Ohio, 1962.

Fillmore, Charles J.: "The Position of Embedding Transformations in a Grammar," *Word,* vol. 19, no. 2, pp. 208–231, 1963.

Fodor, Jerry A., and Jerrold J. Katz (eds.): *The Structure of Language: Readings in the Philosophy of Language,* Prentice-Hall, Inc., Englewood Cliffs, N.J., 1964.

Halle, Morris: "On the Role of Simplicity in Linguistic Descriptions," in *Structure of Language and Its Mathematical Aspects* (*Proceedings of Symposia in Applied Mathematics,* vol. 12), American Mathematical Society, Providence, R.I., 1961, pp. 89–94.

———: "Phonology in a Generative Grammar," *Word,* vol. 18, no. 1–2, pp. 54–72, 1962.

———: *The Sound Pattern of Russian,* chaps. 1, 2, Mouton and Co., The Hague, 1959.

Householder, Fred W., Jr.: "On Linguistic Terms," in Sol Saporta (ed.), *Psycholinguistics: a Book of Readings,* Holt, Rinehart and Winston, Inc., New York, 1961, pp. 15–25.

Katz, Jerrold J., and Paul M. Postal: *An Integrated Theory of Linguistic Descriptions,* The M.I.T. Press, Cambridge, Mass., 1964.

Klima, Edward S.: "Relatedness between Grammatical Systems," *Language,* vol. 40, no. 1, pp. 1–20, 1964.

Koutsoudas, Andreas: "The Handling of Morphophonemic Processes in Transformational Grammars," in *Papers in Memory of G. C. Pappageotes,* Special Publication 5, *Word,* pp. 28–42, 1964.

Lees, Robert B.: *The Grammar of English Nominalizations,* Indiana University Research Center in Anthropology, Folklore, and Linguistics, Publication 12 (*International Journal of American Linguistics,* vol. 26, no. 3, pt. 2, 1960).

———: "Grammatical Analysis of the English Comparative Construction," *Word,* vol. 17, no. 2, pp. 171–185, 1961.

———: "A Multiple Ambiguous Adjectival Construction in English," *Language,* vol. 36, no. 2, pt. 1, pp. 207–221, 1960.

———: Review of Noam Chomsky, *Syntactic Structures* (The Hague, 1957), *Language,* vol. 33, no. 3, pt. 1, pp. 375–408, 1957.

———: "Some Neglected Aspects of Parsing," *Language Learning,* vol. 11, nos. 3 and 4, pp. 171–181, 1961.

Postal, Paul M.: *Constituent Structure: a Study of Contemporary Models of Syntactic Description,* Indiana University Research Center in Anthropology, Folklore, and Linguistics, Publication 30 (*International Journal of American Linguistics,* vol. 30, no. 1, pt. 3, 1964).

———: "Underlying and Superficial Linguistic Structure," *Harvard Educational Review,* vol. 34, no. 2, pp. 246–266, 1964.

Schachter, Paul: Review of Robert B. Lees, *The Grammar of English Nominalizations* (1960), *International Journal of American Linguistics,* vol. 28, no. 2, pp. 134–146, 1962.

———: "Structural Ambiguity in Tagalog," *Language Learning,* vol. 11, nos. 3 and 4, pp. 135–145, 1961.

Smith, Carlota S.: "A Class of Complex Modifiers in English," *Language,* vol. 37, no. 3, pt. 1, pp. 342–365, 1961.

———: "Determiners and Relative Clauses in a Generative Grammar of English," *Language,* vol. 40, no. 1, pp. 37–52, 1964.

Stockwell, Robert P.: "The Place of Intonation in a Generative Grammar of English," *Language,* vol. 36, no. 3, pt. 1, pp. 360–367, 1960.

LANGUAGE INDEX

LANGUAGE INDEX

SUBJECT INDEX

SUBJECT INDEX